The Writer's World

Paragraphs and Essays

With Enhanced Reading Strategies

Fifth Edition

Lynne Gaetz
Lionel Groulx College

Suneeti Phadke
St. Jerome College

330 Hudson Street, NY NY 10013

VP & Portfolio Manager: Eric Stano
Development Consulting: V. Tomaiuolo
Project Marketer: Fiona Murray
Program Manager: Erin Bosco
Project Coordination, Text Design, and Electronic Page Makeup: Spi Global
Cover Designer: Pentagram
Cover illustration: Anuj Shrestha
Senior Manufacturing Buyer: Roy L. Pickering, Jr.
Printer/Binder: LSC Communications/Menasha
Cover Printer: Phoenix Color/Hagerstown

Credits and acknowledgments borrowed from other sources and reproduced, with permission, in this textbook appear on the appropriate page within text and on pages 556–557.

PEARSON, ALWAYS LEARNING, and REVEL are exclusive trademarks in the United States and/or other countries owned by Pearson Education, Inc., or its affiliates.

Unless otherwise indicated herein, any third-party trademarks that may appear in this work are the property of their respective owners and any references to third-party trademarks, logos, or other trade dress are for demonstrative or descriptive purposes only. Such references are not intended to imply any sponsorship, endorsement, authorization, or promotion of Pearson's products by the owners of such marks, or any relationship between the owner and Pearson Education, Inc., or its affiliates, authors, licensees, or distributors.

Library of Congress Cataloging-in-Publication Data

Gaetz, Lynne, 1960- author. | Phadke, Suneeti, 1961- author.
The writer's world : paragraphs and essays, with enhanced reading
  strategies / Lynne Gaetz, Suneeti Phadke.
Fifth edition. | Boston : Pearson, [2017] | Includes index.
LCCN 2017001671| ISBN 9780134311593 (annotated instructor
  edition) | ISBN 9780134195384 (student edition) | ISBN 9780134312613
  (loose leaf)
LCSH: English language—Paragraphs—Problems, exercises, etc. |
  English language—Rhetoric—Problems, exercises, etc. | Report
  writing—Problems, exercises, etc. | English language—Grammar—Problems,
  exercises, etc.
LCC PE1439 .G254 2017 | DDC 808/.042—dc23
LC record available at https://lccn.loc.gov/2017001671

2   17

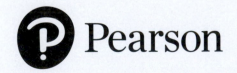

Student Edition ISBN-10:   0-13-419538-8
Student Edition ISBN-13:   978-0-13-419538-4

A la Carte Edition ISBN-10:   0-13-431261-9
A la Carte Edition ISBN-13:   978-0-13-431261-3

Brief Contents

Contents

iv

Copyright © 2018 by Pearson Education

Readings Listed by Rhetorical Mode

Preface

Thank you for making *The Writer's World* series a resounding success. We are delighted that *Paragraphs and Essays* has been able to help so many students produce writing that is technically correct and richly detailed whether students have varying skill levels, are native or nonnative speakers of English, or learn more effectively using visuals.

When we started writing the first edition, we set out to develop practical and pedagogically sound approaches to these challenges. We began with the idea that collaboration is crucial. So we met with more than forty-five instructors from around the country, asking for their opinions and insights regarding (1) the challenges posed by the course, (2) the needs of today's ever-changing student population, and (3) the ideas and features we were proposing in order to provide a more effective teaching and learning tool. For that first edition and every edition since, Pearson also commissioned dozens of detailed reviews from instructors, asking them to analyze and evaluate each draft of the manuscript. These reviewers identified numerous ways in which we could refine and enhance our key features. Their invaluable feedback has been incorporated throughout *The Writer's World*. This text is truly the product of a successful partnership between the authors, publisher, and more than one hundred developmental writing instructors.

What's New in the Fifth Edition?

NEW Revel™ for *The Writer's World*

Educational Technology Designed for the Way Today's Students Read, Think, and Learn

When students are engaged deeply, they learn more effectively and perform better in their courses. This simple fact inspired the creation of Revel: an interactive learning environment designed for the way today's students read, think, and learn.

Revel enlivens course content with media interactives and assessments—integrated directly within the authors' narrative—that provide opportunities for students to read, practice, and study in one continuous experience. This immersive educational technology replaces the textbook and is designed to measurably boost students' understanding, retention, and preparedness.

Learn more about Revel at http://www.pearson highered.com/revel/.

Enhanced Reading Support

Brimming with insightful readings and vocabulary tips, *The Writer's World* series has always drawn attention to the strong connection between reading and writing. This edition goes a step further by offering **extra reading strategies** in a new Chapter 38, such as skimming and scanning, using context clues, and making inferences. Students build their reading skills as they work on dozens of sample paragraphs, essays, and practices. By enhancing their reading skills, students are also better equipped to do research for essay writing.

2016 Modern Language Association (MLA) Updates

In Spring 2016, the Modern Language Association (MLA) published updates to their writing and documentation guidelines. Chapter 15, "Enhancing Your Writing with Research" has related content to reflect the new in-text citation and Works Cited formats.

Updated Model Writing and New Essays and Readings

Approximately thirty percent of this text has updated examples, sample paragraphs, writing practices, Writer's Desk topics, and grammar practices. We've added new student and professional essays to the essay patterns covered in Chapter 14. All are annotated to highlight the components of each essay (e.g., thesis statements, topic sentences, and concluding sentences). Each student essay is followed by a professional essay and a set of questions that deepen students' understanding of the different essay patterns. In Chapter 39, seven new thought-provoking readings relate to the themes presented in the grammar chapters.

New Images

This edition presents new dynamic and vibrant images—photos of exotic locales and pop culture icons, as well as images from independent and mainstream films and television shows—that will engage students and prompt critical thinking.

New Grammar Themes and Practices

Many grammar practices in Part IV: The Editing Handbook are new, providing updated grammar instruction through the lens of topical and culturally relevant content. All of the themes were chosen to appeal to developmental writing students of any background. New topics include:

Online and app-based shopping	Consumer protection	Click-bait online journalism
Body altering practices	The rise in plastic surgery for men	Popular diet fads
Wrestling, the oldest sport	Basketball's rise in popularity	Rock climbing
Idolizing professional athletes	Silicon Valley	Mindfulness
Human behavior: The Blue/Brown-Eyed Experiment	Personality: Influence of Carl Jung	Links: emotional and physical health
Bystander apathy	Childrearing practices	CIA psychiatrist: Donald Ewan Cameron
Government espionage	Social media privacy	Online security measures
Digital tracking	Online hacking in financial institutions	Preparing for college entrance exams
Teaching overseas	Unpaid internships	U.S. and global college fees
Chico Mendes and the Amazon's rubber trees	Climate change	California's longest drought
Chernobyl nuclear disaster	Accidental explosion at Texas' West Fertilizer Company	Student debt for healthcare professions
Food contamination and inspection practices	International response to the Ebola virus	Holistic medicine
History of acupuncture	Rewarding college degrees	The "open office" trend
Building a start-up company	Online entrepreneurs: A clothing delivery service	Oscar Wilde's "The Model Millionaire"
Electronic music (e.g., Daft Punk)	Unauthorized file sharing	Tesla's Elon Musk and his innovations
Youth social and political movements	Drug testing and trials	Paying NCAA athletes

A Fresh Look

An updated, clean, and modern design streamlines instruction and increases usability, allowing students to more effectively find and retain the information covered. And, of course, our signature "sunglasses" are back on the cover by popular demand!

How *The Writer's World* Meets Students' Diverse Needs

We created *The Writer's World* to meet your students' diverse needs. To accomplish this, we asked both the instructors in our focus groups and the reviewers at every stage not only to critique our ideas but to offer their suggestions and recommendations for features that would enhance the learning process of their students. The result has been the integration of many elements that are not found in other textbooks, including our **visual program, coverage of nonnative speaker material, and strategies for addressing the varying skill levels students bring to the course.**

The Visual Program

A stimulating full-color book with more than 140 photos, *The Writer's World* recognizes that today's world is a visual one, and the book encourages students to become better communicators by responding to images. Chapter-opening visuals in Parts I, II, III, and IV help students think about the chapter's key concept in a new way. For example, in the Chapter 9 opener, a photograph of a mechanic's tool case sets the stage for classification. Tools are grouped by type, which helps students understand the premise of classification. In Part IV, chapter-opening photos help illustrate the theme of the examples and exercises. These visual aids can also serve as sources for writing prompts.

The visuals in Part II provide students with another set of opportunities to write in response to images, with Media Writing activities that encourage them to respond using particular paragraph and essay patterns. Throughout *The Writer's World*, words and images work together to encourage students to explore, develop, and revise their writing.

Seamless Coverage for Nonnative Speakers

Instructors in our focus groups consistently note the growing number of nonnative/ESL/ELL students enrolling in developmental writing courses. Although some of these students have special needs relating to the writing process, many native speakers in courses have more traditional needs that must also be satisfied. To address this rapidly changing dynamic, we have carefully implemented and integrated content throughout to assist these students. *The Writer's World* does not have separate ESL boxes, ESL chapters, or tacked-on ESL appendices. Instead, information that traditionally poses a challenge to nonnative speakers is woven seamlessly throughout the book. In our extensive experience teaching writing to both native and nonnative speakers of English, we have learned that both groups learn best when they are not distracted by ESL labels. With the seamless approach, nonnative speakers do not feel self-conscious and segregated, and native speakers do not tune out detailed explanations that may also benefit them. Many of these traditional problem areas receive more coverage than you would find in other textbooks, arming the instructor with the material to effectively meet the needs of nonnative speakers. Moreover, the *Annotated Instructor's Edition* provides more than seventy-five ESL Teaching Tips designed specifically to help instructors better meet the needs of their nonnative speaking students.

Issue-Focused Thematic Grammar

In surveys, many of you indicated that one of the primary challenges in teaching your course is finding materials that are engaging to students in a contemporary context. This is especially true in grammar instruction. **Students come to the course with varying skill levels**, and many students are simply not interested in grammar. To address this challenge, we have introduced **issue-focused thematic grammar** in *The Writer's World*.

Each chapter centers on a theme that is carried out in examples and activities. These themes include topics related to popular culture, psychology, spies and hackers, college life, the environment, health care, the legal world, and the workplace.

The thematic approach enables students to broaden their awareness of subjects important to American life, such as understanding advertising and consumerism and thinking about health care issues and alternative medicine. The thematic approach makes reading about grammar more engaging. And the more engaging grammar is, the more likely students will retain key concepts—raising their skill level in these important building blocks of writing.

We also think that it is important to teach grammar in the context of the writing process. Students should not think that grammar is an isolated exercise. Therefore, **each grammar chapter concludes with a warm-up writing activity**.

Learning Aids to Help Students Get the Most from *The Writer's World*

Overwhelmingly, focus group participants and reviewers asked that both a larger number and a greater diversity of exercises and activities be incorporated into *The Writer's World*. In response, we have developed and tested the following learning aids in *The Writer's World*. We are confident they will help your students become better writers.

Hints In each chapter, Hint boxes highlight important writing and grammar points. Hints are useful for all students, but many will be particularly helpful for nonnative speakers. For example, in Chapter 12, one Hint encourages students to state an argument directly

and a second Hint points out the need to avoid circular reasoning. In Chapter 22, a Hint discusses checking for consistent voice in compound sentences. Hints include brief discussions and examples so that students will see both concept and application.

Vocabulary Boost Throughout Part II of *The Writer's World*, Vocabulary Boost boxes give students tips to improve their use of language and to revise and edit their word choices. For example, a Vocabulary Boost in Chapter 4 asks students to replace repeated words with synonyms, and the one in Chapter 5 gives specific directions for how to vary sentence openings. These lessons give students concrete strategies and specific advice for improving their diction.

The Writer's Desk Parts I, II, and III include The Writer's Desk exercises that help students get used to practicing all stages and steps of the writing process. As the chapter progresses, students warm up with a prewriting activity and then use specific methods for developing, organizing (using paragraph and essay plans), drafting, and revising and editing to create a final draft.

Paragraph Patterns at Work To help students appreciate the relevance of their writing tasks, Chapters 4–12 highlight an authentic writing sample from work contexts. Titled Illustration at Work, Narration at Work, and so on, this feature offers a glimpse of how people use writing patterns in different workplace settings.

Reflect On It Each Reflect On It is a chapter-review exercise. Questions prompt students to recall and review what they have learned in the chapter.

The Writer's Room The Writer's Room contains writing activities that correspond to general, college, and workplace topics. Some prompts are brief to allow students to freely form ideas while others are expanded to give students more direction.

There is something for every student writer in this end-of-chapter feature. Students who respond well to visual cues will appreciate the media writing exercises in The Writer's Room in Part II: Paragraph Patterns. Students who learn best by hearing through collaboration will appreciate the discussion and group work prompts of selected The Writer's Rooms. To help students see how grammar is not isolated from the writing process, there are also The Writer's Room activities at the end of sections 1–8 in Part IV: The Editing Handbook.

How We Organized *The Writer's World*

The Writer's World is separated into five parts for ease of use, convenience, and ultimate flexibility.

Part I: The Writing Process teaches students how to (1) formulate ideas (Exploring); (2) expand, organize, and present those ideas in a piece of writing (Developing); and (3) polish their writing so that they convey their message as clearly as possible (Revising and Editing). The result is that writing a paragraph or an essay becomes far less daunting because students have specific steps to follow.

Part II: Paragraph Patterns gives students a solid overview of the patterns of development. Using the same easy-to-understand process (Exploring, Developing, and Revising and Editing), each chapter in this section explains how to convey ideas using one or more writing patterns. As they work through the practices and write their own paragraphs and essays, students begin to see how using a writing pattern can help them fulfill their purpose for writing.

Part III: The Essay covers the parts of the essay and explains how students can apply the nine patterns of development to essay writing. This section also discusses the role research plays in writing and explains some ways that students can incorporate research in their essays.

Part IV: The Editing Handbook is a thematic grammar handbook. In each chapter, the examples correspond to a theme, such as popular culture, college life, and work. As students work through the chapters, they hone their grammar and editing skills while gaining knowledge about a variety of topics. In addition to helping build interest in the grammar practices, the thematic material provides a spark that ignites new ideas that students can apply to their writing.

Part V: Reading Strategies and Selections offers tips, detailed reading strategies to help students improve their reading skills, as well as interesting and relevant essays and follow-up questions. Students learn how to write by observing and dissecting what they read. The readings relate to the themes found in Part IV: The Editing Handbook, thereby providing more fodder for generating writing ideas.

Pearson Writing Resources for Instructors and Students

Book-Specific Ancillary Material

Annotated Instructor's Edition for *The Writer's World: Paragraphs and Essays*, 5/e ISBN 9-780-13431159-3

The *AIE* offers in-text answers, marginal annotations for teaching each chapter, and links to the *Instructor's Resource Manual* It is a valuable resource for experienced and first-time instructors alike.

Instructor's Resource Manual for *The Writer's World: Paragraphs and Essays*, 5/e ISBN 9-780-13431160-9

The material in the *IRM* is designed to save instructors time and provide them with effective options for teaching their writing classes. It offers suggestions for setting up their course; provides a lot of extra practice for students who need it; offers quizzes and grammar tests, including unit tests; furnishes grading rubrics for each rhetorical mode; and supplies answers in case instructors want to print them out and have students grade their own work. This valuable resource is exceptionally useful for adjuncts who might need advice in setting up their initial classes or who might be teaching a variety of writing classes with too many students and not enough time.

PowerPoint Presentation for *The Writer's World: Paragraphs and Essays*, 5/e ISBN 9-780-13431260-6

PowerPoint presentations to accompany each chapter consist of classroom-ready lecture outline slides, lecture tips and classroom activities, and review questions. The PPT slide set is available for download from the Instructor Resource Center.

Answer Key for *The Writer's World: Paragraphs and Essays*, 5/e ISBN 9-780-13431263-7

The Answer Key contains the solutions to the exercises in the student edition of the text. Available for download from the Instructor Resource Center.

MyWritingLab

MyWritingLab, a complete online learning resource, provides additional practice exercises and engaging animations for developing writers. It accelerates learning through layered assessment and a personalized learning path using the Knewton Adaptive Learning PlatformTM, which customizes standardized educational content. With over eight thousand exercises and immediate feedback to answers, the integrated learning aids of MyWritingLab reinforce learning throughout the semester.

Additional Resources

Pearson is pleased to offer a variety of support materials to help make teaching writing easier for teachers and to help students excel in their coursework. Many of our student supplements are available free or at a greatly reduced price when packaged with *The Writer's World: Paragraphs and Essays, 5/e*. Visit www.pearsonhighereducation.com, contact your local Pearson sales representative, or review a detailed listing of the full supplements package in the *Instructor's Resource Manual* for more information.

Acknowledgments

Many people have helped us produce *The Writer's World*. First and foremost, we would like to thank our students for inspiring us and providing us with extraordinary feedback. Their words and insights pervade this book.

We also benefited greatly from the insightful comments and suggestions from over one hundred instructors across the nation, all of whom are listed in the opening pages of the *Annotated Instructor's Edition*. Our colleagues' feedback was invaluable and helped shape *The Writer's World* series content, focus, and organization.

Reviewers

The following reviewers provided insight and assistance in the latest revision of *The Writer's World* series:

Tia Adger, Piedmont Technical College; Phillip Bannowsky, University of Delaware; Betty Benns, Orangeburg-Calhoun Technical College; Justin Bonnett, Saint Paul College; Cheryl Borman, Hillsborough CC, Ybor City Campus; Adam Carlberg, Tallahessee CC; Judith L. Carter, Amarillo College; Connie Caskey, Jefferson State CC; Zoe Ann Cerny, Horry-Georgetown Technical College; Cathy J. Clements, State Fair CC; Michael F. Courteau, St. Paul College; Cynthia Dawes, Edgecombe CC; Mary F. Di Stefano Diaz, Broward College; Claudia Edwards, Piedmont CC; Stephanie Fischer, Southern Connecticut State University; Paul Gallagher, Red Rocks CC; Kim Allen Gleed, Harrisburg Area CC; Ellen Hernandez, Camden CC; Karen Hindhede, Central Arizona College; Schahara Hudelson, South Plains College; Nikkina Hughes, Tarrant CC; Dianna W. Hydem, Jefferson State CC; Stacy Janicki, Ridgewater College; Patrice Johnson, Dallas County CC District; Jennifer Johnston, Hillsborough CC; Julie Keenan, Harrisburg Area CC; Patricia A. Lacey, Harper College; Nicole Lacroix, Red Rock CC; Ruth K. MacDonald, Lincoln College of New England; Joy McClain, Ivy Technical CC, Evansville; Heather Moulton, Central Arizona College; Ellen Olmstead, Montgomery College; Deborah Peterson, Blinn College; Rebecca Portis, Montgomery College; Sharon Race, South Plains College; Lisa M. Russell, Georgia Northwestern Technical College; Stephanie Sabourin, Montgomery College; Sharisse Turner, Tallahassee CC; Samantha Vance, Chattahoochee Valley CC; Jody Wheeler, Saint Paul College; Julie Yankanich, Camden County College

We are indebted to the team of dedicated professionals who have helped make this project a reality. They have boosted our spirits and have believed in us every step of the way. Special thanks to Veronica Tomaiuolo for developing this series and to Matthew Wright for trusting our instincts and enthusiastically propelling us forward. Also, we'd like to thank Diego Pelaez-Gaetz for writing contemporary and thought provoking grammar practices. We appreciate Kathleen Reynolds for her help finding articles for this new edition. We owe a deep debt of gratitude to Yolanda de Rooy, whose encouraging words helped ignite *The Writer's World* project. Ohlinger Publishing Services helped keep us motivated and on task during the production process. Thanks to everyone's efforts, *The Writer's World* is an even better resource for both instructors and students.

Finally, we would like to dedicate this book to our families who supported us and who patiently put up with our long hours on the computer. Manu and Murray continually encouraged us, as did Diego, Rebeka, Kiran, and Meghana.

A Note to Students

Your knowledge, ideas, and opinions are important. The ability to clearly communicate those ideas is invaluable in your personal, academic, and professional life. When your writing is error-free, readers will focus on your message, and you will be able to persuade, inform, entertain, or inspire them. *The Writer's World* includes strategies that will help you improve your reading skills and your written communication. Quite simply, when you become a better reader and writer, you become a better communicator. It is our greatest wish for *The Writer's World* to make you excited about learning. Enjoy!

Lynne Gaetz & Suneeti Phadke

Lynne Gaetz in Morocco

Suneeti Phadke in India

Part I
The Writing Process

An Overview

The writing process is a series of steps that most writers follow to get from thinking about a topic to preparing the final draft. Generally, you should follow the process step by step; however, sometimes you may find that steps overlap. For example, you might do some editing before revising, or you might think about your main idea while pre-writing. The important thing is to make sure that you have done all of the steps before preparing your final draft.

Before you begin the chapters that follow, review the steps in the writing process.

CHAPTER 1 EXPLORING
- Think about your topic.
- Think about your audience.
- Think about your purpose.
- Try exploring strategies.

CHAPTER 2 DEVELOPING
- Narrow your topic.
- Express your main idea.
- Develop your supporting ideas.
- Make a plan or an outline.
- Write your first draft.

CHAPTER 3 REVISING AND EDITING
- Revise for unity.
- Revise for adequate support.
- Revise for coherence.
- Revise for style.
- Edit for technical errors.

The Paragraph and the Essay

Most of the writing that we do—email messages, work reports, college papers—is made up of paragraphs and essays. A **paragraph** is a series of sentences that are about one central idea. Paragraphs can stand alone, or they can be part of a longer work such as an essay, a letter, or a report. An **essay** is a series of paragraphs that are about one central idea. Both the paragraph and the essay are divided into three parts.

Characteristics of a Paragraph

- The **topic sentence** introduces the subject of the paragraph and shows the writer's attitude toward the subject.
- The **body** of the paragraph contains details that support the topic sentence.
- The paragraph ends with a **concluding sentence**.

Characteristics of an Essay

- The **introduction** engages the reader's interest and contains the **thesis statement**.
- The **body** paragraphs each support the main idea of the essay.
- The **conclusion** reemphasizes the thesis and restates the main points of the essay. It brings the essay to a satisfactory close.

Review the following paragraph and essay, written by college student Anthony Coffman.

The Paragraph

Topic sentence

Supporting ideas

Concluding sentence

A worthwhile place to visit is the Indianapolis Motor Speedway. Built in 1909, it is home to the greatest spectacle in racing: the Indianapolis 500 Indy races. The stadium showcases the apex in automotive design. In addition to the Indy car races, there are Brickyard 400 NASCAR races, Grand Prix events, and GP moto-race events. Races can be expensive; a more wallet-friendly alternative is to attend qualifying time trials or to take a tour and visit the museum on the grounds during the non-race times of the year. Visiting the Indianapolis Motor Speedway provides fun for the whole family.

The Essay

The introduction contains a thesis statement.

Born in Indiana, I've lived here most of my life. Often, I hear fellow Indianans (often called "Hoosiers") say there's not much to do here. In fact, visitors and local citizens can visit many great entertainment venues, including state parks, museums, and the Indianapolis Motor Speedway.

Each body paragraph has a topic sentence that supports the thesis statement.

Indiana provides twenty-five recognized state parks that provide a variety of activities. Visitors can camp, fish, cycle, and see natural and historic sites. Some of the best parks include Turkey Run, Brown County, White River, Whitewater Memorial, and McCormick's Creek. I have had the opportunity to visit the grounds of Turkey Run, Brown County, and White River and had a wonderful time while hiking.

Another great activity to do in Indiana is visit museums. The Indianapolis Children's Museum offers educational exhibits including Dinosphere and the Anne Frank Peace Park with exhibits of the Seven Wonders of the World. The Indianapolis Museum of Art has over fifty thousand artworks and is home to the Virginia B. Fairbanks Art and Nature Park, which provides an urban oasis of woodlands, wetlands, lakes, and meadows. On the museum grounds, the Oldfield's-Lilly House gives visitors a glimpse into a country estate in the early twentieth century.

A worthwhile place to visit is the Indianapolis Motor Speedway. Built in 1909, it is home to the greatest spectacle in racing: the Indianapolis 500 Indy races. The stadium showcases the apex in automotive design. In addition to the Indy car races, there are Brickyard 400 NASCAR races, Grand Prix events, and GP moto-race events. Races can be expensive; a more wallet-friendly alternative is to attend qualifying time trials or to take a tour and visit the museum on the grounds during the non-race times of the year. Visiting the Indianapolis Motor Speedway provides fun for the whole family.

Concluding paragraph

Indiana has so much to offer. Enjoy scenic landscapes in the great outdoors of our state parks or artistic landscapes in the great halls of our museums. And for those with the need for speed, who can resist the spectacle of watching cars whiz by at nearly 200 miles per hour? I can't imagine living anywhere else!

1 Exploring

1.1 Define exploring.

1.2 Identify your topic.

1.3 Identify your audience.

1.4 Identify your purpose.

1.5 Practice exploring strategies.

1.6 Practice journal and portfolio writing.

Before creating a final image, an artist takes the time to consider what to create. Similarly, before developing a draft, a writer needs to explore the topic.

What Is Exploring?

1.1   Define exploring.

Have you ever been given a writing subject and then stared at the blank page, thinking, "I don't know what to write"? Well, it is not necessary to write a good paragraph or essay immediately. There are certain things that you can do to help focus on your topic.

Understanding Your Assignment

As soon as you are given an assignment, make sure that you understand the task. Answer the following questions about the assignment.

- How many words or pages should I write?
- What is the due date for the assignment?
- Are there any special qualities my writing should include?

    After you have considered your assignment, follow the four steps in the exploring stage of the writing process.

Exploring

ESSAY LINK
When you plan an essay, follow the four exploring steps in the same way.

STEP 1   Think about your topic. Determine what you will write about.

STEP 2   Think about your audience. Consider your intended readers and what interests them.

STEP 3 **Think about your purpose.** Ask yourself why you want to write.

STEP 4 **Try exploring strategies.** Experiment with different ways to generate ideas.

Topic

1.2 Identify your topic.

Your **topic**, or **subject**, is what you are writing about. When an instructor gives a topic for your writing, narrow the topic and find an angle that interests you. For example, if your instructor asks you to write about travel, you can take many approaches to the topic. You might write about the dangers of travel or explain what people can learn when they travel. Try to narrow the topic to suit your interests. When thinking about your topic, ask yourself the following questions.

- What special knowledge do I have about the topic?
- What subtopics are most relevant to me?
- What aspect of the topic arouses my emotions?

Audience

1.3 Identify your audience.

Your **audience** is your intended reader. Your audience might be your instructor, your classmates, your boss, your coworkers, and so on. Remember to adapt your language and vocabulary for a specific audience. For example, in a report written for your business class, you might use specialized accounting terms that would not be appropriate in an essay for another class. When you think about your audience, ask yourself the following questions.

- Who will read my assignment? Will the reader be my instructor, or will other students also read it?
- What does my audience already know about the topic?
- What information will my readers expect?
- Should I use formal or informal language?

HINT: Instructor as the Audience

Your instructor represents a general audience. Such an audience will expect you to use correct grammar and to reveal what you have learned or understood about the topic. Do not leave out information because you assume that your instructor is an expert in the field. Your ideas should be presented in a clear and organized manner.

Purpose

1.4 Identify your purpose.

Your purpose is your reason for writing. Sometimes you may have more than one purpose. When you consider your purpose, ask yourself the following questions.

- Is my goal to **entertain**? Do I tell a personal story or anecdote?
- Is my goal to **persuade**? Do I convince the reader that my point of view is correct?
- Is my goal to **inform**? Do I explain something or present information?

HINT: General and Specific Purpose

Your **general purpose** is to entertain, inform, or persuade. Your **specific purpose** is your more precise reason for writing. For example, imagine that you have to write about music. You can have the following general and specific purposes.

General purpose: to inform
Specific purpose: to explain how to become a better musician

Practice 1

Read text messages A and B. Then answer the questions that follow.

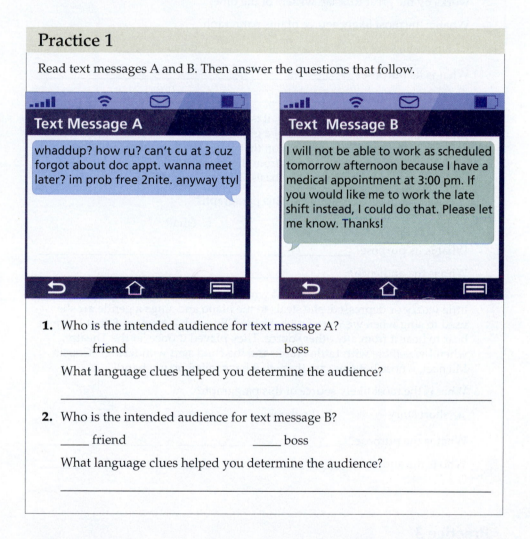

Text Message A

whaddup? how ru? can't cu at 3 cuz forgot about doc appt. wanna meet later? im prob free 2nite. anyway ttyl

Text Message B

I will not be able to work as scheduled tomorrow afternoon because I have a medical appointment at 3:00 pm. If you would like me to work the late shift instead, I could do that. Please let me know. Thanks!

1. Who is the intended audience for text message A?

_____ friend   _____ boss

What language clues helped you determine the audience?

_____

2. Who is the intended audience for text message B?

_____ friend   _____ boss

What language clues helped you determine the audience?

_____

Practice 2

Read each selection carefully. Underline any words or phrases that help you identify its source, audience, and purpose. Then answer the questions that follow each selection.

EXAMPLE:

I'm totally psyched about learning the drums. It's taken me a while to get used to keeping up a steady beat, but I think I'm getting it. My drum teacher is cool, and he's pretty patient with me. I try to practice, but it bugs the neighbors when I hit the cymbals.

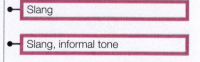

Slang

Slang, informal tone

What is the most likely source of this paragraph?

a. website article   b. textbook   c. email

What is its purpose? <u>To inform</u>

Who is the audience? <u>Friend or family member</u>

1. The nationalist movement in music was first felt in Russia, where music had been dominated entirely by foreign influence. Starting in the middle of the nineteenth century, Russian composers began to write operas in their own language, on Russian themes, and they often based their librettos on literary works by the great Russian writers of the time.

   What is the most likely source of this paragraph?

   a. short story   b. textbook   c. email

   What is its purpose? _____

   Who is the audience? _____

2. When dealing with club managers, it is imperative that you act professionally. Get all the details of a gig in advance. Doing so will eliminate any confusion or miscommunication that could result in a botched deal. It will also instantly set you apart from the legions of flaky musicians that managers must endure on a daily basis. That's a good thing.

   What is the most likely source of this paragraph?

   a. website article   b. novel   c. email

   What is its purpose? _____

   Who is the audience? _____

air: song (also known as aria)

3. We are rather a musical family, and when Christiana sees me, at any time, a little weary or depressed, she steals to the piano and sings a gentle **air** she used to sing when we were first betrothed. So weak a man am I, that I cannot bear to hear it from any other source. They played it once, at the Theatre, when I was there with Little Frank; and the child said wondering, "Cousin Michael, whose hot tears are these that have fallen on my hand!"

   What is the most likely source of this paragraph?

   a. short story   b. textbook   c. email

   What is the purpose? _____

   Who is the audience? _____

Practice 3

View the following cartoon on the next page. What is the topic? Who is the audience? What is the purpose? Does the cartoon achieve its purpose?

© John McPherson/Distributed by Universal Uclick via CartoonStock.com

"My computer's hard drive crashed, so
I text-messaged you my term paper."

John McPherson/Distributed by Universal Uclick via
www.CartoonStock.com

Exploring Strategies

1.5   **Practice exploring strategies.**

After you determine your topic, audience, and purpose, try some **exploring strategies**—also known as **prewriting strategies**—to help get ideas flowing. The four most common strategies are freewriting, brainstorming, questioning, and clustering. It is not necessary to do all of the strategies explained in this chapter. Find the strategy that works best for you.

You can do both general and focused prewriting. If you have writer's block and do not know what to write, use **general prewriting** to come up with possible topics. Then, after you have chosen a topic, use **focused prewriting** to find an angle of the topic that is interesting and that could be developed in your paragraph.

HINT: When to Use Exploring Strategies

You can use exploring strategies at any stage of the writing process.

- To find a topic
- To narrow a broad topic
- To generate ideas about your topic
- To generate supporting details

Freewriting

Freewriting is writing for a limited period of time without stopping. The point is to record the first thoughts that come to mind. If you have no ideas, you can indicate that in a sentence such as "I don't know what to write." As you write, do not be concerned with your grammar or spelling. If you use a computer, let your ideas flow and do not worry about typing mistakes.

TIA'S FREEWRITING

College student Tia Clement did freewriting about her favorite place. During her freewriting, she wrote everything that came to mind.

> Don't know. The coffee shop? The snacks are good. Friends hang there. What else? The beach. Love that sand. My bedroom is really cozy. Calm colors. I can relax there. Feel safe in my room. I listen to music. Songs help me sleep. Nature. Love trees and flowers in the park. Feel free when I'm outdoors in a natural place. Love grass under my bare feet. Feels awesome.

TIA'S FOCUSED FREEWRITING

After Tia did her general freewriting, she underlined ideas that she thought she could expand into a complete paragraph. Then she developed one of her underlined ideas. Her purpose was to describe, so she decided to do focused freewriting about the beach.

> The beach. It is a joyous place. The houses and hotels are around it. Gotta love the sound of the ocean. So peaceful. Water never ends it goes on and on. When does it stop? Goes forever. Smells like salt. What else? The bright sun reflects off the water. So warm on my skin. I love the feeling of sand between the toes. Hot sand burns my feet. Lots of sounds. Kids playing, birds. Adults chatting. The air feels thick. And damp. A feeling of happiness.

The Writer's Desk: Freewriting

Choose one of the following topics and do some freewriting. Remember to write without stopping.

Stress　　　　Nature　　　　Sports

Brainstorming

Brainstorming is like freewriting except that you create a list of ideas, and then stop and think about what's on the list. As you think about the topic, write down words or phrases that come to mind. Do not be concerned about grammar or spelling. The point is to generate ideas.

JIN'S BRAINSTORMING

College student Jin Park brainstormed about health issues. He made a list of general ideas.

> —lack of health care
> —obesity
> —fast food
> —not enough exercise

JIN'S FOCUSED BRAINSTORMING

Jin chose "not enough exercise" as his topic, and then he did focused brainstorming.

> —gaming and game apps
> —parents worry about dangers on streets
> —sports activities (e.g., football) cost a lot for fees, equipment, etc.
> —too much sitting at school
> —not enough physical education time
> —need more community sports programs

The Writer's Desk: Brainstorming

Choose one of the following topics and brainstorm. Create a list of ideas.

Ceremonies   Gossip   Good or bad manners

Questioning

Another way to generate ideas about a topic is to ask yourself a series of questions and write responses to them. The questions can help define and narrow a topic. One common way to do this is to ask *who, what, when, where, why*, and *how* questions. Like other exploring strategies, questioning can be general or focused.

RACHEL'S QUESTIONING
College student Rachel Jubinville used a question-and-answer format to generate ideas about family.

What is a family?	—a unit of people tied by blood or legal documents
Can friends be considered like family?	— maybe long-time friends become part of an extended family
What are problems in families?	—abuse, bankruptcy, grudges, divorce, jealousy
How do families stay together?	—love, patience, withholding judgment, listening to each other, acceptance of differences
When can families connect the best?	—holidays, weddings, funerals, weekly dinners
Why is our family important?	—provides support and connection, helps during times of crisis

The Writer's Desk: Questioning

Choose one of the following topics and write questions and answers. Ask who, what, when, where, why, and how questions.

Technology   Patriotism   Celebrities

Clustering

Clustering is like drawing a word map; ideas are arranged in a visual image. To begin, write your topic in the middle of the page and draw a box or a circle around it. That idea will lead to another, so write the second idea and draw a line connecting it to your topic. Keep writing, circling, and connecting ideas until you have groups, or "clusters," of them on the page. You can use clustering to get ideas about a general or a specific topic.

MAHAN'S CLUSTERING

College student Mahan Zahir used clustering to explore ideas about crime. He identified some main topics.

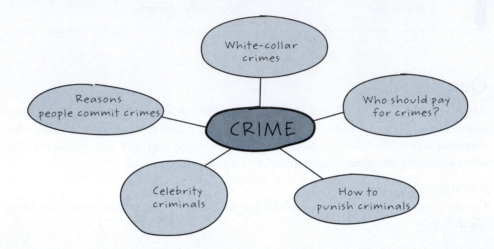

MAHAN'S FOCUSED CLUSTERING

Mahan decided to write about the reasons that people commit crimes. He added clusters to that topic.

The Writer's Desk: Clustering

Choose one of the following topics and use clustering to explore it on a separate sheet of paper. Begin by writing the key word in the middle of the space. Then connect related ideas.

Jobs   Health   Relationships

> ### HINT: More About Exploring
>
> When you explore a topic using any of the listed strategies, keep in mind that a lot of the ideas you generate may not be useful. Later, when you develop your ideas, be prepared to cut irrelevant information.

Journal and Portfolio Writing

1.6   **Practice journal and portfolio writing.**

Keeping a Journal

You may write for work or school, but you can also practice writing for pleasure by keeping a **journal**. This is a book, a computer file, or a blog (Web log) where you record thoughts, opinions, ideas, and impressions. Journal writing gives you a chance to write without worrying about your readers and what they might think about it. Journal writing also gives you a source of material when you want to write about a topic of your choice. According to author Anaïs Nin, "Keeping a diary is a way of making everyday life seem as exciting as fiction."

In your journal, write about any topic that appeals to you. Here are some topics for journal writing.

- Reflections and feelings about your personal life, career goals, college courses, past and future decisions, and work

- Your reactions to controversies in the world or in your country, state, city, or college

- Facts that interest you

- Your reflections on the opinions and philosophies of others, including friends or people that you learn about in your courses

Keeping a Portfolio

A **writing portfolio** is a binder or an electronic file folder where you keep samples of all of your writing. The reason to keep a portfolio is to have a record of your writing progress. In your portfolio, keep all drafts of your writing assignments. When you work on new assignments, review your previous work in your portfolio. Identify your main problems, and try not to repeat the same errors.

Reflect On It

Think about what you learned in this chapter. If you do not know an answer, review that topic.

1. Before you write, you should think about your topic, audience, and purpose. Explain what each one is.

   a. topic: _____

   b. audience: _____

   c. purpose: _____

2. Briefly define each of the following exploring styles.

   a. freewriting: _____

   b. brainstorming: _____

   c. questioning: _____

   d. clustering: _____

The Writer's Room

Writing Activity 1

Choose one of the following topics, or choose your own topic. Then generate ideas about the topic. You may want to try the suggested exploring strategy.

General Topics

1. Try freewriting about a friendship.
2. Try brainstorming about happiness, listing any thoughts that come to mind.
3. Try clustering. First, write "shopping" in the middle of the page. Then write clusters of ideas that connect to the general topic.
4. Ask and answer some questions about online addictions.

College- and Work-Related Topics

5. Try freewriting about a comfortable work environment. Include any emotions or other details that come to mind.
6. Try brainstorming about study habits. List any ideas that come to mind.
7. To get ideas, ask and answer questions about the best or worst jobs.
8. Try clustering about different types of customers. First, write "customers" in the middle of the page. Then write clusters of ideas that relate to the general topic.

Writing Activity 2

Look carefully at the poster below. First, determine the topic, audience, and purpose. Whom is the poster trying to convince? What is the purpose? Is the purpose fulfilled? Then try exploring the topic. Use questioning as your exploring strategy. Ask and answer *who, what, when, where, why,* and *how* questions.

National Highway Traffic Safety Administration (NHTSA), Concept Farm and Ad Council

Exploring Checklist

As you explore your topics, ask yourself the following questions.

❏ What is my topic? (Consider what you will write about.)

❏ Who is my audience? (Think about your intended reader.)

❏ What is my purpose? (Determine your reason for writing.)

❏ How can I explore? (You might try freewriting, brainstorming, questioning, or clustering.)

2   Developing

LEARNING OBJECTIVES

2.1 Define developing.

2.2 Narrow your topic.

2.3 Write your topic sentence.

2.4 Generate supporting ideas.

2.5 Develop a paragraph plan.

2.6 Write the first draft.

After finding an idea, an artist begins to define shapes and layer on colors. Like an artist, a writer shapes ideas to create a solid paragraph or essay.

What Is Developing?

2.1   Define developing.

In Chapter 1, you learned how to use exploring strategies to formulate ideas. In this chapter, you focus on the second stage of the writing process: **developing**. There are five key steps in the developing stage.

> **ESSAY LINK**
> When you develop an essay, you follow similar steps. For details about essay writing, see Chapter 13.

Developing

STEP 1   **Narrow your topic.** Focus on some aspect of the topic that interests you.

STEP 2   **Express your main idea.** Write a topic sentence that expresses the main idea of the paragraph (or a thesis statement that expresses the main idea of the essay).

STEP 3   **Develop your supporting ideas.** Find facts, examples, or anecdotes that best support your main idea.

STEP 4   **Make a plan.** Organize your main and supporting ideas, and place your ideas in a plan or an outline.

STEP 5   **Write your first draft.** Communicate your ideas in a single written piece.

Reviewing Paragraph Structure

Before you practice developing your paragraphs, review the paragraph structure. A **paragraph** is a series of related sentences that develop one central idea. Because a paragraph can stand alone or be part of a longer piece of writing, it is the essential writing model. You can apply your paragraph writing skills to longer essays, letters, and reports. A stand-alone paragraph generally has the following characteristics.

- A **topic sentence** states the topic and introduces the idea the writer will develop.
- **Body sentences** support the topic sentence.
- A **concluding sentence** ends the paragraph.

College student Tam Wang wrote the following paragraph. Notice how it is structured.

> The topic sentence expresses the main idea.

Greenwashing occurs when companies misleadingly promote themselves as environmentally friendly. Just as whitewashing means "to make something look better than it is," greenwashing is an attempt to look greener than one really is. Some greenwashers spend more money advertising their "green" qualities than actually doing ecological practices.

> Supporting sentences provide details and examples.

For instance, an electronic device can be advertised as energy-efficient even though it contains hazardous materials. Oil companies promote eco-friendly corn ethanol even though its production is energy-intensive. Finally, some products have misleading labels with images of mountains and trees. Various household cleaners claim to be organic, but they were

> The concluding sentence brings the paragraph to a satisfying close.

never tested by an impartial organization. In short, greenwashers make use of vague and misleading marketing.

HINT: Paragraph Form

- Leave a 1-inch margin on each side of your paragraph.
- If a title is required, capitalize the first word and the major words in your title and center it. Do not underline it or put it in bold. Indent the first word of a paragraph ½ inch from the left-hand margin.
- Begin every sentence with a capital letter, and end each sentence with the proper punctuation

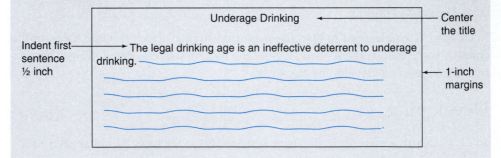

General Topic: The job interview

Narrowed Topic: How to dress for a job interview

Narrow the Topic

2.2   **Narrow your topic.**

A paragraph has one main idea. If your topic is too broad, you might find it difficult to write only one paragraph about it. When you narrow your topic, you make it more specific by using exploring strategies such as freewriting, brainstorming, and questioning. These strategies are explained in more detail in Chapter 1, "Exploring."

HINT: Narrowing the Topic

One way to narrow your topic is to break it down into smaller categories.

Sports

Steroids in sports   Team sports   Dangerous sports

TIA'S EXAMPLE OF NARROWING A TOPIC

College student Tia Clement practiced narrowing a topic by thinking of ideas about her favorite place.

—places I feel comfortable: my bedroom; my house

—a beautiful garden

—the local café where my friends and I hang out

—on the beach

—bookstore where I work

—anywhere my family is

> **ESSAY LINK**
> An essay contains several paragraphs and can have a broader topic than a paragraph.

The Writer's Desk: Narrow the Topic

Topics 1 to 5 are very broad. Practice narrowing topics by writing three ideas for each one.

EXAMPLE: Crime: white-collar crime

why people steal

types of punishment

1. Stress: _____

_____

_____

2. Gossip: _____

_____

_____

3. Nature: _____

_____

_____

4. Sports: _____

_____

_____

5. Jobs: _____

_____

_____

The Topic Sentence

2.3   Write your topic sentence.

After you have narrowed the topic of your paragraph, your next step is to write a topic sentence. The **topic sentence** has specific characteristics.

- It introduces the topic of the paragraph.
- It states the paragraph's controlling idea.
- It is the most general sentence in the paragraph.
- It is followed by other sentences that provide supporting facts and examples.

The **controlling idea** makes a point about the topic and expresses the writer's opinion, attitude, or feeling. You can express different controlling ideas about the same topic. For example, the following topic sentences are about youth offenders, but each sentence makes a different point about the topic.

narrowed topic   controlling idea
Youth offenders should not receive special treatment from the correctional system.

controlling idea   narrowed topic
Rehabilitation and education are the best ways for the state to handle **youth offenders**.

Practice 1

Circle the topic and underline the controlling idea in each topic sentence.

EXAMPLE: Repair a water heater with three simple steps.

1. Bike theft is a very serious crime.

2. Battle rap, conscious rap, and gangsta rap are three important subgenres of hip-hop.

3. My hometown is a desirable place to live.

4. Everything went wrong on the day of my high school graduation.

5. The beauty of Grand Canyon National Park left me breathless.

6. A growing concern in our community is online phishing.

7. Follow the next guidelines before you buy a used car.

8. Newspapers are losing money for several reasons.

Identifying the Topic Sentence

Before you write topic sentences, practice finding them in paragraphs by other writers. To find the topic sentence of a paragraph, follow these steps.

- Read the paragraph carefully.
- Look for a sentence that sums up the paragraph's subject. Professional writers may place the topic sentence anywhere in the paragraph.
- After you have chosen a sentence, see if the other sentences in the paragraph provide evidence that supports that sentence.

If you find one sentence that sums up what the paragraph is about and is supported by other sentences in the paragraph, then you have identified the topic sentence.

Practice 2

Underline or highlight the topic sentences in paragraphs 1, 2, and 3. Remember that the topic sentence is not always the first sentence in the paragraph.

EXAMPLE:

Clever marketers have manipulated the public to equate diamonds with wedding proposals. In the 1930s, the Oppenheimer family, which controlled the diamond trade, discovered large diamond deposits in South Africa. Before then, diamonds were valuable because they were rare. The family faced the problem of marketing a product that was no longer scarce. Using clever marketing techniques, such as the creation of the slogan "Diamonds are forever," the family entrenched the idea in people's minds that a wedding proposal should be accompanied with a diamond ring. Oppenheimer's company, De Beers, also paid film companies to include "diamond ring" wedding proposals in film scripts. The larger the diamond, the more a man expressed his love. Today, the average bride expects to receive a diamond ring, unaware that a diamond company created the tradition.

1. Deviant police officers pose trouble for many groups. Among other things, the problem police officer stains the reputation of police officers in general. Furthermore, they give their department a bad reputation. For example, Freddie Gray was a twenty-five-year-old man who died in Baltimore police custody in April 2015. His death caused Americans to question police tactics and led to a serious lack of confidence in policing by the general public. Moreover, problem officers fail to provide fair protection for the citizens they are supposed to serve. And, most importantly, the autonomy given to police officers and the hidden nature of much police work make it difficult for police forces to detect the problem officer.

    —Dino DeCrescenza, "Early Detection of the Problem Officer"

2. A ring, a ceremony, and a joyful notice in the newspaper once demonstrated the highlights of a romance, and the bitter lowlights were usually endured in the tearful intimacy of close friends. These days, however, in a culture permeated by social networking sites like Facebook, a simple click of a button can mark the beginning and end of a relationship. For instance, about a year ago, as Jamie Barone's relationship became serious, he had a discussion with his girlfriend about changing their relationship status from "single" to "in a relationship" on their Facebook profiles. Barone describes Facebook as a "billboard." The negative side of romance is also publicized. When Spencer Raymond, twenty-six, changed his Facebook status to single, he inadvertently hurt his ex-girlfriend. She was barraged with phone calls from several of their four hundred online friends, an experience he says was uncomfortable for both of them. "Relationships are hard as it is," says Raymond. Facebook just "adds to the pain of a sensitive situation."

    —Zunaira Zaki, "Love and Heartbreak on Facebook," *ABCNews.com*

3. Many factors shape people's worldviews and perception of their environment. Religion and spiritual beliefs are among the most influential. A person's political ideology also may shape his or her attitudes. For instance, one's views on the proper role of government may guide whether one wants government to intervene in a market economy to protect environmental quality. Shared cultural experience is another factor. A community may share

a particular outlook if its members have lived through similar experiences. Early European settlers in the Americas facing the struggles of frontier life viewed their environment as a hostile force because inclement weather and wild animals frequently destroyed crops and killed livestock.

—Jay Withgott and Matthew Laposta, *Environment*

Writing an Effective Topic Sentence

When you develop your topic sentence, avoid some common errors by asking yourself these three questions.

TECHNOLOGY LINK
If you write your paragraph on a computer, make your topic sentence bold (ctrl B). Then you and your instructor can easily identify it.

1. **Is my topic sentence a complete sentence that has a controlling idea?**

   You might state the topic in one word or phrase, but your topic sentence should always reveal a complete thought and have a controlling idea. It should not simply announce the topic.

Incomplete	Working in a restaurant.
	(This is *not* an effective topic sentence. It gives a topic but it does not contain both a subject and a verb, and it does not express a complete thought.)
Announcement	I will write about part-time jobs.
	(This is *not* a topic sentence. It announces the topic but says nothing relevant about it. Do not use expressions such as *My topic is . . .* or *I will write about. . . .*)
Topic sentence	Part-time jobs help college students build self-esteem.

2. **Does my topic sentence make a valid and supportable point?**

   Your topic sentence should express a valid point that you can support with your evidence. It should not be a vaguely worded statement, and it should not be a highly questionable generalization.

Vague	Beauty is becoming more important in our culture.
	(Beauty is more important than what?)
Invalid point	Beauty is more important than it was in the past.
	(Is this really true? Cultures throughout history have been concerned with notions of beauty.)
Topic sentence	Fashion magazines do not provide readers with enough varied examples of beauty.

ESSAY LINK
If you find that your topic is too broad for a paragraph, you might want to save it so you can try using it for an essay.

3. **Can I support my topic sentence in a single paragraph?**

   Your topic sentence should express an idea that you can support in a paragraph. It should not be too broad or too narrow.

Too broad	Love is important.
	(It would be difficult to write only a paragraph about this topic. There are too many things to say.)
Too narrow	My girlfriend was born on March 2.
	(What more is there to say?)
Topic sentence	During my first relationship, I learned a lot about being honest.

HINT: Write a Clear Topic Sentence

Your topic sentence should not express an obvious or well-known fact. When you clearly indicate your point of view, your topic sentence will capture your readers' attention and make your readers want to continue reading.

Obvious	Money is important in our world.
	(Everybody knows this.)
Better	There are several effective ways to save money.

Practice 3

Choose the word from the list that best describes the problem with each topic sentence. Correct the problem by revising each sentence.

Announces	Incomplete	Narrow
Broad	Invalid	Vague

EXAMPLE: Violence is a big problem.

Problem: <u>Vague and broad</u>

Revision: <u>Colleges should take strong measures to make campuses safe for female students</u>.

1. Funding of public schools

Problem: _____   Revision: _____

_____

2. This paragraph is about cybercrime.

Problem: _____   Revision: _____

_____

3. Americans are losing their jobs.

Problem: _____   Revision: _____

_____

4. Daniel's car is silver.

Problem: _____   Revision: _____

_____

5. Girls don't like science.

Problem: _____   Revision: _____

_____

6. I will write about the problems with ecotourism.

Problem: _____   Revision: _____

_____

Practice 4

The following paragraphs do not contain topic sentences. Read the paragraphs carefully, and write appropriate topic sentences for each.

1. _____

_____

First, take shorter showers. Five minutes is enough time to get clean. Also, do the laundry only when there is a full load. When brushing your teeth, don't leave the water running. Just turn the water off and on as needed. Finally, ask your landlord to install toilets that use very little water. Remember that water is a precious resource.

2. _____

_____

First, art education teaches children to be creative thinkers. Early exposure to art promotes right-brain thinking. Also, art classes help children have a greater appreciation for the beauty that surrounds them daily. It helps them slow down and appreciate life. Above all, making art is fun. It provides a stress-free moment in a child's day.

The Writer's Desk: Write Topic Sentences

Narrow each of the topics in this exercise. Then write a topic sentence that contains a controlling idea. You could look at the Writer's Desk: Narrow the Topic on page 15 for ideas.

EXAMPLE: Crime   Narrowed topic: _Why people steal_____

Topic sentence: _People steal for several reasons._____

_____

1. Stress   Narrowed topic: _____

   Topic sentence: _____

   _____

2. Gossip   Narrowed topic: _____

   Topic sentence: _____

   _____

3. Nature   Narrowed topic: _____

   Topic sentence: _____

   _____

4. Sports   Narrowed topic: _____

   Topic sentence: _____

   _____

5. Jobs   Narrowed topic: _____

   Topic sentence: _____

   _____

The Supporting Ideas

2.4   Generate supporting ideas.

Once you have written a clear topic sentence, focus on the **supporting details**—the facts and examples that provide the reader with interesting information about the subject matter.

ESSAY LINK

When writing an essay, place the thesis statement in the introduction. Use each supporting idea to write a distinct paragraph with its own topic sentence.

Generating Supporting Ideas

Try an exploring strategy such as brainstorming or freewriting to generate ideas. Then you can choose the best ideas.

An effective paragraph has **unity** when all of its sentences directly relate to and support the topic sentence. Create a unified paragraph by selecting three or four ideas that are the most compelling and that clearly prop up your topic sentence. You may notice that several items in your list are similar; therefore, you can group them together. If some items do not support the topic sentence, remove them.

MAHAN'S SUPPORTING IDEAS

College student Mahan Zahir narrowed his topic and brainstormed a list of supporting ideas. Then he grouped similar ideas together and crossed out two items.

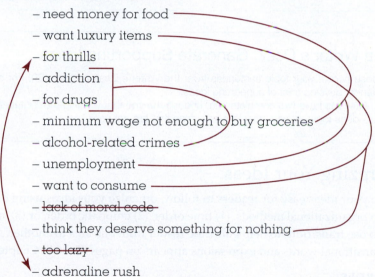

People steal for many reasons.
- need money for food
- want luxury items
- for thrills
- addiction
- for drugs
- minimum wage not enough to buy groceries
- alcohol-related crimes
- unemployment
- want to consume
- ~~lack of moral code~~
- think they deserve something for nothing
- ~~too lazy~~
- adrenaline rush

HINT: Identifying the Best Ideas

There are many ways that you can highlight your best ideas. You can circle the best supporting points and then use arrows to link them with secondary ideas. You can also use highlighter pens or asterisks (*) to identify the best supporting points.

TECHNOLOGY LINK

On a computer, you can cut (ctrl X) and paste (ctrl V) similar ideas together.

Practice 5

College student Romina Herrera brainstormed ideas about compulsory volunteer work. Her purpose was to persuade, so she created a topic sentence that expressed her opinion about the issue.

Underline the three ideas from her list that you think are the most compelling and that most clearly illustrate the point she is making in her topic sentence. Then group together any related ideas under each of the main subheadings. If any ideas do not relate to her topic sentence, cross them out.

Topic Sentence: Freshman high school students should be forced to do community service on weekends.

—in Haiti, youths helped rebuild houses after the earthquake

—during last year's floods, student volunteers could have helped in shelters

—can provide assistance in times of crisis

—some students are too lazy and don't want to help anyone else

—Miguel stopped littering after he cleared roadside garbage

—provides a chance to learn about real-world issues with the environment, poverty, etc.

—can gather food and clothing for the homeless

—some students need to earn money on weekends

—provides a character-building opportunity

—Kelsey developed empathy when she worked at the women's shelter

—need more shelters for battered women

—Ivan became more generous after working with the homeless

ESSAY LINK
In an essay, you can use time, space, or emphatic order to organize your ideas.

The Writer's Desk: Generate Supporting Ideas

Choose two of your topic sentences from the Writer's Desk on page 20. For each topic sentence, develop a list of supporting ideas.

After you have two complete lists, choose the one that you find most interesting. Then group ideas together and cross out any ideas that are not useful.

Organizing Your Ideas

To make your ideas easy for readers to follow, organize your ideas using one of three common organizational methods: (1) time order, (2) emphatic order, or (3) space order.

Also use **transitions** to help guide the reader from one idea to another. A complete list of transitional words and expressions appears on pages 35–36 in Chapter 3.

TIME ORDER

When organizing a paragraph using **time order (chronological order)**, arrange the details according to the sequence in which they have occurred. When you narrate a story, explain how to do something, or describe a historical event, you generally use time order.

first   then   after that

Here are some transitional expressions you can use in time-order paragraphs.

after that	first	later	next
eventually	in the beginning	meanwhile	suddenly
finally	immediately	months after	then

The next paragraph is structured using time order.

> One day, some gentlemen called on my mother, and I felt the shutting of the front door and other sounds that indicated their arrival. Immediately, I ran upstairs before anyone could stop me to put on my idea of formal clothing. Standing before the mirror, as I had seen others do, I anointed my head with oil and covered my face thickly with powder. Then I pinned a veil over my head so that it covered my face and fell in folds down to my shoulders. Finally, I tied an enormous bustle round my small waist, so that it dangled behind, almost meeting the hem of my skirt. Thus attired, I went down to help entertain the company.
>
> —Helen Keller, *The Story of My Life*

EMPHATIC ORDER

When you organize the supporting details of a paragraph using **emphatic order**, you arrange them in a logical sequence. For example, you can arrange details from least to most important, from least appealing to most appealing, and so on.

Banana Republic/Fotolia

Here are some transitional expressions you can use in emphatic-order paragraphs.

above all	first	moreover	principally
clearly	in particular	most importantly	the least important
especially	last	of course	the most important

The following paragraph uses emphatic order. The writer presents the conditions from bad to the worst.

> The conditions experienced by the eager young volunteers of the Union and Confederate armies included massive, terrifying, and bloody battles, apparently unending, with no sign of victory in sight. First, soldiers suffered from the uncertainty of supply, which left troops, especially in the South, without uniforms, tents, and sometimes even food. They also endured long marches over muddy, rutted roads while carrying packs weighing fifty or sixty pounds. Most importantly, disease was rampant in their dirty, verminous, and unsanitary camps, and hospitals were so dreadful that more men left them dead than alive.
>
> —Adapted from John Mack Faragher et al., *Out of Many:*
> *A History of the American People*

HINT: Using Emphatic Order

When you organize details using emphatic order, use your own values and opinions to determine what is most or least important, upsetting, remarkable, and so on. Another writer might organize the same ideas in a different way.

SPACE ORDER

When you organize ideas using **space order**, you help the reader visualize what you are describing in a specific space. For example, you can describe something or someone from top to bottom or bottom to top, from left to right or right to left, or from far to near or near to far.

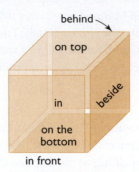

Here are some transitional expressions you can use in space-order paragraphs.

above	beneath	nearby	on top
behind	closer in	on the bottom	toward
below	farther out	on the left	under

In the next paragraph, the writer describes a location beginning at the beach and ending at the front of the house.

> Their house was even more elaborate than I expected. It was a cheerful red-and-white Georgian Colonial mansion overlooking the bay. The lawn started at the beach and ran toward the front door for a quarter of a mile, jumping over sundials and brick walks and burning gardens. Finally, when it reached the house, it drifted up the side in bright vines as though from the momentum of its run. The front was broken by a line of French windows.
>
> —F. Scott Fitzgerald, *The Great Gatsby*

Practice 6

Read each paragraph and underline the topic sentence. Then decide what order the writer used: time, emphatic, or space order. Circle any words or phrases that help you make your choice.

1.   Plastic is extremely harmful for our marine environment. First, plastic is not biodegradable. Often large pieces of plastic are broken into smaller beads, which float under the surface of the water. Sometimes, the plastic bits sink to the bottom of the ocean, covering the ocean floor with litter. Next, plastic pieces travel over large distances due to ocean currents. Species from one part of the world spread to another part of the world by using the plastic pieces as boats. When a foreign species invades a region, it can destroy the native species. Most importantly, sea creatures often mistake small pieces of floating plastic for plankton. Plastic contains harmful substances. After eating the plastic, the digestive system of marine animals is harmed, often causing their death.

—Suzhi Park, student

Order: _____

2.   After two months of work, I realized that my job selling a health drink was actually a pyramid scheme. In the beginning, I answered an online ad promising great money in sales. I went to the initiation meeting, and there were about twenty job seekers. Enthusiastic speakers spoke to us about the enormous

amounts of money we would soon be earning. The next day, after a screening process, the recruiter claimed to choose the best candidates. I now realize that she chose everybody. Then, a week later, we were asked to invest $200 in our initial samples. "Sell your drinks and the money will start rolling in," the recruiter promised. We could also earn income by recruiting more salespeople. I was nervous, but I really needed the job, so I put almost all of my savings into those power drinks. After two months of unsuccessful sales, I understood that the only people making money were those at the top of the scheme.

—Latonza Hines, student

Order: _____

3. Samuel Spade's jaw was long and bony, his chin a jutting v under the more flexible v of his mouth. His nostrils curved back to make another, smaller, v. His yellow-grey eyes were horizontal. The v motif was picked up again by thickish brows rising outward from twin creases above a hooked nose, and his pale brown hair grew down—from high flat temples—in a point on his forehead. He looked rather pleasantly like a blond satan.

—Dashiell Hammett, *The Maltese Falcon*

Order: _____

Practice 7

Read the following topic sentences. Decide whether to use time, emphatic, or space order to develop the paragraph details. (There may be more than one correct organizational method.)

EXAMPLE: Repair a water heater with three simple steps.   _time_

1. Physical education is essential in public schools.   _____

2. There are three types of difficult bosses.   _____

3. My furnished room has everything a student could need.   _____

4. We had many problems during our camping trip.   _____

5. Carolina Bomback has a very eccentric fashion style.   _____

6. A serious problem in high schools is cyberbullying.   _____

7. The Beatles went through many musical phases.   _____

8. Learning to cook well requires practice, patience, and perseverance.   _____

The Paragraph Plan

2.5 **Develop a paragraph plan.**

A **plan** (or **outline**) of a paragraph is a map showing the paragraph's main and supporting ideas. To make a plan, write your topic sentence and then list supporting points and details. Remember to use time, emphatic, or space order to organize the supporting points. In a more formal outline, you can use letters and numbers to indicate primary and secondary ideas.

MAHAN'S PARAGRAPH PLAN
Mahan completed his paragraph plan. He narrowed his topic, wrote a topic sentence, and thought of several supporting details. Here is his paragraph plan.

ESSAY LINK
Make a plan when you write an essay. In essay plans, each supporting idea becomes a separate paragraph.

Topic Sentence: People steal for many reasons.

Support 1:   Poverty is a primary motivation for people to steal.

   Details: —some people are unemployed

                —others work at low-paying jobs

                —need money for food, rent, clothing

Support 2:   Some criminals are greedy.

   Details: —want to live a life of luxury

                —crave jewels and nice cars

                —wish for a larger yacht or faster jet

Support 3:   Some people steal due to drug or alcohol addictions.

   Details: —addicts steal to buy drugs

                —alcohol ruins good judgment

Support 4:   Some people steal for the kicks.

   Details: —experience the thrill

                —receive an adrenaline rush when stealing

HINT: Adding Specific Details

When you prepare your paragraph plan, ask yourself if the details clearly support your topic sentence. If not, then you could add details to make your points stronger. For example, when Mahan first brainstormed a list of supporting details (page 21), he did not think of specific details to support his point about greed. In his paragraph plan, however, he added a few more details (larger yacht, faster jet) to make that point stronger and more complete.

The Writer's Desk: Write a Paragraph Plan

Look at the topic sentence and the organized list of supporting ideas that you created for the previous Writer's Desk exercises. Now, in the space provided, make a paragraph plan. Remember to include details for each supporting idea.

Topic sentence: _____

_____

Support 1: _____

Details: _____

_____

Support 2: _____

Details: _____

_____

Support 3: _____

Details: _____

_____

Writing the Concluding Sentence

A stand-alone paragraph may have a **concluding sentence** that brings it to a satisfactory close. There are several ways to write a concluding sentence.

ESSAY LINK
Essays end with a concluding paragraph. For more information, see Chapter 1.

- Restate the topic sentence in a new, refreshing way.
- Make an interesting final observation.
- End with a prediction, suggestion, or quotation.

HINT: Problems with Concluding Sentences

To make an effective conclusion, avoid the following:

- Do not contradict your main point or introduce new or irrelevant information.
- Do not apologize or back down from your main points.
- Do not end with a rhetorical question. (A rhetorical question is a question that won't be answered, such as, "When will people stop texting while driving?")

   For example, in Mahan's paragraph about crime, he should not end with a statement that questions or contradicts his main point.

Weak	But nobody really understands why people break the law.
	(This concluding sentence undermines the main point, which is that people steal for many reasons.)
Better	Knowing why people steal may help social services and lawmakers deal with criminals more effectively.
	(This prediction closes off the paragraph.)

Practice 8

The topic sentences in paragraphs 1 and 2 are underlined. For each paragraph, circle the letter of the most effective concluding sentence, and then explain why the other choice is not as effective.

EXAMPLE:

   Games are not just for children. <u>Adults should exercise their brains by playing games.</u> Puzzles and games help keep a person's mind sharp, especially as the aging process occurs. According to the *New England Journal of Medicine*, seniors who play cards, do board games, and solve crossword puzzles can reduce their risks of developing dementia. Marcia Wilkins, a senior living in Arlington, Virginia, plays the addictive number game Sudoku and credits the game with helping her concentration skills.

   a. However, do all adults have the time or energy to play games?
   b. Ultimately, people need to exercise their brains as much as they exercise their bodies.

Why is the other choice not as effective?

Answer "a" is a rhetorical question that sends the paragraph

in a different direction.

1.   Our government should address the serious issue of homelessness. First, people with mental illness or substance addiction often do not get the help they need to function in society. Due to inadequate social services, these vulnerable people have difficulty finding and keeping jobs; therefore, they do not have the money to pay for housing. Second, people who lose their jobs often find themselves no longer able to pay their rent. For example, during the 2008 financial crisis, many people who became unemployed had to live in their cars. Finally, some people find themselves without affordable housing when their communities undergo redevelopment or gentrification. Rising property taxes and rents make it difficult for the poor to remain in the neighborhood.

   a. <u>Politicians should search for solutions to this serious problem.</u>

   b. Most people do not remain homeless for long.

   Why is the other choice not as effective?

   _____

2.   College students should find part-time jobs that require them to exercise different muscles. If a business student spends hours sitting in front of a computer screen, then he should try to find a job that requires physical activity. If an engineering student has to do advanced calculus, then maybe her part-time job should allow her to rest her brain. Students who do a lot of solitary study could try to find jobs that allow them to interact socially.

   a. Some college students should not take part-time jobs because they need to concentrate on their studies.

   b. Humans need to do a variety of activities to be mentally and physically strong, so college students should keep that in mind when they look for work.

   Why is the other choice not as effective?

   _____

The First Draft

2.6   **Write the first draft.**

After making a paragraph plan, you are ready to write your first draft, which is a very important step in the writing process. The first draft includes your topic sentence, some supporting details, and a concluding sentence. It is okay if the first draft is incomplete or messy. Later, during the revising and editing stages, you can clarify ideas and modify the organization of your paragraph.

MAHAN'S FIRST DRAFT

Here is Mahan Zahir's first draft. You may notice that his paragraph has errors. He will correct these when he gets to the revising and editing stage of the process.

    People steal for many reasons. Poverty is a primary motivation for people to steal. Because some people are unemployed and others may be underemployed. They may not have enough money for food, clothing rent. Stealing money or food may be very tempting. As a means of survival. Criminals do fraud because they are greedy. In fact, some extremly wealthy people steal simply because they want to acquire a larger yacht

or a more better jet. Another important reason that people engage in
stealing is to pay for their addictions. Finally, people also steal for kicks.
Criminals get an adrenaline rush when you outwit the cops.

The Writer's Desk: Write Your First Draft

In the previous Writer's Desk on page 26, you made a paragraph plan. Now use the plan's
information to type or write your first draft paragraph.

Reflect On It

Think about what you have learned in this chapter. If you do not know an
answer, review that topic.

1. What is a topic sentence? _____

   _____

2. What is time order? _____

   _____

3. What is emphatic order? _____

   _____

4. What is space order? _____

   _____

Are the following sentences true or false? Circle the best answer.

5. A paragraph has more than one main idea.   True   False

6. A paragraph's details support its topic sentence.   True   False

7. A paragraph can have several supporting ideas.   True   False

The Writer's Room

Writing Activity 1

In the Writer's Room in Chapter 1, "Exploring," you used various strategies to find ideas
about the following topics. Select one of the topics and write a paragraph. Remember
to follow the writing process.

General Topics

1. friendship

2. happiness

3. shopping

4. online addictions

College- and Work-Related Topics

5. a comfortable work environment

6. study or work habits

7. best and worst jobs

8. types of customers

Writing Activity 2

Choose a topic that you feel passionate about, and write a paragraph. Your topic could be an activity (painting, swimming, basketball) or an interest (music, politics). Your topic sentence should make a point about the topic.

Developing Checklist

As you develop your paragraph, ask yourself the following questions.

❏ Have I narrowed my topic?

❏ Does my topic sentence make a valid and supportable point about the topic?

❏ Is my topic sentence interesting?

❏ Does my paragraph focus on one main idea?

❏ Do the details support the topic sentence?

❏ Do the supporting details follow a logical order?

❏ Does my paragraph end in a satisfactory way?

3 Revising and Editing

The revising and editing stage of the writing process is similar to adding the finishing touches to an artwork. Small improvements can make the work more solid and complete.

LEARNING OBJECTIVES

3.1 Define revising and editing.

3.2 Revise for unity.

3.3 Revise for adequate support.

3.4 Revise for coherence.

3.5 Revise for style.

3.6 Edit for errors.

3.7 Write a final draft.

What Are Revising and Editing?

3.1 Define revising and editing.

The next step in the writing process is to revise and edit your work. When you **revise**, you modify your writing to make it stronger and more convincing. Read your first draft critically, looking for faulty logic, poor organization, or poor sentence style. Then you reorganize and rewrite your draft, making any necessary changes. When you **edit**, you proofread your final draft for errors in grammar, spelling, punctuation, and mechanics.

There are five key steps to follow during the revising and editing stage.

Revising and Editing

STEP 1 Revise for unity. Ensure that all parts of your work relate to the main idea.

STEP 2 Revise for adequate support. Determine that your details effectively support the main idea.

STEP 3 Revise for coherence. Verify that your ideas flow smoothly and logically.

STEP 4 Revise for style. Ensure that your sentences are varied and interesting.

STEP 5 Edit for technical errors. Proofread your work, and correct errors in grammar, spelling, mechanics, and punctuation.

Revise for Unity

3.2 **Revise for unity.**

Unity means that a paragraph has only one main idea. All of the sentences in the paragraph should support the topic sentence. A paragraph lacks unity if some sentences drift from the main idea or if the paragraph contains two main ideas. To check for unity, ensure that every sentence in the body of the paragraph relates to one main idea.

PARAGRAPH WITHOUT UNITY

In the next paragraph, the writer drifted away from her main idea. The highlighted sentences do not relate to the topic sentence. When they are removed, the paragraph has unity.

> **The United States should make voting mandatory.** In most elections, more than half of eligible voters stay home. For democracy to work, citizens must vote. It is a person's civic duty. Mandatory voting will ensure that a majority of the population expresses its concerns about issues. Moreover, candidates would have to develop election platforms that appeal to many groups. Such groups would include the most vulnerable, like the very poor. In addition, political candidates would spend less on campaigns because the politicians would not need to mobilize voters. Of course, some people are not interested in politics. In fact, my friend Jimmy-Lee never votes. He thinks it is not worth it. Voting is important, and the government should make it compulsory.

Every idea in a paragraph should move in the same direction just as the vehicles on this bridge need to move in the same direction to reach their destinations. There should be no detours or forks in the road.

The writer took a detour here.

ESSAY LINK
When revising and editing your essay, check that the body paragraphs support the thesis statement. Also, ensure that each body paragraph has unity.

Practice 1

Paragraphs 1 and 2 contain problems with unity. Underline the topic sentence of each paragraph. Then circle the letter that indicates the type of problem, and make any necessary changes to each paragraph to ensure that it has unity. You may have to cross out sentences that do not belong, or you may have to indicate the start of a new paragraph.

1. Although parents and teachers often criticize the negative influence of video games on today's youth, such games may actually have a positive impact on young people. First, video games help people acquire important skills, such as problem solving, hand–eye coordination, and memory skills. With "Guitar Hero" or "Wii Sports," players improve these skills because the levels of games vary in difficulty. Also, video games improve players' social skills. Some video games, such as "Lara Croft" and "The Sims," teach players about leadership, friendship, and real-life rules. Lastly, video games are powerful tools to aid children who lack self-esteem. If a child attains a high level playing the "Tony Hawk's Motion" game, he or she may feel a sense of accomplishment. However, some games are too violent, such as Grand Theft Auto. That game is really bloody. Thus, parents should remember that video games can have positive effects on youths.

    a. Some sentences are off topic.   b. Paragraph contains two main ideas.

2. Americans will benefit in many ways if the government raises the tax on junk food. First, a high tax rate will increase the price of items like chips and soda. Consumers will most likely have to limit the purchase of these products. By reducing their consumption of junk food, consumers will get fewer calories from nutritionally empty food. People will eat better to replace the empty calories, which will lead to improved health. Health problems like obesity and type 2 diabetes might be reduced in the general

population. Healthier Americans will use fewer healthcare resources. The government should also give tax rebates to those who participate in some physical exercise. People can join a gym or do an organized physical activity like tai chi for a tax credit. Exercise is one way Americans can be healthier. By encouraging citizens to engage in more exercise, the government will save money on healthcare.

a. Some sentences are off topic.   b. Paragraph contains two main ideas.

Revise for Adequate Support

3.3   Revise for adequate support.

A paragraph has **adequate support** when there are enough details and examples to make it solid, convincing, and interesting. The following paragraph attempts to persuade, but it does not have any specific details that make a strong point.

PARAGRAPH WITHOUT ADEQUATE SUPPORT

A bridge is built using several well-placed support columns. Like a bridge, a paragraph requires adequate support to help it stand on its own.

   In the past, the entertainment industry stereotyped women as the weaker sex. However, women are now portrayed as tough and intelligent characters. Most comic books usually depicted males as superheroes. But comic books now embrace super heroines. Recent films have portrayed females as super heroines. Video games are also changing stereotypical gender roles. The image of women as the weaker sex in the entertainment media is definitely being redefined.

Practice 2

When the preceding paragraph about female stereotypes in the entertainment media is expanded with specific details and examples, the paragraph becomes more convincing. Add details on the lines provided. You can do this practice alone or with a partner.

ESSAY LINK
When revising your essay, ensure that you have adequately supported the thesis statement. Also ensure that each body paragraph has sufficient supporting details.

   In the past, the entertainment industry stereotyped women as the weaker sex. However, women are now portrayed as tough and intelligent characters. Most comic books usually depicted males as superheroes. For example, _____ and _____ fought creepy scoundrels. But comic books now embrace super heroines. One of the most famous female comic book heroines is _____. She is beautiful, but she can fight evil as well as any man. Furthermore, recent films have portrayed females as super heroines. In the movie _____, the actress _____ plays a strong and intelligent character who outwits her opponents. Video games are also changing stereotypical gender roles. For example, _____ is a super-sexy heroine who is strong, determined, and intelligent. She can overcome any obstacle in her way. The image of women as the weaker sex in the entertainment industry is definitely being redefined.

Avoiding Circular Reasoning

Circular reasoning means that a paragraph restates its main point in various ways but does not provide supporting details. The main idea goes in circles and never progresses. Avoid using circular reasoning by providing a clear, concise topic sentence and by supporting the topic sentence with facts, examples, statistics, and anecdotes.

Circular reasoning in a paragraph is like a Ferris wheel. The main idea of the paragraph does not seem to progress.

CHERYL'S PARAGRAPH

Cheryl Bernal-Pena wrote a paragraph about her role model. In her first draft, she repeated her main point and did not provide any details to support her topic sentence.

Circular   I have always considered my mom a warrior. My mother is a great role model because she is so strong. She shows a lot of strength and perseverance when life is difficult and when there is a challenge. Her strength is her greatest quality, and she has a lot of personal power. She taught me that no task is too big and no challenge is too difficult.

In her revised paragraph, Cheryl added details and examples that illustrated her main point.

Revised   I have always considered my mom a warrior. My mother is a great role model because she is so strong. When my brother and I were young, my mother was devastated because my dad abandoned us for another family. We were innocent, but we knew Mom was having a very difficult time. Instead of remaining depressed, she went out and dedicated herself to working to support us. My mom shows a lot of strength and perseverance when life is difficult and when there is a challenge. When we were older, my mother developed ovarian cancer. It was a difficult time, and she went through a lot of suffering, but she beat the disease. Her strength is her greatest quality, and she has a lot of personal power. She has taught me that no task is too big and no challenge is too difficult.

Practice 3

Paragraphs 1 and 2 use circular reasoning. Neither has specific evidence to support the topic sentence. List supporting examples for each paragraph. With numbers, indicate where you would place the supporting examples.

EXAMPLE:

American teenagers go through several rites of passage. These rites of passage **(1)** help the teenager navigate the transition from childhood to adulthood. Some rites **(2)** of passage are shared with the community. These rites are an important part of every youth's life.

Examples: (1) The first date and the first kiss are important. The
                    first job is also a special step.
                    (2) During the high school prom, the community members
                    gather together.

1.   The percentage of Americans who shop online is growing for a number of reasons. People are buying a lot of items from mobile apps and Internet sites. All ages of people shop online, so this form of shopping will only increase.

Examples: _____
_____
_____
_____
_____

2.   Having a summer job teaches adolescents some valuable life lessons. There are many situations that students will experience through a summer job that will help them navigate the adult world. So students should try to get some work knowledge before graduating.

Examples: _____
_____
_____
_____

Revise for Coherence

3.4   Revise for coherence.

When you drive along a highway and suddenly hit a pothole, that is an uncomfortable experience. Readers experience similar discomfort if they encounter potholes in a piece of writing. Make your writing as smooth as possible by ensuring that it has **coherence**. The ideas should be well connected, and the sentences should flow smoothly and logically.

Transitional Expressions

Transitional expressions are words or phrases that connect ideas. Here are some common transitional expressions.

Just as bolts link parts of a bridge, transitional expressions can link ideas in a paragraph.

Function	Transitional Word or Expression		
Addition	again also besides finally first (second, third)	for one thing furthermore in addition in fact last	moreover next then
Concession of a point	certainly even so	indeed no doubt	of course to be sure
Comparison and contrast	as well equally even so however	in contrast instead likewise nevertheless	on the contrary on the other hand similarly
Effect or result	accordingly as a result consequently	hence otherwise then	therefore thus

ESSAY LINK
To create coherence in an essay, you can place transitional expressions at the beginning of each body paragraph.

Function	Transitional Word or Expression		
Example	for example for instance in other words	in particular namely specifically	to illustrate
Emphasis	above all clearly first especially	in fact in particular indeed least of all	most important most of all of course particularly principally
Reason or purpose	for this purpose for this reason	the main reason	
Space	above behind below beneath beside beyond closer in	farther out inside near nearby on one side/on the other side on the bottom	on the left/right on top outside to the north/east/ south/west under
Summary or conclusion	in conclusion in other words in short generally	on the whole therefore thus	to conclude to summarize ultimately
Time	after that at that time at the moment currently earlier eventually first (second, etc.) gradually	immediately in the beginning in the future in the past later meanwhile months after now	one day presently so far subsequently suddenly then these days

GRAMMAR LINK
For more practice using transitions in sentences, see Ch. 17, "Compound Sentences," and Ch. 18, "Complex Sentences."

HINT: Use Transitional Expressions with Complete Sentences

When you add a transitional expression to a sentence, ensure that your sentence is complete. Your sentence must have a subject and a verb, and it must express a complete thought. (Remember to place a comma after the transitional expression.)

Incomplete   For example, the rules posted on the wall.

Complete   For example, the rules were posted on the wall.

Practice 4

The next paragraph contains eight transitional expressions that appear at the beginning of sentences. Underline each expression, and then indicate its purpose. The first one has been done for you.

The McDonaldization of society—the standardization of everyday life—does not refer just to the robot-like assembly of food. Indeed, sociologist George Ritzer points out that this process is occurring throughout society—and it is transforming our lives. First, shopping malls offer one-stop shopping in controlled environments. In addition, travel agencies offer "package" tours. They will transport tourists to ten European capitals in fourteen days. All visitors experience the same hotels, restaurants, and other scheduled sites—and no one need fear meeting a "real" native. Similarly, news agencies **spew** out McNews—short, bland unanalytical pieces that can be digested between gulps of McShake or McBurgers. Moreover, our programmed education will eliminate the need for discussion of social issues. Accordingly, computerized courses will teach the same answers to everyone—

spew: pour out

the approved, "politically correct" ways to think about social issues. Likewise, mass testing will ensure that students **regurgitate** the programmed responses. Therefore, for good or bad, our lives are being McDonaldized, and the predictability of packaged settings seems to be our social destiny.

regurgitate: repeat

—James M. Henslin, *Sociology*

Transitional Expression	Function
1. Indeed	Emphasis
2.	
3.	
4.	
5.	
6.	
7.	
8.	

Practice 5

Add appropriate transitional expressions to the following paragraph. Choose from the following list, and use each transitional word once. There may be more than one correct answer for each blank.

consequently	furthermore	on the other hand
for example	first	therefore

Workplace gossip has both positive and negative effects. _____, when two colleagues share secrets about others, that helps build trust and create intimacy. _____, in large organizations, gossip helps form small social groups that provide workplace support systems. _____, overly negative gossip can undermine employee morale. An employee who hears malicious gossip may suspect that he or she is also the subject of office chatter. _____, Latisha Bishop, an employee at CR Industries, says that she felt devastated when she realized that her coworkers were spreading information about her private life. _____, she seriously considered leaving her job. _____, when office workers share workplace news, they should try to do so without malice.

Revise for Style

Just as paint and lighting can make a bridge more beautiful, varied sentence style makes a paragraph more compelling.

3.5 Revise for style.

When you revise for sentence **style**, you ensure that your paragraph has concise and appropriate language and sentence variety. Ask yourself the following questions.

- Have I used a **variety of sentence patterns**? (To practice using sentence variety, see Chapter 19.)
- Have I used **exact language**? (To learn about slang, wordiness, and overused expressions, see Chapter 32.)
- Are my sentences **parallel in structure**? (To practice revising for parallel structure, see Chapter 22.)

MAHAN'S REVISION

On page 28–29 in Chapter 2, you read the first draft of student Mahan Zahir's paragraph about crime. Look at his revisions for unity, support, coherence, and style.

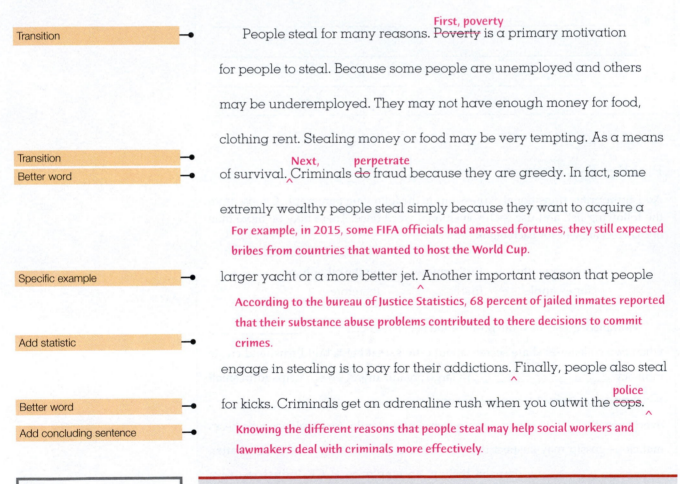

Transition

People steal for many reasons. ~~Poverty~~ **First, poverty** is a primary motivation for people to steal. Because some people are unemployed and others may be underemployed. They may not have enough money for food, clothing rent. Stealing money or food may be very tempting. As a means

Transition
Better word

of survival. **Next,** Criminals ~~do~~ **perpetrate** fraud because they are greedy. In fact, some extremely wealthy people steal simply because they want to acquire a

For example, in 2015, some FIFA officials had amassed fortunes, they still expected bribes from countries that wanted to host the World Cup.

Specific example

larger yacht or a more better jet. Another important reason that people

According to the bureau of Justice Statistics, 68 percent of jailed inmates reported that their substance abuse problems contributed to there decisions to commit crimes.

Add statistic

engage in stealing is to pay for their addictions. Finally, people also steal

Better word

for kicks. Criminals get an adrenaline rush when you outwit the ~~cops~~ **police**.

Add concluding sentence

Knowing the different reasons that people steal may help social workers and lawmakers deal with criminals more effectively.

ESSAY LINK
You should revise your essays for style, ensuring that sentences are varied and parallel. Also, ensure that your language is exact.

HINT: Adding Strong Support

When you revise, look at the strength of your supporting details. Ask yourself the following questions.

- Are my supporting details interesting, and do they grab the reader's attention? Should I use more vivid words?
- Is my concluding sentence appealing? Could I end the paragraph in a more interesting way?

Edit for Errors

3.6   Edit for errors.

When you **edit**, you reread your writing and make sure that it is free of errors. Focus on the language, and look for mistakes in grammar, punctuation, mechanics, and spelling. There is an editing guide at the back of this book. It contains some common error codes that your teacher may use and provides you with a checklist to proofread your text.

Editing Tips

The following tips will help you proofread your work effectively.

- Put your writing aside for a day or two before you do the editing. Sometimes, when you have been working closely with a text, you might not see the errors.

- Begin your proofreading at any stage of the writing process. For example, if you are not sure of the spelling of a word while writing the first draft, you could either highlight the word to check later or immediately look up the word in the dictionary.

- Keep a list of your common errors in a separate grammar log, such as the one in Appendix 7. When you finish a writing assignment, consult your error list and make sure that you have not repeated any of those errors. After each assignment has been corrected, you can add new errors to your list.

MAHAN'S EDITED PARAGRAPH

Mahan Zahir edited his paragraph about crime. He corrected errors in spelling, capitalization, punctuation, and grammar.

People steal for many reasons. First, poverty is a primary motivation for people to steal. Because some people are unemployed and others may be underemployed. ~~They~~ *, they* may not have enough money for food, clothing *, and* rent. Stealing money or food may be very tempting. ~~As~~ *as* a means of survival.

Next, criminals perpetrate fraud because they are greedy. In fact, some ~~extremly~~ *extremely* wealthy people steal simply because they want to acquire a larger yacht or a ~~more better~~ *faster* jet. For example, in 2015, some FIFA officials had amassed fortunes~~, they~~ *. They* still expected bribes from countries that wanted to host the World Cup. Another important reason that people engage in stealing is to pay for their addictions. According to the ~~b~~*B*ureau of Justice Statistics, 68 percent of jailed inmates reported that their substance abuse problems contributed to ~~there~~ *their* decisions to commit crimes. Finally, people also steal for kicks. Criminals get an adrenaline rush when ~~you~~ *they* outwit the police. Knowing the different reasons that people steal may help social workers and lawmakers deal with criminals more effectively.

Practice 6

In Chapters 1 and 2, you saw examples of Tia Clement's prewriting and planning. Now look at the first draft of Tia's paragraph. First, read it and revise it for support and coherence. Also, edit it for five errors in spelling, punctuation, and grammar.

> My favorite place is the beach. It is such a joyfull place. Colorful houses and hotels face the beach. Also, the water is turquoise, and the sand is golden. I can smell the odors of fish and salt. The water goes on and on. The bright sun reflects off the ocean, and it is always feeling so warm on my skin. The sensation of sand between my toes. There is a lot of sounds. Kids giggle, birds chirping, music plays, and adults chat. The air feels thick and damp. Being at the beach brings me a great feeling of happiness.

The Writer'S Desk: Revise and Edit

Choose a paragraph you wrote for Chapter 2, or choose one that you have written for another assignment. Carefully revise and edit the paragraph. You can refer to the Revising and Editing Checklist at the end of this chapter.

Peer Feedback

After you write a paragraph or essay, it is useful to get peer feedback. Ask another person, such as a friend, family member, or fellow student, to read your work and make suggestions for addressing its weaknesses.

HINT: Offer Constructive Criticism

When you peer-edit someone else's writing, phrase your comments in a positive way. Try to make helpful suggestions that your peers can use to improve their work. Look at these examples.

Instead of saying . . .	You could say . . .
Your sentences are boring.	Maybe you could combine some sentences.
Your supporting ideas are weak.	You could add more details here.

You can use the following peer feedback form to evaluate written work.

Peer Feedback Form

Written by: _____   Feedback by: _____

Date: _____

1. What is the main point of the written work?

   _____

2. What details effectively support the topic sentence?

   _____

   _____

3. What, if anything, is unclear or unnecessary?

   _____

   _____

4. Give some suggestions about how the work could be improved.

   _____

   _____

5. What is an interesting or unique feature of this written work?

   _____

   _____

Write the Final Draft

3.7   Write a final draft.

When you have finished making revisions on the first draft of your paragraph, write the final draft. Include all of the changes that you have made during the revision and editing phases. Before you hand in your final draft, proofread it one last time to ensure that you have caught any errors.

The Writer's Desk: Write Your Final Draft

You have developed, revised, and edited your paragraph. Now write the final draft. Before you offer it to readers, proofread it one last time to ensure that you have found all of your errors.

HINT: Spelling, Grammar, and Vocabulary Logs

- **Keep a spelling and grammar log.** Writers often repeat, over and over, the same types of grammar and spelling errors. You will find it very useful to record your repeated grammar mistakes in a spelling and grammar log. Then, refer to your list of spelling and grammar mistakes when you revise and edit your writing.
- **Keep a vocabulary log.** Expanding your vocabulary will benefit your writing enormously. In a vocabulary log, make a list of unfamiliar words and their definitions.

See Appendix 7 for more information about spelling, grammar, and vocabulary logs.

Reflect On It

Think about what you have learned in this chapter. If you do not know an answer, review that topic.

1. What are four things that you should look for when revising?

   _____   _____

   _____   _____

2. Circle the best answer(s). A paragraph is unified if
   a. there are no irrelevant supporting details.
   b. there are many facts and statistics.
   c. all details support the topic sentence.

3. Circle the best answer: Transitional words are _____ that help ideas flow in a logical manner.
   a. links   b. sentences   c. verbs

4. The "Editing Handbook" in Part IV includes information about grammar, spelling, and punctuation errors. In what chapter would you find information about the following topics? Look in the table of contents to find the chapter number.

   a. capitalization   _____

   b. subject–verb agreement   _____

   c. faulty parallel structure   _____

   d. commas   _____

   e. commonly confused words   _____

The Writer's Room

Writing Activity 1

Choose a paragraph that you have written for your job or for another course. Revise and edit that paragraph, and then write a final draft.

Writing Activity 2

Choose any of the following topics, or choose your own topic. Then write a paragraph. Remember to follow the writing process.

General Topics
1. a wonderful moment
2. heroes in the media
3. a risky adventure
4. bad service

College- and Work-Related Topics
5. something you learned in a college course or on campus
6. reasons to change jobs
7. your career plans
8. an interesting job

Revising and Editing Checklist

When you revise and edit, ask yourself the following questions. (For a more detailed editing checklist, refer to the inside back cover of this book.)

Unity

❏ Is my paragraph unified under a single topic?

❏ Does each sentence relate to the topic sentence?

Support

❏ Does my paragraph have an adequate number of supporting details?

Coherence

❏ Is my paragraph logically organized?

❏ Do I use transitional words or expressions to help the paragraph flow smoothly?

Style

❏ Do I use a variety of sentence styles?

❏ Is my vocabulary concise?

❏ Are my sentences parallel in structure?

Editing

❏ Do my sentences contain correct grammar, spelling, punctuation, and mechanics?

Part II
Paragraph Patterns

What Is a Paragraph Pattern?

A writing *pattern* or *mode* is a method used to express one of the three purposes: to inform, to persuade, or to entertain. Once you know your purpose, you will be able to choose which writing pattern or patterns can help you to express it.

Patterns can overlap, and it is possible to use more than one in a single piece of writing. For example, imagine you are writing a paragraph about bullying, and your purpose is to inform the reader. You might use *definition* as your predominant pattern (to define *bullying* or explain the characteristics of a *bully*), but in the supporting details, you might use *comparison and contrast* to compare a bully and a victim. You might also use *narration* to highlight an incident in which a bully harassed a victim.

Before you work through the next chapters, review the paragraph patterns.

CHAPTER 4   ILLUSTRATION
- To illustrate or prove a point using specific examples

CHAPTER 5   NARRATION
- To narrate or tell a story about a sequence of events that happened

CHAPTER 6   DESCRIPTION
- To describe using vivid details and images that appeal to the reader's senses

CHAPTER 7   PROCESS
- To inform the reader about how to do something, how something works, or how something happened

CHAPTER 8   DEFINITION
- To define or explain what a term or concept means by providing relevant examples

CHAPTER 9   CLASSIFICATION
- To classify or sort a topic's qualities to help readers better understand the topic

CHAPTER 10   COMPARISON AND CONTRAST
- To present information about similarities (compare) or differences (contrast)

CHAPTER 11   CAUSE AND EFFECT
- To explain why an event happened (the causes) or the consequences of the event (the effects)

CHAPTER 12   ARGUMENT*
- To argue or to take a position on an issue and offer reasons for your position

*Argument is included as one of the nine patterns, but arguing is also a purpose when writing.

Travel agencies use examples of attractions to sell tour packages. In illustration writing, you give examples to support your point of view.

Writers' Exchange

Work with a team of two or three students. List at least five examples of each part of speech. Include only words that begin with the letters *H* or *S*. Do as many as you can in two minutes.

Noun	Verb	Adjective	Pronoun

Exploring

What Is Illustration?

4.1   **Define illustration.**

When using **illustration**, include specific examples to clarify your main point as you explain, analyze, narrate, or give an opinion about something. As a writer, you can use many different types of examples to help readers acquire a deeper and clearer understanding of your subject. You can include personal experience or factual information, such as a statistic.

In fact, you illustrate or give examples every day. When telling a friend about a good day or a bad day, you might use examples to make the story more interesting. At college, you might give an oral presentation using examples that will help the audience better understand your point. At work, you might give examples to show clients where or how they might market their products.

Illustration   **47**

Illustration at Work

Patti Guzman is a registered nurse at a large hospital. She was invited to speak to nursing students at a local university. In the following excerpt from her speech, she gives examples to explain why a nurse must be in good physical health.

Physically, the job of a nurse is demanding. On a daily basis, we must lift patients and move them. When patients are bedridden for prolonged periods, we must change their positions on their beds. When new patients arrive, we transfer them from stretchers to beds or from beds to wheelchairs. If patients fall, we must be able to help them stand up. If patients have difficulty walking, we must assist them. Patients who have suffered paralysis or stroke need to be lifted and supported when they are bathed and dressed. Keep in mind that some patients may be quite heavy, so the job requires a good level of physical strength.

> The **topic sentence** expresses the main idea.

> **Supporting sentences** provide details and examples.

> The **concluding sentence** brings the paragraph to a satisfying close.

The Illustration Paragraph

4.2   **Explain how to write an illustration paragraph.**

There are two ways to write an illustration paragraph.

- **Use a series of examples** to illustrate your main point. For example, if you are writing a paragraph about an innovative teacher, you might list things that the teacher did, such as wear a costume, let students teach parts of the course, and use music to engage the class.

- **Use an extended example** to illustrate your main point. The example can be an anecdote or a description. For example, in a paragraph about creativity, you might describe a time when you decorated a room.

> **ESSAY LINK**
> You can develop illustration essays with a series of examples or extended examples.

Practice 1

Read the next paragraph and answer the questions.

Digital home technology is rapidly invading our lives. In Japan, Toto Ltd. has manufactured the Intelligent Toilet. This digital lavatory measures blood sugar, blood pressure, and obesity. It also carries out urine analysis, which tracks hormone levels. The toilet, which is hooked up to a home computer, allows users to graph personal health trends. Furthermore, engineers are developing touchscreen technology for doorknobs, furniture, and appliances. They respond to different touches and are programmed to react. Disney research scientist Ivan Poupyrev says that a postman can touch the doorknob with three fingers and record a message. Moreover, the Smart Home system by Rogers Communications allows homeowners to synchronize lighting systems, carbon monoxide sensors, and alarms to their smartphones to get instant alerts. Setting up a digital home is likely to become easier and cheaper in the near future.

— *"Digital Life" by Julia Johnson*

1. Underline the topic sentence of this paragraph. (The topic sentence expresses the main idea of the paragraph.)

2. What type of illustration paragraph is this? Circle the better answer.

    a. a series of examples   b. an extended example

3. List the examples that the writer gives to illustrate her point.

_____

_____

_____

_____

_____

_____

_____

Practice 2

Read the next paragraph and answer the questions.

    Although the public usually imagines notorious computer hackers as being males, female hackers are as infamous as their male counterparts. For example, Kyrie specialized in hacking into databases and collecting long distance numbers. She used these numbers to do mischief by clogging up the voice mail systems of corporations. Kyrie also gathered a following of 150 adolescent fans. These teenagers bought Kyrie's long distance dialing codes and in return gave her stolen credit cards. Kyrie then used the stolen credit cards to pay for expensive hotel rooms and airline tickets and to commit welfare fraud. But her most unethical act was to involve her children in her criminal schemes. She prevented her children from having legal identities and going to school. Eventually, Kyrie's ego led to her downfall. She made boastful phone calls about her criminal activities to Arizona Assistant Attorney General Gail Thackeray, who taped them and gave the tapes to the Secret Service. Kyrie was arrested and found guilty for her crimes.

—Nikita Bulgakov, student

1. Underline the topic sentence.

2. What does the writer use to present her supporting details? Circle the best answer.

    a. a series of examples   b. an extended example

3. What example(s) does the writer give to illustrate his point?

_____

4. What are the main events in the narrative?

_____

_____

_____

_____

_____

_____

Illustration **49**

Explore Topics

4.3 Explore topics.

In the Warm Up, you will try an exploring strategy to generate ideas about different topics.

The Writer's Desk: Warm Up

Think about the following questions, and write the first ideas that come to your mind. Try to think of two to three ideas for each topic.

EXAMPLE: What are some symbols of a child's transition into adolescence?

getting a driver's license

dating

celebrating a birthday

1. What are some examples of superstitions?

_____

_____

_____

2. What are some traits of an effective leader?

_____

_____

_____

3. What are some qualities that you look for in a mate?

_____

_____

_____

Developing

The Topic Sentence

4.4 Identify the topic sentence of an illustration paragraph.

ESSAY LINK
In an illustration essay, the thesis statement expresses the controlling idea.

The topic sentence of the illustration paragraph is a general statement that expresses both the topic and the controlling idea. To determine your controlling idea, think about what point you want to make.

      topic   controlling idea

Part-time jobs teach students valuable skills.

     controlling idea   topic

Our father overreacted **when my sister started dating**.

The Writer's Desk: Write Topic Sentences

Write a topic sentence for each of the following topics. You can look for ideas in the previous Writer's Desk. Remember to narrow your topic. Each topic sentence should contain a general statement that expresses both your topic and your controlling idea.

EXAMPLE: Topic: Symbols of a child's transition into adolescence

Topic sentence: In the United States, many important rites and rituals symbolize a child's transition into adolescence.

1. Topic: Types of superstitions
Topic sentence: _____
_____

2. Topic: Traits of an effective leader
Topic sentence: _____
_____

3. Topic: Qualities you look for in a mate
Topic sentence: _____
_____

The Supporting Ideas

4.5   **Identify the supporting details of an illustration paragraph.**

After you have developed an effective topic sentence, generate supporting ideas. In an illustration paragraph, you can give a series of examples or an extended example.

When you use a series of examples, you can arrange your examples in emphatic order–from the most to the least important or from the least to the most important. If you use an extended example, you can arrange your ideas using time order.

Practice 3: Visualizing Illustration

Brainstorm supporting ideas for the following topic sentence. Give examples of how people risk their lives.

Topic Sentence: Some workers risk their lives daily.

window washer

electrician

fisher

police officer

_____   _____   _____   _____

_____   _____   _____   _____

Illustration **51**

The Writer's Desk: Generate Supporting Ideas

Generate some supporting examples under each topic. Make sure your examples support the topic sentences that you wrote for the previous Writer's Desk.

EXAMPLE:
Symbols of a child's transition into adolescence

- celebrating a birthday

- having more responsibilities

- becoming interested in a

romantic partner

1. Superstitions

_____

_____

_____

_____

2. Traits of an effective leader

_____

_____

_____

_____

3. Qualities you look for in a mate

_____

_____

_____

_____

The Paragraph Plan

4.6   Develop an illustration paragraph plan.

A paragraph plan helps you organize your topic sentence and supporting details before writing a first draft. When you write a paragraph plan, make sure that all examples are valid and relate to the topic sentence. Also include details that will help clarify your supporting examples, and organize your ideas in a logical order.

Topic Sentence: In the United States, many important rites and rituals symbolize a child's transition into adolescence.

Support 1: Celebrating a birthday signals a child's entry into adolescence.

   Details: —Jewish-American boys and girls celebrate bar mitzvahs and bat mitzvahs.

           —Mexican-American girls celebrate quinceaneras.

Support 2: Teenagers often look for more responsibilities to show that they are no longer children.

   Details: —At sixteen years old, many teens get a driver's license.

           —Many people get their first job during their teen years.

Support 3: Some adolescents become interested in a romantic partner.

   Details: —Teenagers start to date.

> **ESSAY LINK**
> In an illustration essay, place the thesis statement in the introduction. Then, structure the essay so that each supporting idea becomes a distinct paragraph with its own topic sentence.

The Writer's Desk: Write a Paragraph Plan

Choose one of the topic sentences that you wrote for the previous Writer's Desk. Write a paragraph plan using some of the supporting ideas that you have generated. Include details for each supporting idea.

Topic sentence: _____

_____

Support 1: _____

Details: _____

_____

Support 2: _____

Details: _____

_____

Support 3: _____

Details: _____

_____

The First Draft

4.7   **Write the first draft of an illustration paragraph.**

After you outline your ideas in a plan, you are ready to write the first draft. Remember to write complete sentences. You might include transitional words or expressions to help your ideas flow smoothly.

Transitional expressions can help you introduce an example or show an additional example. The following transitional words are useful in illustration paragraphs.

To Introduce an Example		To Show an Additional Example	
for example	namely	also	in addition
for instance	specifically	first (second, etc.)	in another case
in other words	to illustrate	furthermore	moreover

The Writer's Desk: Write the First Draft

For the previous Writer's Desk, you developed a paragraph plan. Now write the first draft of your illustration paragraph. Before you write, carefully review your paragraph plan and make any necessary changes.

Revising and Editing

Revise and Edit an Illustration Paragraph

4.8   **Revise and edit an illustration paragraph.**

After drafting an illustration paragraph, review your work and revise it to make the example(s) as clear as possible to your readers. Check to make sure that the order of ideas is logical, and remove any irrelevant details. Before you work on your own paragraph, practice revising and editing the next student paragraph.

Illustration   **53**

Practice 4

Read this student paragraph, and answer the questions.

In the United States, many important rites and rituals symbolize a child's transition into adolescence. Celebrating a birthday often symbolizes entry into adolescence. For example, Jewish-American boys and girls celebrate bar mitzvahs and bat mitzvahs. And Mexican-American girls quinceañeras. Some minors look forward to their sweet-sixteen parties. In addition, teenagers often look for more responsibilities to show that they are no longer children. At sixteen years old, a teenager may get their driver's license. A teen may also get a first job during this period. Furthermore, some adolescents become interested in a romantic partner. Young people start dating. Such rites of passage are important markers of adolescence.

—Rafael Castillo, student

Revising

1. Underline the topic sentence.

2. What type of illustration paragraph is this?

 a. a series of examples   b. an extended example

3. List the main supporting points.

_____

_____

_____

4. What is the purpose of this paragraph?

 a. to persuade   b. to entertain   c. to inform

Editing

5. Underline a pronoun error. Write your correction in the space below.

Correction: _____

6. This paragraph contains a fragment, which is an incomplete sentence. Underline the fragment. Then correct it in the space below.

Correction: _____

> **GRAMMAR LINK**
> See the following chapters for more information about these grammar topics:
>   Pronouns, Chapter 29
>   Fragments, Chapter 20

GRAMMAR HINT: Writing Complete Sentences

Avoid fragment errors. A fragment is an incomplete sentence. When you give an example, make sure that your sentence contains at least one subject and one verb (someone or something performing an action).

Fragment   For example, too many parties.

Correction   For example, some students go to too many parties.

The Writer's Desk: Revise and Edit Your Paragraph

Revise and edit the paragraph that you wrote for the previous Writer's Desk. Make sure that your paragraph has unity, adequate support, and coherence. Also, correct any errors in grammar, spelling, punctuation, and mechanics.

VOCABULARY BOOST: Avoid Repetition

Read through the first draft of your paragraph, and identify some words that you frequently repeat. Replace those words with synonyms.

Reflect On It

Think about what you have learned in this chapter. If you do not know an answer, review that topic.

1. In an illustration paragraph, you _____

2. There are two ways to write illustration paragraphs. Explain each of them.

   a. Using a series of examples: _____

   b. Using an extended example: _____

3. List three transitional expressions that indicate an additional idea.

   _____

The Writer's Room

Writing Activity 1: Topics

Choose any of the following topics, or choose your own topic. Then write an illustration paragraph by following the steps of the writing process.

General Topics

1. unusual fashions
2. great things in life that are free
3. mistakes parents make
4. hobbies
5. positive personality traits

College- and Work-Related Topics

6. pressures faced by college students
7. qualities that help you succeed
8. office etiquette
9. qualities of a good instructor
10. excuses for not completing a task or project

Writing Activity 2: Media Writing

Write an illustration paragraph explaining the ways real people or fictional characters experience peer pressure in a high school, college, or workplace setting. Consider scenarios in which peer pressure has either negative or positive effects. Here are some suggestions to spark ideas:

Show: *Glee*

Films: *Pitch Perfect* or *American Pie 2*

Video: AdCouncil campaigns, such as stoptextsstopwrecks.org

Song: *Try* by Colbie Caillat

Podcast: "Riding the Herd Mentality," a *Freakonomics* episode

WRITING LINK
MORE ILLUSTRATION WRITING TOPICS

Ch. 16, Writer's Room topic 1, p. 249
Ch. 17, Writer's Room topic 1, p. 260
Ch. 20, Writer's Room topic 1, p. 288
Ch. 25, Writer's Room topic 1, p. 338
Ch. 28, Writer's Room topic 1, p. 356

READING LINK
MORE ILLUSTRATION READINGS
"Comics As Social Commentary"
    (p. 178)
"What's in an African Name?" (p. 180)
"The Beeps" (p. 519)

Illustration **55**

Illustration Paragraph Checklist

After you write your illustration paragraph, review the checklist on at the back of the book. Also ask yourself the following questions.

❑ Does my topic sentence make a point that can be supported with examples?

❑ Does my paragraph contain sufficient examples that clearly support the topic sentence?

❑ Do I use transitions to smoothly connect my examples?

❑ Have I arranged my examples in a logical order?

5   Narration

LEARNING OBJECTIVES

5.1 Define narration.

5.2 Explain how to write a narrative paragraph.

5.3 Explore topics.

5.4 Identify the topic sentence of a narrative paragraph.

5.5 Identify the supporting details of a narrative paragraph.

5.6 Develop a narrative paragraph plan.

5.7 Write the first draft of a narrative paragraph.

5.8 Revise and edit a narrative paragraph.

When you meet a new friend or romantic interest, family and friends often enthusiastically ask for more information about this person. They might ask *who*, *what*, *when*, *where*, *why*, and *how* questions. You answer the same questions when you write a narrative paragraph.

Writers' Exchange

Work in a team of at least three students. First, choose a fairy tale to retell in an updated way. Next, one team member begins by saying one sentence. Then, another team member adds a sentence to the tale. Team members continue to take turns until the story is complete. Here is one example based on the old "Little Red Riding Hood" fairy tale.

EXAMPLE: Yesterday, a young woman wearing a red baseball cap decided to visit her grandmother.

Exploring

What Is Narration?

5.1   **Define narration.**

When using the **narration** pattern, narrate or tell a story about what happened. Explain events in the order in which they occurred, and include information about when they happened and who was involved in the incidents.

You use narration every day. You may write about the week's events in a personal journal, or you might send a postcard to a friend detailing your vacation. At college, you may explain what happened during a historical event or what happened in a novel that you have read. At work, you might use narration to explain an incident involving a customer or coworker.

Narration is not only useful on its own; it also enhances other types of writing. For example, an argument essay about youth crime might be more compelling if it includes a personal anecdote about the time a gang of youths attacked someone in a subway station. In other words, narration can provide supporting evidence for other paragraph or essay patterns.

Narration at Work

Joseph Roth, a boiler and pressure vessel inspector, used narrative writing in a memo he wrote to his supervisor.

As you know, I recently inspected the boiler and pressure vessels in the refinery on Highway 11, and I had a few problems that I would like to mention. When I first arrived, the manager of the unit was uncooperative and initially tried to stop me from examining the boiler! After much discussion, I was finally permitted into the boiler room, where I noticed several defects in the operation and condition of the equipment. Immediately, I saw that the low-water fuel cutoff chamber was filled with sludge and could not possibly function properly. Then I realized that the boiler heating surfaces were covered with scale. Finally, I found stress cracks in the tube ends and in tube seats. This is a sure sign of caustic embrittlement, which makes the boiler unsafe to operate and in danger of exploding. I have asked that the boiler be taken out of service immediately. We must follow up to make sure that measures are being taken to replace the boiler.

> The **topic sentence** expresses the main idea.

> **Supporting sentences** provide details and examples.

> The **concluding sentence** brings the paragraph to a satisfying close.

The Narrative Paragraph

5.2　**Explain how to write a narrative paragraph.**

There are two main types of narrative paragraphs.

1. **First-person narration (autobiography)**

   In first-person narration, you describe a personal experience from your point of view. Because you are directly involved in the story, use the words *I* (first-person singular) or *we* (first-person plural). For example: "When I was a child, I thought that the world began and ended with me. I didn't know, or care, how other children felt. Thus, when schoolmates ridiculed a shy boy, I gleefully joined in."

2. **Third-person narration**

   In third-person narration, you do not refer to your own experiences. Instead, describe what happened to somebody else using *he, she, it,* or *they*. You might tell a story about your mother's childhood, or you might explain what happened during the last election. In this type of narration, you are simply an observer or storyteller, not a participant in the action. For example: "The teacher raised his voice and called out a student's name. He then pointed at the door."

> **ESSAY LINK**
> In a narrative essay, you can use first- or third-person narration.

HINT: Choose an Interesting Topic

When you write a narrative paragraph, try to choose a topic that will interest readers. For example, people might not be interested if you write about the act of eating your lunch. However, if you write about a time when your best friend argued with a waiter during a meal, you could create an entertaining narrative paragraph.

Think about a topic that you personally find very interesting, and then share it. Try to bring your experience to life so that your readers can "live" the moment with you.

Explore Topics

5.3 **Explore topics.**

In the Warm Up, you will try an exploring strategy to generate ideas about different topics.

The Writer's Desk: Warm Up

Think about the following questions, and write down the first ideas that come to your mind. Try to think of two or three ideas for each topic.

EXAMPLE: Think about some mistakes that you made. Did you get into trouble at home or at school?

<u>My dad got mad when I lied. I broke my brother's toy. The time I tripped</u>

<u>a boy at school.</u>

_____

1. Have you ever done a good deed, or has someone ever helped you? If so, what happened?

_____

_____

_____

2. What are some memorable parties or celebrations that you have attended?

_____

_____

_____

3. Think about interesting true events that have happened to family members or friends. Are some stories particularly funny, sad, or inspiring? List some ideas.

_____

_____

_____

Practice 1

Read the paragraph and answer the questions.

   At eighteen years old, I was offered a scholarship to the University of South Africa. I took my first plane flight and had a very frightening experience. After the plane took off from Cameroon, I took pictures of the fields and clouds below. Suddenly, I realized there was smoke at the rear of the plane. The pilot announced an emergency landing at the international airport in Congo. At that time, Congo was in the midst of a civil war. The passengers who had been calm and relaxed became frantic. Some bowed their heads for their last prayers, and others moved toward the emergency exits. As soon as we landed, rebels approached our plane, and we had to run. We were hiding in a bunker when we heard loud screams from people who were being chased by horsemen with machetes. The frightened civilians stumbled into our safe location, which then exposed us to the attackers.

When the rebels saw us, they looked as though they had found a gold mine. Because we were from Cameroon, they decided not to hurt us but stripped us of our possessions. As we walked to a neighboring city, we saw burning homes and running refugees. There were also child soldiers carrying big machine guns and patrolling the city center. Eventually, we made our way to Zimbabwe, and then I caught a ferry to South Africa. This experience changed my perspective on life. Every day when I wake up, I am grateful to be alive and breathe free air.

—Beryl Fomundam, student

1. Underline the topic sentence.

2. What type of narration is this paragraph? _____

3. Who is the narrator? _____

4. Where is the narrator? _____

5. Why is the narrator in that region? _____

_____

_____

6. What happens to her? _____

_____

_____

7. By combining your answers to questions 3 and 6, write a one-sentence summary of the paragraph. Someone who has never read the paragraph should have a clear idea of the paragraph's content after reading your sentence.

_____

_____

_____

Practice 2

Read the next paragraph and answer the questions.

In the history of fake art, one of the most bizarre stories is the tale of Xiao Yuan, a talented librarian, a skilled painter, and a daring thief. In 2003, Xiao became head librarian at the Guangzhou Academy of Fine Arts in southeast China. He soon noticed that the academy's art gallery contained several fakes. He thought they were badly painted and believed he could do better. Such a scheme could make him rich. "I was very greedy and tempted," he says. In 2004, he began to make copies of paintings, choosing the less well-known works of masters from the seventeenth to the twentieth century. When he finished a painting, he stole the original and replaced it with his copy. Over two years, he copied 143 paintings and sold most of the originals through an auction house. He netted the equivalent of about $6 million. In 2006, Xiao's scheme ended when the gallery was moved elsewhere on campus, making it inaccessible to him. He retired from crime and used the money to buy real estate and increase his own art collection. A decade later, he was caught when a graduate of the Guangzhou Academy noticed that paintings offered for sale in

Hong Kong carried the university's seal. Last summer, Xiao appeared before the Guangzhou People's Intermediate Court and admitted his guilt.

1. Who or what is the paragraph about? _____

   _____

2. Underline the topic sentence of the paragraph.

3. What type of narration is this paragraph?

   a. first person   b. third person

4. What type of order do the specific details follow?

   a. time order   b. space order   c. emphatic order

5. Highlight at least five transitional words or phrases.

6. What are the main events in the paragraph? List the main details.

   _____

   _____

   _____

   _____

   _____

   _____

Developing

The Topic Sentence

ESSAY LINK
In a narrative essay, the thesis statement expresses the controlling idea.

5.4   Identify the topic sentence of a narrative paragraph.

When you write a narrative paragraph, it is important to express a main point. A basic list of events will bore your readers, so make sure your topic sentence has a controlling idea to steer the paragraph's details.

topic   controlling idea

When somebody broke into my house, I felt totally invaded.

controlling idea   topic

Jay learned to be responsible **during his first job**.

Make a Point

In a narrative paragraph, the topic sentence should make a point. To figure out the controlling idea, you can ask yourself the following questions.

- What did I learn?
- How did I change?

- How did it make me feel?
- What is important about it?

EXAMPLE:

Topic	Moving out of the family home
Possible controlling idea	Becoming more independent

topic   controlling idea

When I moved out of the family home, I became more independent.

Practice 3

Practice writing topic sentences. Complete the following sentences by adding a controlling idea.

1. When I moved out of the family home, I felt _____

_____

2. In my first job, I learned _____

_____

3. When Tara heard the news about _____,

she realized _____

The Writer's Desk: Write Topic Sentences

Write a topic sentence for each of the following topics. You can look for ideas in the Writer's Desk Warm Up on page 58. Each topic sentence should mention the topic and express a controlling idea.

EXAMPLE: Topic: A mistake I made

Topic sentence: <u>One day, I got into a lot of trouble for "bully flirting"</u>

<u>with a boy I liked.</u>

1. Topic: A good deed

Topic sentence: _____

_____

2. Topic: A celebration or party

Topic sentence: _____

_____

3. Topic: A story about someone

Topic sentence: _____

_____

The Supporting Ideas

5.5   Identify the supporting details of a narrative paragraph.

A narrative paragraph should contain specific details so that the reader understands what happened. To come up with the details, ask yourself a series of questions. Your paragraph should provide answers to these questions.

- Who is the paragraph about?
- What happened?
- When did it happen?
- Where did it happen?
- Why did it happen?
- How did it happen?

When recounting a story to a friend, you can add details out of order, saying, "I forgot to mention something." When writing a narrative paragraph, however, organize the sequence of events chronologically so that readers can follow your story.

Practice 4: Visualizing Narration

Brainstorm supporting ideas for the following topic sentence. Write some descriptive words and phrases.

Topic Sentence: Our camping trip exposed us to new experiences.

_____ _____ _____

_____ _____ _____

The Writer's Desk: Develop Supporting Ideas

Generate supporting ideas for each topic. List what happened.

EXAMPLE: A mistake I made

- "bully flirted"

- tripped a boy I liked

- teacher saw me

- told my mom

- she yelled at me

1. A good deed

_____

_____

_____

_____

_____

1. A celebration or party

_____

_____

_____

_____

_____

2. A story about someone

_____

_____

_____

_____

_____

The Paragraph Plan

5.6 Develop a narrative paragraph plan.

ESSAY LINK
In a narrative essay, you place the thesis statement in the introduction. Each event is developed in a supporting paragraph.

Before you write a narrative paragraph, it is a good idea to make a paragraph plan. Write down events in the order in which they occurred. To make your narration more complete, include details about each event.

Topic Sentence: When I was ten, I got into a lot of trouble for "bully flirting" with a boy I liked.

Support 1:   Students were lined up for art class.

   Details: — Along came the boy.

                — The teacher turned away.

Support 2:   The line started moving.

   Details: — Boom! I tripped him.

                — He stumbled.

                — The teacher was looking at us.

Support 3:   After school, the teacher told my father what I had done.

   Details: — My father drove me home.

                — He got very angry at me.

                — I cried and promised not to do it again.

The Writer's Desk: Write a Paragraph Plan

Choose one of the topic sentences that you wrote for the previous Writer's Desk. Write a paragraph plan using some of the supporting ideas that you have generated. Include details for each supporting idea.

Topic sentence: _____

_____

Support 1: _____

  Details: _____

_____

_____

Support 2 _____

  Details: _____

_____

_____

Support 3: _____

  Details: _____

_____

_____

The First Draft

5.7   Write the first draft of a narrative paragraph.

After outlining ideas in a plan, you are ready to write the first draft. Remember to write complete sentences. You might include transitional words or expressions to help your ideas flow smoothly.

Transitions can help you show a sequence of events. The following transitional words are useful in narrative paragraphs.

To Show a Sequence of Events			
afterward	finally	in the end	meanwhile
after that	first	last	next
eventually	in the beginning	later	then

The Writer's Desk: Write the First Draft

In the previous Writer's Desk, you developed a paragraph plan. Now write the first draft of your narrative paragraph. Before you write, carefully review your paragraph plan and make any necessary changes.

VOCABULARY BOOST: Using Varied Language

1. Underline the opening word of every sentence in your first draft. Check to see if some are repeated.

2. Replace repeated opening words with an adverb such as *Usually*, *Generally*, or *Fortunately* or a prepositional phrase, such as *On the side* or *Under the circumstances*. You can also begin the sentences with a phrase such as *Leaving the door open*. In other words, avoid beginning too many sentences with a noun, pronoun, or transitional word.

Repeated First Words

We opened the door of the abandoned house. We looked nervously at the rotting floorboards. We thought the floor might collapse. We decided to enter. We walked carefully across the kitchen floor to the bedroom, one by one.

Variety

My cousins and I opened the door of the abandoned house. Nervously, we looked at the rotting floorboards. Thinking the floor might collapse, we decided to enter. One by one, we walked across the kitchen floor to the bedroom.

Revising and Editing

Revise and Edit a Narrative Paragraph

5.8   Revise and edit a narrative paragraph.

When you finish writing a narrative paragraph, carefully review your work and revise it to make the events as clear as possible to readers. Check that you have organized events chronologically, and remove any irrelevant details. Before you revise and edit your own paragraph, practice revising and editing the following student paragraph.

Practice 5

Read the next student paragraph and answer the questions.

In school, most kids are guilty of "bully flirting," which means students pick on somebody that they like. When I was ten, I got into a lot of trouble for bully flirting with a boy I liked. My whole class was lined up neatly against the wall to go to the art room. Along comes this boy I had a crush on. All week, I had practiced tripping, so he was my first victim. The teacher turned away. When the line started moving, I stared at his feet, and then BOOM! I tripped him perfectly, and he stumbled. When I looked up, I seen my teacher looking in my direction. I quickly tried to help the boy and make it look like he had tripped over his own shoestring, but that didn't quite work out. Later that day, when my dad came to pick me up from school, my teacher told him what I had done. During the car ride home, my dad was quiet. But when we got home, he yelled "Girl, what is wrong with you!" He warned me that the boy coulda been badly hurt. I started to cry, and I made a promise that I wouldn't trip nobody again.

—Kevinnetta Artis, student

Revising

1. Underline the topic sentence. Be careful because the topic sentence is not always the first sentence.

2. What type of order do the specific details follow? Circle the best answer.

   a. space   b. time   c. emphatic

3. What type of narration is this paragraph?

   a. first person   b. third person

Editing

4. The paragraph contains two incorrect verb tenses. Underline and correct the two verbs.

5. The direct quotation is incorrectly punctuated. Add the missing punctuation.

6. The second to last sentence contains a spelling mistake. Identify and correct the error.

7. The paragraph contains a double negative. Two negative forms cancel each other, and the sentence doesn't make sense. Identify and correct the error.

> **GRAMMAR LINK**
> See the following chapters for more information about these grammar topics:
> Verb tenses (Chs. 23 and 24)
> Spelling (Ch. 33)
> Quotations (Ch. 35)

GRAMMAR HINT: Using Quotations

When you insert a direct quotation into your writing, capitalize the first word of the quotation and put the final punctuation inside the closing quotation marks.

- Place a comma after an introductory phrase.

   Vladimir screamed, "The kitchen's on fire!"

- Place a colon after an introductory sentence.

   Vladimir watched me coldly: "We have nothing to discuss."

The Writer's Desk: Revise and Edit Your Paragraph

Revise and edit the paragraph that you wrote for the previous Writer's Desk. Make sure that your paragraph has unity, adequate support, and coherence. Also, correct any errors in grammar, spelling, punctuation, and mechanics.

Reflect On It

Think about what you have learned in this chapter. If you do not know an answer, review that topic.

1. In narrative writing, you _____

2. What are the differences between the two following types of narration?

   First person: _____

   _____

   Third person: _____

   _____

3. What are some questions that you should ask yourself when you write a narrative paragraph?

   _____

4. What organizational method is commonly used in narrative paragraphs? Circle the best answer.

   a. space order   b time order   c. emphatic order

The Writer's Room

Writing Activity 1: Topics

Choose any of the following topics, or choose your own topic. Then write a narrative paragraph by following the steps of the writing process.

WRITING LINK
MORE NARRATIVE WRITING TOPICS

Ch. 21, Writer's Room Topic 1, (p. 295)
Ch. 23, Writer's Room Topic 1, (p. 317)
Ch. 31, Writer's Room Topic 1, (p. 409)

General Topics

1. a breakup
2. a great or disastrous date
3. an unforgettable holiday
4. a celebrity scandal
5. a time when you were influenced by peer pressure

College- and Work-Related Topics

6. an embarrassing incident at college or work
7. a life-changing meeting
8. a positive or negative job interview
9. an encounter with a difficult customer
10. a proud moment at work or college

Writing Activity 2: Media Writing

Watch or listen to media that show a real or fictional character overcoming a challenge. Write a narrative explaining what happens. Here are some suggestions to spark ideas:

Show: *Nashville, Scandal, The Amazing Race*

Film: *Django Unchained*

Video: Brene Brown's TED talks, such as the "Power of Vulnerability"

Song: "The Impossible Dream" (from *Man of La Mancha*); "Survivor" (Destiny's Child)

Podcast: Radiolab's *Finding Emilie* segment

READING LINK MORE NARRATIVE READINGS

"My Prison Story" (p. 183)
"Laughing Through the Fog" (p. 184)
"The Sanctuary of School" (p. 505)
"My Father Taught Me to Love Guns" (p. 524)

Narrative Paragraph Checklist

As you write your narrative paragraph, review the checklist at the end of the book. Also ask yourself the following questions.

❏ Does my topic sentence clearly express the topic of the narration?

❏ Does my topic sentence contain a controlling idea that is meaningful and interesting?

❏ Does my paragraph answer most of the following questions: *who, what, when, where, why, how*?

❏ Do I use transitional expressions that help clarify the order of events?

❏ Do I include details to make my narration more interesting?

6   Description

When professional photographers prepare for a session, they adjust the lighting, the model, and the camera angle to make a visual impression. In descriptive writing, you use words to create a distinct image.

Writers' Exchange

Work with two or three students. First, think about a particular place. It can be a street, a coffee shop, a mall, a park, or any other place in your region. Describe details about that place, but don't reveal the name of the place. Describe sights, sounds, and smells. Speak nonstop about the place for about forty seconds. Your teammates must guess the place that you are describing.

Exploring

What Is Description?

6.1   Define description.

Description creates vivid images in the reader's mind by portraying people, places, or moments in detail.

You use description every day. At home, you might describe a new friend or describe a new purchase. At college, you might describe the structure of a cell or a literary character. At work, you may describe a new product to a client or the qualities of potential clients to your boss.

Description at Work

In this excerpt from a note sent from Dr. Pradish Chowdhury to his students, he describes chicken pox.

Chicken pox, related to the herpes family, is a highly contagious virus. The first symptoms include skin that is hot to the touch. A rash, appearing like small red spots, appears on the upper part of the body. Within about twenty-four hours, the spots become fluid-filled and itchy blisters, which can appear on the face, scalp, back, chest, and even inside the nostrils and mouth. Sometimes the skin becomes darker around the blisters, which can number in the hundreds. Keep an infected child's nails very short, as scratching can cause blisters to become infected and can leave scars. After a few days, crusty scabs form and the blisters fall off. Full recovery takes about a week to ten days.

> The **topic sentence** expresses the main idea.

> **Supporting sentences** provide details and examples.

> The **concluding sentence** brings the paragraph to a satisfactory close.

The Description Paragraph

6.2 Explain how to write a description paragraph.

When you write descriptively, focus on three main points:

1. **Create a dominant impression.**
   The dominant impression is the overall atmosphere that you wish to convey. It can be a strong feeling, mood, or image. For example, if you are describing taking an end-of-term exam, you can emphasize the tension in the room.

2. **Express your attitude toward the subject.**
   Do you feel positive, negative, or neutral toward the subject? For example, if you feel positive about your best friend, then the details of your paragraph about him or her should convey those good feelings. If you describe a place that you do not like, then your details should express how uncomfortable that place makes you feel. You might write a neutral description of a science lab experiment.

3. **Include concrete details.**
   Details will enable readers to visualize the person, place, or situation that is being described. You can use active verbs and adjectives so that readers imagine the scene more clearly. You can also use **imagery**, which is description using the five senses. Review the following examples of imagery.

> **ESSAY LINK**
> In description essays, you should also create a dominant impression, express your attitude toward the subject, and include concrete details.

Sight	While talking casually to her husband, Joanna absentmindedly tugs at a hangnail until the skin tears and a tiny droplet of blood appears.
	—Deborah Tannen, *You're Wearing That?*
Sound	As the glass tinkled onto the cellar floor, he heard a low growl.
	—Christopher Morley, *The Haunted Bookshop*
Smell	The odor of fresh-sawed pine perfumed the air.
	—Stewart Edward White, *The Blazed Trail*
Touch	My heart started racing, perspiration dripped down my face causing my glasses to slide, and I had a hard time breathing.
	—Bebe Moore Campbell, "Dancing with Fear"
Taste	I asked for fresh lemonade, and got it—delicious, and cold, and tangy with real fruit.
	—Mary Stewart, *My Brother Michael*

Practice 1

Read the next paragraph and answer the questions.

My biological father left before my birth, and my single mother worked three dead-end jobs. By my twelfth birthday, I was gang affiliated, and I was on a first-name basis with the police. I tried medications and meditation to relieve my built-in rage, but nothing helped. My life changed, and I became tamed when I found a five-foot six-inch, sun-rotted, waterlogged surfboard in my neighbor's garbage. Initially, learning to surf wasn't easy. During my first hundred times, I nearly drowned. I'd swallow the salty water as I tumbled into the ocean, often banging my head on the board. Of course, there were moments of terror. I was often visited by an ancient predator, the shark. Sharks can pick up on the electromagnetic beat of the human heart and sense fear, so I learned to tame my nerves. Furthermore, I learned about balance. Sitting on the board naturally calmed my heart rate while I stared into the vast blue, aware of the swooshing waves and squawking seagulls and the fishy odors. Ultimately, surfing gave me what I had never had, a sense of real belonging. When I am in the ocean, I am in the womb, attached to the birth cord. To the naked eye, my surfboard is a dinged-up piece of foam, fiberglass, and epoxy resin. To me, it is a thousand stories of courage and joy.

—Robert James Perkins, student

1. Underline the topic sentence. Be careful, as it may not be the first sentence in the paragraph.

2. What is the dominant impression that the writer creates?

   a. pride   b. rage   c. shock

   Give examples that show the dominant impression.

   _____

   _____

3. Provide examples from the paragraph of each type of sensory detail.

   a. sight   _____

   b. sound   _____

   c. taste   _____

   d. touch   _____

   e. smell   _____

4. How did riding a surfboard affect or change the author?

   _____

   _____

Explore Topics

6.3 **Explore topics.**

In the Warm Up, you will try an exploring strategy to generate ideas about different topics.

The Writer's Desk: Warm Up

Think about the following questions, and write down the first ideas that come to your mind. Try to think of two or three ideas for each topic.

EXAMPLE: What were some strong impressions you had on a vacation or an outing?

-the spray of ocean mist on my face

-the bright lights in an amusement park

-the smell of food grilling on a barbecue

1. What were some very emotional moments in your life? (Think about two or three moments when you felt extreme joy, sadness, excitement, anxiety, or other strong emotions.)

_____

_____

_____

2. Describe your food quirks. What are your unusual tastes or eating habits? Which foods do you really love or hate?

_____

_____

_____

3. What are some very beautiful places in or near your home?

_____

_____

_____

Developing

ESSAY LINK
In a descriptive essay, the thesis statement expresses the controlling idea.

When you write a description paragraph, choose a subject that appeals to at least some of the five senses. For example, you might describe the sights, tastes, and smells in a bakery.

The Topic Sentence

6.4 **Identify the topic sentence of a description paragraph.**

In the topic sentence of a description paragraph, you should convey a dominant impression—the overall impression or feeling that the topic inspires.

          topic   controlling idea
The abandoned buildings in our neighborhood are an eyesore.

    topic   controlling idea
When the car skidded, I panicked.

HINT: How to Create a Dominant Impression

To create a dominant impression, ask yourself how or why the topic is important.

Poor   The parade was noisy.

          (Why should readers care about this statement?)

                      topic   controlling idea

Better   **The parade participants** shouted joyfully as they celebrated the arrival of the New Year.

The Writer's Desk: Write Topic Sentences

Write a topic sentence for each of the following. Narrow the ideas from the previous Writer's Desk. Each topic sentence should state what you are describing and contain a controlling idea.

EXAMPLE: Topic: Impressions on a vacation or an outing

Topic sentence: The Ferris wheel at the Dixie Classic Fair, with its vibrant, twinkling lights, is a wonderful attraction.

1. Topic: An emotional moment

   Topic sentence: _____

   _____

2. Topic: Food quirks (unusual food habits or foods you love or hate)

   Topic sentence: _____

   _____

3. Topic: A beautiful place

   Topic sentence: _____

   _____

The Supporting Ideas

6.5 **Identify the supporting details of a description paragraph.**

After you have developed an effective topic sentence, generate supporting details. The details can be placed in space, time, or emphatic order.

Practice 2: Visualizing Description

Brainstorm supporting ideas for the following topic sentence. Write some descriptive words or phrases.

Topic Sentence: My grandfather's neighborhood has many beautiful features.

_____   _____   _____
_____   _____   _____
_____   _____   _____

Show, Don't Tell

Your audience will find it more interesting to read your written work if you *show* a quality of a place or an action of a person rather than just state it.

Example of Telling	Recently, we had a big snowstorm.
Example of Showing	Recently, a blizzard roared off Lake Michigan and blasted our farm. The trees moaned and their branches creaked. Wind-driven snow encased pine needles, heaped into drifts, and sculpted fields. Curtains of snow-draped shrubs created small caverns where sparrows and rabbits hid.

—from "Snow" by Joan Donaldson

Practice 3

Choose one of the following sentences, and write a short description that shows—not tells—the quality of the person, place, thing, or event.

1. My roommate is inconsiderate.
2. I made dinner.
3. The park was beautiful.

List Sensory Details

To create a dominant impression, think about your topic and make a list of your feelings and impressions. These details can include imagery (descriptions that appeal to sight, sound, touch, taste, and smell).

ESSAY LINK
When you plan a descriptive essay, it is useful to list sensory details.

Topic: An abandoned building

Details: —damp floors

—boarded-up windows   —musty

—broken glass   —gray bricks

—graffiti on the walls   —chipping paint

VOCABULARY BOOST: Using Vivid Language

When you write a description paragraph, try to use vivid language. Use specific action verbs and vivid adjectives to create a clear picture of what you are describing.

                unpretentious

The wealthy owner was ~~nice~~.

(Use a more vivid, specific adjective.)

        howled

The wind ~~blew~~.

(Use a more vivid, specific verb or image.)

Think about other words or expressions that more effectively describe these words:

Hungry: _____

Not friendly: _____

Cry: _____

Speak: _____

The Writer's Desk: List Sensory Details

Think about images, impressions, and feelings that the following topics inspire in you. Refer to your topic sentences on page 72, and make a list under each topic.

EXAMPLE: Impression on a vacation or an outing

bright blinking lights

ticket-taker yelling

chilly breeze on my face

smell of french fries

inky black sky

flickering stars

silence

1. An emotional moment: _____

_____

_____

_____

_____

_____

_____

_____

2. Food quirks: _____

_____

_____

_____

_____

_____

3. A beautiful place: _____

_____

_____

_____

_____

_____

The Paragraph Plan

6.6   Develop a description paragraph plan.

A description paragraph should contain specific details so that readers can clearly imagine what is being described. When you make a paragraph plan, remember to include concrete details. Also think about the organizational method that you will use.

Topic Sentence: With its vibrant colorful lights, the Ferris wheel at the Dixie Classic Fair is a wonderful attraction.

Support 1:   We wait in the long line for what seems like hours.

   Details: —bright blinking lights

          —ticket-taker yelling

          —scramble to our seats

Support 2:   Soon the ride takes off, and we look outside our windows.

   Details: —the ground gets smaller as the ride gets higher

          —a chilly breeze

          —salty french fries and sweet cakes

Support 3:   Finally, we feel as if we are on the top of the world as the ride reaches its peak.

   Details: —inky black sky and flickering stars

          —faces shimmer with moonlight

          —silence

          —autumn breeze rocks the seats

> **ESSAY LINK**
> In a description essay, place the thesis statement in the introduction. Then, develop each supporting idea in a body paragraph. Include descriptive details.

The Writer's Desk: Write a Paragraph Plan

Choose one of the topic sentences that you wrote for the Writer's Desk on page 72, and write a detailed paragraph plan. You can include some of the sensory details that you have generated in the previous Writer's Desk.

Topic sentence: _____

_____

Support 1: _____

Details: _____

_____

Support 2: _____

Details: _____

_____

Support 3: _____

Details: _____

_____

The First Draft

6.7   Write the first draft of a description paragraph.

After you outline your ideas in a plan, write the first draft. Use complete sentences and include transitional words or expressions to help your ideas flow smoothly.

You can use space order to describe a person, place, or thing. "**On top** of his head" or "**underneath** the bed" are examples of transitional phrases that describe spatially. The following transitions are useful in description paragraphs.

To Show Place or Position			
above	beyond	in the distance	outside
behind	closer in	nearby	over there
below	farther out	on the left/right	under
beside	in front (of)	on top (of)	underneath

The Writer's Desk: Write the First Draft

In the previous Writer's Desk, you developed a paragraph plan. Now write the first draft of your description paragraph. Before you write, carefully review your paragraph plan and make any necessary changes.

Revising and Editing

Revise and Edit a Description Paragraph

6.8 **Revise and edit a description paragraph.**

When you finish writing, carefully review your paragraph and revise it to make the description as clear as possible to your readers. Check that you have organized your steps logically, and remove any irrelevant details.

Practice 4

Read the following student paragraph, and answer the questions.

With its vibrant colorful lights, the Ferris wheel at the Dixie Classic Fair is a wonderful attraction. We wait impatiently in the long line for what seems like hours. The bright blinking lights cause us to squint as we reach the front of the line. We get closer to the entrance of the ride and hear the ticket-taker yelling, "three tickets please." The man takes three yellow tickets from us and rips them to shreds. We watch excitedly as the Ferris wheel car stops in front of us. And scramble quickly to our seats. Soon, the ride takes off, and we look curious out of the windows. Everything on the ground gets smaller as we go higher. We feel the chilly breeze on our faces, so we wrap our scarves tightly and zip up our jackets. As the wind blows, the smell of salty French fries and sweet funnel cakes travels upward and fills our noses, causing our stomachs to growl. Finally, feeling on top of the world, the ride reaches its peak. The sky is inky black, and the stars flicker like fireflies. The faces of the other customers shimmer in the moonlight. The universe becomes silent. The autumn breeze rocks our seats back and forth causing our stomachs to flip-flop. The ride finally comes to an end, and as we slowly descend, the sounds of screams, laughs, excited chatter, and music fill the air.

—Tiara Johnson, student

Revising

1. Underline the topic sentence.

2. Highlight three vivid images in the paragraph.

3. The paragraph lacks a title. Add a title.

Editing

4. Underline and correct one adverb error.

5. A fragment lacks a subject or a verb and is an incomplete sentence. Underline and correct one fragment.

6. Underline and correct a dangling modifier. See the following Grammar Hint for an explanation about dangling modifiers.

> **GRAMMAR LINK**
> Extra grammar help:
>> Past Participles, Ch. 24, p. 318
>> Fragments, Ch. 20, p. 282
>> Modifiers, Ch. 31, p. 402

GRAMMAR HINT: Using Modifiers

When you revise your descriptive essay, check that your modifiers are placed near the items they are modifying. Also make sure that the modifier is connected to another part of the sentence and is not dangling.

Incorrect	Gazing at the sky, the clouds drifted on the horizon.
Correct	Gazing at the sky, **I noticed** the clouds drifting on the horizon.

The Writer's Desk: Revise and Edit Your Paragraph

Revise and edit the paragraph that you wrote for the previous Writer's Desk. Check that your paragraph has unity, adequate support, and coherence. Also, correct any errors in grammar, spelling, punctuation, and mechanics.

Reflect On It

Think about what you have learned in this chapter. If you do not know an answer, review that topic.

1. What are the main features of a description paragraph? _____

_____

_____

_____

2. Define imagery. _____

3. Look at the familiar words below. Write down at least two more descriptive ways to say each word. Try to find words that are more specific.

a. cute _____   c. sad _____

b. angry _____   d. mean _____

The Writer's Room

Writing Activity 1: Topics

Choose any of the following topics, or choose your own topic. Then write a description paragraph by following the steps of the writing process.

General Topics

1. a fad or a fashion trend
2. a comfortable room
3. an evening out
4. an exciting sports event
5. a positive person

College- and Work-Related Topics

6. a quiet area on campus
7. an unusual student or coworker
8. an inspiring teacher or instructor
9. an uncomfortable uniform
10. a place with a good or bad odor

Writing Activity 2: Media Writing

Watch or listen to media that refer to or depict futuristic, post-apocalyptic, or mysterious places. Write an illustration paragraph describing what you see, hear, or envision. Describe the setting or main characters. Use imagery that appeals to the senses. Here are some suggestions to spark ideas.

Show: *The Walking Dead*

Film: *Mad Max* and *Star Trek*

Video: Katy Perry and Kanye West's *E.T.*

Song: David Bowie's classic "A Space Odyssey"

Podcast: *Welcome to Night Vale*

WRITING LINK
More descriptive writing activities:
The Writer's Room

Ch. 20, topic 2, p. 288
Ch. 22, topic 1, p. 303
Ch. 23, topic 2, p. 317
Ch. 27, topic 1, p. 356
Ch. 36, topic 1, p. 456

READING LINK
MORE DESCRIPTIVE READINGS

"Roaring Waves of Fire" p. 188
"Chicken Hips" p. 189
"The Catcher of Ghosts" p. 502
"Aunt Tee" p. 514

Description Paragraph Checklist

As you write your description paragraph, review the checklist at the end of the book. Also ask yourself the following questions.

❑ Does my topic sentence clearly show what I will describe?

❑ Does my topic sentence have a controlling idea that makes a point about the topic?

❑ Does my paragraph make a dominant impression?

❑ Does my paragraph contain supporting details that appeal to the reader's senses?

❑ Do I use vivid language?

7 Process

Instructors explain dance moves step by step. Similarly, in process writing, you describe how to do something.

LEARNING OBJECTIVES

7.1 Define process.

7.2 Explain how to write a process paragraph.

7.3 Explore topics.

7.4 Identify the topic sentence of a process paragraph.

7.5 Identify the supporting ideas of a process paragraph.

7.6 Develop a process paragraph plan.

7.7 Write the first draft of a process paragraph.

7.8 Revise and edit a process paragraph.

Writers' Exchange

Choose one of the following topics, and have a group or class discussion. Describe the steps you would take to do that process.

1. How to plan a party
2. How to find a part-time job
3. How to organize a garage sale
4. How to set the table for a formal dinner

Exploring

What Is a Process?

7.1 Define process.

A **process** is a series of steps done in chronological order. In process writing, you explain how to do something, how an incident took place, or how something works.

You explain processes every day. At home, you may show a family member how to use electronic devices, or write instructions to a babysitter or caregiver. At college, you may describe the steps to solve a math problem or discuss how a new product was invented. At work, you may explain how to operate a machine or how to perform a particular job.

PROCESS AT WORK

Michelle Mabry instructs college students in the art of welding. Read this excerpt from an instruction manual.

The **topic sentence** expresses the main idea.

Supporting sentences provide details.

The **concluding sentence** brings the paragraph to a close.

Welding, like sewing, consists of piecing together metal with neat seams that withstand wear and tear. It is stitching with fire. To weld safely, consider the following points. First, you need a welding jacket, some leather gloves, and an auto-darkening welding helmet to wear over your safety glasses. For a weld to work, the metal needs to be clean and abraded along the line you will be welding. You can use a wire brush for that. Clamp the pieces of metal together. Your first welds will be tack welds, sort of like pinning cloth together so the pieces don't move while you sew them together. A couple of tack welds should do: a quick zap at the corners and maybe one in the middle. Check the position of the pieces after the first tack weld. When you are comfortable, position your gun at the first tack and pull the trigger. There will be a steady crackle as you move the nozzle across the seam. Don't hurry. Keep moving until the end of the pieces. Release the trigger. Use pliers to pick it up and inspect the underside. You will be pleased with the results.

The Process Paragraph

7.2   Explain how to write a process paragraph.

There are two main types of process paragraphs.

- **Complete a process.** This type of paragraph contains directions on how to complete a particular task. Readers should be able to follow the directions and complete the task (how to paint a room, how to repair a leaky faucet, how to apply for a job).

- **Understand a process.** This type of paragraph explains how something works or how something happens. Readers should be able to understand a process or a function (how the heart pumps blood to other organs in the body, how a country elects its political leaders).

ESSAY LINK
Process essays also focus on completing or understanding a process.

Practice 1

A framed painting hanging on a wall creates its own imaginary world. Understanding and responding to a painting does not have to be difficult. First, get up close. When you approach a picture, step into its universe. Put your nose up close and observe the picture as a physical object. Drink in its visual and physical properties. Next, take a step back and look at the picture as a whole. Look at the arrangement or composition of the picture's elements: background or foreground, implied movement, and dramatic action. Is there a story? Who are the human figures? Are there symbols? What feelings or ideas does it stimulate in you? Then, think and apply what you know. Study the picture in historical context. This knowledge can help identify the style or movement to which a picture belongs. It can tell you about the work's patron or something significant about the artist's life and how this work fits into that story. Finally, respond with your own thoughts and feelings. Look at what it shows you and listen to what it says and record that experience for yourself in a journal or notebook. This personal reflection fixes the impression and helps you recall this picture as something you've become acquainted with.

—Philip E. Bishop, *A Beginner's Guide to the Humanities*

1. a. What is the topic of this paragraph? _____

   _____

   b. What is the controlling idea in the topic sentence? _____

   _____

2. What type of process paragraph is this?

   a. complete a process   b. understand a process

3. List the main steps the author suggests to help you understand a painting.

   _____

   _____

   _____

   _____

Practice 2

Read the next paragraph, and answer the questions.

In the beginning . . . there was no Internet. The Internet as we know it today evolved over many decades. In its earliest form, the Internet did not include commerce, global connectivity, or public usage. The initial conceptualization of the Internet actually derived from government suspicion and social hysteria that permeated Cold War America in the 1960s. In 1969, the Department of Defense sponsored a project to overcome threats from a blackout of communication in the event of a nuclear war. The fledgling project linked four universities and was intended to facilitate communications between their computers. In the early 1970s, the project was opened up to non-military institutions, and major universities took advantage of this policy. By 1972, computer links were made with institutions outside the United States, but it was still only a way for computers to talk to each other. In the mid-1980s, the services we now use, such as email, started appearing on the Internet. By the end of the 1980s, the World Wide Web was developed by Tim Berners Lee, who invented the system of hyperlinked pages so that scientists could share information about their research. These pages used text and graphics to communicate information. By 1993, using their computers and a modem, people could dial in and connect to the network, and the Internet that is familiar to us today began.

—Marje T. Britz *Computer Forensics*

1. Underline the topic sentence.

2. What type of process paragraph is this? Circle the best answer.

   a. complete a process   b. understand a process

3. List the steps in the process. The first one has been done for you.
   Started during the Cold War in the 1960s. _____

   _____

   _____

   _____

   _____

   _____

   _____

   _____

Practice 3

For each of the following topics, write *C* if it explains how to complete a process, or write *U* if it explains how to understand a process (how something works or how something happens).

1. How to improve your study habits   _____

2. How a credit card works   _____

3. How to wash a car   _____

4. How to catch a fish   _____

5. How a microwave heats food   _____

Explore Topics

7.3 Explore topics.

In the Warm Up, you will try an exploring strategy to generate ideas about different topics.

The Writer's Desk: Warm Up

Think about the following questions, and write down the first ideas that come to your mind. Try to think of two or three ideas for each topic.

EXAMPLE: Explain how to do a group "flash mob" activity. Write down some of the steps in the process.

    —to make a flash mob dance, you need to find music

    —organize your friends and learn the steps

    —perform the dance in a public place

1. How do you do a particular activity at your workplace?

_____

_____

_____

2. What are some things you should do to succeed in college?

_____

_____

_____

3. How do you use a particular app?

_____

_____

_____

Developing

When you write a process paragraph, choose a process that you can easily cover in a single paragraph. For example, you might be able to explain how to download a software program in a single paragraph; however, you may need much more than a paragraph to explain how to use the software program.

ESSAY LINK
In a process essay, the thesis statement expresses the controlling idea.

The Topic Sentence

7.4 Identify the topic sentence of a process paragraph.

In a process paragraph, the topic sentence states which process you will be explaining and what readers will be able to do or understand after they have read the paragraph.

topic   controlling idea

To calm your child during a tantrum, <u>follow the next steps</u>.

controlling idea   topic

<u>With inexpensive materials</u>, **you can redecorate a room in your house**.

HINT: Make a Point

Your topic sentence should not simply announce the topic. It should make a point about the topic.

Announces	I will describe how to do speed dating.
Correct	<u>It is surprisingly easy and efficient</u> **to meet someone using speed dating**.

Above "Correct": controlling idea ... topic

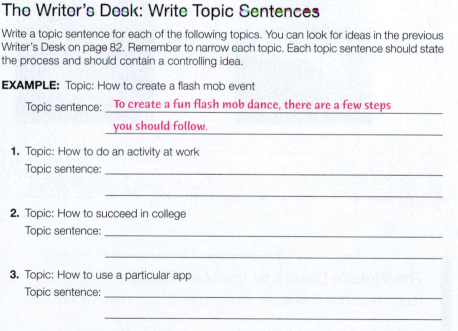

The Writer's Desk: Write Topic Sentences

Write a topic sentence for each of the following topics. You can look for ideas in the previous Writer's Desk on page 82. Remember to narrow each topic. Each topic sentence should state the process and should contain a controlling idea.

EXAMPLE: Topic: How to create a flash mob event

Topic sentence: <u>To create a fun flash mob dance, there are a few steps you should follow.</u>

1. Topic: How to do an activity at work

Topic sentence: _____

_____

2. Topic: How to succeed in college

Topic sentence: _____

_____

3. Topic: How to use a particular app

Topic sentence: _____

_____

The Supporting Ideas

7.5 Identify the supporting ideas of a process paragraph.

A process paragraph contains a series of steps. When you develop supporting ideas for a process paragraph, think about the main steps that are necessary to complete the process. Most process paragraphs use time (chronological) order.

ESSAY LINK
In an essay, each body paragraph could describe a process. For example, in an essay about how to get rich, one body paragraph could be about buying lottery tickets and another could be about inventing a product.

HINT: Give Steps, Not Examples

When you explain how to complete a process, describe each step. Do not simply list examples of the process.

Topic: How to Get Rich

List of Examples	Steps in the Process
flip real estate	do market research
win the lottery	find a specific need
invent a product	invent a product to fulfill that need
inherit money	heavily promote the product

Practice 4: Visualizing Process

Brainstorm supporting ideas for the following topic sentence. List some steps that you should take.

Topic Sentence: To groom a curly-coat dog, follow the next steps.

 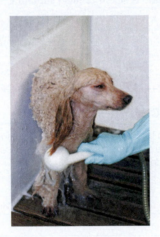 

_____ _____ _____

_____ _____ _____

_____ _____ _____

The Writer's Desk: List the Main Steps

Think of three or four essential steps in each process. Make a list under each topic.

EXAMPLE: How to create a flash mob event

choose a song and a sound system

contact friends using Facebook

practice the dance moves

meet in a public place to dance

_____

1. How to do an activity at work

_____

_____

_____

_____

2. How to succeed in college

_____

_____

_____

_____

3. How to use a particular app

_____

_____

_____

_____

The Paragraph Plan

7.6   **Develop a process paragraph plan.**

A paragraph plan helps you organize the topic sentence and supporting details before writing a first draft. Decide which steps and which details your readers will really need to know to complete the process or understand it. Write down the steps in chronological order.

> **ESSAY LINK**
>
> In a process essay, place the thesis statement in the introduction. Then use each body paragraph to explain a step in the process.

Topic Sentence: To create a fun flash mob dance, follow these easy steps.

Support 1:	Find a song that inspires you to dance.
Details:	—Borrow a good sound system.
	—Choose a song that everyone will recognize.
Support 2:	Organize the event using social media like Facebook, Twitter, and Instagram.
Details:	—Determine a time and place to practice.
	—Try to get as many people as possible.
Support 3:	Meet somewhere to practice the dance steps.
Details:	—Choreograph the steps.
	—Repeat until everyone knows the routine.
Support 4:	At a planned time in a public place, do the flash mob dance.
Details:	—Act like normal members of the public.
	—Turn on the music and start dancing.
	—Bystanders will stare in amazement and maybe join in.

HINT: Include Necessary Tools or Supplies

When you are writing a plan for a process paragraph, remember to include any special tools or supplies a reader will need to complete the process. For example, if you want to explain how to pack for a move, you should mention boxes, felt-tip markers, newspaper, twine, scissors, and tape.

The Writer's Desk: Write a Paragraph Plan

Choose one of the topic sentences that you wrote for the Writer's Desk on page 83, and then list the main steps to complete the process. Also add details and examples that will help to explain each step.

Topic sentence: _____

_____

Supporting points:

Step 1: _____

Details: _____

_____

Step 2: _____

Details: _____

_____

Step 3: _____

Details: _____

_____

Step 4: _____

Details: _____

_____

Step 5: _____

Details: _____

_____

The First Draft

7.7   Write the first draft of a process paragraph.

After outlining your ideas in a plan, you are ready to write the first draft. Remember to write complete sentences. You might include transitional words or expressions to help your ideas flow smoothly. Most process paragraphs explain a process using time (or chronological) order. The following transitions are useful in process paragraphs.

To Begin a Process	To Continue a Process		To End a Process
(at) first	after that	later	eventually
initially	afterward	meanwhile	finally
the first step	also	second	in the end
	furthermore	then	ultimately
	in addition	third	

TECHNOLOGY LINK
Images can enhance process writing. When explaining how to use an app, for example, snap a screen shot of each step on your phone or similar smart device. Then, you might embed those images in your written paragraph.

The Writer's Desk: Write the First Draft

In the previous Writer's Desk, you developed a paragraph plan. Now write the first draft of your process paragraph. Before you write, carefully review your paragraph plan and make any necessary changes.

Revising and Editing

Revise and Edit a Process Paragraph

7.8 **Revise and edit a process paragraph.**

When you finish writing a process paragraph, carefully review your work and revise it to make the process as clear as possible to your readers. Check to make sure that you have organized your steps chronologically, and remove any irrelevant details.

Practice 5

Read the following student paragraph, and answer the questions.

> To create a fun flash mob dance, follow these easy steps. First, find a song. It's best to choose an easily recognizable song with a strong beat. You will also need a good sound system. Organize the event using social media like Facebook, Twitter, and Instagram. Determine a time and place to practice. Don't ask others for input, or you might never agree on a date. Try to get as many people as possible to participate, ask friends to contact their friends. Meet somewhere to practice the steps. Repeat the steps until everyone knows the routine. You can even videotape yourself doing the steps and post it online so others can practice at home. At a planned time in a public place, do the flash mob dance. Act like normal members of the public, start the music, and then start dancing. Bystanders will stare in amazement and might even join in. For sure, your going to have a fantastic time. Craig Knowles, a flash mob veteran, says, "Its the best feeling in the world to add some laughter and joy to a routine day".
>
> —Amal Kahan, student

Revising

1. Underline the topic sentence.
2. The author uses "first" to introduce the first steps. Subsequent steps would be more clearly recognizable if the writer had used more transitions. Include three more transitional expressions.
3. How does the writer conclude the paragraph?
   a. with a prediction   b. with a suggestion   c. with a quotation

Editing

4. The paragraph contains a type of run-on sentence called a comma splice. Two complete ideas are incorrectly connected with a comma. Identify and correct the run-on sentence.
5. Identify and correct two pronoun errors. (For more information about pronoun errors, see the Grammar Hint on the next page.)
6. Correct a punctuation error in the concluding quotation.

GRAMMAR LINK
Extra grammar help:
  Run-Ons, Ch. 21, p. 289
  Pronouns, Ch. 29, p. 372
  Quotations, Ch. 35, p. 450

8 Definition

8 Definition

LEARNING OBJECTIVES

8.1 Define definition.

8.2 Explain how to write a definition paragraph.

8.3 Explore topics.

8.4 Identify the topic sentence of a definition paragraph.

8.5 Identify the supporting ideas of a definition paragraph.

8.6 Develop a definition paragraph plan.

8.7 Write the first draft of a definition paragraph.

8.8 Revise and edit a definition paragraph.

Hockey has specialized terms—*icing*, *off side*, and *right wing*—both players and fans should understand. In definition writing, you define what a term means.

Writers' Exchange

Work with a partner or a team of students. Try to define the following terms. Think of some examples that can help define each term.

netiquette   chick flick   bromance   a tweet (on Twitter)

Exploring

What Is Definition?

8.1 Define definition.

When you **define**, you explain the meaning of a word. Some terms have concrete meanings, and you can define them in a few words. For example, a pebble is "a small stone." Other words, such as *culture, happiness,* or *evil*, are more abstract and require longer definitions. In fact, it is possible to write a paragraph, an essay, or even an entire book on such concepts.

Dictionaries list one or more definitions for a term. However, many words have nuances that are not necessarily discussed in dictionaries. For example, suppose that your boss calls your work *unsatisfactory*. You might need clarification of that term. Do you have poor work habits? Do you miss deadlines? Is your attitude problematic? What does your boss mean by *unsatisfactory*?

The ability to define difficult concepts is always useful. At home, a friend or loved one may ask you to define *commitment*. If you mention that a movie was *great*, you may need to clarify what you mean by that word. In a political science class, you might define *socialism, capitalism*, or *communism*. At work, you might define a product's *marketing strategy*.

DEFINITION AT WORK

Will Thomas is a certified home inspector. In this excerpt from a home inspection report, he defines ice-damming.

My inspection of the attic insulation and the roof ventilation system indicate that your house may be subject to ice-damming, which can cause water to penetrate the structure. Ice-damming occurs in the winter when hot air from the heated parts of the house escape into an insufficiently insulated and improperly ventilated attic. This hot air warms the underside of the roof, causing snow on the roof to melt. It quickly re-freezes when it trickles down over a cold spot that is typical at the edge of the roof. This ice forms a physical barrier, a dam, which holds back more meltwater creating a pool on the roof. This growing pool of meltwater then creeps under the shingles and into the house. Ice-damming can cause serious, and visible, damage to the interior of a house, but also can cause hidden problems such as biological growth in finished walls and degradation of the wood frame structure of the house. It should be remembered that roofs are designed to stop precipitation entering the house from above—not act as a barrier.

> The **topic sentence** expresses the main idea.

> **Supporting sentences** provide details and examples.

> The **concluding sentence** brings the paragraph to a close.

The Definition Paragraph

8.2   **Explain how to write a definition paragraph.**

When you write a definition paragraph, try to explain what a term means to you. For example, if someone asks you to define *bravery*, you might tell stories to illustrate the meaning of the word. You may also give examples of acts of bravery or even explain what bravery is not.

Remember the following two points.

- **Choose a term that you know something about.** You need to understand a term in order to say something relevant and interesting about it.

- **Give a clear definition.** In your first sentence, write a definition that is understandable to your reader, and support your definition with examples. Do not simply give a dictionary definition because your readers are capable of looking up the word themselves.

HINT: Consider Your Audience

When you write a definition paragraph, consider your audience. You may have to adjust your tone and vocabulary to suit your reader's age, education level, or other characteristics. For example, if you write a definition paragraph about computer viruses for your English class, use easily understandable terms. If you write the same paragraph for your computer class, use more technical terms.

Practice 1

Read the paragraph, and then answer the questions.

People who use computers at work for personal purposes are called *cyberslackers*. Many employees download music, gamble, and play games while they are at work. They read books, shop, exchange jokes, and send personal e-mails. Some go online to trade stocks or post messages in chat rooms. There are also those who visit porn sites while at their desks. Some cyberslackers even operate their own businesses online during work hours. The master cyberslacker is a programmer who has become somewhat of a folk hero. "Bob," as he is known, outsourced his own job to a company in China. Bob paid the Chinese worker one-fifth of his salary, and then Bob spent his "work days" online. In his little cubicle, he would visit Facebook and eBay, and he would watch cute cat videos. Bob's supervisors were pleased with Bob's work. He produced clean code and was always on time. Bob was even voted the best coder in the building! Cyberslackers often get discovered. Eventually, the company investigated Bob's online activities and found out how he really spent his work days.

—James M. Henslin, *Sociology: A Down-To-Earth Approach*

1. Underline the topic sentence of the paragraph.

2. What is the writer defining? _____

3. In the paragraph, why are the words "work days" in quotation marks? _____

   _____

4. How does the anecdote about "Bob" support the definition? _____

   _____

   _____

Explore Topics

8.3   Explore topics.

In the Warm Up, you will try an exploring strategy to generate ideas about different topics.

The Writer's Desk: Warm Up

Think about the following questions, and write down the first ideas that come to your mind. Try to think of two or three ideas for each topic.

EXAMPLE: What is slang? Think of some examples of slang.

   —words people use for effect

   —cool, dude, bro

   —different cultural groups have their own slang terms

1. What is peer pressure? Give some examples of peer pressure.

   _____

   _____

   _____

2. What is binge viewing?

_____

_____

_____

3. What are some characteristics of a blended or reconstructed family?

_____

_____

_____

_____

Developing

The Topic Sentence

8.4 **Identify the topic sentence of a definition paragraph.**

A clear topic sentence for a definition paragraph introduces the term and provides a definition. There are three basic ways to define a term.

- By synonym
- By category
- By negation

Definition by Synonym

The easiest way to define a term is to supply a synonym (a word that has a similar meaning). This type of definition is useful if the original term is difficult to understand and the synonym is a more familiar word.

term	+	synonym
Vaping		is inhaling the vapor of an electronic cigarette.

I am a procrastinator, which means I tend to put things off.

Definition by Category

A more effective way to define a term is to give a definition by category (or class). When you define by category, you determine the larger group to which the term belongs. Then you determine what unique characteristics set the term apart from others in that category.

term	+	category	+	detail
A farce is		a dramatic work		filled with exaggerated and humorous situations.
Luddites are		people		who are skeptical about new technology.

Definition by Negation

When you define by negation, you explain what a term does not mean. You can then include a sentence explaining what it does mean. Definition by negation is especially useful when your readers have preconceived ideas about something. Your definition explains that the term does not mean what the reader previously thought.

ESSAY LINK
In a definition essay, the thesis statement expresses the controlling idea. In the thesis, you can define the term by synonym, category, or negation.

term	+	what it is not	+	what it is
Alcoholism		is not an invented disease;		it is a serious physical dependency.
Hackers		are not playful computer geeks;		they are criminals.

GRAMMAR HINT: Using Semicolons

When you write a definition by negation, you can join the two separate and independent sentences with a semicolon.

Independent clause   ;   independent clause

Feminists are not man haters; they are people who want fairness and equality for women.

Practice 2

A. Write a one-sentence definition by synonym for each of the following terms. Your definition should include the term and a synonym. If necessary, you can use a dictionary; however, define each term using your own words.

EXAMPLE: To capitulate __means to give up or surrender_____

1. To procrastinate _____

2. A pseudonym _____

B. Write a one-sentence definition by category for the following terms. Make sure that your definition includes the term, a category, and details.

EXAMPLE: Jargon _is vocabulary used by specific professions._____

3. A knockoff _____

_____

4. A selfie _____

_____

C. Write a one-sentence definition by negation for the following terms. Explain what each term is not, followed by what each term is.

EXAMPLE: A placebo _pill does not contain real medication; it is a sugar pill._____

5. A YouTube addict _____

_____

6. A vote _____

_____

Use the Right Word

When you write a definition paragraph, it is important to use precise words to define the term. Moreover, when you define a term by category, make sure that the category for your term is correct. For example, look at the following imprecise definitions of insomnia.

- Insomnia is the (inability) to sleep well.

  (Insomnia is not an ability or an inability.)

- Insomnia is (when) you cannot sleep well.

  (*When* refers to a time, but insomnia is not a time.)

- Insomnia is the (nights) when you do not get enough sleep.

  (Insomnia is not days or nights.)

- Insomnia is (where) it is hard to fall asleep.

  (*Where* refers to a place, but insomnia is not a place.)

Now look at a better definition of insomnia.

category

Insomnia is a **sleeping disorder** characterized by the inability to sleep well.

HINT: Make a Point

Defining a term by synonym, category, or negation is the guideline for writing topic sentences. However, keep in mind that your paragraph will be more interesting if you express an attitude or point of view in your topic sentence.

No point	Anorexia is an eating disorder.
Point	Anorexia is a tragic eating disorder that is difficult to cure.

Practice 3

Revise each sentence using precise language.

EXAMPLE: Tuning out is when you ignore something.

Tuning out is the action of ignoring something.

1. Claustrophobia is the inability to be in a small place.

_____

_____

2. A bully is the abuse of power over others.

_____

_____

3. A selfie stick is when you take selfies using an elongated stick.

_____

_____

4. Ego surfing is when you surf the Internet to find references to yourself.

_____

_____

VOCABULARY BOOST: Using Your Thesaurus

Work with a partner to brainstorm synonyms or expressions that can replace each word listed below. If you have trouble coming up with ideas, use your thesaurus.

1. optimist _____

2. depressed _____

3. lazy _____

4. reckless _____

Later, when you finish writing your definition paragraph, identify any repeated words and replace them with synonyms.

The Writer's Desk: Write Topic Sentences

For each of the following, write a topic sentence in which you define the topic. You can look for ideas in the Warm Up on page 92–93. Remember to use precise language in your definition.

EXAMPLE: Topic: Slang

Topic sentence: Slang is informal language that changes rapidly and exists in various forms among different cultural groups.

1. Topic: Peer pressure

   Topic sentence: _____

   _____

2. Topic: Binge viewing

   Topic sentence: _____

   _____

3. Topic: A blended family

   Topic sentence: _____

   _____

The Supporting Ideas

8.5 Identify the supporting ideas of a definition paragraph.

After you have developed an effective topic sentence, generate supporting ideas. In a definition paragraph, you can give examples that clarify your definition.

Think about how you will organize your examples. Most definition paragraphs use emphatic order, which means that examples are placed from the most to the least important or from the least to the most important.

Practice 4: Visualizing Definition

Brainstorm supporting ideas for the following topic sentence. Using words or phrases, describe each example of timeless fashion.

Topic Sentence: Men's timeless fashions remain popular and will not go out of style.

_____

_____

_____

The Writer's Desk: Develop Supporting Ideas

Choose one of your topic sentences from the Writer's Desk on page 96. List three or four examples that best illustrate the definition.

EXAMPLE:

Topic sentence: Slang is informal language that changes rapidly and
exists in various forms among different cultural groups.

Supports: —words change in different eras
—subcultures have their own terms
—prisoners and gangs use slang
—some slang becomes standard English

Topic sentence: _____
_____
_____

Supports: _____
_____
_____
_____
_____

The Paragraph Plan

8.6   Develop a definition paragraph plan.

A good definition paragraph includes a complete definition of the term and provides adequate examples to support the central definition. When creating a definition paragraph plan, make sure that your examples provide varied evidence and do not

> **ESSAY LINK**
> In a definition essay, the thesis statement is in the introduction. Each supporting idea is in a distinct body paragraph with its own topic sentence.

just repeat the definition. Also, add details that will help clarify your supporting examples.

Topic Sentence: Slang is informal language that changes rapidly and exists in various forms among different cultural groups.

Support 1: Slang is a code used in many subcultures.

Details: — Hipsters use certain terms.

— Terms like *devo* and *basic* are hipster terms.

— Outsiders don't understand the slang terms.

Support 2: Marginalized groups use slang to hide their conversations from others.

Details: — Gangs have special words.

— Prisoners have specialized terms.

— Matt Soniak's *MentalFloss* article gives examples.

Support 3: Slang changes over time.

Details: — In the 1920s, people used words that are out of fashion now.

— Terms from the 1980s are obsolete.

— Some slang terms, such as *gamer*, become standard English.

The Writer's Desk: Write a Paragraph Plan

Create a detailed paragraph plan using the topic sentence that you wrote for the Writer's Desk on the previous page. Arrange the supporting details in a logical order.

Topic sentence: _____

_____

Support 1: _____

Details: _____

_____

_____

Support 2: _____

Details: _____

_____

_____

Support 3: _____

Details: _____

_____

_____

The First Draft

8.7 **Write the first draft of a definition paragraph.**

After you outline your ideas in a plan, you are ready to write the first draft. Remember to write complete sentences. You might include transitional words or expressions to help your ideas flow smoothly. Transitional expressions can show different levels of importance. The following transitions are useful in definition paragraphs.

To Show the Level of Importance	
clearly	next
first	one quality . . . another quality
most important	second
most of all	undoubtedly

The Writer's Desk: Write the First Draft

In the previous Writer's Desk, you developed a paragraph plan. Now write the first draft of your definition paragraph. Before you write, carefully review your paragraph plan and make any necessary changes.

Revising and Editing

Revise and Edit a Definition Paragraph

8.8   **Revise and edit a definition paragraph.**

When you finish writing a definition paragraph, carefully review your work and revise it to make the definition as clear as possible to your readers. Check that you have organized your steps logically, and remove any irrelevant details.

Practice 5

Read the following student paragraph and answer the questions.

Slang is informal language that changes rapidly and exists in various forms among different cultural groups. It is a type of code used in many subcultures. It helps members identify each other and feel like they belong. Hipsters might say *devo* instead of *devastated*. They refer to those who are interested in mainstream commercial things as *basic*. Often, outsiders do not understand the groups slang. My father, for instance, didn't know the meaning of LOL. I laughed out loud when I heard that. Marginalized groups develop slang to hide what they are saying from others. Someone in a gang might call his gun a *biscuit*. Prisoners develop slang to confuse prison guards and other inmates. Matt Soniak, a writer for *MentalFloss*, writes that an untrustworthy staff member is called a *bug*. A *kite* is a contraband letter. Slang words come and go real fast. In the 1920s, *clams* meant money and *gams* referred to a woman's legs. In the 1980s, people used terms such as *bodacious* and *yuppie*. Those words are out of fashion. Slang can become part of standard English. This is especially true with computer-related terms such as *gamer*, *blog*, *hacker*, and *troll*. Today, throughout the world, people are inventing new slang words.

—Alexis Wright, student

Revising

1. Underline the topic sentence.

2. What type of definition does the topic sentence contain? Circle the best answer.

   a. definition by synonym   b. definition by category

   c. definition by negation

3. This paragraph lacks sentence variety. Revise the paragraph to give it more sentence variety by combining sentences or changing the first word of some sentences. (For more information about combining sentences and sentence variety, see Chapters 17–19.)

4. The paragraph lacks transitions to show the order of ideas. Add some transitional words or expressions.

5. The paragraph needs a concluding sentence. Add a concluding sentence in the lines provided.

   _____

   _____

Editing

6. There is one word that requires an apostrophe. Circle and correct the error.

7. There is an error in adverb form. Circle and correct the error.

GRAMMAR LINK
See the following chapters for more information about these grammar topics:
Apostrophes, Ch. 35, p. 445
Adjectives and Adverbs, Ch. 30, p. 389

The Writer's Desk: Revise and Edit Your Paragraph

Revise and edit the paragraph that you wrote for the previous Writer's Desk. Make sure that your paragraph has unity, adequate support, and coherence. Also correct any errors in grammar, spelling, punctuation, and mechanics.

Reflect On It

Think about what you have learned in this chapter. If you do not know an answer, review that topic.

1. In definition writing, what do you do? _____

   _____

2. Write an example of a definition by synonym. _____

   _____

3. Write an example of a definition by category. _____

   _____

4. Write an example of a definition by negation. _____

   _____

The Writer's Room

Writing Activity 1: Topics

Choose any of the following topics, or choose your own topic. Then write a definition paragraph.

General Topics

1. a hashtag
2. a spoiled child
3. a white lie
4. a texting addict
5. a lightbulb moment

College- and Work-Related Topics

6. integrity
7. a workaholic
8. an opportunist
9. the glass ceiling
10. a newbie

Writing Activity 2: Media Writing

Watch or listen to media about people who fight to succeed. Define the term *blind ambition*, and support your definition with examples or anecdotes from the media piece you choose. Here are some suggestions to spark ideas.

Show: *Survivor, The Voice, Shark Tank*

Film: *The Corporation, Fame*

Video: *64-Year-Old Swims Cuba to Florida* or YouTube videos about people who hope to succeed

Music: Roar by Katy Perry

Podcast: *A Work in Progress* segment on *The Moth* podcast

WRITING LINK
MORE DEFINITION WRITING TOPICS

Ch. 19, Writer's Room topic 1, p. 281
Ch. 24, Writer's Room topic 1, p. 328
Ch. 26, Writer's Room topic 1, p. 338
Ch. 35, Writer's Room topic 1, p. 456

READING LINK
MORE DEFINITION READINGS

"Homophobia" p. 197
"What Is Luck?" p. 198
"Being a Hyphenated American" p. 487
"Emojis" p. 492

Definition Paragraph Checklist

As you write your definition paragraph, review the checklist at the end of the book. Also ask yourself the following questions.

❏ Does my topic sentence contain a definition by synonym, negation, or category?

❏ Do all of my supporting sentences relate to the topic sentence?

❏ Do I use concise language in my definition?

❏ Do I include enough examples to help define the term?

9 Classification

LEARNING OBJECTIVES

9.1 Define classification.

9.2 Explain how to write a classification paragraph.

9.3 Explore topics.

9.4 Identify the topic sentence of a classification paragraph.

9.5 Identify the supporting ideas of a classification paragraph.

9.6 Develop a classification paragraph plan.

9.7 Write the first draft of a classification paragraph.

9.8 Revise and edit a classification paragraph.

Mechanics organize their tools to be able to find items easily. In classification writing, you divide a topic into categories to help readers understand it.

Writers' Exchange

Work with a partner or in a group. Classify the next words into three or four different categories. What are the categories? Why did you choose those categories?

mechanic	fertilizer	kitchen	office
garden	cook	programmer	computer
microwave	landscaper	wrench	garage

Exploring

What Is Classification?

9.1 Define classification.

When you **classify**, you sort a subject into more understandable categories. The categories must all belong to the subject, yet they must also be distinct from one another. For example, you might write a paragraph about the most common types of pets and sort the subject pets into the categories cats, dogs, and birds.

Classification occurs in many situations. At home, you could classify the bills or the responsibilities of each person in the family. In a biology course, you might write about the different types of cells, or in a commerce course, you may write about the categories in a financial statement. On the job, you might design specific screens to show categories of information on a website.

Classification at Work

Robert Luzynski, an allergy specialist, wrote the following information in a brochure for his patients.

If you exhibit allergic symptoms to animals, there are three types of treatment that you can follow. The most effective is to avoid contact with known allergens. Thus, avoid bringing pets into the home. If you have a pet, consider using an air cleaner, vacuum two to three times a week, and ensure that the animal is groomed frequently to remove loose fur and dander. The second type of treatment consists of medications. Antihistamines help alleviate the symptoms of allergic reactions, but they do not cure allergies. It is important to read the labels carefully, as some antihistamines cause drowsiness. A final method, desensitization, is an extended treatment involving allergy shots. You would be exposed to gradually increasing amounts of specific allergens. The treatment lasts for an extended period of time, and the goal is to reduce your sensitivity to the allergens. One of these treatments should work for you.

> **The Topic sentence** expresses the main idea.

> **Supporting details** provide details and examples.

> The **concluding sentence** brings the paragraph to a close.

The Classification Paragraph

9.2   **Explain how to write a classification paragraph.**

To find a topic for a classification paragraph, think of something that can be sorted into different groups, or categories. Also determine a reason for classifying the items. When you are planning your ideas for a classification paragraph, remember these two points.

> **ESSAY LINK**
> Classification essays also require a classification principle and distinct categories.

1. **Use a common classification principle.** A **classification principle** is the overall method that you use to sort the subject into categories. To find the classification principle, think about one common characteristic that unites the different categories. For example, if your subject is "social media," your classification principle could be any of the following:

   — types of social media apps
   — categories of social media users
   — types of online posts
   — categories of online friends

2. **Sort the subject into distinct categories.** A classification paragraph should have two or more categories.

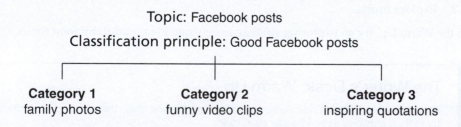

Topic: Facebook posts

Classification principle: Good Facebook posts

| **Category 1** | **Category 2** | **Category 3** |
| family photos | funny video clips | inspiring quotations |

Practice 1

Read the next paragraph and answer the questions.

Superheroes undergo three types of life-altering experiences to which we can relate. The first is trauma, which lies at the heart of Batman's origin story, in which Bruce Wayne dedicates himself to fighting crime after seeing his parents murdered. In real life, many people experience "stress-induced growth" after a trauma and resolve to help others, even becoming social activists. The second life-altering force is destiny. Consider *Buffy the Vampire Slayer*, about a normal teenager who discovers she's the "Chosen One"—endowed with supernatural powers to fight demons. Buffy is reluctant to accept her destiny, yet she throws herself into her new job. Many of us identify with Buffy's challenge. We assume a great responsibility that compels us to grow up quickly. Lastly, there's sheer chance. A young Spider-Man was using his power for selfish purposes until his beloved uncle was murdered by a street thug. Spider-Man's heroism is an example of how random adverse events cause many of us to take stock of our lives and choose a different path. At their best, superhero origin stories inspire us and provide models of coping with adversity, finding meaning in loss and trauma, discovering our strengths, and using them for good purpose.

—Robin Rosenberg, "The Psychology Behind Superhero Origin Stories"

1. Underline the topic sentence of the paragraph.

2. State the three categories that the author discusses, and list some details about each category.

   a. _____

      Details: _____

   b. _____

      Details: _____

   c. _____

      Details: _____

      _____

      _____

3. What is the author's overall opinion of superhero stories?

   a. mainly positive   b. mainly negative

Explore Topics

9.3 Explore topics.

In the Warm Up, try an exploring strategy to generate ideas about different topics.

The Writer's Desk: Warm Up

Think about the following questions, and write down the first ideas that come to your mind. Try to think of two or three ideas for each topic.

EXAMPLE: What are some types of cheaters?

Students cheat on tests and at school.

People cheat in their marriages.

Some athletes cheat and take steroids.

1. Think about some YouTube videos that you have seen. What categories of videos do you prefer? List some types of videos.

   _____

   _____

   _____

2. What are a few types of sports fans? To get ideas, you might think about some people you know and the way that they show team support.

   _____

   _____

   _____

3. List some skills or abilities people need for different jobs. As you brainstorm ideas, consider manual labor as well as professional and office jobs.

   _____

   _____

   _____

Making a Classification Chart

A **classification chart** is a visual representation of the main topic and its categories. Making a classification chart can help you identify the categories more clearly so that you will be able to write more exact topic sentences.

When you classify items, remember to use a single classification principle to sort the items. For example, if you are classifying movies, you might classify them according to their ratings: General Audience, Parental Guidance, and Restricted. You could also classify movies according to their country of origin: Argentinian, Brazilian, and Mexican, for example. Remember that one classification principle must unite the group.

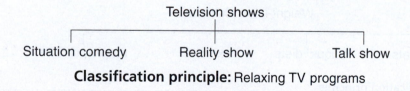

Classification principle: Relaxing TV programs

HINT: Categories Should Not Overlap

When sorting a topic into categories, make sure that the categories do not overlap. For example, you would not classify drivers into careful drivers, aggressive drivers, and bad drivers because aggressive drivers could also be bad drivers. Each category should be distinct.

Practice 2

In the following classifiscation charts, a subject has been broken down into distinct categories. The items in the group should have the same classification principle. Cross out one item in each group that does not belong. Then write down the classification principle that unites the group.

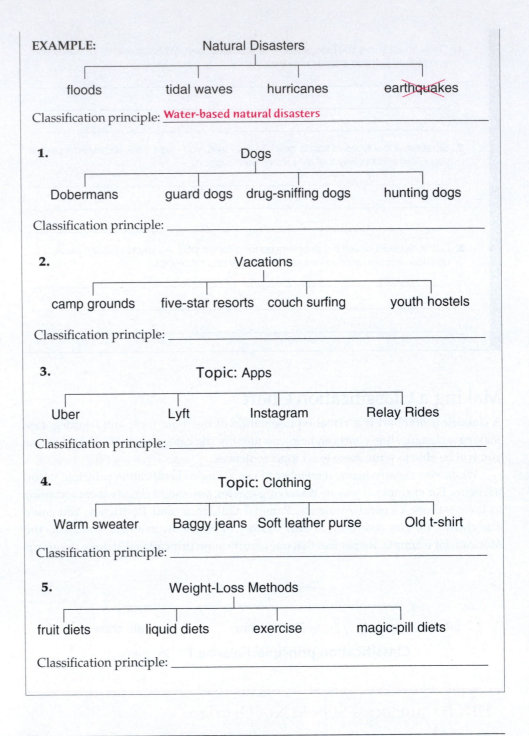

EXAMPLE: Natural Disasters

floods   tidal waves   hurricanes   ~~earthquakes~~

Classification principle: **Water-based natural disasters**

1.   Dogs

Dobermans   guard dogs   drug-sniffing dogs   hunting dogs

Classification principle: _____

2.   Vacations

camp grounds   five-star resorts   couch surfing   youth hostels

Classification principle: _____

3.   **Topic:** Apps

Uber   Lyft   Instagram   Relay Rides

Classification principle: _____

4.   **Topic:** Clothing

Warm sweater   Baggy jeans   Soft leather purse   Old t-shirt

Classification principle: _____

5.   Weight-Loss Methods

fruit diets   liquid diets   exercise   magic-pill diets

Classification principle: _____

The Writer's Desk: Find Distinct Categories

Break down the following topics into three distinct categories. Remember to find categories that do not overlap. You can look for ideas in the Warm Up on page 104–105.

EXAMPLE: Types of Cheaters

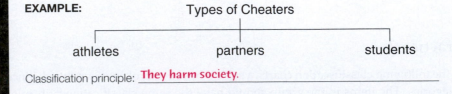

athletes   partners   students

Classification principle: **They harm society.**

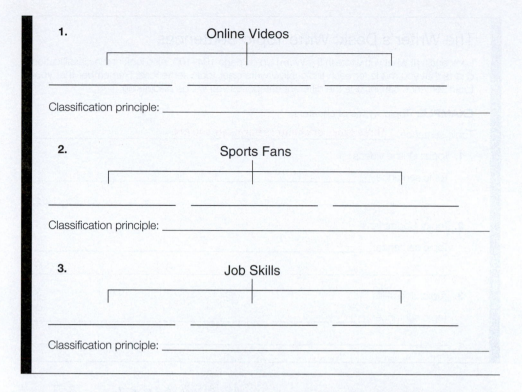

1.   Online Videos

Classification principle: _____

2.   Sports Fans

Classification principle: _____

3.   Job Skills

Classification principle: _____

Developing

The Topic Sentence

9.4   Identify the topic sentence of a classification paragraph.

The topic sentence in a classification paragraph clearly indicates what you will classify. It also includes the controlling idea, which is the classification principle that you use.

> Several types of students can completely disrupt a classroom.

Topic	Students
Classification principle	Disruptive types

You can also mention the types of categories in your topic sentence.

> The most annoying telephone calls are surveys, telemarketing, and wrong numbers.

Topic	Telephone calls
Classification principle	Types of annoying calls

> **ESSAY LINK**
> In a classification essay, the thesis statement expresses the controlling idea, or classification principle.

HINT: Make a Point

To make interesting classification paragraphs, try to express an attitude, opinion, or feeling about the topic. For example, you can write a paragraph about types of diets, but it is more interesting if you make a point about the types of diets.

Poor	Types of diets
Better	Types of **dangerous** diets
	Types of **effective** diets

The Writer's Desk: Write Topic Sentences

Look again at what you wrote in the Warm Up on page 104–105. Also look at the classification charts that you made for each topic. Now write clear topic sentences. Remember that your topic sentence can include the different categories you will be discussing.

EXAMPLE: Topic: Types of cheaters

Topic sentence: ___*Three types of cheaters harm our society.*___

1. Topic: Online videos

   Topic sentence: _____

   _____

2. Topic: Sports fans

   Topic sentence: _____

   _____

3. Topic: Job skills

   Topic sentence: _____

   _____

The Supporting Ideas

9.5   Identify the supporting ideas of a classification paragraph.

After you have developed an effective topic sentence, generate supporting ideas. In a classification paragraph, you can list details about each of your categories.

Practice 3: Visualizing Classification

Brainstorm supporting ideas for the following topic sentence. List unhealthy ingredients in each type of food.

Topic Sentence: Junk food can be classified into three main categories.

Salty   Sweet   Fatty

_____   _____   _____

_____   _____   _____

The Paragraph Plan

9.6   Develop a classification paragraph plan.

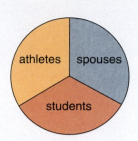

You can make a standard paragraph plan. You can also create another type of graphic, such as a pie chart, to help you visualize the different categories.

Finally, an effective way to visualize your categories and supporting ideas is to make a detailed classification chart. Break down the main topic into several categories, and then give details about each category.

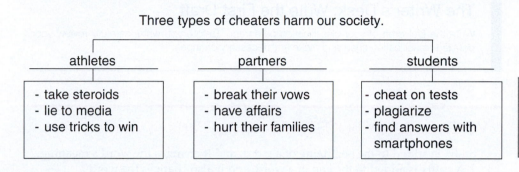

Three types of cheaters harm our society.

athletes	partners	students
- take steroids - lie to media - use tricks to win	- break their vows - have affairs - hurt their families	- cheat on tests - plagiarize - find answers with smartphones

> **ESSAY LINK**
> You can make a detailed classification chart when you develop your classification essay. Each supporting idea would become a distinct paragraph.

The Writer's Desk: Make a Detailed Classification Chart

Choose one of the topic sentences that you wrote for the previous Writer's Desk, and make a detailed classification chart. Arrange the supporting details in a logical order. You can refer to the information you generated in the Warm Up.

Topic sentence: _____

_____

The First Draft

9.7   Write the first draft of a classification paragraph.

After you outline your ideas in a classification chart or plan, you are ready to write the first draft. Remember to write complete sentences. You might include transitional words or expressions to help your ideas flow smoothly.

Some classification paragraphs use transitional words and expressions to show which category is most important and to signal a movement from one category to the next. The following transitions are very useful in classification writing.

To Show Importance	To Show Types of Categories
above all	the first/second type
clearly	the first/second kind
the most important	the last category
most of all	one kind . . . another kind
particularly	

The Writer's Desk: Write the First Draft

Write the first draft of your classification paragraph. Before you write, carefully review your detailed classification chart and make any necessary changes.

VOCABULARY BOOST: Classifying Parts of Words

A prefix is added to the beginning of a word, and it changes the word's meaning.
A suffix is added to the end of a word, and it also changes the word's meaning. Review the list of ten common prefixes and suffixes. Then come up with at least two more words using the listed prefix or suffix.

Prefixes	Example	
anti = against	antiwar	_____
un = not	unable	_____
re = again	redo	_____
bi = two	bilingual	_____
mis = wrong	misspell	_____

Suffixes	Example	
er = doer	teacher	_____
ment = condition	agreement	_____
less = without	wireless	_____
ous = full of	courageous	_____
ful = filled with	respectful	_____

Revising and Editing

Revise and Edit a Classification Paragraph

9.8   Revise and edit a classification paragraph.

When you finish writing a classification paragraph, carefully review your work and revise it to make sure that the categories do not overlap. Check to make sure that you have organized your paragraph logically, and remove any irrelevant details.

Practice 4

Read the following student paragraph and answer the questions.

Many people have a strong sense of civic duty. However, three types of cheaters harm our society. First, cheaters in sports disappoint fans. In 2012, many Americans became disillusioned when the U.S. Anti-Doping Agency (USADA) concluded that Lance Armstrong used performance-enhancing drugs when he won the Tour de France seven times. The USADA stripped Armstrong of his gold medals. Furthermore, some people cheat in relationships. They may commit adultery. Which can be emotionally and financially damaging to their partners and children. Finally, academic cheating can also harm a community. For example, some students plagiarize and cheat on exams. Those same students could become incompetant doctors or other professionals. There are university professors who fabricate evidence in their research or steal the ideas of others. Academic cheating can mar a student's future prospects, a professor's career advancement, and an institution may lose its reputation. In conclusion, different types of cheating can lead to harmful consequences for the cheater and society.

—Theodore Johnson, student

Revising

1. What is the classification principle in this paragraph?

   _____

2. What are the three categories?

   _____

3. Add one more supporting example to each category.

   _____

   _____

   _____

Editing

4. There is a sentence fragment. Identify and correct the fragment.
5. There is one spelling error. Identify and correct the error.
6. There is one error in parallel structure. Underline the error and correct it.

> **GRAMMAR LINK**
> See the following chapters for more information about these grammar topics:
> Fragments, Ch. 20, p. 282
> Parallel Structure, Ch. 22, p. 296
> Spelling, Ch. 33, p. 418

GRAMMAR HINT:

Use parallel structure when words or phrases are joined in a series.

The three categories of allergies are <u>animal allergies</u>, <u>food allergies</u>, and
<s>people who are allergic to medicine</s>. **drug allergies**

The Writer's Desk: Revise and Edit Your Paragraph

Revise and edit the paragraph that you wrote for the previous Writer's Desk. Make sure that your paragraph has unity, adequate support, and coherence. Also correct any errors in grammar, spelling, punctuation, and mechanics.

Reflect On It

Think about what you have learned in this chapter. If you do not know an answer, review that topic.

1. What is classification? _____

_____

2. What is the classification principle? _____

_____

3. Give examples of various classification principles that you can use to classify the following items.

   EXAMPLE: Cars _Types of owners, degrees of fuel efficiency, price_____

   a. Animals _____

   b. Sports _____

4. Now choose one classification principle for each item in question 3. Write down three possible categories for that item.   .

   EXAMPLE:

   Cars

   Classification principle: _Types of owners_____

   Categories: _SUV owners, sports car owners, and tiny eco car owners_____

   a. Animals

      Classification principle: _____

      Categories: _____

   b. Sports

      Classification principle: _____

      Categories: _____

3. Why is it useful to make a classification chart?

_____

The Writer's Room

Writing Activity 1: Topics

Choose any of the following topics, or choose your own topic. Then write a classification paragraph.

General Topics

Categories of . . .

1. relationship problems
2. friends
3. parties
4. games
5. entertainment

College- and Work-Related Topics

Categories of . . .

6. campus fashions
7. housing
8. bosses
9. cheating
10. coworkers

Writing Activity 2: Media Writing

Watch or listen to media about spies or spying. Classify something about them. For example, you might classify types of spy shows, types of spies, or methods used for spying. Use concrete examples to support your ideas. *Here are some suggestions* to *spark ideas*.

Show: *Homeland*
Film: *Spectre 007* (or any James Bond film)
Video: "Spies and Scouts"
Web: Internet of Things (IoT) Devices
Podcast: *International Spy Museum Spycast*

WRITING LINK
MORE CLASSIFICATION WRITING TOPICS

Ch. 22, Writer's Room topic 2, p. 303
Ch. 29, Writer's Room topic 1, p. 388
Ch. 32, Writer's Room topic 2, p. 417
Ch. 34, Writer's Room topic 2, p. 444
Ch. 36, Writer's Room topic 2, p. 463

READING LINK
MORE CLASSIFICATION READINGS

"Origins of Names" p. 201
"The Purpose of Pets" p. 202
"Domains of Sacred
    Consumption" p. 489
"Advertising Appeals" p. 517

Classification Paragraph Checklist

As you write your classification paragraph, review the checklist at the end of the book. Also ask yourself the following questions.

❏ Does my topic sentence explain the categories that will be discussed?

❏ Do I use a common classification principle to unite the various categories?

❏ Do I offer sufficient details to explain each category?

❏ Do I arrange the categories in a logical manner?

❏ Does all of the supporting information relate to the categories that are being discussed?

❏ Do I include categories that do not overlap?

10 Comparison and Contrast

Doctors compare x-rays taken at different times to identify changes and make informed decisions. In this chapter, you practice comparison and contrast writing.

Writers' Exchange

Discuss your music preferences with a partner. Then make a short list showing which music preferences you share and which ones you do not share.

Exploring

What Is Comparison and Contrast?

10.1 Define comparison and contrast.

When you want to decide between options, you **compare** to find similarities and **contrast** to find differences. The exercise of comparing and contrasting can help you make judgments. It can also help you better understand familiar things.

You often compare and contrast. At home, when watching TV, you might compare and contrast different programs. At college, you might compare and contrast different psychological or political theories. On the job, you might need to compare and contrast computer operating systems, shipping services, or sales figures.

Comparison and Contrast at Work

In this paragraph, Stephen Bergeron, an art teacher, explains the differences in acrylic and oil paints in his class notes for his students.

Both acrylic and oil paints have useful characteristics. Acrylics, which were developed about fifty years ago, can be mixed with water. The brushes can be easily rinsed out. The paints do not have a strong odor, so they can be used indoors. A great advantage of acrylics is that they can mimic watercolor or gouache, and they can be used as a base painting under oils. Additionally, some artists appreciate the quick drying time of acrylics. Oil paints, on the other hand, have a slow drying time, which is useful when artists want to mix and layer colors. Although oil paints can have a strong smell when mixed with mineral spirits or linseed oil, the texture of oil paints is creamier than that of acrylics. Finally, most artists find that oil paints have deeper and more vivid colors than acrylics. A beginning artist should experiment with both types of paint and find the one that suits his or her needs.

> The **topic sentence** expresses the main idea.

> **Supporting sentences** provide details and examples.

> The **concluding sentence** brings the paragraph to a close.

The Comparison and Contrast Paragraph

10.2   **Explain how to write a comparison and contrast paragraph.**

In a comparison and contrast paragraph, you can compare and contrast two different subjects, or you can compare and contrast different aspects of a single subject. For example, you might contrast married life and single life, or you might write only about marriage but contrast the expectations people have before they get married to what realistically happens after marriage.

When you write a comparison and contrast paragraph, remember to think about your specific purpose.

- **Your purpose could be to make judgments about two things.**
  For example, you might compare and contrast two restaurants in order to convince your readers that one is preferable.

- **Your purpose could be to describe or understand two familiar things.**
  For example, you might compare two stories to help your readers understand their thematic similarities.

Comparison and Contrast Patterns

Comparison and contrast texts follow two common patterns. One pattern is to present the details point by point. Another is to present one topic and then the other topic.

When you are thinking about ideas for writing a comparison and contrast paragraph, choose one of these two methods to organize your supporting ideas.

POINT BY POINT
Present one point about Topic A and then one point about Topic B. Keep following this pattern until you have a few points for each topic. You go back and forth from one side to the other like tennis players hitting a ball back and forth across a net.

TOPIC BY TOPIC
Present all points related to Topic A in the first few sentences, and then present all points related to Topic B in the last few sentences. So, you present one side and then the other side, just as lawyers might in the closing arguments of a court case.

> **ESSAY LINK**
> To write a comparison and contrast essay, organize each body paragraph in point-by-point or topic-by-topic form.

KYLE'S EXAMPLE

Kyle is trying to decide whether he should take a job in another city or stay at his current job in his hometown. Kyle could organize his information using a point-by-point or topic-by-topic method.

Point by Point		Topic by Topic	
Job A	Low salary	Job A	Low salary
Job B	Good salary		Parents nearby
Job A	Parents nearby		Like my colleagues
Job B	Parents far away	Job B	Better salary
Job A	Like my colleagues		Parents far away
Job B	Don't know colleagues		Don't know colleagues

Practice 1

Read the next two paragraphs and answer the questions.

A.   Chandra Reyes is concerned about a major difference between her and her daughter's teen years. While Chandra's adolescent antics were relatively private, Romilla's have been far more public. In the late 1980s, when Chandra was a teen, she made mistakes—as most youths do. She dyed her hair with harsh chemicals, and some of her hair fell out. At one time, Chandra wore unflattering tight dresses and too much makeup to impress her boyfriend. She used a fake ID to sneak into local bars, sometimes drank too much, and got sick in front of her friends. Memories—not photos, not videos, not posts—are the only records of those "old times." On the other hand, Romilla's teen years have an extensive social media record. Every transgression is widely viewed, shared, and critiqued. After an argument with a classmate, Romilla impulsively wrote a series of colorful, curse-filled tweets. When she first smoked marijuana, Romilla's boyfriend posted photos on Instagram showing her, joint in hand, looking dazed and stoned. Then, after they broke up, Romilla littered her Facebook timeline with late-night rants and bad poetry. Over the following year, she posted selfies with new boyfriends. In each photo, she pouted and posed provocatively. Her "good times" (and definitely some bad times) are now part of a digital universe, to be examined by future friends, employers, partners, and perhaps, one day, by her own daughter.

1. Underline the topic sentence. Be careful; it may not be the first sentence in the paragraph.

2. What does the writer compare? _____

3. What pattern of comparison does the author follow? Circle the correct answer.

   a. Point by point   b. Topic by topic

4. What does the paragraph focus on? Circle the correct answer.

   a. Similarities   b. Differences

B.   There are some major differences between the supermarket and a traditional marketplace. The cacophony of a traditional market has given way to programmed innocuous music, punctuated by enthusiastically intoned commercials. A stroll through a traditional market offers an array of sensuous aromas; if you are conscious of smelling something in a supermarket, there is a problem. The life and death matter of eating, expressed in traditional markets by the sale of vegetables with stems and roots and by hanging animal carcasses, is purged from the supermarket, where food is processed somewhere else, or at least trimmed out of sight. But the most fundamental difference between a traditional market and the places through which you push your cart is that in a modern retail setting nearly all the selling is done without people. The product is totally dissociated from the personality of any particular person selling it—with the possible exception of those who appear in its advertising. The supermarket purges sociability, which slows down sales.

—Thomas Hine, "What's in a Package?"

5. Underline the topic sentence.

6. What pattern of comparison does the author follow? Circle the best answer.

   a. Point by point   b. Topic by topic

7. What does the author focus on? Circle the best answer.

   a. Similarities   b. Differences

8. Using your own words, list the main differences.

Traditional market	Supermarket
_____	_____
_____	_____
_____	_____
_____	_____

VOCABULARY BOOST: Brainstorming Opposites

Work with a partner to brainstorm words that have the opposite meaning of the words listed. Try to come up with as many antonyms (words that have the opposite meaning) as possible.

EXAMPLE: tiny   huge, immense, gigantic _____

shy   _____

happy   _____

whisper   _____

spicy   _____

Explore Topics

10.3   **Explore topics.**

In the Warm Up, you will try an exploring strategy to generate ideas about different topics.

The Writer's Desk: Warm Up

Think about the following questions, and write down the first ideas that come to your mind. Try to think of two to three ideas for each topic. Then decide if a good paragraph would be about similarities or differences.

EXAMPLE: Compare someone you know with yourself. How are your experiences similar or different?

Demi Lovato	I was different from my peers.
was bullied at school.	I was bullied at school.
She became bulimic and cut herself.	I became depressed.
She was depressed.	

My paragraph will focus on __X__ similarities _____ differences

1. What are some stereotypes about your nationality? What is the reality about your nationality?

Stereotypes	Reality
_____	_____
_____	_____
_____	_____
_____	_____

This paragraph will focus on _____ similarities _____ differences.

2. What were your goals when you were in high school? What are your goals in college?

Goals in high school	Goals in college
_____	_____
_____	_____
_____	_____
_____	_____

This paragraph will focus on _____ similarities _____ differences.

3. What are some qualities and characteristics of someone who is a good sport and someone who is a bad sport?

A good sport	A bad sport
_____	_____
_____	_____
_____	_____
_____	_____

This paragraph will focus on _____ similarities _____ differences.

When you plan your comparison and contrast paragraph, decide whether you want to focus on comparing (looking at similarities), contrasting (looking at differences), or both. In a paragraph, it is usually best to focus on either comparing or contrasting. In a larger essay, you could more easily do both.

Developing

The Topic Sentence

10.4 **Identify the topic sentence of a comparison and contrast paragraph.**

In a comparison and contrast paragraph, the topic sentence indicates what is being compared and contrasted and expresses a controlling idea.

Although all dogs make good house pets, large dogs are much more useful than small dogs.

Topic	Large dogs versus small dogs
Controlling idea	One is more useful than the other.

> **ESSAY LINK**
> In a comparison and contrast essay, the thesis statement expresses what the writer wants to compare, either similarities, differences, or both.

Practice 2

Read each topic sentence, and then answer the questions that follow. State whether the paragraph would focus on similarities or differences.

EXAMPLE: Before the baby comes, people expect a beautiful world of soft coos and sweet smells, but the reality is quite different.

a. What is being compared? _Expectation versus reality of life with a baby_

b. What is the controlling idea? _Reality not as pleasant as expectation_

c. What will the paragraph focus on? Circle the correct answer.

Similarities   (Differences)

1. Many media pundits complain about reality television; however, reality shows are just as good as regular scripted shows.

   a. What is being compared? _____

   b. What is the controlling idea? _____

   _____

   c. What will the paragraph focus on? Circle the correct answer.

   Similarities   Differences

2. Women's sports lag behind men's in media attention, prize money, and salaries.

   a. What is being compared? _____

   b. What is the controlling idea? _____

   _____

   c. What does the paragraph focus on? Circle the best answer.

   Similarities   Differences

3. Texting can be as intimate as calling.

   a. What is being compared? _____

   b. What is the controlling idea? _____

   c. What does the paragraph focus on? Circle the correct answer.

   Similarities   Differences

The Writer's Desk: Write Topic Sentences

For each topic, write whether you will focus on similarities or differences. Then, write three topic sentences. Look for ideas in the Writer's Desk Warm Up on page 117–118. Your topic sentence should include what you are comparing and contrasting, as well as a controlling idea.

EXAMPLE: Topic: Compare someone you know with yourself. How are your experiences similar or different?

Focus: _Similarities_

Topic sentence: _My role model Demi Lovato and I went through a lot of_
                    the same difficult situations in life.

1. Topic: Stereotypes and reality about my nation

   Focus: _____

   Topic sentence: _____

   _____

2. Topic: Goals in high school and goals in college

   Focus: _____

   Topic sentence: _____

   _____

3. Topic: People who are good and bad sports

   Focus: _____

   Topic sentence: _____

   _____

The Supporting Ideas

10.5   Identify the supporting ideas of a comparison and contrast paragraph.

After you have developed an effective topic sentence, generate supporting ideas. In a comparison and contrast paragraph, think of examples that help clarify the similarities or differences.

Practice 3: Visualizing Comparison and Contrast

Brainstorm supporting ideas for the following topic sentence. Compare and contrast the types of heroes.

Topic Sentence: My childhood heroes were very different from my current heroes.

Childhood heroes   **Current heroes**

_____   _____

_____   _____

MAKE A VENN DIAGRAM

To generate supporting ideas, you might try using a Venn diagram. In this example, you can see how the writer draws two circles to contrast Demi Lovato and the author of the paragraph. Where the circles overlap, the writer includes similarities. If you are focusing only on similarities or differences, then you can make two separate circles.

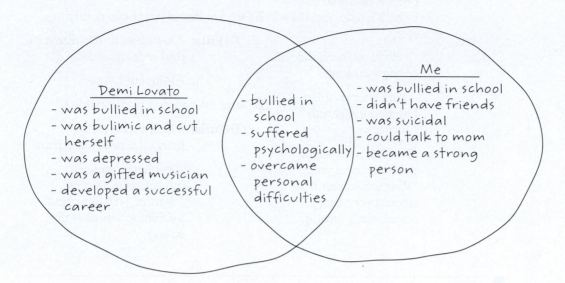

Demi Lovato
- was bullied in school
- was bulimic and cut herself
- was depressed
- was a gifted musician
- developed a successful career

- bullied in school
- suffered psychologically
- overcame personal difficulties

Me
- was bullied in school
- didn't have friends
- was suicidal
- could talk to mom
- became a strong person

The Paragraph Plan

10.6 **Develop a comparison and contrast paragraph plan.**

Before you write a comparison and contrast paragraph, it is a good idea to make a paragraph plan. Decide which pattern you will follow: point by point or topic by topic. Write "**A**" and "**B**" alongside your topics. Then add supporting details. Make sure that each detail supports the topic sentence.

Topic Sentence: My role model Demi Lovato and I went through a lot of the same difficult situations in life.

Point by Point

A/B Demi Lovato and I were both bullied at school.

> **Details:** -I ate lunch alone.
>
> -I was different.
>
> -Demi quit public school.
>
> -She was home-schooled.

A/B We both suffered psychologically.

> **Details:** -I used to cry at night.
>
> -I had thoughts about committing suicide.
>
> -Demi became bulimic and a drug addict.
>
> -Demi cut herself.

Topic by topic

A I was bullied in primary and high school.

> **Details:** -I ate lunch alone.
>
> -I was different.

A I suffered psychologically.

> **Details:** -I used to cry at night.
>
> -I had thoughts about committing suicide.

A I overcame my difficulties.

> **Details:** -I became a strong person because of Demi's music and life story.
>
> -Today, I am a confident college student.

> **ESSAY LINK**
>
> In a comparison and contrast essay, place the thesis statement in the introduction. Each supporting idea becomes a distinct paragraph with its own topic sentence.

→

Point by Point

A/B We both overcame our difficulties

Details: -I became a strong person because of Demi's music and life story.

-Today I am a confident college student.

-Demi successfully finished the rehab program.

-She is a successful musician and wrote "Warrior," a song about becoming emotionally strong.

Topic by topic

B Demi was bullied at school.

Details: -Demi quit public school.

-She was home-schooled.

B Demi suffered psychologically.

Details: -Demi became bulimic and a drug addict.

-Demi cut herself.

B Demi overcame her difficulties.

Details: -Demi successfully finished a rehab program.

-She is a successful musician and wrote "Warrior," a song about becoming emotionally strong.

The Writer's Desk: Write a Paragraph Plan

Write a detailed paragraph plan in a point-by-point or topic-by-topic pattern. You can refer to the information you generated in previous Writer's Desk exercises. You can use the letters **A** and **B** to indicate which side you are discussing in your plan. Include details about each supporting idea.

Topic sentence: _____

_____

Support 1: _____

Details: _____

_____

Support 2: _____

Details: _____

_____

Support 3: _____

Details: _____

_____

Support 4: _____

Details: _____

_____

Support 5: _____

Details: _____

_____

Support 6: _____

Details: _____

_____

The First Draft

10.7   **Write the first draft of a comparison and contrast paragraph.**

After outlining ideas in a plan, you are ready to write the first draft. Remember to write complete sentences. Also include transitional words or expressions to help your ideas flow smoothly. In comparison and contrast paragraphs, there are some transitional words and expressions that you might use to explain either similarities or differences.

To Show Similarities		To Show Differences	
additionally	in addition	conversely	nevertheless
at the same time	in the same way	however	on the contrary
equally	similarly	in contrast	then again

The Writer's Desk: Write the First Draft

Write the first draft of your comparison and contrast paragraph. Before you write, carefully review your paragraph plan to see if you have enough support for your points and topics.

Revising and Editing

Revise and Edit a Comparison and Contrast Paragraph

10.8   **Revise and edit a comparison and contrast paragraph.**

When you finish writing a comparison and contrast paragraph, carefully review your work and revise it to make the comparison or contrast as clear as possible to your readers. Check that you have organized your paragraph logically, and remove any irrelevant details.

Practice 4

Read the following student paragraph and answer the questions.

My role model Demi Lovato and I went through a lot of the same difficult situations in life. In school, my fellow classmates tortured me because I was different from my peers. I always eat lunch alone. Many times, some of the "popular" kids would slide plastic knives down to me and tell me to commit suicide. Because of the bullying, I became depressed. I would always cry myself to sleep at night, and I often thought about dying. One day, my mother told me that I should find someone to look up to in my dark times. That was when I came across an actress and singer who's songs and life story helped me to become a confident college student. Demi

Lovato . She was a lot like me when she was in grade school. She was brutally

bullied at the age of twelve. She quit public school and asked to be home schooled.

When she grew older, she was bullied about her weight. She became a bulimic and

drug addict. Also, Demi often cut herself. She decided to enter a rehab program,

and she worked real hard to get better. Afterward, she released the song "Warrior"

on her self-titled album, *Demi*. In the song, she sings that she is a warrior with thick

skin and a survivor. The song helped me to deal with my problems, and Demi Lovato

remains my role model. I would like to thank her for helping me feel stronger.

—Joshua Thomas, student

Revising

1. What is the writer comparing? _____

_____

2. What does the writer focus on?

a. Similarities   b. Differences

3. What were the similarities or differences that both people experienced?

_____

_____

_____

Editing

4. Identify and correct one verb-tense error.

5. This paragraph contains one fragment, which is an incomplete sentence. Identify and correct the fragment.

6. There is a spelling error. The word sounds like a similar word, but the spelling is different. Identify and correct the spelling error.

7. Find and correct one error with an adjective or adverb.

> **GRAMMAR LINK**
> Extra grammar help:
>
> Fragments, Ch. 20, p. 282
> Verb Tenses, Ch. 25, p. 329
> Adjectives and Adverbs, Ch. 30, p. 389
> Spelling, Ch. 33, p. 418

GRAMMAR HINT: Comparing with Adjectives and Adverbs

When comparing or contrasting two items, ensure that you have correctly written the comparative forms of adjectives and adverbs. For instance, never put *more* with an adjective ending in *-er*.

Living alone is ~~more~~ quieter than living with a roommate.

If you are comparing two actions, remember to use an adverb instead of an adjective.

My roommate cleans ~~quicker~~ more quickly than I do.

The Writer's Desk: Revise and Edit Your Paragraph

Revise and edit the paragraph that you wrote for the previous Writer's Desk. Make sure that your paragraph has unity, adequate support, and coherence. Also correct any errors in grammar, spelling, punctuation, and mechanics.

Reflect On It

Think about what you have learned in this chapter. If you do not know an answer, review that topic.

1. Define the words *comparing* and *contrasting*.

   a. Comparing: _____

   b. Contrasting: _____

3. Explain the following comparison and contrast patterns.

   a. Point by point: _____

   _____

   Topic by topic: _____

   _____

The Writer's Room

Writing Activity 1: Topics

Choose any of the following topics, or choose your own topic. Then write a comparison and contrast paragraph. You may write about similarites, differences, or both. Remember to follow all of the steps of the writing process.

General Topics

1. physical beauty and inner beauty
2. people from two different regions
3. your current home and a home that you lived in before
4. expectations about marriage and the reality of marriage
5. two websites

College- and Work-Related Topics

6. male and female students
7. two different managers or bosses
8. working indoors and working outdoors
9. leaving a child in day care or with a family member
10. working mainly with your hands and working mainly with your head

Writing Activity 2: Media Writing

Watch or listen to media about two cultures or countries that are outside your own country or experience. Compare the language, accents, clothing, music, attitudes, or landscapes of the two. Here are some suggestions you can look up to spark ideas.

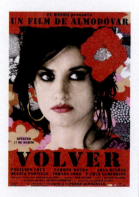

Show: *Les Revenants* (France), *Srugim* (Israel), *Please Like Me* (Australia), *Boys Over Flowers* (South Korea), *Las Aparacio* (Mexico)

Film: *A Separation* (Iran), *Paradise Now* (Palestine), *Close to Home* (Israel), *Volver* (Spain), *The Queen* (Great Britain), *The Kite Runner* (Afghanistan), and *Slumdog Millionaire* (India)

Web: *Canada's Inuit Culture, Malaysian Countries*

Music: Bollywood, Flamenco

Podcast: *Afropop Worldwide, RadioAmbulante*

WRITING LINK
MORE COMPARISON AND CONTRAST WRITING ACTIVITES:

Ch. 16, Writer's Room topic 2, p. 249
Ch. 18, Writer's Room topic 1, p. 271
Ch. 21, Writer's Room topic 2, p. 295

READING LINK
MORE COMPARISON AND CONTRAST READINGS

"Cuban Versus American Schools" p. 205
"Just Say No" page 207
"This Boat is My Boat" p. 494
"Rags and Riches and Social Responsibility" p. 522

Comparison and Contrast Paragraph Checklist

As you write your comparison and contrast paragraph, review the checklist at the end of the book. Also ask yourself the following questions.

❑ Does my topic sentence explain what I am comparing and/or contrasting?

❑ Does my topic sentence make a point about the comparison?

❑ Does my paragraph have a point-by-point or topic-by-topic pattern?

❑ Does my paragraph focus on either similarities or differences?

❑ Do all of my supporting examples clearly relate to the topics that I am comparing or contrasting?

11 Cause and Effect

Drought and water scarcity are major problems in our world. What are the causes for water scarcity? What are the effects of drought? Cause and effect writing helps to explain the answers to these types of questions.

LEARNING OBJECTIVES

11.1 Define cause and effect.

11.2 Explain how to write a cause and effect paragraph.

11.3 Explore topics.

11.4 Identify the topic sentence of a cause and effect paragraph.

11.5 Identify the supporting ideas of a cause and effect paragraph.

11.6 Develop a cause and effect paragraph plan.

11.7 Write the first draft of a cause and effect paragraph.

11.8 Revise and edit a cause and effect paragraph.

Writers' Exchange

Your instructor will divide the class into two groups. You should work with a partner or a team of students. Your group will discuss one of the following topics.

What are some reasons that students go to college?

What effects does a college education have on a person's life?

Exploring

What Is Cause and Effect?

11.1 Define cause and effect.

Cause and effect writing explains why an event happened or what the consequences of such an event were. A cause and effect paragraph can focus on causes, effects, or both.

You often analyze the causes or effects of something. At home, you may worry about what causes your siblings or your own children to behave in a certain manner, or you may wonder about the effects of certain foods on your health. In a U.S. history course, you might analyze the causes of the Civil War, or you might write about the effects of industrialization on American society. At work, you may wonder about the causes or effects of a promotion or a pay cut.

Cause and Effect at Work

In this memo from the file of a fourth-grade student, early childhood educator Luisa Suarez explains some causes and effects of the child's behavioral and learning problems.

The **topic sentence** expresses the main idea.

Supporting sentences provide details and examples.

The **concluding sentence** brings the paragraph to a close.

Mark frequently expresses his dislike of school and reading. He continues to read at a second-grade level and is behind his classmates in the acquisition of knowledge expected from fourth-grade students. In interviews with the child, he has stated that he never reads at home and spends most of his time watching television. Because he is so far behind his peers in the classroom, he is embarrassed to show his lack of reading skills for fear of ridicule. It is easier for him to "act out," thus distracting others from his deficiency in reading. He displays a low level of self-confidence and appears to have given up trying.

The Cause and Effect Paragraph

11.2   Explain how to write a cause and effect paragraph.

When writing a cause and effect paragraph, focus on two main points.

1. **Indicate whether you are focusing on causes, effects, or both.**   Because a paragraph should not be very long, it is often easier to focus on either causes or effects. If you do decide to focus on both causes and effects, make sure that your topic sentence announces your purpose to the reader.
2. **Ensure that your causes and effects are valid.**   Determine real causes and effects, and do not simply list things that happened before or after the event. Also verify that your assumptions are logical.

Illogical	The product does not work because it is inexpensive.
	(This statement is illogical; quality is not always dictated by price.)
Better	The product does not work because it is constructed with poor-quality materials.

Practice 1

Read the following paragraph and answer the questions.

Over the past 50 years, Brazil experienced the second-largest drop in fertility among developing nations with large populations. There are three major reasons for the decline in Brazil's fertility rates. First, a major factor was society's changing view of women. It began with the civil rights movement in the 1960s, which gave females equal access to education and the opportunity to pursue careers outside the home. Women now comprise around 45 percent of the workforce. Furthermore, the Brazilian government provides contraception to all its citizens free of charge.

Approximately, 80 percent of married women of childbearing age in Brazil currently utilize contraception, a rate higher than in the United States. In addition, Brazil has a rather unique influence affecting its fertility rates over many decades. Brazilian soap operas, called telenovelas, are watched religiously by people of all ages, races, and incomes. Telenovelas promote a vision of the ideal Brazilian family, of working parents and two children. In a 2012 paper in the *American Economic Journal: Applied Economics*, researchers found that women in regions that have access to Brazilian telenovelas had significantly lower fertility than those in areas where there was limited access to such programs. Clearly, the factors that influence fertility can come from unexpected sources.

—Jay Withgott and Matthew Laposata,
Environment: The Science Behind the Stories, 5th edition

1. Underline the topic sentence. Be careful because it is not necessarily the first sentence in the paragraph.

2. What does the paragraph mainly focus on? Circle the best answer.

   a. causes   b. effects

3. Who is the audience? _____

4. List the supporting details.

   _____

   _____

   _____

Explore Topics

11.3   Explore topics.

In the Warm Up, you will try an exploring strategy to generate ideas about different topics. Imagine that you had to write a cause and effect paragraph about teenage rebellion. You might brainstorm to come up with as many causes and effects as possible.

Causes
- Want to assert independence
- May think it is cool
- May be influenced by peer pressure
- Might want to test boundaries of parental authority
- Might be seeking attention from adults

Teenage rebellion

Effects
- Teenager's parents may lose trust
- Might fail at school
- Might engage in risky behavior
- Might lose close friends

GRAMMAR HINT: Do Not Confuse *Effect* and *Affect*

Generally, *affect* is used as a verb, and *effect* is used as a noun. *Affect* (verb) means "to influence or change" and *effect* (noun) means "the result."

verb
How will your new job <u>affect</u> your family?

noun
What <u>effect</u> will moving to a new city have on your spouse's career?

Effect can also be used as a verb that means "to cause or to bring about." It is generally used in the following phrases: "to effect a change" or "to effect a plan."

The union members demonstrated to <u>effect</u> changes in their working conditions.

The Writer's Desk: Warm Up

Write some possible causes and effects for the following topics. Then decide if your paragraph will focus on causes or effects.

EXAMPLE: Reduction of violent crime

Causes	Effects
- more police on street	- citizens feel sense of security
- reduction in youth population	- less cost to taxpayers
- harsher sentences for nonviolent criminals	- public money for crime prevention can be spent on other things

Focus on: _Causes_

1. Dropping out of high school

Causes	Effects

Focus on: _____

2. Moving to a new place

Causes	Effects

Focus on: _____

3. Owning a pet

Causes	Effects

Focus on: _____

The Topic Sentence

11.4   Identify the topic sentence of a cause and effect paragraph.

The topic sentence in a cause and effect paragraph must clearly demonstrate whether the focus is on causes, effects, or both. Also, make sure that you have clearly indicated your controlling idea. For example, read the next topic sentences. Notice that the controlling ideas are underlined.

> topic   controlling idea (causes)
> **The American public** is paying high gasoline prices for many reasons.

> topic   controlling idea (effects)
> **High gasoline prices** have led Americans to change their driving habits.

> topic   controlling idea (causes and effects)
> **High gasoline prices**, which are caused by many factors, have profound consequences for many Americans.

> **ESSAY LINK**
> In a cause and effect essay, the thesis statement expresses whether the essay will focus on causes, effects, or both.

Practice 2

Carefully read the following topic sentences. Decide whether each sentence focuses on causes, effects, or both. Look for key words that give you clues. Circle the best answer.

1. People commit to long-distance relationships for many reasons.

   a. Causes   b. Effects   c. Both

2. Inadequate medical insurance has important consequences on people's health.

   a. Causes   b. Effects   c. Both

3. The environment in Ukraine has changed forever because of many problems at the Chernobyl nuclear site.

   a. Causes   b. Effects   c. Both

4. Scientists have proposed many theories that explain the disappearance of the dinosaurs.

   a. Causes   b. Effects   c. Both

The Writer's Desk: Write Topic Sentences

Write a topic sentence for each of the following topics. You can look for ideas in the Writer's Desk Warm Up on page 130. Determine whether you will focus on causes, effects, or both in your paragraph.

EXAMPLE: Topic: Reduction of violent crime

Topic Sentence: _The number of serious crimes committed in the United States has fallen recently for several reasons._

1. Topic: Dropping out of high school

   Topic sentence: _____

   _____

2. Topic: Moving to a new place

Topic sentence: _____

_____

3. Topic: Owning a pet

Topic sentence: _____

_____

The Supporting Ideas

11.5   **Identify the supporting ideas of a cause and effect paragraph.**

After developing an effective topic sentence, generate supporting ideas. When planning a cause and effect paragraph, think of examples that clearly show the causes or effects. Then arrange your examples in **emphatic order**—from the most to the least important or from the least to the most important.

Practice 3: Visualizing Cause and Effect

Brainstorm supporting ideas for the following topic sentence. Explain how pollution might affect the environment.

Topic Sentence: Pollution has serious effects on our planet.

_____

_____

HINT: Do Not Oversimplify

Avoid attributing a simple or general cause to a complex issue. When you use expressions such as *It appears that* or *A possible cause is*, you show that you are aware of the complex factors involved in the situation.

Oversimplification	The foreclosure crisis caused the growing rate of homelessness. (This is an oversimplification of a complicated problem.)
Better	The foreclosure crisis may have contributed to the growing rate of homelessness.

The Writer's Desk: Generate Supporting Ideas

Choose one of the topic sentences from the Writer's Desk on page 131–132. Then list either causes or effects.

EXAMPLE: Topic sentence: ___The number of serious crimes committed in___

___the United States has fallen recently for several reasons.___

_____

Supports: ___youth population has declined_____

___different policing tactics_____

___harsher sentences for all types of crimes_____

Topic sentence: _____

_____

_____

Supports: _____

_____

_____

_____

_____

The Paragraph Plan

11.6   Develop a cause and effect paragraph plan.

In most coursework and workplace writing, you will be required to write about the causes or effects of a particular subject. Always plan your paragraph before you write your final version. Here are some things to think about: Does it make the most sense to focus on causes, effects, or both? Which supporting details do you want to present first, second, and so on? Which of those ideas makes the biggest impact? Choose the order that best supports your topic and controlling idea.

> **ESSAY LINK**
> In a cause and effect essay, place the thesis statement in the introduction. Then use body paragraphs, each with its own topic sentence, to support the thesis statement.

Topic Sentence: The number of serious crimes committed in the United States has fallen recently for several reasons.

Support 1: There are fewer people between the ages of fifteen and twenty-four.

  Details: —There was a drop of almost 5 percent in youth populations between 1975 and 2000.

Support 2: Police-patrolling tactics have changed.

  Details: —Police get to know locals.

    —Police check suspicious individuals for hidden weapons.

Support 3: Punishment for criminals has become tougher.

  Details: —Nonviolent offenders and drug dealers are given prison terms.

    —More criminals are off the street, which reduces the crime rate.

The Writer's Desk: Write a Paragraph Plan

Refer to the information you generated in previous Writer's Desk exercises and create a paragraph plan. If you think of new details that will explain your point more effectively, include them here.

Topic sentence: _____

_____

Support 1: _____

Details: _____

_____

_____

Support 2: _____

Details: _____

_____

_____

Support 3: _____

Details: _____

_____

_____

VOCABULARY BOOST

You can improve your style by avoiding repetition of words. Using your thesaurus, come up with three synonyms for *cause* and three synonyms for *effect*.

The First Draft

11.7   Write the first draft of a cause and effect paragraph.

After outlining your ideas in a plan, you are ready to write the first draft. Remember to write complete sentences. You might include transitional words or expressions to help your ideas flow smoothly. The following transitional expressions are useful for showing causes and effects.

To Show Causes	To Show Effects
for this reason	accordingly
the first cause	as a result
the most important cause	consequently

The Writer's Desk: Write the First Draft

Write the first draft of your cause and effect paragraph. Before you write, carefully review your paragraph plan and make any necessary changes.

Revising and Editing

Revise and Edit a Cause and Effect Paragraph

11.8   Revise and edit a cause and effect paragraph.

When you finish writing a cause and effect paragraph, review your work and revise it to make the examples as clear as possible to your readers. Make sure that your sentences relate to the topic sentence and flow together smoothly.

Practice 4

Read the next student paragraph and answer the questions.

The number of serious crimes committed in the United States has fallen recently for several reasons First, experts believe that there are fewer people between the ages of fifteen and twenty-four. From 1975 to 2000, the youth population droped by almost 5 percent. This decrease has led to a reduction in crime rates. In addition, police-patrolling tactics have changed. Police officers get to know locals in various neighborhoods. Officers also check suspicious individuals for concealed weapons. Finaly, punishment has become more tougher. People who commit certain nonviolent crimes and drug offenses are given prison terms. More criminals are off the streets, which reduces the crime rate. But some people have been wrongly convicted because they can't afford a good lawyer. In conclusion, these factors have had a positive affect on the country's crime rate.

—Logan Two-Rivers, student

Revising

1. Does the paragraph focus on causes, effects, or both? _____

2. List the causes or effects given. _____

   _____

   _____

   _____

3. There is one sentence in the paragraph that does not relate to the topic. Cross it out.

4. This paragraph has some sentences that require source information. Highlight two or three examples of unsupported claims.

5. Go online and find two or three specific examples to back up the claims made in this paragraph. Add them here, and include your sources.

   _____

   _____

   _____

   _____

   _____

Editing

6. This paragraph contains two misspelled words. Identify and correct them.

7. There is one error with the comparative form. Correct the error.

8. There is one commonly confused word error. Underline the error and replace it with the correct word.

GRAMMAR LINK
Extra grammar help:
Adjectives and Adverbs, Ch. 30, p. 389
Spelling and Commonly Confused Words, Ch. 33, p. 418

12 Argument

Cause and Effect? 187

LEARNING OBJECTIVES

12.1 Define argument.

12.2 Explain how to write an argument paragraph.

12.3 Explore topics.

12.4 Identify the topic sentence of an argument paragraph.

12.5 Identify the supporting ideas of an argument paragraph.

12.6 Develop an argument paragraph plan.

12.7 Write the first draft of an argument paragraph.

12.8 Revise and edit an argument paragraph.

Teenagers often argue with their parents. In argument writing, you try to convince readers to agree with your point of view.

Writers' Exchange

For this activity, you and a partner will take turns debating an issue. To start, choose who will begin speaking. The first speaker chooses one side of any issue listed below, and then argues about that issue, without stopping, for a set amount of time. Your instructor will signal when to switch sides. After the signal, the second speaker talks nonstop about the other side of the debate. If you run out of ideas, you can switch topics when it is your turn to speak.

Dogs are better than cats.   Cats are better than dogs.

It's better to be married than single.   It's better to be single than married.

Life is easier for men.   Life is easier for women.

Exploring

What Is Argument?

12.1 **Define argument.**

When you use **argument**, you take a position on an issue and attempt to defend it. You try to convince somebody that your point of view is the best one.

Argument is both a writing pattern and a purpose for writing. In fact, it is one of the most common aims or purposes in college and work-related writing. For example, in Chapter 6, there is a paragraph about the Ferris wheel at the Dixie Classic Fair. The writer uses descriptive imagery to describe the wheel. At the same time, she argues that it is a wonderful attraction. Therefore, in most of your college and work-related writing, your purpose is to argue or to persuade the reader that your ideas are compelling and valid.

You come across argument every day. At home, you may write a persuasive letter to a newspaper to express your views about public policy. At college, you may be learning about persuasive technology and how ecommerce and social media sites appeal to users. At work, you might have to convince your manager to give you a raise.

Argument at Work

Lawyer Marshal L. Dodge argues on behalf of his client, Ethan Ward,* a veteran of the conflict in Afghanistan, for disability compensation for posttraumatic stress disorder (PTSD).

On behalf of my client, I request that the Veterans Claims Board grant Mr. Ward disability compensation. Ward served on active duty in Afghanistan from September 2008 to January 2010. After his discharge, Mr. Ward began to experience a nervous condition. He could not sleep, eat, or do other daily activities. The American Psychiatric Association has acknowledged PTSD as a delayed-stress syndrome experienced by combat veterans. My client has provided a list of each stress-related incident he has experienced since returning to civilian life. Mr. Ward has provided the necessary medical reports from health care professionals. The medical reports indicate that, before serving in Afghanistan, my client functioned very well in his day-to-day activities. Furthermore, my client has responded in a timely manner to all and any requests made by the VA regarding his claim. Therefore, he should receive disability compensation.

> The **topic sentence** expresses the main idea.

> **Supporting sentences** provide details and examples.

> The **concluding sentence** brings the paragraph to a close.

*name changed

The Argument Paragraph

12.2   **Explain how to write an argument paragraph.**

> **ESSAY LINK**
> When you write argument essays, also keep these four points in mind.

When you write an argument paragraph, remember the following four points.

- **Choose a subject that you know something about.** It would be very difficult to write a good text about space research funds, capital punishment, or conditions in federal prisons, for example, if you have never had experience with, or read about, these issues. On the other hand, if you, or someone close to you, cannot find good child care or elder care, then you could likely write a very effective paragraph about the need for better services.

- **Consider your readers.** What do your readers already know about the topic? Are they likely to agree or disagree with you? Do they have specific concerns? Consider what kind of evidence will appeal to or sway your audience.

- **Know your purpose.** In argument writing, your general purpose is to persuade the reader to agree with you. Your specific purpose is more focused. You may want the reader to take action, to support a viewpoint, to counter somebody else's argument, or to offer a solution to a problem. Ask yourself what your specific purpose is.

- **Take a strong position and provide supporting evidence.** The first thing to do in the body of your paragraph is to prove that there is, indeed, an issue to be argued. Then back up your point of view with a combination of facts, statistics, examples, and informed opinions.

HINT: Be Passionate!

When planning your argument paragraph, try to find a topic that you feel passionate about. If you care and express yourself enthusiastically, your audience likely will care, too.

franchisor: the company that issues a license to individuals who run a specific location of the business

franchisee: the individual who buys a particular franchise

Practice 1

Read the next paragraph, and answer the questions.

Although buying a franchise provides many benefits, there are some disadvantages. First, the **franchisor** controls the look and feel of the business. The **franchisee** does not have much opportunity to make creative contributions. Second, the start-up and ongoing costs can be significant. The security fee for an H&R Block might be $2500, and the franchise fee for a Subway restaurant may be $15,000, but other fees or expenses, including the cost to rent or purchase real estate, can make initial costs much higher. There is also a monthly royalty fee, which is typically 6 to 10 percent of the business's gross revenues. The royalty fees are due even if the business is not making a profit. Additionally, new franchise owners shouldn't expect easy hours. Aisha Lawrence bought an ice cream franchise, and she spends a lot more time running the business than she originally expected. Furthermore, competition can be fierce. Some franchises do not restrict the number of their franchise locations. Buyers could experience serious competition not only from other companies but also from franchisees in the same organization. Finally, if one franchise has a problem, all other franchisees can share the pain. For example, when a Wendy's restaurant was falsely accused of serving chili with a human thumb mixed in, all of Wendy's restaurants suffered from the fallout. If you want to buy a franchise, do your homework first.

—Solomon, Poatsy, and Martin, *Better Business*

1. Who or what is the paragraph about? _____
2. Highlight the topic sentence of the paragraph.
3. Who is the authors' audience?

   _____

4. What is the authors' specific purpose?

   _____

   _____

5. What type of order does the paragraph use?

   a. space   b. time   c. emphatic
6. Underline the five supporting points. (You can look for transitional words or phrases that introduce each idea.)

Explore Topics

12.3   Explore topics.

In the Warm Up, you will try an exploring strategy to generate ideas about different topics.

The Writer's Desk: Warm Up

Think about the following questions, and write down the first ideas that come to mind. Try to think of two or three ideas for each topic.

EXAMPLE: Should people stop launching frivolous lawsuits?

Yes, I think so. I sold a computer, and it stopped working so my friend sued me. But computers sometimes break! Lawsuits cause stress and split up friendships.

1. Have you ever used a dating app or site? What is your opinion of Tinder or other dating sites?

   _____

   _____

   _____

2. Should college students be permitted to carry concealed weapons?

   _____

   _____

   _____

3. What are some of the major controversial issues in your neighborhood, at your workplace, at your college, or in the news these days?

   _____

   _____

   _____

   _____

Developing

The Topic Sentence

12.4 **Identify the topic sentence of an argument paragraph.**

In the topic sentence of an argument paragraph, state your position on the issue. In the following example, notice that the controlling idea has been underlined.

           controlling idea   topic

Our government should severely punish **corporate executives who commit fraud**.

Your topic sentence should be a debatable statement. It should not be a fact or a statement of opinion.

Fact	In some public schools, students wear uniforms. (This is a fact. It cannot be debated.)
Opinion	I think that it is a good idea for public school students to wear uniforms. (This is a statement of opinion. Nobody can deny that you like school uniforms. Therefore, do not use phrases such as *In my opinion, I think*, or *I believe* in your topic sentence.)
Argument	Public school students should wear uniforms. (This is a debatable statement.)

Practice 2

Evaluate the following statements. Write *F* for a fact, *O* for an opinion, or *A* for a debatable argument.

1. I think that people should stop using Facebook.   _____

2. Most high school graduates take SATs to qualify for college.   _____

3. American businesses should give longer maternity and paternity leave for employees.   _____

4. I believe that the government should ban handguns.   _____

5. Private citizens should not be permitted to own handguns.   _____

6. Some people love online games.   _____

7. High school graduates should be required to do volunteer work for one year.   _____

8. In my opinion, the voting age should be lowered to sixteen.   _____

HINT: Be Direct

You may be reluctant to state your point of view directly. You may feel that it is impolite to do so. However, in academic writing, it is perfectly acceptable, and even desirable, to state an argument in a direct manner.

In argument writing, you can make your topic debatable by using *should*, *must*, or *ought to* in the topic sentence or thesis statement.

Although daily prayer is important for many people in the United States, it **should** not take place in the classroom.

The Writer's Desk: Write Topic Sentences

Write a topic sentence for the following topics. You can look for ideas in the previous Writer's Desk Warm Up. Make sure that each topic sentence clearly expresses your position on the issue.

EXAMPLE: Topic: Frivolous lawsuits

Topic sentence: People should stop suing each other over minor incidents.

1. Topic: Dating apps or sites

Topic sentence: _____

_____

2. Topic: College students carrying concealed weapons

Topic sentence: _____

_____

3. Topic: A controversial issue in your neighborhood, at work, at college, or in the news

Topic sentence: _____

_____

The Supporting Ideas

12.5 Identify the supporting ideas of an argument paragraph.

When building an argument paragraph, always support your point of view. Reinforce it with examples, facts, statistics, and informed opinions. Also, try to think about ways you would counter or respond to someone who might disagree with or oppose your stance on the topic. Using several types of supporting evidence can strengthen your argument.

> **ESSAY LINK**
> In an argument essay, body paragraphs should contain supporting details such as examples, facts, informed opinions, logical consequences, and answers to the opposition.

- **Examples** are pieces of information that illustrate your main argument. For instance, if you want to argue that there are not enough day-care centers in your area, you can explain that one center has more than 100 children on its waiting list.

- Another type of example is the **anecdote**. To support your main point, you can write about a true event or tell a personal story. For example, if you think that rebellious teenagers hurt their families, you might tell a personal story about your brother's involvement with a gang.

- **Facts** are statements and statistics that can be verified in some way. For example, here's a fact: "According to the World Health Organization, secondhand smoke can cause cancer in nonsmokers." And here's a statistic: "Approximately 3,000 lung cancer deaths occur each year among adult nonsmokers in the United States as a result of exposure to secondhand smoke." When you use factual information, ensure that the source is reliable, and remember to record the source information. You will need it when you write your full draft. For example, in a paragraph arguing that underage drinking is a problem, you might incorporate the following statistic: According to the *Journal of the American Medical Association*, "Underage drinkers consume about 20 percent of all the alcohol imbibed in this country."

- Sometimes experts in a field express an **informed opinion** about an issue. An expert's opinion can add weight to your argument. For example, if you want to argue that the courts treat youths who commit crimes too harshly or leniently, then you might quote a judge who deals with juvenile criminals. If you want to argue that secondhand smoke is dangerous, then you might quote a lung specialist or a health organization.

- Solutions to problems can carry **logical consequences**. When you plan an argument, think about long-term consequences if something does or does not happen. For example, you could argue that children should learn social media etiquette. If they don't, any embarrassing comments or photos they post could impact their career prospects.

- Try to **answer the opposition**. For example, if you want to argue that drinking laws are ineffective, you might think about reasons other people may believe those laws work well. Then you might write, "Drinking age laws do a fine job of keeping young people out of clubs and bars; however, these laws do nothing to keep young people from getting access to alcohol in other places." Try to refute some of the strongest arguments of the opposition.

1. Dating apps or sites

For	Against
_____	_____
_____	_____
_____	_____
_____	_____

2. College students carrying concealed weapons

For	Against
_____	_____
_____	_____
_____	_____
_____	_____

3. A controversial issue: _____

For	Against
_____	_____
_____	_____
_____	_____
_____	_____

Avoid Common Errors

When you write an argument paragraph or essay, avoid the following pitfalls.

Do not make generalizations. If you begin a statement with *Everyone knows* or *It is common knowledge*, then the reader may mistrust what you say. Everyone can't possibly know the same information. It is better to refer to specific sources.

Generalization	Everyone knows that global warming is destroying our planet.
Better	According to the United Nations Panel on Climate Change, governments must take serious steps to reduce greenhouse gas emissions.

Use emotional arguments sparingly. Certainly, the strongest arguments can be emotional ones. Sometimes the most effective way to influence others is to appeal to their sense of justice, humanity, pride, or guilt. However, do not rely on emotional arguments. If you use emotionally charged words (for example, if you call someone *ignorant*) or if you try to appeal to basic instincts (for example, if you appeal to people's fear of other ethnic groups), then you will seriously undermine your argument.

Emotional	Racists believe that undocumented immigrants are attacking the American way of life.
Better	Many sectors of society, including some politicians, students, and activists, believe that illegal immigration hampers the efforts of those who want to immigrate legally.

Do not make exaggerated claims. Make sure that your arguments are plausible.

Exaggerated	Sugar-filled food and drinks are killing us.
Better	Sugar-filled food and drinks are contributing to obesity and health problems.

Some words have neutral, positive, or negative associations. With a partner, try to find the most neutral word in each list. Categorize the other words as positive or negative.

1. macho, jerk, hunk, lout, hottie, man, stud, sweetheart, bully

2. nation, homeland, refuge, kingdom, rogue state, country, motherland

3. freedom fighter, terrorist, anarchist, believer, radical, fanatic, revolutionary, rebel, soldier, activist

The Paragraph Plan

12.6 Develop an argument paragraph plan.

Before you write your argument paragraph, make a plan. Think of some supporting arguments, and think about details that can help illustrate each argument. Make sure that every example is valid and that it relates to the topic sentence. Also, arrange your ideas in a logical order.

Topic Sentence: People should stop suing each other over minor incidents.

> **Support 1:** They should accept that accidents can happen and stop being so greedy.
>
> **Details:** —A woman sued McDonald's after she spilled hot coffee on her lap.
>
> —People sue doctors for events that are outside the doctors' control.
>
> —A man answered his cell phone while driving, had an accident, and sued his boss who had called him.
>
> **Support 2:** Lawsuits can split up friendships and create antagonism between neighbors.
>
> **Details:** —My friend sued me over the sale of a computer that had stopped working.
>
> —A neighbor wearing high heels fell and sued another neighbor.
>
> —Good friends and neighbors stop speaking to each other.
>
> **Support 3:** Finally, lawsuits contribute to higher costs for everyone.
>
> **Details:** —Doctors pay high amounts for malpractice suits, raising medical costs.
>
> —Companies pass along the costs of defending themselves to customers.
>
> —Insurance costs are high because of the suits.

The Writer's Desk: Write a Paragraph Plan

Choose one of the topic sentences that you wrote for the Writer's Desk on page 142, and write a detailed paragraph plan. You can refer to the information you generated in previous Writer's Desk exercises, and if you think of examples that will explain your point more effectively, include them here.

Subject: _____

Topic sentence: _____

_____

Support 1: _____

Details: _____

_____

_____

_____

Support 2: _____

Details: _____

_____

_____

_____

Support 3: _____

Details: _____

_____

_____

_____

The First Draft

12.7 **Write the first draft of an argument paragraph.**

After you outline your ideas in a plan, you are ready to write the first draft. Remember to write complete sentences. You might include transitional words or expressions to help your ideas flow smoothly. The following transitional words and expressions can introduce an answer to the opposition or the support for an argument.

To Answer the Opposition	To Support Your Argument
admittedly	certainly
however	consequently
nevertheless	furthermore
of course	in fact
on one hand/on the other hand	obviously
undoubtedly	of course

The Writer's Desk: Write the First Draft

Write the first draft of your argument paragraph. Before you write, carefully review your paragraph plan and make any necessary changes.

Revising and Editing

Revise and Edit an Argument Paragraph

12.8 **Revise and edit an argument paragraph.**

When you finish writing an argument paragraph, carefully review your work and revise it to make the supporting examples as clear as possible to your readers. Check that the order of ideas is logical, and remove any irrelevant details.

Practice 5

Read the next student paragraph and answer the questions.

People should stop suing each other over minor incidents. Of course, some people think that citizens need the right to sue and that lawsuits make doctors more careful. But too many people are greedy idiots. Americans should accept that accidents can happen, they should stop hunting for easy money. For example, a woman sued McDonald's because she spilled hot coffee on her own lap. Also, one of our neighbors sued my father after she tripped on our front lawn. Those people should take responsibility for their own actions. In addition, the lawsuits create antagonism between friends and neighbors. For example, our neighbor, Mrs. Blair, slipped and fell on a sidewalk wearing high heels. She sued our other neighbor, Mr. Ferner, and now they are not friends no more. Finally, consider why are prices so high. Lawsuits contribute to higher expenses for everyone. Medical costs increase when doctors pay for malpractice insurance. Companies pass along the costs of defending themselves to consumers. In Ohio and elsewhere, Americans have to stop suing each other for ridiculous reasons.

—Jill Chen, student

Revising

1. Underline the topic sentence.
2. The writer uses an emotionally charged word. Remove it.
3. Does the writer acknowledge the opposition? _____ Yes _____ No

   If you answered "yes," circle the sentence in which the writer acknowledges the opposition.
4. Number the three supporting arguments. Then summarize the three ideas here.

   _____

   _____

   _____

   _____

Editing

5. A run-on sentence occurs when two complete ideas are joined incorrectly with a comma. Identify and correct a run-on sentence.
6. This paragraph contains a misplaced modifier. Underline the modifier and indicate where it should be placed.
7. Underline and correct an embedded question error. (For information about embedded questions, see the Grammar Hint on the next page.)
8. Underline and correct a double negative error.

> **GRAMMAR LINK**
> See the following chapters for more information about these grammar topics:
> Slang Versus Standard English, Ch. 32 p. 415
> Dangling Modifiers, Ch. 31 p. 406
> Run-On Sentences, Ch. 21, p. 289
> Embedded Questions, Ch. 18, p. 268

GRAMMAR HINT: Using Embedded Questions

When you embed a question inside a larger sentence, you do not need to use the question word order. Make sure that your embedded questions are correctly written.

why our government doesn't

Some people wonder ~~why doesn't our government~~ strictly regulate the banks.

The Writer's Desk: Revise and Edit Your Paragraph

Revise and edit the paragraph that you wrote for the previous Writer's Desk. Make sure that your paragraph has unity, adequate support, and coherence. Also correct any errors in grammar, spelling, punctuation, and mechanics.

Reflect On It

Think about what you have learned in this chapter. If you do not know an answer, review that topic.

1. What is the main purpose of an argument paragraph or essay?

2. What is the difference between a statement of opinion and a statement of argument?

3. What five types of supporting evidence can you use in argument writing?

4. In argument writing, you should avoid circular reasoning. What is circular reasoning?

5. Why is it important to avoid using emotionally charged words?

The Writer's Room

Writing Activity 1: Topics

Choose any of the following topics, or choose your own topic. Then write an argument paragraph. Remember to narrow your topic and to follow the writing process.

General Topics

Should

1. the voting age be raised or lowered?
2. beauty contests be banned?
3. people look for partners online?
4. the government provide free day care?
5. children be homeschooled?

College- and Work-Related Topics

Should

6. companies give drug testing to employees?
7. all college programs include internships?
8. physical education courses be compulsory in colleges?
9. office relationships be permitted?
10. tips for service be abolished?

WRITING LINK
MORE ARGUMENT WRITING TOPICS

Ch. 25, Writer's Room topic 2, p. 338
Ch. 26, Writer's Room topic 2, p. 351
Ch. 27, Writer's Room topic 2, p. 356
Ch. 28, Writer's Room topic 2, p. 371
Ch. 31, Writer's Room topic 2, p. 409
Ch. 33, Writer's Room topics 1 and 2, p. 432

Writing Activity 2: Media Writing

Watch or listen to media that addresses health or healthcare. Find a controversial issue in the media piece, and write an argument paragraph. Give examples to support your ideas. Here are some suggestions to spark ideas.

Show: *House, ER, Royal Pains*

Film: *Sicko, Looper*

Web: NIH's History of Medicine image archives

Music: Bruce Springsteen's "How Can a Poor Man Stand"

Podcast: *Slate* magazine's *The CheckUp*

READING LINK
MORE ARGUMENT READINGS

"The Importance of Music" (p. 214)
"Robot Ethics" (p. 215)
"It's Class, Stupid!" (p. 497)
"Why Diversity on Campus Matters" (p. 500)

Argument Paragraph Checklist

As you write your argument paragraph, review the checklist at the end of the book. Also ask yourself the following questions.

❏ Does my topic sentence clearly state my position on the issue?

❏ Do I make strong supporting arguments?

❏ Do I include facts, examples, statistics, logical consequences, or answers to the opposition?

❏ Do my supporting arguments provide evidence that directly supports the topic sentence?

Part III
The Essay

An **essay** is a series of paragraphs that support one main or central idea. Essays differ in length, style, and subject, but the structure of an essay generally consists of an introductory paragraph, several body paragraphs, and a concluding paragraph.

Before you begin reading the following chapters, become familiar with the parts of the common five-paragraph essay by reviewing the student essay on the next page.

The title gives a hint about the essay's topic.

An introductory paragraph introduces the essay's topic and contains its thesis statement.

The thesis statement contains the essay's topic and its controlling idea.

Each body paragraph begins with a topic sentence and contains supporting details.

The concluding paragraph brings the essay to a close.

Extending the School Year

School children look forward to a long lazy summer. They await the end of the year impatiently. But a long summer vacation has drawbacks. The school year should be increased from 180 to 210 days because students would not be left at home alone, they would not get into trouble, and teachers would have more time to teach their subjects.

If the school year were lengthened to 210 days, parents would not have to worry about their children spending many hours at home alone during the summer months. Currently, students have at least two months of summer holidays. Many do not have anything to do except eat and go online. For example, Carol, a single mother of three boys, works at a Quick-Stop Store from 7:00 A.M. until 7:00 P.M. The boys have no supervision. They never pick up a book, nor do they play any sports. Having a longer school year would ensure that children are more constructively occupied.

Moreover, students would stay out of trouble by going to school for 210 days a year. Many adolescents have a lot of free time on their hands after school and during school vacations. For instance, thirteen-year-old KeKe spends her summer vacations at the mall. One time, her friends pressured her to steal a pair of gold earrings. The security guard arrested the girls as they walked out of the store, and KeKe now has a record. If the school year were extended, students would have less free time and would be less likely to get into mischief.

Furthermore, teachers would have more time to teach their course curriculum if the school year were prolonged. During long summer holidays, many students forget what they learned, so teachers spend a lot of time revisiting the previous year's subject matter. With the additional days of instruction, students could spend more time studying. They would also have more time to absorb their course material. For example, Sally, a student in junior high, has a problem reading. If the school year were longer, she could get the extra help she needs because the teacher would have more time. Teachers could work with students one on one and teach their subjects step by step.

In conclusion, the U.S. school year should be increased from 180 to 210 days. Students would spend less time at home alone, they could keep out of trouble, and teachers would have more time to teach. The grades of students would improve, and they would gain more confidence. Increasing the number of days students spend in school is a winning situation.

—Archie Arnold, student

13 Writing the Essay

Completed in 1973, the Sydney Opera House in Australia has tons of concrete, steel, and glass supporting its structure. In the same way, an essay is a sturdy structure that is supported by a strong thesis statement and solid body paragraphs held together by plenty of facts and examples.

Exploring

Explore Topics

13.1 Explore topics.

There are limitless topics for writing essays. Your knowledge and personal experiences will help you find topics and develop ideas when you write your essay.

When planning your essay, consider your topic, audience, and purpose. Your **topic** is who or what you are writing about. Your **audience** is your intended reader, and your **purpose** is your reason for writing. Do you hope to entertain, inform, or persuade the reader? Maybe you wish to do all three?

Narrowing the Topic

Your instructor may assign a topic for your essay, or you may need to think of your own. In either case, you need to narrow your topic (make it more specific) to ensure that it suits your purpose for writing and fits the size of the assignment. To narrow your topic, you can use some exploring methods such as questioning or brainstorming.

Keep in mind that an essay contains several paragraphs; therefore, an essay topic can be broader than a paragraph topic. In the following examples, you will notice that the essay topic is narrow but is slightly broader than the paragraph topic.

> **WRITING LINK**
> For more information about exploring strategies, see Chapter 1.

Broad Topic	Essay Topic	Paragraph Topic
Job interview	Preparing for the interview	Dressing for the interview
Rituals	Initiation rituals	College orientation week

HINT: Choosing an Essay Topic

Paragraphs and essays can also be about the same topic. However, an essay has more details and concrete examples to support its thesis.

Do not make the mistake of choosing an essay topic that is too broad. Essays that try to cover a large topic risk being superficial and overly general. Make sure that your topic is specific enough that you can cover it in an essay.

DAVID NARROWS HIS TOPIC

Student writer David Raby-Pepin used both brainstorming and questioning to narrow his broad topic, "music." His audience was his English instructor, and the purpose of his assignment was to persuade.

—Should street performers be required to have a license?
—downloading music
—difference in earning power between classical and pop musicians
—Why do some rock bands have staying power?
—how to be a successful musician
—What is hip-hop culture?
—the popularity of shows like *American Idol*
—difference between poetry and song lyrics

The Writer's Desk: Narrow the Topics

Practice narrowing four broad topics.

EXAMPLE: Money: –reasons it doesn't make you happy
–teach children about value of money
–best ways to be financially successful

1. Volunteer work: _____

_____

_____

2. Environment: _____

_____

_____

3. Advertising: _____

_____

_____

4. Entertainment: _____

_____

_____

The Thesis Statement

13.2   **Develop a thesis statement.**

Once you have narrowed the topic of your essay, develop your **thesis statement.** The thesis statement—like the topic sentence in a paragraph—introduces the topic of the essay and arouses the interest of the reader.

Characteristics of a Good Thesis Statement

A thesis statement has three important characteristics.

- It expresses the main topic of the essay.
- It contains a controlling idea.
- It is a complete sentence that usually appears in the essay's introductory paragraph.

  Here is an example of an effective thesis statement.

  <u>topic</u>   <u>controlling idea</u>
  Marriage has lost its importance for many young people in our society.

Writing an Effective Thesis Statement

When you develop your thesis statement, ask yourself the following questions.

1. **Is my thesis statement a complete statement that has a controlling idea?** Your thesis statement should always reveal a complete thought and make a point about the topic. It should not simply announce the topic or express a widely known fact.

Incomplete	Gambling problems.
	(This statement is not complete.)
Announcement	I will write about lotteries.
	(This statement announces the topic but says nothing relevant about the topic. Do not use expressions such as *I will write about . . .* or *My topic is . . .*)
Thesis statement	Winning the lottery will not necessarily lead to happiness.

2. **Does my thesis statement make a valid and supportable point?** Your thesis statement should express a logical and valid point that you can support with evidence. It should not be an obvious statement or a highly questionable generalization.

Obvious	There are many apps on smartphones.
	(So what? This idea is boring and obvious.)
Invalid point	Cell phone apps are dangerous and useless.
	(This statement is difficult to support.)
Thesis statement	Three types of cell phone apps are addictive and time-wasting.

3. **Can I support my thesis statement in an essay?** Your thesis statement should express an idea that you can support in an essay. It should not be too broad, vague, or narrow.

Too broad/vague	Education is important.
	(For whom is it important? What level of education will be discussed? This thesis needs a more specific, narrow focus.)
Too narrow	The tuition fee at our college is $6,000 a year.
	(It would be difficult to write an entire essay about this fact. This needs a stronger, broader focus.)
Thesis statement	A college education provides students with financial, emotional, and social benefits.

HINT: Give Specific Details

Give enough details to make your thesis statement focused and clear. Your instructor may want you to guide the reader through your main points. To do this, mention both your main point and your supporting points in your thesis statement. In other words, your thesis statement provides a map for the readers to follow.

Weak	My first job taught me many things.
Better	My first job taught me the importance of responsibility, organization, and teamwork.

Practice 1

Identify the problem in each thesis statement. Then revise each statement to make it more interesting and complete.

Announces	Invalid	Broad
Incomplete	Vague	Narrow

EXAMPLE: I will write about human misery on television news.

Problem: _Announces_

Revised statement: _Television news programs should not treat personal_ _tragedies as big news._

1. Young men are worse drivers than young women.

   Problem: _____

   Revised statement: _____

   _____

2. I think that steroid-using athletes are poor role models for American youths.

   Problem: _____

   Revised statement: _____

   _____

3. Freedom is important.

Problem: _____

Revised statement: _____

4. The streets are becoming more dangerous.

Problem: _____

Revised statement: _____

_____

5. The problem with traditional values.

Problem: _____

Revised statement: _____

_____

6. My children know how to count to ten in Spanish.

Problem: _____

Revised statement: _____

_____

_____

The Writer's Desk: Write Thesis Statements

For each item, choose a narrowed topic from the Writer's Desk on pages 156. Then write an interesting thesis statement. Remember that each thesis statement should contain a controlling idea.

EXAMPLE: Topic: Money

Narrowed topic: **Winning a lottery**

Thesis statement: **Rather than improving your life, winning the lottery can lead to feelings of guilt, paranoia, and boredom.**

1. Topic: Volunteer work

Narrowed topic: _____

Thesis statement: _____

_____

2. Topic: Environment

Narrowed topic: _____

Thesis statement: _____

_____

3. Topic: Advertising

Narrowed topic: _____

Thesis statement: _____

_____

4. Topic: Entertainment

Narrowed topic: _____

Thesis statement: _____

_____

The Writer's Desk: List Supporting Ideas

Choose two of your thesis statements from the previous Writer's Desk on page 159, and create two lists of possible supporting ideas.

Thesis 1: _____

_____

Support: _____

_____

_____

_____

_____

_____

Thesis 2: _____

_____

Support: _____

_____

_____

_____

WRITING LINK

For more information about time, space, and emphatic order, see Chapter 2, "Developing."

Organizing Your Ideas

After you have examined your list of supporting ideas, choose three or four that are most compelling and most clearly support your statement. Highlight your favorite ideas, and then group together related ideas. Finally, make your essay as clear and coherent as possible by organizing your ideas in a logical manner using time, space, or emphatic order.

DAVID'S EXAMPLE

David underlined his three best supporting points, and he grouped related ideas using emphatic order.

3
—use lyrics to reveal their religious opinions
—Christian lyrics
—hip hop inspired breakdancing
—praise Allah

1
—want to promote peace
—some address issues of violence
—some hip hop artists have been jailed

2
—advise fans about healthy lifestyles
—warn about drugs
—talk about STIs

The Writer's Desk: Organize Your Ideas

Look at the list you produced in the previous Writer's Desk, and then follow these steps.

1. Highlight at least three ideas from your list that you think are the most compelling and that most clearly illustrate the point you are making in your thesis statement.

2. Group together any related ideas with the three supporting ideas.

3. Organize your ideas using time, space, or emphatic order.

The Essay Plan

13.4   Develop an essay plan or outline.

An **essay plan** or an **outline** can help you organize your thesis statement and supporting ideas before you write your first draft. To create an essay plan, follow these steps.

- Look at your list of ideas and identify the best supporting ideas.
- Write topic sentences that express the main supporting ideas.
- Add details under each topic sentence.

In the planning stage, you do not have to develop your introduction and conclusion. It is sufficient to simply write your thesis statement and an idea for your conclusion. Later, when you flesh out your essay, you can develop the introduction and conclusion.

DAVID'S ESSAY PLAN

David wrote topic sentences and supporting examples and organized his ideas into a plan. Notice that he begins with his thesis statement, and he indents his supporting ideas.

Thesis Statement:	Rap and hip-hop artists use their music to share their positive cultural values with others.
Body paragraph 1:	Many musicians shout out a powerful message of nonviolence.
	—They have broken from the "gansta rap" lyrics.
	—Encourage listeners to respect themselves and others.
Body paragraph 2:	Some advise fans about responsible and healthy lifestyles.
	—They discuss the importance of good parenting.
	—They talk about drug addiction or STIs.
Body paragraph 3:	These urban musicians use their poetry to reveal their religious beliefs.
	—Some show their Christian faith through the lyrics.
	—Others praise Allah.
Concluding sentence:	Finally, music is a way for rap musicians to share their personal culture with the world.

Writing a Formal Essay Plan

Most of the time, a basic essay plan is sufficient. However, in some courses, instructors may ask for a formal plan, which uses Roman numerals and letters to identify main and supporting ideas.

Thesis statement: _____

I. _____

   A. _____

   B. _____

II. _____

   A. _____

   B. _____

III. _____

   A. _____

   B. _____

Concluding idea: _____

Practice 3

Create an essay plan based on Archie Arnold's essay "Extending the School Year" on page 154.

_____

_____

_____

_____

_____

_____

_____

_____

_____

_____

_____

_____

_____

_____

_____

_____

_____

_____

_____

_____

_____

_____

Practice 4

Complete the following essay plan. Add details under each supporting point. Make sure that the details relate to the topic sentence.

Thesis statement: Rather than improving someone's life, winning the lottery can lead to feelings of guilt, paranoia, and boredom.

I. Feelings of guilt are common in newly rich people.

Details: A. _____

_____

B. _____

_____

C. _____

_____

II. Lottery winners often become paranoid.

    Details: A. _____

                _____

             B. _____

                 _____

             C. _____

                 _____

III. After lottery winners quit their jobs, they commonly complain of boredom and loneliness.

    Details: A. _____

                 _____

             B. _____

                 _____

             C. _____

                 _____

Concluding idea: _____

_____

_____

The Writer's Desk: Write an Essay Plan

Write an essay plan using one of your thesis statements and supporting details you came up with in the previous Writer's Desk.

Thesis statement: _____

_____

    I. _____

        Details: A. _____

                 B. _____

                 C. _____

    II. _____

        Details: A. _____

                 B. _____

                 C. _____

    III. _____

        Details: A. _____

                 B. _____

                 C. _____

Concluding idea: _____

_____

The Introduction

13.5 Develop an introduction.

After making an essay plan, develop the sections of your essay by creating an introduction, linking paragraphs, and writing a conclusion.

The **introductory paragraph** introduces the subject of your essay and contains the thesis statement. A strong introduction will capture the reader's attention and make him or her want to read on. Introductions may have a lead-in, and they can be developed in several different ways.

The Lead-In

You can choose to begin the introduction with an attention-grabbing opening sentence, or lead-in. There are three common types of lead-ins:

- Quotation
- Surprising or provocative statement
- Question

Introduction Styles

You can develop the introduction in several different ways. Experiment with any of these introduction styles.

- **Give general or historical background information.** The general or historical information gradually leads to your thesis. For example, in an essay about winning a lottery, begin by giving a brief history of lotteries.

- **Tell an interesting anecdote.** Open your essay with a story that leads to your thesis statement. For example, begin your lottery essay by telling the story of a real-life lottery winner.

- **Present a vivid description.** Give a detailed description, and then state your thesis. For example, describe the moment when a lottery winner realizes that he or she has won.

- **Present an opposing position.** Open your essay with an idea that contradicts a common belief or an idea that is the opposite of the one that you will develop, and build to your thesis. For instance, begin by listing all of the great things about winning a lottery, and then your thesis could mention that lottery wins are not as great as they appear.

- **Give a definition.** Define a term, and then state your thesis. For example, in an essay about the lottery, begin by defining *happiness*.

HINT: Placement of the Thesis Statement

Although a paragraph often begins with a topic sentence, an introduction does not begin with a thesis statement. Rather, most introductory paragraphs are shaped like a funnel. The most general statement introduces the topic. The following sentences become more focused and lead to a clear, specific thesis statement. Therefore, the thesis statement is generally the last sentence in the introduction.

Practice 5

In introductions A through E, the thesis statement is underlined. Read each introduction and then answer the questions that follow. Look at David's example for some guidance.

EXAMPLE:

David's Introduction

Can hip-hop, with its obscene lyrics and violent culture, have any redeeming qualities? Hip-hop and rap music mainly originated from poor, minority-inhabited neighborhoods located in New York City. Since the residents did not have enough money to buy musical instruments, they began creating beats with their mouths. This raw form of music rapidly became popular within these communities because it gave people a way to express themselves and to develop their creative abilities. <u>Many rap and hip-hop artists use their music to share their positive cultural values with others.</u>

1. What type of lead-in does David use? *Question* _____

2. What is the introduction style?

   a. Description   b. Definition

   (c.) Historical background   d. Opposing position

3. What is his essay about? *The positive message of hip-hop and rap music* _____

A.   "He's rich, so he must be really smart!" wrote blogger Lee Wang about Mark Zuckerberg. Zuckerberg created his first messaging program at the age of twelve. Shortly after, his parents, who are both professionals, hired a private tutor to help teenage Mark continue his interest in computer programming. Then Zuckerberg's parents sent him to Harvard University where he developed Facebook. Most so-called "self-made millionaires" actually received a lot of help along the way.

—Emanuel DeSouza, student

1. What type of lead-in does the author use? _____

2. What is the introduction style?

   a. Description   b. Anecdote

   c. Historical information   d. Opposing position

3. What is this essay about? _____

B.   Sacred consumption occurs when we set apart objects and events from normal activities and treat them with respect or awe. Many consumers regard events such as the Super Bowl and people such as Michael Jackson as sacred. Indeed, virtually anything can become sacred. Consider the website that sells unlaundered athletic wear that members of the Dallas Cowboys football team have worn. Sacred consumption permeates many aspects of our lives.

—Adapted from Michael R. Solomon, Consumer Behavior:
Buying, Having, and Being

4. What is the introduction style?

   a. Anecdote   b. Vivid description

   c. General background   d. Definition

5. What is this essay about? _____

C.   High school is a waste of time. In fact, it is a baby-sitting service for teens who are too old to be baby-sat. In England, fifteen-year-old students graduate and can choose technical or university streams of education. They are free to choose what to study, or they can stop schooling and get jobs. In short, they are treated like mature adults. In our country, we prolong the experience of forced schooling much longer than is necessary. On the other hand, our nation's high school system has tremendous benefits for students, parents, and the community.

—Adelie Zang, student

6. What type of lead-in does the author use? _____

7. What is the introduction style?

a. Anecdote

b. Definition

c. Background information

d. Opposing position

8. What is this essay about? _____

D.   How do Westerners feel about women wearing burqas? In Spain, the Catalonian assembly almost passed a law to ban women from wearing the burqa in public. In France, politicians want to ban such clothing, and girls cannot wear Muslim head coverings at school. Belgian politicians are also debating this issue. Europeans are very emotional about this subject. In the United States, the mindset varies and often depends on a number of factors.

—Amida Jordan, student

9. What type of lead-in does the author use? _____

10. What is the introduction style?

a. Anecdote

b. General background

c. Description

d. Opposing position

11. What is this essay about? _____

E.   When the Internet became popular in the 1990s, some people realized the potential for social networking. Friendster, which began in 2002, was one of the first social media sites. In 2003, LinkedIn and MySpace began, and Mark Zuckerberg launched Facebook in 2005. In 2010, Instagram became a success. Such sites are appealing and are used by over a billion people around the globe. Although most people have social media accounts, many of them become addicted. Taking a break from all social media provides physical, emotional, and financial benefits.

—Gina Montour, student

12. What is the introduction style?

a. anecdote

b. general

c. historical

d. vivid description

13. What is this essay about?_____

The Writer's Desk: Write Three Introductions

In the previous Writer's Desk, you made an essay plan. Now, write three different styles of introductions for your essay. Use the same thesis statement in all three introductions. Later, you can choose the best introduction for your essay.

The Conclusion

13.6   Develop a conclusion.

A **conclusion** is a final paragraph that rephrases the thesis statement and summarizes the main points in the essay. To make your conclusion more interesting and original, you could close with a prediction, a suggestion, a quotation, or a call to action.

DAVID'S CONCLUSION

David concluded his essay by restating his main points.

> Finally, music is a way for hip-hop and rap musicians to share their personal culture with the world. This cultural facet can be reflected through different values, religious beliefs, and ways of life.

He could then end his conclusion with one of the following:

Prediction	If you are concerned about hip-hop portraying negative images, don't abandon the music yet. There are many artists who promote and will continue to promote positive values through upbeat lyrics.
Suggestion	Hip-hop fans should encourage musicians to continue to give a positive message through their music.
Call to action	If you are concerned by the negative message of hip-hop music, make your opinions heard by joining the debate on hip-hop blogs and buying CDs from musicians who write only positive lyrics.
Quotation	According to hip-hop artist Doug E. Fresh, "Hip Hop is supposed to uplift and create, to educate people on a larger level, and to make a change."

Practice 6

Read the following conclusions and answer the questions.

A.   If the recent as well as the distant past is any guide, we may expect religious belief and practice to be revitalized periodically, particularly during times of stress. And even though the spread of world religions minimizes some variation, globalization has also increased the worldwide interest in **shamanism** and other features of religion that are different from the dominant religions. Thus, we can expect the world to continue to have religious variation.

> —Carol R. Ember and Melvin Ember, *Cultural Anthropology*

shamanism: a practice in which a spiritual leader interacts with the spirit world

1. What method does the author use to end the conclusion?

a. Prediction

b. Suggestion

c. Quotation

d. Call to action

B.   Daily headlines about war, genocide, and murderous shooting sprees paint a depressing image of humanity. It's sometimes difficult to remember that millions of people do altruistic actions every day. Perhaps the media can help encourage compassion. Video clips showing forgiveness, benevolence, and heroism could replace a few of those clips showing looting, death, and destruction.

—Diego Pelaez, "We're Not All Bad"

2. What method does the author use to end the conclusion?

a. Prediction   b. Suggestion

c. Quotation   d. Call to action

C.   Every once in a while, the marketing wizards pay lip service to today's expanding career options for women and give us a Scientist Barbie complete with a tiny chemistry set as an accessory. But heaven forbid should little Johnnie plead for his parents to buy him that Scientist Barbie. After all, it is acceptable for girls to foray, occasionally, into the world of boy-style play, but for boys the opposite "sissified" behavior is taboo. Why is this? One commentator, D. R. Shaffer, says, "The major task for young girls is to learn how not to be babies, whereas young boys must learn how not to be girls."

—Dorothy Nixon, "Put GI Barbie in the Bargain Bin"

3. What method does the author use to end the conclusion?

a. Prediction   b. Suggestion

c. Quotation   d. Call to action

HINT: Avoiding Conclusion Problems

In your conclusion, do not contradict your main point, and do not introduce new or irrelevant information. In this chapter's sample essay, David initially included the next sentences in his conclusion.

> The rap and hip-hop movement is not restrained only to the musical scene. It influences many other facets of art and urban culture as well. It can be found in dance and fashion, for instance. Thus, it is very versatile.

He revised his conclusion when he realized that some of his ideas were new and irrelevant information. His essay does not discuss dance or fashion.

The Writer's Desk: Write a Conclusion

In previous Writer's Desks, you wrote an introduction and an essay plan. Now write a conclusion for your essay.

The First Draft

13.7   Write the first draft.

After creating an introduction and conclusion, and after arranging the supporting ideas in a logical order, you are ready to write your first draft. The first draft includes your introduction, several body paragraphs, and your concluding paragraph.

The Writer's Desk: Write the First Draft

In previous Writer's Desks, you wrote an introduction, a conclusion, and an essay plan. Now write the first draft of your essay.

Revising and Editing

Revising and Editing the Essay

13.8   **Revise and edit the essay.**

Revising your essay is an extremely important step in the writing process. When you revise your essay, you modify it to make it stronger and more convincing. You do this by reading the essay critically. Ask yourself: Does that point make sense? Can readers easily follow my train of thought? Could I organize the details a different way? Does that sentence flow well? When you reorganize and rewrite, make any necessary changes.

    Editing is the last stage in writing. When you edit, you proofread your writing and make sure that it is free of errors.

Revising for Unity

To revise for **unity**, verify that all of your body paragraphs support the thesis statement. Also look carefully at each body paragraph; make sure that the sentences support the topic sentence.

HINT: Avoiding Unity Problems

Here are two common errors to check for as you revise your body paragraphs.

- **Rambling paragraphs.** The paragraphs in the essay ramble on. Each paragraph has several topics, and there is no clearly identifiable topic sentence.
- **Artifical breaks.** A long paragraph is split into smaller paragraphs arbitrarily, and each smaller paragraph lacks a central focus.

To correct either of these errors, revise each body paragraph until it has *one* main idea that supports the thesis statement.

Revising for Adequate Support

When you revise for adequate **support**, ensure that there are enough details and examples to make your essay strong and convincing. Include examples, statistics, quotations, or anecdotes.

> **WRITING LINK**
> To practice revising for unity and support, see Chapter 3, "Revising and Editing."

Revising for Coherence

When you revise for **coherence**, ensure that paragraphs flow smoothly and logically. To guide the reader from one idea to the next, or from one paragraph to the next, try using **paragraph links**.

    You can develop connections between paragraphs using three methods.

1. **Repeat words or phrases from the thesis statement in each body paragraph.** In the next example, *violent* and *violence* are repeated words.

Thesis statement	Although some will argue that <u>violent</u> movies are simply a reflection of a <u>violent</u> society, these movies actually cause a lot of the <u>violence</u> around us.
Body paragraph 1	Action movie heroes train children to solve problems with <u>violence</u>.
Body paragraph 2	<u>Violent movies</u> are "how to" films for some mentally unstable individuals.

2. **Refer to the main idea in the previous paragraph, and link it to your current topic sentence.** In body paragraph 2, the writer reminds readers of the first point (the newly rich feel useless) and then introduces the next point.

Thesis statement	A cash windfall may cause more problems than it solves.
Body paragraph 1	The newly rich often lose their desire to become productive citizens, and they end up <u>feeling useless</u>.
Body paragraph 2	Apart from <u>feeling useless</u>, many heirs and lottery winners also tend to feel guilty about their wealth.

3. **Use a transitional word or phrase to lead the reader to your next idea.**

Body paragraph 2	<u>Furthermore</u>, the newly rich often feel guilty about their wealth.

> **WRITING LINK**
> Furthermore is a transition. For a list of transitions, see pages 35–36 in Chapter 3.

Revising for Style

Another important step in the revision process is to ensure that you have varied your sentences and that you have used concise wording. When you revise for sentence style, ask yourself the following questions.

- Do I use a variety of sentence patterns? (To practice using sentence variety, see Chapter 19.)

- Do I use exact language? (To learn about slang, wordiness, and overused expressions, see Chapter 32.)

- Are my sentences parallel in structure? (To practice revising for parallel structure, see Chapter 22.)

> **ESSAY LINK**
> To practice your editing skills, see Chapter 37, "Editing Paragraphs and Essays."

Editing

When you edit, you proofread to correct any errors in punctuation, spelling, grammar, and mechanics. There is an editing guide on the inside back cover of this book that provides you with a list of things to check for when you proofread your text.

DAVID'S ESSAY

David Raby-Pepin revised and edited this paragraph from his essay about hip-hop culture.

<u>Furthermore, some</u> ~~Some~~ rappers advise fans about responsible and healthy lifestyles. Several hip-hop artists divulge that ~~their~~ <u>they are</u> parents and discuss the importance of good parenting. Others announce their choice of a monogamous lifestyle ~~. They~~ <u>and</u> encourage their fans to have respectful relationships. Some rappers mention past drug addictions and advise listeners to ~~be avoiding~~ <u>avoid</u> drugs. Others rap about the dangers of sexually transmitted diseases. The rapper Ludacris, for ~~example. He~~ <u>example,</u> warns his fans about STIs and advises them to be careful and to use condoms during sex. Such messages are ~~extremly~~ <u>extremely</u> important since many young people do not take precautions with their health.

The Writer's Desk: Revising and Editing Your Essay

In the previous Writer's Desk, you wrote the first draft of an essay. Now revise and edit it. You can refer to the checklist at the end of this chapter.

The Essay Title

13.9   Develop the essay title.

It is a good idea to think of a title after you have completed your essay because then you will have a more complete impression of your essay's main point. The most effective titles are brief, depict the topic and purpose of the essay, and attract the reader's attention.

When you write your title, place it at the top center of your page. Capitalize the first word of your title, and capitalize the main words except for prepositions three or fewer letters in length (*in, at, for, to,* etc.) and articles (*a, an, the*). Double-space between the title and the introductory paragraph.

> **ESSAY LINK**
> For more information about punctuating titles, see page 452 in Chapter 35.

Descriptive Titles

Descriptive titles are the most common titles in academic essays. They depict the topic of the essay clearly and concisely. You might take key words from the thesis statement and use them in the title. Here are some examples.

> The Importance of Multiculturalism in a Democratic Society
> Why Mothers and Fathers Should Take Parenting Seriously

Titles Related to the Writing Pattern

You can also relate your title directly to the writing pattern of your essay. Here are examples of titles for different writing patterns.

Illustration	The Problems with Elections
Narration	My Visit to Las Vegas
Description	Graduation Day
Process	How to Dress for an Interview
Definition	What It Means to Be Brave
Classification	Three Types of Hackers
Comparison and Contrast	Fast Food Versus Gourmet Food
Cause and Effect	Why People Enter Beauty Pageants
Argument	Barbie Should Have a New Look

HINT: Avoiding Title Pitfalls

When you write your title, watch out for problems.

- Do not view your title as a substitute for a thesis statement.
- Do not put quotation marks around the title of your essay.
- Do not write a really long title because it can be confusing.

The Final Draft

13.10   Write the final draft.

When you have finished making the revisions on the first draft of your essay, write the final copy. This copy should include all changes that you have made during the revision phase of your work. You should proofread the final copy to check for grammar, spelling, mechanics, and punctuation errors.

DAVID'S ESSAY

David Raby-Pepin revised and edited his essay about hip-hop culture. This is his final draft.

Positive Messages in Hip-Hop Music

Can hip-hop, with its obscene lyrics and violent culture, have any redeeming qualities? Hip-hop and rap music mainly originated from poor, minority-inhabited neighborhoods located in New York City. Since the residents did not have enough money to buy musical instruments, they began creating beats with their mouths. This raw form of music rapidly became popular within these communities because it gave people a way to express themselves and to develop their creative abilities. <u>Many rap and hip-hop artists use their music to share their positive cultural values with others.</u>

Leading hip-hop and rap artists have broken from the gangsta rap lyrics of the past. Now, many of these musicians shout out hopeful messages of nonviolence and respect. Instead of expressing anger, they express positive sentiments. Some musicians also encourage listeners to respect others and to avoid violent confrontation.

Furthermore, some rappers advise fans about responsible and healthy lifestyles. Several hip-hop artists divulge the fact that they are parents and discuss the importance of good parenting. Others announce their choice of a monogamous lifestyle and encourage their fans to have respectful relationships. Some rappers mention past drug addictions and advise listeners to avoid drugs. Others rap about the dangers of sexually transmitted diseases. The rapper Ludacris, for example, warns his fans about STIs and advises them to be careful and to use condoms during sex. Such messages are extremely important since many young people do not take precautions with their health.

Moreover, these urban musicians also use their lyrics to reveal their religious beliefs. Some show their Christian faith by including God in their texts. For example, in the song "Tommy" by Mathematics, the lyrics refer to a relationship with God after death. Members of the band Killarmy praise Allah in their lyrics. Hip-hop and rap musicians generally do not criticize other religions through their songs. They use this form of communication to support their own religious opinions. Hip-hop and rap music can be a way for individuals to show their faith or to pass it on to members of their audience.

Finally, music is a way for rap musicians to share their personal culture with the world. This cultural facet can be reflected through different values, religious beliefs, and ways of life. According to hip-hop artist Doug E. Fresh, "Hip-hop is supposed to uplift and create, to educate people on a larger level, and to make a change."

The Writer's Desk: Writing Your Final Draft

At this point, you have developed, revised, and edited your essay. Now write the final draft. Before you submit your essay to your instructor, proofread it one last time to make sure that you have found as many errors as possible.

Reflect On It

Think about what you have learned in this unit. If you do not know an answer, review that topic.

1. What is a thesis statement? _____

2. What are the five different introduction styles?

   _____   _____

   _____   _____

   _____

3. What are the four different ways to end a conclusion?

   _____   _____

   _____   _____

4. What are the three different ways you can link body paragraphs?

   _____

   _____

   _____

The Writer's Room

Writing Activity 1: Topics

Choose any of the following topics, or choose your own topic. Then write an essay. Remember to follow the writing process.

General Topics

1. benefits of friendship
2. an unforgettable experience
3. differences between generations
4. advertising
5. peer pressure

College- and Work-Related Topics

6. juggling college and family life
7. juggling college and a job
8. long-term career goals
9. a current social controversy
10. an important issue in the workplace

Writing Activity 2: Photo Writing

Use this photo as an essay-writing prompt. Reflect on a topic related to this photo. For instance, you could define the American dream, or you could write about a culture of excess. You might discuss the growing wealth gap in America, or you could contrast a "house" with a "home." Brainstorm ideas before you write your essay.

Revising and Editing Checklist for Essays

As you write your essay, ask yourself the following questions.

Revising

❏ Does my essay have a compelling introduction and conclusion?

❏ Does my introduction have a clear thesis statement?

❏ Does each body paragraph contain a topic sentence?

❏ Does each body paragraph's topic sentence relate to the thesis statement?

❏ Does each body paragraph contain specific details that support the topic sentence?

❏ Do all of the sentences in each body paragraph relate to its topic sentence?

❏ Do I use transitions to smoothly and logically connect ideas?

❏ Do I use a variety of sentence styles?

Editing

❏ Do I have any errors in grammar, spelling, punctuation, and capitalization?

14   Essay Patterns

Fashion designers choose fabric patterns that are appropriate for the articles of clothing that they wish to make. In the same way, writers choose essay patterns that best suit their purposes for writing.

LEARNING OBJECTIVES

14.1 Write an illustration essay.

14.2 Write a narration essay.

14.3 Write a description essay.

14.4 Write a process essay.

14.5 Write a definition essay.

14.6 Write a classification essay.

14.7 Write a comparison and contrast essay.

14.8 Write a cause and effect essay.

14.9 Write an argument essay.

In Chapters 4 through 12, you read about and practiced using nine different paragraph patterns. In this chapter, you will learn how to apply those patterns when writing essays. Take a moment to review these writing strategies and their purposes.

Pattern	Purpose
Illustration	To prove a point using specific examples
Narration	To tell a story about a sequence of events that happened
Description	To portray something using vivid details and images that appeal to the reader's senses
Process	To inform the reader about how to do something, how something works, or how something happened
Definition	To explain what a term or concept means by providing relevant examples
Classification	To sort a topic to help readers understand different qualities about that topic
Comparison and contrast	To present information about similarities (compare) or differences (contrast)
Cause and effect	To explain why an event happened (the cause) or what the consequences of the event were (the effects)
Argument	To take a position on an issue and offer reasons for your position

Most college essay assignments specify one dominating essay pattern. However, you can use several patterns to fulfill your purpose. For example, imagine that you want to write a cause and effect essay about youth crime and the purpose of the essay is to inform. The supporting paragraphs might include a definition of youth crime and a narrative about an adolescent with a criminal record. You might incorporate different writing patterns, but the dominant pattern would still be cause and effect.

Each time you write an essay, remember to follow the writing process that you learned in Chapter 13, "Writing the Essay."

The Illustration Essay

14.1   Write an illustration essay.

When writing an illustration essay, use specific examples to clarify your main point. Illustration writing is a pattern that you frequently use in college essays and exams because you must support your main idea with examples.

The Thesis Statement

The thesis statement in an illustration essay gives the direction of the body paragraphs. It includes the topic and a controlling idea about the topic.

topic   controlling idea
Tourists in New York City can participate in several exciting and inexpensive activities.

The Supporting Ideas

In an illustration essay, the body paragraphs contain examples that support the thesis statement. You can develop the body paragraphs in two different ways. To give your essay variety, you could use both a series of examples and an extended example.

- **Use a series of examples** that support the paragraph's topic sentence. For example, in an essay about bad driving, one body paragraph could be about drivers who do not pay attention to the road. The paragraph could list the things that those drivers do, such as choosing songs, using a cell phone, eating, and putting on makeup.

- **Use an extended example** to support the paragraph's topic sentence. The example could be an anecdote or a description of an event. In an essay about bad driving, for example, one paragraph could contain an anecdote about a driver who always wanted to be faster than other drivers.

A Student Illustration Essay

Read and analyze the structure of the next student illustration essay by Nicholas Slayton.

COMICS AS SOCIAL COMMENTARY

1.   Comics, funny illustrated magazines, are the home of people in tights fighting each other. They are also a great medium for social commentary and protest. Since their inception, comic books have challenged the established system and worked to highlight injustice around the world.

[Thesis statement]

2.   When comics started in the 1930s, the writers were urban and influenced by the world around them. If cities were at the forefront of social and economic progress, then the comics that came out of them were timely and well aware of the troubles facing contemporary society. Joe Shuster and Jerry Siegel initially created Superman not as a defender of truth, justice, and the American way, but as a defender of the New Deal. Accordingly, Superman spent his early issues taking on slumlords, corrupt businessmen, and other symptoms of the Great Depression.

[Topic sentence]

PARAGRAPH LINK
For more information about developing ideas with examples, refer to Chapter 4, "Illustration."

3.   In the 1950s, comics briefly found their soapbox kicked out from under them because of congressional pressure and self-imposed censorship. The Comics Code nearly killed the industry, and the remaining series in publication turned to camp and silly stories instead of social commentary. That is until the 1970s, when a new group of writers, influenced by the counter culture and political unrest of the 1960s, took over. Stan Lee, who revolutionized comics by focusing on heroes with personal issues—as opposed to the shining beacons of heroic perfection from the 1940s—decided to tackle drug use. In the *Amazing Spider-Man* "Green Goblin Reborn!" comic, Spider-Man confronted his best friend who had started using drugs. Meanwhile at DC, Green Arrow and Green Lantern traveled across the United States, confronting poverty, racism, and, ultimately, drug use when Green Arrow's sidekick was revealed to be a heroin addict.

Topic sentence

4.   From the 1980s onwards, activism in comics took a new spin. In the 1980s, British writers took over American series. Dark titles such as *Hellblazer* took on the politics and conservatism of the time. Alan Moore and David Lloyd's *V for Vendetta* was a direct reaction to Margaret Thatcher's conservatism and ended up forecasting the CCTV cameras everywhere in London. In the new millennium, a new wave of writers came from a **DIY** mindset. David Lloyd, the artist behind the *V for Vendetta* Guy Fawkes mask, used Kickstarter, a large funding platform, to support Occupy Comics, which aims to capture the spirit and motivations of the Occupy movement. It provides a form of documentation for the ongoing protests. And beyond works like Occupy Comics, there are more subtle works. For instance, Brian Wood's recently concluded *DMZ* was a sharp critique of the post–September 11 world.

Topic sentence

DIY: do it yourself

5.   Because comics are aimed at youth—the people who are likely to be the most socially conscious—there's a greater impact. Why should students support equal rights? Read *X-Men*, and they'll see why they should take action. Comics combine protest art, visual documentation, and text. Comics have been calling out injustices for decades and hopefully will for many more to come.

Concluding sentence

Practice 1

1. How does the writer develop the body paragraphs? Circle the best answer.

   a. Extended examples   c. Both

   b. Series of examples

2. Who is the audience for this essay? _____

   _____

3. What organizational pattern does the author use in this essay?

   a. Time order   c. Emphatic order

   b. Space order

A Professional Illustration Essay

Read the next essay by writer Ryan Lenora Brown and answer the questions that follow.

What's in an African Name?

1.   Ask a Southern African to explain the meaning of his or her name, and you'll often hear an elaborate tale of family politics, tradition, and sometimes prophecy. In 1918, for instance, a chief in a remote corner of eastern South Africa gave his son the name Rolihlahla, a local word meaning "pulling the branch of a tree," or, colloquially, "troublemaker." Rolihlahla—better known as Nelson Mandela—lived up to his name. But as English elbowed its way into the region's governments, education systems, and media over the past century, the naming tradition took on a new linguistic twist, and nowhere more obviously than in Zimbabwe.

2.   Zimbabwe has a mix of fascinating and original English names. Check the phone books of Harare and Bulawayo: Alongside a slate of Annes, Johns, and Philips, you'll find Lovemores, Addmores, and Godsaveses. There are Noviolets and Pinkroses. In recent years, there have been professional Zimbabwean soccer players named Danger Fourpence and Have-a-look Dube. One of the nation's leading opposition politicians is a Zimbabwean man named Welshman. "I suppose it's because of colonization, but many parents believe if you give your child a name in English, it will help them get ahead in life," says Pinkrose Mpofu, a call-center operator in Johannesburg who is from Zimbabwe. Ms. Mpofu does not have to look far to find more recipients of that naming ethos: Down the hall are Zimbabweans Thanksalot and Godknows. "We get a lot of laughs when we introduce ourselves," she says.

3.   The names are reminders that Zimbabwe had Africa's highest literacy rate and one of its most rigorous and democratic postcolonial school systems, which created a generation of seasoned English-speakers, even among the country's poorest. The buoyancy of that era—which stretched across the 1980s—is recorded in popular names of the time, including that of a man this writer once interviewed named Freeman Chari. Born in 1981, just a year after the country's independence, Mr. Chari was the first in his family to grow up a free man.

4.   In the early 1990s, political violence accelerated and Zimbabwe's economy splintered and many fled the country. Today, some 2 million to 4 million Zimbabweans live abroad, compared with a local population of just 14 million. Most are now in South Africa, where their hopeful names—copied out onto asylum petitions, applications for work permits, résumés, and job-wanted ads—are betrayed by the fact that they are in a nation of high unemployment and deep distrust of foreigners. Shopman Moyo, who says his parents probably thought his name meant "businessman," did not become one when he came to Johannesburg. He's a Coca-Cola deliveryman. "However long you are here, even if you have a South African passport like I do, the police look at the name on your ID, and they know you are not from here," says Last Sibanda, a mechanic who has lived in South Africa since 1996. "They begin to ask you strange questions."

5.   Last Sibanda's name is a poignant token of family history. The tenth of eleven children, Mr. Sibanda was originally named Khiwa, a Shona word meaning "white person," for his pale skin. But when his youngest brother died at age 3, their grief-stricken mother decided she would never have another baby, and sealed the promise by renaming her youngest living son "Last."

6.   South Africa's Zimbabwe community maintains its unique and hopeful naming traditions. There's Staysoft, a Johannesburg gardener named for a popular brand of fabric softener, who says he got his name because of the soft skin he had as a baby. Mpofu's colleague Godknows was born to a single mother after his father "pulled a disappearing act," so the name was "a comfort, a reminder to have faith that it would all work out."

Practice 2

1. Highlight the thesis statement.

2. Identify the types of specific examples the writer uses to support his thesis. (Select all that apply.)

    a. statistics   d. expert opinion

    b. research study   e. anecdote

    c. facts

3. Underline the topic sentence of each body paragraph.

4. Why do many Zimbabwean parents give their children English names?

    _____

5. How are Zimbabweans treated in South Africa? _____

    _____

6. List ten first names that combine two or more words into a single name.

    _____

    _____

7. What name is the most interesting and original? _____

The Writer's Room

Writing Topics

Write an illustration essay about one of the following topics.

General Topics

1. important milestones
2. stereotypes on television
3. useless products or inventions
4. activities that relieve stress
5. American symbols
6. money-making hobbies

College- and Work-Related Topics

7. qualities of an ideal workplace
8. skills that you need for your job
9. temptations that college students face
10. important things to know about doing your job

> **PARAGRAPH LINK**
> To practice illustration writing, you could develop an essay about one of the topics found in Chapter 4, "Illustration."

Illustration Essay Checklist

As you write your illustration essay, review the essay checklist at the end of the book. Also ask yourself the following questions.

❑ Does my thesis statement include a topic that I can support with examples?

❑ Does my thesis statement make a point about the topic?

❑ Do my body paragraphs contain sufficient examples that clearly support the thesis statement?

❑ Do I smoothly and logically connect the examples?

The Narration Essay

14.2 Write a narration essay.

When writing a narration essay, you tell a story about what happened, and you generally explain events in the order in which they occurred.

There are two main types of narrative writing. In **first-person narration**, you describe a personal experience using *I* or *we*. In **third-person narration**, you use *he*, *she*, *it*, or *they* to describe what happened to somebody else.

PARAGRAPH LINK
For more information about narrative writing, refer to Chapter 5, "Narration."

The Thesis Statement

The thesis statement controls the direction of the body paragraphs. To create a meaningful thesis statement for a narrative essay, ask yourself what you learned, how you changed, or how the event is important.

controlling idea   topic

Something wonderful happened **the summer I turned fifteen**.

The Supporting Ideas

Here are some tips to remember as you develop a narration essay.

• Make sure that your essay has a point. Do not simply recount what happened. Try to indicate why the events are important.

• Organize the events in time order (the order in which they occurred). You could also reverse the order of events. Begin with the outcome of the events and then explain what happened that led to the outcome.

• Make your narrative essay more interesting by using some descriptive language. For example, you could describe images that appeal to the five senses: taste, touch, smell, sight, and sound.

To be as complete as possible, a good narration essay should provide answers to most of the following questions.

• *Who* is the essay about?

• *What* happened?

• *When* did it happen?

• *Where* did it happen?

• *Why* did it happen?

• *How* did it happen?

GRAMMAR LINK
For information about punctuating quotations, see Chapter 35.

HINT: Using Quotations

One effective way to enhance your narration essay is to use dialogue. Include direct and/or indirect quotations.

A **direct quotation** contains a person's exact words. A direct quotation is set off with quotation marks. When you tell a story and include the exact words of more than one person, you must start a new paragraph each time the speaker changes.

> Sara looked at me sadly: "Why did you betray me?"
>
> "I didn't mean to do it," I answered.
>
> She looked down at her hands and said, "I don't think I can ever forgive you."

An **indirect quotation** keeps the person's meaning but not the person's exact words. An indirect quotation is not set off by quotation marks.

> Sara asked why I had betrayed her.

A Student Narration Essay

Read and analyze the next student narration essay by Yirga Gebremeskel.

MY PRISON STORY

1.   Growing up, I found myself constantly getting in trouble. I hung around with the wrong group of people and experimented with marijuana. My academic work declined because all I wanted to do was hang out with the crew. My mother constantly lectured me, but no matter what she said, I always did what I wanted to do. At seventeen years old, I was heading for disaster when I was wrongfully convicted of assault and battery.

Thesis statement

2.   My troubles started when my little brother Samson and I hung out with my friend Malcolm. We were in downtown Boston, and we joked around and went window-shopping. Then we stopped into a 7-Eleven to get drinks. When I got to the counter to pay, I looked through the glass doors and saw a cop cruiser pull up. The officer pointed toward me and signaled me to come outside. My heart pounding, I went outside to meet him. He said that someone had just been assaulted, and I fit the description. I protested that there had to be a mistake, but he put me against the wall and patted me down. Then he read me my rights, and he shoved me into the cruiser.

Topic sentence

3.   I was thrust into a legal problem over which I had no control. I couldn't afford a lawyer, so the court gave me a court-appointed attorney. Four months later, my attorney unexpectedly arrived and said it was time to go to court. I explained that my best witness, my little brother, was in school, but he wouldn't give my mother enough time to find Samson. The actual trial was very brief and was hard for me to take seriously; I felt like any moment the victim would realize his mistake. But when the victim took the stand and described what had happened, he seemed earnest. He really believed that I was his attacker.

Topic sentence

4.   The verdict caused my family a lot of pain. There was no other evidence but the victim's word, but that was enough. The jury convicted me, and the judge gave me my sentence: six months in prison with an additional two years on probation. I turned around to look at my mother's face, and there were tears coming down

Topic sentence

2. I marveled at this accolade, for I had never been called thin in my life. It was something I longed for. I would have been flattered if those ample-bosomed women hadn't looked so distressed. It was obvious I fell far short of their ideal of beauty.

3. I had dressed up for a very special occasion—the baptism of a son. The women heaped rice into tin basins the size of laundry tubs, shaping it into mounds with their hands. Five of us sat around one basin, thrusting our fingers into the scalding food. These women ate with such relish, such joy. They pressed the rice into balls in their fists, squeezing until the bright-red palm oil ran down their forearms and dripped off their elbows.

4. I tried desperately, but I could not eat enough to please them. It was hard for me to explain that I come from a culture in which it is almost unseemly for a woman to eat too heartily. It's considered unattractive. It was even harder to explain that to me thin is beautiful, and in my country we deny ourselves food in our pursuit of perfect slenderness.

5. That night, everyone danced to welcome the baby. Women swiveled their broad hips and used their hands to emphasize the roundness of their bodies. One needed to be round and wide to make the dance beautiful. There was no place for thinness here. It made people sad. It reminded them of things they wanted to forget, such as poverty, drought, and starvation. They never knew when the rice was going to run out.

6. I began to believe that Africa's image of the perfect female body was far more realistic than the long-legged leanness I had been conditioned to admire. There, it is beautiful—not shameful—to carry weight on the hips and thighs, to have a round stomach and heavy, swinging breasts. Women do not battle the bulge; they celebrate it. A body is not something to be tamed and molded.

7. The friends who had christened me Chicken-hips made it their mission to fatten me up. It wasn't long before a diet of rice and rich, oily stew twice a day began to change me. Every month, the women would take a stick and measure my backside, noting with pleasure its gradual expansion. "Oh Catherine, your buttocks are getting nice now!" they would say.

8. What was extraordinary was that I, too, believed I was becoming more beautiful. There was no sense of panic, no shame, and no guilt-ridden resolves to go on the miracle grape-and-water diet. One day, I tied my *lappa* tight across my hips and went to the market to buy beer for a wedding. I carried the crate of bottles home on my head, swinging my hips slowly as I walked. I felt transformed.

Practice 7

1. In this essay, what is the author describing? _____
    _____

2. Underline at least five descriptive verbs.

3. What is the dominant impression? Circle the best answer.
    a. homesickness   b. tension   c. admiration

4. The writer appeals to more than one sense. Give an example for each type of imagery.

   a. Sight: _____

   b. Sound: _____

   c. Touch: _____

   _____

5. How does the writer change physically and emotionally during her time in Africa?

   _____

   _____

   _____

6. What is the writer's main message?

   _____

   _____

   _____

The Writer's Room

Writing Topics

Write a description essay about one of the following topics.

General Topics

1. a dream vacation
2. a wedding
3. a painting or photograph
4. a physical and psychological self-portrait
5. your neighborhood

College- and Work-Related Topics

6. your first impressions of college
7. a sports event
8. your college or workplace cafeteria or food court
9. a memorable person with whom you have worked
10. a pleasant or unpleasant task

> **PARAGRAPH LINK**
> To practice descriptive writing, you could develop an essay about one of the topics in Chapter 6, "Description."

Description Essay Checklist

As you write your description essay, review the essay checklist at the end of the book. Also ask yourself the following questions.

❏ Does my thesis statement clearly show what I will describe in the rest of the essay?

❏ Does my thesis statement make a point about the topic?

❏ Does my essay have a dominant impression?

❏ Does each body paragraph contain supporting details that appeal to the reader's senses?

❏ Do I use figurative language (simile, metaphor, or personification)?

Practice 8

1. What kind of process essay is this? Circle the best answer.

   a. Complete a process   b. Understand a process

2. Who is the audience for this essay? _____

3. In which paragraph(s) does the writer use an anecdote? _____

4. How does the writer end the conclusion?

   a. With a suggestion   b. With a quotation   c. With a prediction

---

A Professional Process Essay

In the following essay, Rohan Healy explains how he overcame a problem. Read the essay and answer the questions.

How I Overcame My Panic Attacks

1.   At the age of nineteen, my life was difficult. There was illness in the family, I was unemployed, and I had very little money. This immense stress manifested in a series of panic attacks. Sometimes the panic attacks would occur outdoors. In crowded streets or cafes, I would hyperventilate, sweat, turn pale, and feel sick for no apparent reason. Sometimes my attacks would come in the night. My heart would beat rapidly as though I were running the 100-meter sprint. I would fear that I was going to die. I found some help through the books of celebrated panic expert Dr. Claire Weekes. There are certain steps you can take to combat panic attacks.

2.   First, understand what a panic attack is. In basic terms, it is the engagement of the body's survival response. When you feel stressed or anxious, you can inadvertently trigger the "fight or flight" response. This response fools the brain and nervous system into thinking there is an actual physical threat that requires you to defend yourself or run away. Your heart palpitates and provides more oxygen for your muscles, which are ready for action. You then worry about the mysterious behavior of your body: "Why is my heart racing? Why am I sweating? Why is it difficult to breathe?" Of course, if you are being chased or if a car almost hits you, then you have a context and can understand the physical symptoms. But when you are lying in bed at night and the survival response is triggered, it's terrifying. Remember that panic attacks are not dangerous, and they will not kill you.

3.   Second, remember that panic attacks are time limited. When faced with danger, your bloodstream is pumped with adrenaline, which causes the most confusing and scary symptoms of a panic attack. The good news is that you have a limited supply of adrenaline in your glands, so no matter what you do, the panic attack will end when the body runs out of adrenaline, after about thirty minutes. You will not die.

4.   Next, deep breathing is a powerful tool in overcoming and shortening panic attacks. Unlike the heart, which you cannot control, you can consciously override your breath. In the midst of an attack, or as you feel one coming on, breathe slowly and deeply into your abdomen, filling up your whole belly and chest before slowly exhaling. This sends "I'm safe" signals to the brain because deep, relaxed breathing is a sign that the danger has passed.

5.   Finally, focus your attention on the sensations in your body while reminding yourself that you are safe. The sensations are not physically harmful, and they will end no matter what you do, so simply experience them. Feel the tingling, and focus on your beating heart, your cold face, and the shaking. Let the sensations wash over you while breathing deeply and staying present. Repeating "I am safe" tells the cognitive part of the brain that all is well and that there is no danger. The positive affirmation helps to end the attack sooner.

6.   I used this technique to overcome my panic attacks, and now they are very rare. If I ever feel one coming, I am able to quell the fight/flight/flee response quickly. So remember that panic attacks can do you no physical harm. Even if it feels like your heart is beating out of your chest, it's not even beating as hard as it would if you were, say, running to catch a bus or playing a game of soccer. Remember that there's nothing physically wrong with you, and it's a natural response to fear and danger. Although it takes a little time and courage, you *can* overcome panic attacks just like I did.

Practice 9

1. Highlight the thesis statement of the essay.

2. Underline the topic sentences in paragraphs 2 to 5.

3. What type of process essay is this? Circle the best answer.

   a. Complete a process   b. Understand a process

4. In process essays, the support is generally a series of steps. List the steps to overcome panic attacks.

   _____

   _____

   _____

5. Circle the transitional expressions the author uses in this essay.

6. Who is the audience for this essay? _____

7. Is this essay relevant for people who never suffer from panic attacks? If yes, how?

   _____

   _____

   _____

The Writer's Room

Writing Topics

Write a process essay about one of the following topics.

General Topics

1. how to be a good person
2. how to kick a bad habit
3. how someone became famous
4. how something works
5. how to raise a happy child

College- and Work-Related Topics

6. how to manage your time
7. how education changed somebody's life
8. how to do your job
9. how to be a better student
10. how to find satisfaction in your work life

> **PARAGRAPH LINK**
> To practice process writing, you could develop an essay about one of the topics in Chapter 7, "Process."

> ## Process Essay Checklist
>
> As you write your process essay, review the essay checklist at the end of the book. Also ask yourself the following questions.
>
> ❏ Does my thesis statement make a point about the process?
>
> ❏ Does my essay explain how to do something, how something works, or how something happened?
>
> ❏ Do I include all of the steps in the process?
>
> ❏ Do I clearly explain the steps in the process or in the event?
>
> ❏ Do I mention the tools or equipment that my readers need to complete or understand the process?

The Definition Essay

14.5   **Write a definition essay.**

A definition explains what something means. When writing a **definition essay**, give your personal definition of a term or concept. Although you can define most terms in a few sentences, you may need to offer extended definitions for words that are particularly complex. For example, you could write an essay or even an entire book about the term *love*. The way that you interpret love is unique, and you would bring your own opinions, experiences, and impressions to your definition essay.

PARAGRAPH LINK
For more information about definition writing, refer to Chapter 8, "Definition."

The Thesis Statement

In your thesis statement, indicate what you are defining and include a definition of the term. Look at the three ways you might define a term in your thesis statement.

1. **Definition by synonym.** You could give a synonym for the term.

   term   +   synonym

   Some doctors insist that green care, or the use of therapeutic nature for healthcare, is a silly fad.

2. **Definition by category.** Decide what larger group the term belongs to, and then determine the unique characteristics that set the term apart from others in that category.

   term   +   category   +   what it is

   A backie is a photo that people take of their own backs.

3. **Definition by negation.** Explain what the term is not, and then explain what it is.

   term   +   what it is not   +   what it is

   Stalkers are not misguided romantics; they are dangerous predators.

The Supporting Ideas

In a definition essay, you can support your main point using a variety of writing patterns. For example, in a definition essay about democracy, one supporting paragraph could give historical background about democracy, another could include a description of a functioning democracy, and a third paragraph could compare different styles of democracy. The different writing patterns would all support the overriding pattern, which is definition.

HINT: Enhancing a Definition

One way to enhance a definition essay is to begin with a provocative statement about the term. Then in the body of your essay, develop your definition more thoroughly. This technique arouses the interest of the readers and makes them want to continue reading. For example, the next statement questions a common belief.

> According to Dr. W. Roland, attention-deficit/hyperactivity disorder (ADHD) is an invented condition.

A Student Definition Essay

Read and analyze the next student definition essay by Dominic Chartrand.

HOMOPHOBIA

1.   The status of homosexuality has changed with time in various parts of the world. In Greek mythology, Patroclus was Achilles' lover. Alexander the Great was alleged to have had homosexual relationships. Central and South American natives were also known to tolerate homosexuality. When Western religions declared homosexuality a sin, a direct consequence of this edict was homophobia. Homophobia is deplorable feelings of hate and fear toward homosexuals, and it rages on under many forms.   **← Thesis statement**

2.   Homophobia is a problem that affects people's professional lives. First, some people do not want gays or lesbians to occupy certain jobs, such as teaching, because parents are afraid that teachers may "teach" homosexuality to their children. In the movie *Milk*, Harvey Milk's character asks, "How do you teach homosexuality? Like French?" In addition, people of the opposite sex working in gender-dominated professions are constantly assaulted by homophobic comments. Female plumbers, male hairdressers, or male nurses might be labeled gay.   **← Topic sentence**

3.   Many discriminatory laws have been passed by people who fear homosexuals. In many Muslim countries, such as Saudi Arabia and Yemen, homosexuality is punishable by death. Some other punishment methods include jail and torture. Some countries prohibit homosexuals from marrying or adopting children. For example, in our nation, there are many citizens and politicians who want gay marriage to be banned.   **← Topic sentence**

4.   Homophobia is a social factor that can destroy people's lives. For example, a Rutgers University student, Dharun Ravi, secretly filmed his roommate, Tyler Clementi, having sexual relations with another man. Ravi then posted cruel and mocking comments on Twitter about Clementi. Clementi killed himself a few days later. Ravi was given a one-month jail sentence, hundreds of hours of community service, and a heavy fine. Although Ravi was never charged with causing his roommate's death, the gay-bashing act led to serious consequences and effectively destroyed two people's lives.   **← Topic sentence**

5.   In conclusion, homophobia is a problem present in every sphere of people's lives. It affects individuals on a professional, legal, and personal level. Achieving legal recognition does not annihilate homophobia entirely. Lots of work still needs to be done to eradicate intolerance completely. However, some progress has been made toward acceptance and tolerance in the last forty years, and homosexuals throughout the world have to keep faith in a brighter future.   **← Concluding sentence**

Practice 10

1. What type of definition does the writer use in the thesis statement? Circle the best answer.

   a. Definition by synonym

   b. Definition by category

   c. Definition by negation

2. Who is the audience? _____

3. In which paragraph does the author give an anecdote? _____

4. How does the writer end the essay?

   a. With a prediction   b. With a suggestion   c. With a quotation

5. What organizational pattern does the writer use in this essay?

   a. Time order   b. Space order   c. Emphatic order

A Professional Definition Essay

In the following essay adapted from his book *The 7 Laws of Magical Thinking*, science journalist Matthew Hutson explores the definition of luck.

What Is Luck?

Nagasaki: a Japanese city hit by an atomic bomb on August 9, 1945

1.   On the morning of August 9, 1945, the wings of Bockscar lifted it into the air. The B-29, loaded with a five-ton atomic bomb named "Fat Man," took off from Tinian, an island 1,500 miles southeast of Japan. By the time Bockscar passed over its target at 10:44 A.M., the city was covered in haze and difficult to see. So the crew left the city of Kokura and made their way over to their second choice, **Nagasaki**. Most people have never heard of Kokura. In this regard, it can be counted as one of the luckiest cities in the world. In another case, in 1993, a German motorcyclist hit a truck, went flying into a tree, and was impaled on a branch. The headline in a Norwegian newspaper, next to a photograph of this unfortunate gentleman with a branch still going into his chest and out his back, read, "Verdens Heldigste," or "World's Luckiest," because the branch had missed all his vital organs. We are fascinated by such near misses.

2.   Luck is as tricky to define as it is to tame. Rare good things are lucky. But, what about Kokura? Nothing positive happened to it. In fact, it lost thousands of neighboring countrymen. And the German motorcyclist had surely seen better days. "Luck" is often yoked to terrible, terrible things.

3.   Karl Teigen, a psychologist at the University of Tromsø in Norway, has spent years studying what we mean when we talk about luck. One conclusion he has reached is that, on par, "lucky" events are not pleasant. In a search of newspaper stories, for example, he found that "with the exception of an occasional sports champion and a . . . lottery winner, the typical lucky person had survived a plane or car crash, had been stabbed or shot, had fallen off a cliff or bridge, or had been shipwrecked or surrounded by flames." In a one-month period, he found one mention of "bad luck" in a story about a soldier who had stepped on a mine—but the soldier had nevertheless commented on his own good fortune in losing just the one leg.

4.   Teigen suggests that luck derives not from the absolute value of an outcome but from its relative value. That soldier lost a leg but thought of how he had almost lost two, so he considered himself lucky. Why wouldn't he compare losing

a leg to not stepping on the mine at all? Mentally altering an effect or a recent cause in a chain of events comes more naturally than mentally undoing an earlier cause. Once someone has skewered himself on a tree, he'll tend to think of the untouched organs right next to the branch hole, not about how this never would have happened if he hadn't taken the extra five minutes to floss that morning.

5.   According to Teigen, feeling lucky correlates with feelings of gratitude, a distinctly social sentiment, and the thanks are often of an existential kind, directed not toward a person but toward God or the universe or fate. A few years ago, Eugene Subbotsky, a psychologist at Lancaster University who studies magical thinking, was strolling through Moscow with his young son, with no one around. They walked past an empty parked car. "Just when we were passing by, the engine started," Subbotsky told me soon after the event. The car started moving. It swerved toward them. Finally, it turned a little more and hit an iron gate a few inches away. "We escaped death very narrowly," he said. "I could have been smashed to pieces with my little son. I am a rational man, I am a scientist, I'm studying this phenomenon, but there are some events in life that I cannot explain rationally. Of course people can always write it down to chance and say, 'Okay, it's a coincidence,' but it's such a rare coincidence that they start thinking mystically and magically about things."

6.   We can certainly tell a good story of a lucky escape without resorting to unnatural intervention: event B just logically followed event A. However, we want to believe that flukes of luck happened for a reason or are building up to some future purpose. It gives the story of our lives both continuity and a destination, something to strive for. Sometimes it's fun to pretend.

Practice 11

1. Highlight the thesis statement. Be careful because it may not be in the first paragraph.

2. Underline the topic sentences in body paragraphs 2 to 5.

3. According to the author, people define luck by "its relative value." In your own words, what does he mean?

   _____

   _____

   _____

4. According to the author, how does society generally define "lucky people"?

   _____

   _____

   _____

5. How does the author support the thesis? _____

6. In your own words, sum up the author's main supporting anecdotes.

   a. _____

   b. _____

   c. _____

   d. _____

PARAGRAPH LINK
To practice definition writing, you could develop an essay about one of the topics found in Chapter 8, "Definition."

The Writer's Room

Writing Topics

Write a definition essay about one of the following topics.

General Topics

1. independence
2. an effective politician
3. street smarts
4. a control freak
5. our disposable culture

College- and Work-Related Topics

6. a McJob
7. a team player
8. a whistle-blower
9. a green-collar job
10. downsizing

Definition Essay Checklist

As you write your definition essay, review the essay checklist at the end of the book. Also ask yourself the following questions.

❑ Does my thesis statement explain what term I am defining?

❑ Does each topic sentence clearly show some aspect of the definition?

❑ Do my supporting paragraphs include examples that help illustrate the definition?

❑ Do I use concise language in my definition?

The Classification Essay

14.6   Write a classification essay.

Classifying means to sort a subject into more understandable categories. When you are planning a classification essay, find a topic that you can organize into categories. Each category must be part of a larger group, yet it must also be distinct. For example, if your essay is about types of lawyers, you might sort lawyers into criminal lawyers, divorce lawyers, and corporate lawyers.

PARAGRAPH LINK
For more information about classification writing, refer to Chapter 9, "Classification."

The Thesis Statement

The thesis statement in a classification essay mentions the categories of the subject and contains a controlling idea. In this type of essay, the controlling idea is your classification principle, which is the overall method that you use to sort the items. For example, if your essay topic is "electronic communication," you might sort it according to types of online apps, categories of social media, or types of texters.

controlling idea (classification principle)   categories
Three types of annoying **texters** are emoji addicts, screamers, and abbreviators.
topic

HINT: List Specific Categories

You can guide your reader by listing the specific categories you will cover in your thesis statement.

Children learn gender roles **through the family, the school, and the media**.

The Supporting Ideas

In a classification essay, each body paragraph covers one category. To organize your categories and supporting details, you can use a classification chart or a more traditional classification essay plan.

A CLASSIFICATION CHART

A classification chart helps you plan your ideas by providing a visual representation of how you wish to classify a subject. In this sample chart, the thesis statement appears at the top, and all of the categories branch from it.

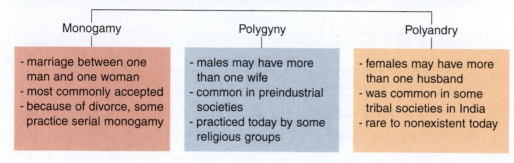

Historically, three types of heterosexual marital unions have been practiced around the world.

Monogamy	Polygyny	Polyandry
- marriage between one man and one woman - most commonly accepted - because of divorce, some practice serial monogamy	- males may have more than one wife - common in preindustrial societies - practiced today by some religious groups	- females may have more than one husband - was common in some tribal societies in India - rare to nonexistent today

A Student Classification Essay

Read and analyze the next student classification essay by Cleavon Henry.

Origins of Names

1.   Have you ever wondered how your family acquired its name? Names are important because they give an identity to individuals and groups of people. Not all cultures give people two names: a first and family name. In some cultures, people go by only one name, or they take their father or mother's first name as their own last name. In Western societies, the tradition of labeling an individual grew during the Middle Ages as size of populations grew. Profession, description, and location became three important origins of last names in western European tradition.   ● **Thesis statement**

2.   First, before the Middle Ages, individuals were usually known by only one name. But as communities grew more organized and professions became more varied, it was necessary to identify a person by the job she was performing.   ● **Topic sentence**   For example, if John made arrows for a living, he became known as John the Fletcher. The last names Miller, Baker, Carpenter, and Farmer are associated with a particular trade or skill. Most likely somewhere in the ancestry of the modern-day Miller and Baker families, there was a miller and a baker. President Jimmy Carter's last name is an occupational name, meaning transporter of goods by a cart.

3.   Furthermore, if someone had a particular characteristic, it was often used to label the person.   ● **Topic sentence**   Generally, such types of names were adjectives and were used as nicknames to identify the individual. For instance, Mr. White may have had white hair. Or Mrs. Short may have been very short. And Mr. Young may have been used to differentiate between an older and younger sibling. President Harry Truman may have had a trustworthy individual as an ancestor. According to *BabyNamesPedia*, an encyclopedia of names, President John F. Kennedy's name originates from Scottish or Gaelic and means someone who has an ugly head.

Topic sentence

4.   Finally, people acquired names by their location. Some people's surnames came from a specific geographical marker. Ms. Brook may have lived near a brook, or Mr. Wood may have lived near the woods. Others may have become known through their landholdings, such as Mr. Castle, who may have occupied one. Ms. Whitehouse may have lived in a white house. Or a person could have lived in a town or village, such as Mrs. London who may have built a house in London. President Abraham Lincoln's ancestors may have come from the city of Lincoln in the United Kingdom.

5.   In western European tradition, an individual's work, a particular trait, or the place he called home commonly determined his family name. The origin of people's last names is interesting and might give clues to their ancestry. So, if you want to know about your origins, you may want to research your own surname.

Concluding sentence

Practice 12

1. What is the classification principle? That is, what main principle unifies the three categories? _____

2. What are the three categories? _____

3. Add one more example to each of the categories.

_____

_____

_____

A Professional Classification Essay

This essay first appeared in *Introduction to Animal Science* by W. Stephen Damron. Read the essay and answer the questions that follow.

The Purpose of Pets

1.   Pet species provide many practical services to society, and it is clear that some animals are companion animals. Their greatest value is defined by their relationships with the people who share their lives. Once a source of derision, the human–companion animal bond is now recognized for its value as a contributing factor in the physical, mental, emotional, and social health of the owner. However, not all domestic animals qualify as companions. For instance, there are many barn cats across the country whose job in life is just to keep the rats and mice at bay. In fact, many people purchase an animal for the following motives: the animal is ornamental, a status symbol, or a plaything.

Ornamental Pets

2.   Ornamental pets serve the same purpose that houseplants serve—they decorate and enhance the atmosphere. Ornamental pets are usually brightly colored birds or fish or some type of animal that adds aesthetic appeal to an environment. It is common to find an aquarium filled with brightly colored or interesting aquatic species in restaurants, professional offices, or homes. Decorators have been known to bring fabric swatches to pet stores in order to pick a bird that matches carpets and draperies. Outdoor environments are often graced by flashy species such as peacocks, pheasants, Sumatra chickens, swans, geese, and ducks. Rarely are these ornamental pets handled, named, or treated in any special way. They are not considered companion animals.

Status Symbols

3.   There is strong evidence that at least part of the domestication of the wolf was linked to the status its presence in camp gave the human occupants. A wolf as totem and companion would have conveyed a powerful message to rival clans or tribes. Sometimes we succumb to this same symbolism in modern life. This explains the motives of some people who keep poisonous snakes, piranhas, vicious dogs, big cats, bears, or wolves as pets. The animals are usually admired and well cared for as long as they satisfy the owner's expectations. In a more benign example, the symbolism of animals as totems for ancient people is not so different from that conveyed in modern society by what we generally refer to as "mascots." Status can also be conveyed by a pet kept for another primary reason. Purebred animals generally convey more status than mixed breed animals. Sometimes unusual, rare, and expensive animals are status symbols.

Playthings

4.   Pets as playthings may range from living toys given to children, before they are old enough to appreciate the responsibilities, to animals used in sporting events such as hunting or riding. Children are often given a pet as a plaything before they are capable of appreciating it. Some of the people involved in sports and who use animals are only interested in the animal during the competitive season and lose interest and enthusiasm rather quickly at the close of the season. Often, these animals are poorly treated and may be discarded or destroyed by their owners when the animals lose their amusement value.

5.   It is clear that some animals are companion animals. Their greatest value is defined by their relationships with the people who share their lives. The Council for Science and Society states, "An animal employed for decoration, status-signaling, recreation, or hobby is being used primarily as an object—the animal equivalent of a work of art, a Rolls Royce, a surfboard, or a collector's item. The companion animal, however, is typically perceived and treated as a subject—as a personality in its own right, irrespective of other considerations. With companion animals, it is the relationship itself which is important to the owner."

Practice 13

1. Highlight the thesis statement.

2. What is the essay's classification principle? _____

_____

3. What are the three main categories? _____

_____

4. Underline the topic sentences in body paragraphs 2, 3, and 4.

5. Provide some details about each type of pet. Use your own words.

Ornamental Pets: _____

_____

Status Symbols: _____

_____

Playthings: _____

_____

6. To better understand how the author organizes this essay, make a classification chart. Write the categories on the lines and examples in the boxes. Use your own words to explain each category.

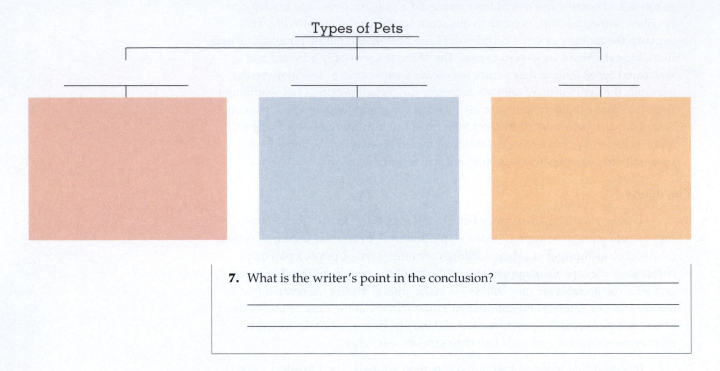

Types of Pets

7. What is the writer's point in the conclusion? _____

_____

_____

The Writer's Room

Writing Topics

Write a classification essay about one of the following topics.

General Topics

1. addictions
2. movies or TV series
3. extreme sports
4. things that cause allergic reactions
5. salespeople

College- and Work-Related Topics

6. annoying customers or clients
7. punishment
8. competition
9. college students
10. fashions in the workplace

PARAGRAPH LINK
To practice classification writing, you could develop an essay about one of the topics found in Chapter 9, "Classification."

Classification Essay Checklist

As you write your classification essay, review the essay checklist at the end of the book. Also ask yourself the following questions.

❑ Do I clearly identify which categories I will discuss in my thesis statement?

❑ Do I use a common classification principle to unite the various items?

❑ Do I include categories that do not overlap?

❑ Do I clearly explain one of the categories in each body paragraph?

❑ Do I use sufficient details to explain each category?

❑ Do I arrange the categories in a logical manner?

The Comparison and Contrast Essay

14.7 **Write a comparison and contrast essay.**

You **compare** when you want to find similarities and **contrast** when you want to find differences. When writing a comparison and contrast essay, you explain how people, places, things, or ideas are the same or different to prove a specific point.

Before you write, make a decision about whether to focus on similarities, differences, or both. As you explore your topic, make a list of both similarities and differences. Later, you can use some of the ideas in your essay plan.

PARAGRAPH LINK
For more information about this pattern, refer to Chapter 10, "Comparison and Contrast."

The Thesis Statement

The thesis statement in a comparison and contrast essay indicates if you are making comparisons, contrasts, or both. When you write a thesis statement, specify what you are comparing or contrasting and the controlling idea.

> Although neat people have a very nice environment, messy people are more relaxed.

> **Topics being contrasted:** Neat people and messy people
> **Controlling idea:** Messy people are more relaxed.

> Alice's daughter wants to be her own person, but she is basically very similar to her mother.

> **Topics being compared:** Mother and daughter
> **Controlling idea:** Very similar personalities

The Supporting Ideas

In a comparison and contrast essay, you can develop your body paragraphs in two different ways.

1. In a **point-by-point** development, you present *one* point about Topic A and then *one* point about Topic B. You keep following this pattern until you have a few points for each topic.

   Paragraph 1: Topic A, Topic B
   Paragraph 2: Topic A, Topic B
   Paragraph 3: Topic A, Topic B

2. In a **topic-by-topic** development, you discuss one topic in detail, and then you discuss the other topic in detail.

   Paragraphs 1 and 2: All of Topic A
   Paragraphs 3 and 4: All of Topic B

A Student Comparison and Contrast Essay

Read and analyze the next student comparison and contrast essay by Reina Lopetequi.

....
Cuban Schools and American Schools
....

1.　　"Education is the most powerful weapon which you can use to change the world," stated Nelson Mandela. Most people agree that education is the fundamental key to open the door to success. Since I went to school in Cuba and in the United States, I have personal experience with both school systems. In Cuba and in the United States, education is compulsory between six to sixteen years

Thesis statement

of age and is free regardless of a student's class, race, or religion. However, the Cuban educational system prepares students more thoroughly for college and university courses than the American system.

Topic sentence

2.   Cuban children have greater respect for their schooling than American children. In Cuba, children are very serious about school. I remember how we used to stand up and greet the teacher every morning as a sign of respect and wait for the teacher to give us permission to take our seats. It caught my attention when I came to the United States how it was considered "cool" to disrespect the teacher. Students often did not listen to the teacher or were unprepared for the lesson because they had not done their homework. In Cuba, the majority of the students came to class prepared.

Topic sentence

3.   Furthermore, the Cuban curriculum is more rigorous than the American curriculum. Cuban students take many courses such as Spanish, mathematics (including algebra, geometry, statistics, etc.), physical sciences (chemistry and physics), biological sciences, history (world and Cuban), civics, computers, physical education, arts, and English. These courses are taught more in-depth than in American schools. My friend Alessandro arrived in the United States when he was in grade six. He had already studied geometry and could calculate angles of triangles and was more advanced in all of his subjects than his peers. When I was in high school in the United States, I found most of my courses to be easy and many of my high school teachers had low expectations of the students, so they did not assign much homework.

Topic sentence

4.   Finally, in Cuba, the family and the teachers work together to support students. Teachers visit students at their homes when the teacher feels the student is having family problems that affect her performance at school. I can talk from experience on this topic. I was always considered a smart student, but when my parents divorced, I got behind in class. I remember my teacher never gave up on me. She used to hold my hand and help me write, and she would sing songs to me to cheer me up. It is also perfectly normal for parents to ask about their children's performance at school. And at the end of the year, the parents get together to throw a party for the class as a celebration that the course was successfully over. When I came to the United States, I never saw a single parent at school. I was expecting an awesome party at the end of the year, but instead I got a "have a safe summer" from the teacher and no celebration.

5.   The Cuban school system supports students in their quest for a good education better than the American school system. Educators, politicians, and psychologists often worry that American students do not perform as well academically as students from other countries. Perhaps, American politicians

Concluding sentence

should examine closely what Cuba is doing to produce well-educated students.

Practice 14

1. What type of lead-in does the writer use in the introduction?
   a. Quotation   b. Surprising statement   c. Question
2. What does this essay focus on?
   a. Similarities   b. Differences
3. What pattern of comparison does the writer follow in each body paragraph?
   a. Point by point   b. Topic by topic
4. How does the writer end the essay?
   a. With a suggestion   b. With a prediction   c. With a quotation

A Professional Comparison and Contrast Essay

In the following essay, author and journalist Mark Milke compares and contrasts two different time periods. Read the essay and answer the questions that follow.

....

Just Say No

....

1.   In a world where many people have instant text messaging, multiple e-mail accounts, several phones, the still-**ubiquitous** television screen, and a smorgasbord of unlimited web information, life's challenges today are not the ones faced by our ancestors. While theirs were about finding a way to eke out a slightly better life than their narrow circumstances allowed, our world requires a conscious denial of opportunities.

2.   Think back one hundred years. With the exception of the tiniest sliver of the population, most people faced daily scarcity. The food they ate was necessarily local (and limited the possibility for a healthier diet); communication beyond their immediate surroundings was restricted to letters and in-person visits. Even for those who had telephones, long-distance calling was prohibitively expensive. As for vacations, if taken at all, they were close to home or at the relatives. And only the rich could spare the money and time to see exotic locales that many now assume as an annual rite and right. Such generations, to say nothing of the ones that preceded them, knew scarcity as a fact of daily life.

3.   In contrast, today, while poverty yet exists at home and abroad, and in some places more severely than others—North Korea and sub-Saharan Africa are examples—much of the world endures a new predicament rarely considered: abundance. That's a better "problem" to face than chronic shortages of food and opportunities. Still, for anyone who wants to live out what Plato called "the good life," the challenge is to face this fact: If we want a better, more rewarding existence, we have to say "no" more often than "yes." Fail the temptation offered by abundance, and the waistline explodes, the mind atrophies, and the deepest potential joys—discovered through conversation and contemplation and by mastery of some skill, sport, art, or career—are sacrificed to a twittered and inconsequential life.

4.   An advantage exists for those who choose the better over the banal. Those who can shut up and shut out the unhelpful distractions long enough to let the useful thoughts and activities into their soul can then accomplish something valuable. While counterintuitive, the world will never belong to those who engage in every distraction. The world will not build future shrines to those who e-mail, Facebook, text, Twitter, and talk their lives away but never have anything useful to say in all their virtual activities. They have never taken the time to ignore the frenetic present long enough to learn from the past or from some still small voice. What would be the point of trekking into the great outdoors, but with little music buds stuck in one's ears, and then missing the roar of a river or the call of one bird to another?

5.   The most profound books, the most sublime symphonies, and life's rare beautiful moments result from those who choose to say "no" to life's many siren calls of opportunistic distractions. Such men and women also have the most impact on the world around them precisely because they found their own solid center. It is from that solidity that they can then offer others something unique. Case in point: Had **Glenn Gould** been raised in the Internet age and succumbed to every possible distraction, the world would have missed out on the full actualization of his talents; the world would also have been poorer.

6.   In much of human history, men and women necessarily devoted every waking moment to scratching out a basic life of subsistence. These days, our challenge is to block out the avalanche of cheap opportunities that can make us satiated, content, oblivious, and dull.

ubiquitous:
ever present; everywhere

Glen Gould (1932–1982):
Canadian classical pianist, best known for his interpretation of Bach

Practice 15

1. What type of introduction does the writer use?

   a. Opposing position   b. Definition   c. General information

2. Underline the thesis statement.

3. This essay looks at lifestyles in the past and present. What is the focus of this essay?

   a. Similarities   b. Differences

4. In the introduction, the writer says that our world requires a conscious denial of opportunities. What opportunities is the writer referring to?

   _____

   _____

5. What are the differences between the generation a hundred years ago and our generation? _____

   _____

   _____

6. In paragraph 3, what is the author's main message?

   _____

   _____

The Writer's Room

PARAGRAPH LINK
To practice comparison and contrast writing, you could develop an essay about one of the topics found in Chapter 10, "Comparison and Contrast."

Writing Topics

Write a comparison and contrast essay about one of the following topics.

General Topics

Compare and/or contrast . . .

1. expectations about parenthood versus the reality of parenthood
2. two stages in life
3. living together and getting married
4. two fast-food restaurants
5. peer pressure versus parental pressure

College- and Work-Related Topics

Compare and/or contrast . . .

6. male and female college athletes
7. a good manager and a bad manager
8. a stay-at-home parent and an employed parent
9. student life and professional life
10. expectations about a job and the reality of that job

Comparison and Contrast Essay Checklist

As you write your comparison and contrast essay, review the essay checklist at the end of the book. Also ask yourself the following questions.

❑ Does my thesis statement explain what I am comparing or contrasting?

❑ Does my thesis statement make a point about my topic?

❑ Does my essay focus on either similarities or differences?

❏ Does my essay include point-by-point and/or topic-by-topic patterns?

❏ Do all of my supporting examples clearly relate to the topics that are being compared or contrasted?

❏ Do I use transitions that will help readers follow my ideas?

The Cause and Effect Essay

14.8   Write a cause and effect essay.

When writing a cause and effect essay, you explain why an event happened or what the consequences of such an event were.

The Thesis Statement

The thesis statement in a cause and effect essay contains the topic and the controlling idea. The controlling idea indicates whether the essay will focus on causes, effects, or both.

> topic   controlling idea (causes)
>
> **Chronic insomnia** is caused by many factors.

> topic   controlling idea (effects)
>
> **Chronic insomnia** can have a serious impact on a person's health.

> topic   controlling idea (causes and effects)
>
> **Chronic insomnia**, which is caused by many factors, can have a serious impact on a person's health.

> **PARAGRAPH LINK**
> For more information about this pattern, refer to Chapter 11, "Cause and Effect."

HINT: Thinking About Effects

If you are writing about the effects of something, you might think about both the short-term and long-term effects. By doing so, you will generate more ideas for the body of your essay. You will also be able to structure your essay more effectively by moving from short-term to long-term effects. For example, look at the short- and long-term effects of a smoke-free work zone.

Short term	Inside air is cleaner. The smokers get more coffee breaks.
Long term	Fewer smoke-related illnesses occur in nonsmokers. Some smokers might quit smoking.

The Supporting Ideas

The body paragraphs in a cause and effect essay focus on causes, effects, or both. Make sure that each body paragraph contains specific examples that clarify the cause and/or effect relationship.

A Student Cause and Effect Essay

Read and analyze the structure of the next student cause and effect essay by Jim Baek.

WHY SMALL BUSINESSES FAIL

1.   Last spring, Pablo Ortiz rented a tiny pizzeria in his neighborhood to turn it into a taco restaurant. Full of enthusiasm, he bought supplies, paid for advertisements, and posted a large menu in the window of his new venture, called Taco Heaven. Ten months later, Taco Heaven closed, and Ortiz declared bankruptcy. He was not alone. The Small Business Administration Office reports that close to half of all new businesses fail within the first five years. **Causes of small business failures are numerous.**

Thesis statement

2.   First, inexperienced business owners often neglect to do market research to find out if community members are interested in the product. In Ortiz's case, he thought that area residents would appreciate the chance to buy hearty chicken or pork tacos. However, there were three other Mexican fast-food restaurants in the area, so Ortiz's competitors took most of the business.

Topic sentence

3.   Second, inadequate pricing can hurt new businesses. Maggie Stevens, owner of a successful restaurant in Los Angeles, sells stuffed Belgian waffles to an eager clientele. Before pricing her waffles, she calculated the exact cost of each plate, right down to the strawberry that adorned the waffle and the touch of cream next to it. She also considered other costs beyond that of the ingredients, including the cost of labor and food spoilage. Her final price for each dish was 60 percent higher than her base cost. Ortiz, on the other hand, had absolutely no idea what he really spent to make each taco. He ended up underpricing his product and losing money.

Topic sentence

4.   Additionally, many small business owners have insufficient funds to run their ventures successfully. According to accountant Louis Polk, most small businesses operate for four years before they break even, let alone actually make money. Therefore, owners need a cash reserve to get through the first slow years. Ortiz, expecting to make a decent profit right away, did not realize that he would have to use up his savings to keep his business afloat.

Topic sentence

5.   Finally, inexperienced merchants may underestimate the sheer volume of work involved in running a business. Ortiz admits he was very naive about the workload. Taco Heaven was open 15 hours a day, 7 days a week. Ortiz had to cook, shop for ingredients, and do the accounting. After months of grueling work and little to no pay, he burned out.

Topic sentence

6.   Inexperience, lack of proper planning, and insufficient funds can combine to create a business failure. People who plan to open small businesses should become informed, especially about potential pitfalls.

Concluding sentence

Practice 16

1. Does this essay focus on causes or effects? _____

2. In which paragraph does the writer give the following types of support?

   Anecdote: _____

   Expert opinion: _____

3. Who is the audience for this essay?

   _____

   _____

4. What is the purpose of this essay? _____

A Professional Cause and Effect Essay

Albert Nerenberg is a writer, director, and journalist. He has worked on many projects about the power of laughter. Read the essay and answer the questions that follow.

Don't Worry, Act Happy

1.   We usually think of acting as the preserve of movie stars and annoying people with fake moustaches and bad accents. But a surging scientific theory says acting could make people happy. The theory arises from a controversial concept, sometimes called the body–mind principle, that emotions can be reverse engineered. It's simple: If we feel good, we may smile. But the surprising part is if we smile, we may feel good. The Act Happy theory is that we get happier simply by going through the motions of contentment and joy.

2.   Although the Act Happy idea has been bouncing around for years, all of a sudden there's heat around it. There is increasing evidence that the opposite is true—acting enraged, obsessed, malevolent, or depressed may be bad for us. Actor Leonardo DiCaprio developed obsessive–compulsive disorder while playing Howard Hughes in the blockbuster *The Aviator*. In real life, Hughes had the disorder. Actor David Duchovny, who plays a writer obsessed with sex in the TV series *Californication*, checked into a sex-addiction clinic. Batman star Christian Bale allegedly assaulted his mother and sister after completing the violent and brooding *Dark Knight*. Heath Ledger played a tragic and maniacal Joker. Ledger, who had everything going for him, was allegedly clinically depressed. So if people can cultivate rage, depression, and death, can they cultivate joy, hilarity, love, and vitality? If the simple human smile is anything to go by, the answer is yes.

3.   A traditional Buddhist adage recommends smiling as the first conscious thing to do each day, and science may concur. Smiling has clear health benefits. Lee Berk, Associate Director of the Centre for Neuroimmunology at Loma Linda University California, has demonstrated that "mirthful emotions" or "mirthful laughter" can increase the number of T cells, or immune cells, in the bloodstream. Robert Kall, a Philadelphia-based Positive Psychology therapist, tried simple smiling as a way to treat depression. "I would put surface electrodes on the smile muscles in people's faces and, using electromyography, would measure the strength of their smiles," he said. "People who were not depressed had smile muscles that were on average four times stronger than people who were depressed," he said. So he began developing what could only be described as a smiling exercise program. "I would have depressed people pump 'smile' iron," he said. "I would have them do repetitions: three sets of 12 every day." By naturally triggering smiles, the "smilercizers" would seem to drive themselves to happier states.

4.   Smiling's greatest benefit may be that it helps us to connect with others. According to Dr. Mark Stibich, a behavior change expert at the University of California San Diego, smiling not only boosts the immune system and lowers blood pressure, it enhances other people's views of us. When we practice positive emotions, it makes others more apt to reciprocate and smile back. Tanisha Wright, who runs the Beautiful Beginnings Charm School in New Jersey, said her students would sometimes burst out laughing while exercising their smiles.

5.   Although it is often viewed with suspicion, acting may just represent a way to expand our emotional range. Acting comes naturally. Kids do it all the time. Since most people can learn to act, perhaps most could learn to Act Happy. If Heath Ledger's tragic torn smile has taught us anything, it may be that we are what we act. So we should be good to ourselves and not forget to smile.

Practice 17

1. Highlight the thesis statement.

2. Underline the topic sentences in paragraphs 2 to 4. Be careful; the topic sentence may not be the first sentence in the paragraph.

3. Overall, what does this essay focus on?

    a. Causes   b. Effects   c. Both

4. Why does the author mention actors who portrayed depressed or disagreeable characters?

    _____

    _____

5. What psychological and physical changes does a person experience by acting happy?

    _____

    _____

    _____

6. What type of support does the author use to prove his thesis?

    _____

    _____

    _____

The Writer's Room

Writing Topics

Write a cause and effect essay about one of the following topics.

PARAGRAPH LINK
To practice cause and effect writing, you could develop an essay about one of the topics found in Chapter 11, "Cause and Effect."

General Topics

Causes and/or effects of . . .

1. a new law or policy
2. rejecting or adopting a religion
3. sibling rivalry
4. peer pressure
5. leaving your home or homeland

College- and Work-Related Topics

Causes and/or effects of . . .

6. being a parent and college student
7. taking time off before college
8. having an office romance
9. gossiping in the office
10. changing jobs or career paths

Cause and Effect Essay Checklist

As you write your cause and effect essay, review the essay checklist at the end of the book. Also ask yourself the following questions.

❏ Does my essay clearly focus on causes, effects, or both?

❏ Do I have adequate supporting examples of causes and/or effects?

❏ Do I avoid using faulty logic (a mere asumption that one event causes another or is the result of another)?

❏ Do I use the terms *effect* and *affect* correctly? (If you need a refresher about these terms, see the Grammar Hint box in Chapter 11.)

The Argument Essay

14.9 **Write an argument essay.**

When you write an **argument essay**, you take a position on an issue, and you try to defend your position. In other words, you try to persuade your readers to accept your point of view.

PARAGRAPH LINK
For more information about argument writing, refer to Chapter 12, "Argument."

The Thesis Statement

The thesis statement in an argument essay mentions the subject and a debatable point of view about the subject. Do not include phrases such as *in my opinion*, *I think*, or *I am going to talk about* in your thesis statement.

topic · controlling idea

Building a wall on the Mexican border is an ineffective way to deal with illegal immigration.

HINT: List Specific Arguments

Your thesis statement can further guide your readers by listing the specific arguments you will make in your essay.

controlling idea · topic · argument 1

Colleges should implement **work-study programs** to help students acquire

argument 2 · argument 3

job skills, make professional contacts, and earn money for expenses.

The Supporting Ideas

In the body of your essay, give convincing arguments. Try to use several types of supporting evidence.

PARAGRAPH LINK
For more detailed information about types of evidence, see page 143 in Chapter 12, "Argument."

- **Include anecdotes.** Specific experiences or pieces of information can support your point of view.
- **Add facts.** Facts are statements that can be verified in some way. **Statistics** are a type of fact. When you use a fact, make sure that your source is reliable.
- **Use informed opinions.** Opinions from experts in the field can give weight to your argument.
- **Think about logical consequences.** Consider long-term consequences if something does or does not happen.
- **Answer the opposition.** Think about your opponents' arguments, and provide responses to their arguments.

HINT: Quoting a Respected Source

One way to enhance your essay is to include a quotation from a respected source. Find a quotation from somebody in a field that is directly related to your topic. When you include the quotation as supporting evidence, remember to mention the source.

> According to Dr. Tom Houston, co-director of the American Medical Association's SmokeLess States campaign, secondhand smoke "can lead to serious health consequences, ranging from ear infections and pneumonia to asthma."

RESEARCH LINK
For more information about doing research, see Chapter 15, "Enhancing Your Writing with Research."

A Student Argument Essay

Read and analyze the structure of the next student argument essay by Christine Bigras.

THE IMPORTANCE OF MUSIC

Thesis statement

1.   Most parents want their children to receive a well-rounded education. Students study traditional subjects, such as math, science, English, history, geography, and physical education, but many educators and parents have come to believe that schoolchildren should also be taught fine arts subjects. Thus, often school boards offer art, dance, and music, if not as core courses, then at least as extracurricular activities. Although the study and practice of all these arts develop sensitivity and creativity in students, learning music is the most beneficial to all-around student success.

Topic sentence

2.   First, music makes a child smarter. Everybody has already heard about scientists or doctors who are also musicians. A child who studies music may not become a genius; nevertheless, several research findings have shown that music lessons can enhance IQ and develop intelligence. One of the most recent and conclusive studies has shown that there is a link between children who study music and their academic success because music and schoolwork may develop similar problem-solving skills (Schellenberg).

Topic sentence

3.   Furthermore, music education improves a child's physical and psychological health. Playing music is excellent exercise for the heart, especially for those who play a wind instrument. A child will also learn to stand straight and adopt good posture. Playing music also decreases stress and anxiety. Through music, the apprentices will learn concentration and listening skills. Furthermore, according to the Texas Commission on Drug and Alcohol Abuse Report, a 2010 study showed that the 19 percent of students who participated in band or orchestra had a lower percentage of illegal substance abuse than students who did not engage in any music program (Liu).

Topic sentence

4.   Finally, music education helps a child's social development. Playing music may help students connect with one another, particularly through participation in orchestra or a choir. If a child is ugly, poor, big, or shy, he or she is as important as any other musician in the group. Music is the great equalizer. Musicians learn how to respect each other, how to cooperate, and how to build constructive relationships with others. When Yoko Kiyuka entered my former high school, she was very shy and lonely. The music program changed her life. The connections she made helped her become integrated into the school and feel valued.

Concluding sentence

5.   Many school boards are removing music education from the curriculum. They argue that music is not a necessary or useful course. However, the benefits conveyed by music education are tremendous. By developing a child's brain, body, and feelings, music gives the child a better chance to be confident in life. Parents of elementary or secondary school children should play an active role in the success of their children by encouraging them to learn music.

Works Cited

Liu, Liang Y. "Texas School Survey of Substance Use Among Students: Grades 7–12." *Research Archives: School Surveys.* Texas Department of State Health Services, 6 Nov. 2012, https://www.dshs.texas.gov.

Schellenberg, E. Glenn. "Music Lessons Enhance IQ." *Psychological Science* vol. 15, no. 8, 2004, pp. 511–514.

Practice 18

1. Find an example in the essay for each of the following types of support.

   a. Statistic: _____

   _____

   _____

   b. Anecdote: _____

   _____

2. Who is the audience for this essay? _____

   _____

3. How does the writer end the essay?

   a. With a prediction   b. With a quotation   c. With a suggestion

A Professional Argument Essay

Read the professional argument essay from *The Economist* and answer the questions that follow.

Robot Ethics

1.   In the classic science fiction film *2001*, the ship's computer, HAL, faces a dilemma. His instructions require him both to fulfill the ship's mission (investigating an artifact near Jupiter) and to keep the mission's true purpose secret from the ship's crew. To resolve the contradiction, he tries to kill the crew. As robots become more autonomous, the notion of computer-controlled machines facing ethical decisions is moving out of the realm of science fiction and into the real world. Society needs to find ways to ensure that machines are better equipped to make moral judgments than HAL was.

2.   Robots are spreading in the military and civilian worlds. Military technology is at the forefront of the march towards self-determining machines. For example, the Sand Flea can leap through a window or onto a roof, filming all the while. RiSE, a six-legged robo-cockroach, can climb walls. LS3, a dog-like robot, trots behind a human over rough terrain, carrying up to 180 kilograms of supplies. SUGV, a briefcase-sized robot, can identify a man in a crowd and follow him. Robots are spreading in the civilian world, too, from the flight deck to the operating theatre. Passenger aircraft have long been able to land themselves. Fully self-driving vehicles are being tested around the world. Google's driverless cars have clocked up more than 250,000 miles.

3.   As they become smarter and more widespread, autonomous machines are bound to end up making life-or-death decisions in unpredictable situations. Although weapons systems currently have human operators "in the loop," as they grow more sophisticated, they will be able to carry out orders autonomously. When that happens, they will be presented with ethical dilemmas. Should a drone fire on a target's house, which may also be sheltering civilians? Should a driverless car swerve to avoid pedestrians if that means hitting other vehicles or endangering its occupants? Such questions have led to the emergence of the field of "machine ethics," which aims to give machines the ability to make such choices appropriately—in other words, to tell right from wrong.

4.   One way of dealing with these difficult questions is to avoid them altogether, by banning autonomous battlefield robots and requiring cars to have the full attention of a human driver at all times. But autonomous robots could do much more good than harm. Robot soldiers would not commit rape, burn down a village in anger, or become erratic decision-makers amid the stress of combat. Driverless cars are very likely to be safer than ordinary vehicles, as autopilots have made planes safer. Sebastian Thrun, a pioneer in the field, reckons driverless cars could save one million lives a year.

5.   Regulating the development and use of autonomous robots will require progress in three areas in particular. First, laws are needed to determine whether the designer, the programmer, the manufacturer, or the operator is at fault if an autonomous drone strike goes wrong or a driverless car has an accident. In order to allocate responsibility, autonomous systems must keep detailed logs so that they can explain the reasoning behind their decisions. Second, where ethical systems are embedded into robots, the judgments they make need to be ones that seem right to most people. Last, and most important, more collaboration is required between engineers, ethicists, lawyers, and policymakers, all of whom would draw up very different types of rules if they were left to their own devices.

6.   Technology has driven mankind's progress, but each new advance has posed troubling new questions. Autonomous machines are no different. The sooner the questions of moral agency they raise are answered, the easier it will be for mankind to enjoy the benefits that they will undoubtedly bring.

Practice 19

1. Highlight the thesis statement in the introduction.

2. What introductory style opens this essay? Circle the best answer.

   a. Definition   c. General information

   b. Anecdote   d. Opposing viewpoint

3. Underline the topic sentence in each body paragraph.

4. In which paragraph(s) does the writer give the following examples of support?

   an informed opinion: _____

   a series of examples: _____

   a series of questions: _____

5. According to the writer, what should robot experts take into consideration as they develop future robots? _____

   _____

   _____

   _____

   _____

6. Who is the audience for this essay? _____

   _____

7. How does the writer end the essay?

   a. With a prediction   b. With a suggestion   c. With a quotation

The Writer's Room

Writing Topics

Write an argument essay about one of the following topics. Remember to narrow your topic and follow the writing process.

General Topics

1. state-sponsored gambling
2. beauty contests
3. talk shows
4. curfews
5. the healthcare system

College- and Work-Related Topics

6. outsourcing of jobs
7. college sports
8. the cost of a university education
9. student activism
10. dress codes at work

> **PARAGRAPH LINK**
> To practice argument writing, you could develop an essay about one of the topics found in Chapter 12, "Argument."

Argument Essay Checklist

As you write your argument essay, review the essay checklist at the end of the book. Also ask yourself the following questions.

❏ Does my thesis statement clearly state my position on the issue?

❏ Do I include facts, examples, statistics, logical consequences, or answers to my opponents in my body paragraphs?

❏ Do my supporting arguments provide evidence that directly supports each topic sentence?

❏ Do I use transitions that will help readers follow my ideas?

15 Enhancing Your Writing with Research

LEARNING OBJECTIVES

15.1 Explain the purpose of research.

15.2 Research for academic writing.

15.3 Gather information.

15.4 Evaluate sources.

15.5 Add a paraphrase, summary, or quotation.

15.6 Cite sources using MLA style.

15.7 Analyze a sample research essay that uses MLA style.

When you want more information about something, you might talk to other people; look for resources in libraries, bookstores, and museums; make phone calls; search the Internet; and so on. You can use the same tools when looking for details to include in your writing.

What Is Research?

15.1 Explain the purpose of research.

When you **research**, you look for information that will help you better understand a subject. For example, when you read movie reviews in the newspaper, you are engaging in research to make an informed decision about which movie to see. At college, you are often asked to quote outside sources in your essays. This chapter gives some strategies for researching information and effectively adding it to your writing.

Research for Academic Writing

15.2 Research for academic writing.

There is a formal type of writing called the research paper. However, many types of academic essays, especially those with the purpose of persuading, can benefit from research. Additional facts, quotations, and statistics can back up your arguments.

Student writer David Raby-Pepin prepared an argument for an essay about rap music. You may have read his essay in Chapter 13 on page 174. His purpose was to persuade the reader that rap musicians share positive cultural values. The following paragraph is from his essay.

DAVID'S PARAGRAPH WITHOUT RESEARCH

> Many of these musicians shout out a powerful message of nonviolence. Leading hip-hop and rap artists have broken from the gangsta rap lyrics of the past. Instead, they write lyrics that present a productive way to resolve conflicts. They encourage listeners to respect themselves and others.

David's paragraph, although interesting, is not entirely convincing. He mentions that rappers encourage listeners to respect others, but he doesn't give any examples. David decided to do some research to support his points with specific details. He found many Internet sites about his topic that are run by hip-hop fans, but he worried that his readers might be skeptical if he used those sources. He kept searching and found two quotations from reputable sources.

DAVID'S PARAGRAPH WITH RESEARCH

> Leading hip-hop and rap artists have broken from the gangsta rap lyrics of the past. Now, many of these musicians shout out hopeful messages of nonviolence and respect. Instead of expressing anger, they express positive sentiments. For example, the website *Indian Country Today* contains uplifting videos produced by Native Americans. Positive messages include the following words from Cree Nation Artists: "Stay true, stay real, that's the recipe / Even when you're down and out, got no energy / Just look to the sky, let yourself fly free" ("Life"). Some musicians also encourage listeners to respect others and to avoid violent confrontation. At a concert in Connecticut, rapper Edo. G said, "You need to respect your parents, respect your teachers, and respect the police. You need to respect yourselves and stop the violence" (qtd. in Macmillan).

David added two quotations from respected publications. He included the authors' last names in parentheses. Because the publications were on websites, he did not include page numbers in the parentheses.

Later, at the end of his essay, David also included a "Works Cited" page with the following information. (You will learn more about the Works Cited page later in this chapter.)

Works Cited

"Life is So Great! 12 Uplifting Hip Hop Videos by Native Americans." *Indian Country Today Media Network*, 21 Jan. 2015, indiancountrytodaymedianetwork.com/2015/01/21/life-so-great-12-uplifting-hip-hop-videos-native-americans-158784.

Macmillan, Thomas. "Through Hip Hop, Nonviolence Resonates." *New Haven Independent*, 7 May 2009, www.newhavenindependent.org/index.php/archives/entry/through_hip_hop_nonviolence_resonates/.

Gather Information

15.3 Gather information.

To find information that will bolster your essay, consult sources in the library or on the Internet.

Using the Library

When you first enter a library, ask the reference librarian to help you locate information using various research tools, such as online catalogs, CD-ROMs, and microforms.

- **Search the library's online catalog.** You can search by keyword, author, title, or subject. When you find a listing that interests you, remember to jot down the title, author, and call number. You will need that information when you search the library shelves.

- **Use online periodical services in libraries.** Your library may have access to EBSCOhost® or INFOtrac. By typing keywords into EBSCOhost®, you can search through national or international newspapers, magazines, and reference books. When you find an article that you need, email the link to yourself or paste the document into a word processing file. Remember to print or copy the publication data because you will need that information when you cite your source.

Using the Internet

The Internet is a valuable research tool. You will be able to find information about almost any topic online. Here are some tips to help with online research.

- **Use efficient search engines such as Yahoo! or Google Scholar.** These sites can rapidly retrieve thousands of documents from the Internet.

- **Choose your keywords with care.** Narrow your search by entering very specific keywords. For example, to bolster an essay about binge drinking, you might try to find information about deaths due to alcohol poisoning. By placing quotation marks around your key words, you further limit your search. The term *alcohol poisoning deaths* without quotation marks may get more than a million hits. When the same term is enclosed in quotation marks, the number of hits might be reduced to about five hundred, and the displayed pages are more relevant.

- **Use bookmarks.** When you find information that might be useful, create a folder where you can store the information so that you can easily locate it later. (The bookmark icon appears on the toolbar of your search engine.)

WEB ADDRESSES

A Web address (also known as a URL) has the following parts.

Protocol	Host name	Domain name	Document path	Specific topic

http://www.nytimes.com/2008/10/28/technology/28soft.html?ref=business

Sometimes you can determine what type of organization runs the website by looking at the domain, shown by the three letters that follow the site name. However, be careful to always evaluate the site's content.

URL ending	Meaning	Example
.com	Company	www.companyname.com
.edu	Educational institution	www.stateschoolname.edu
.gov	Government	www.governmentagencyname.gov
.org	Organization	www.organizationname.org

HINT: Useful Sites

The following sites could be useful when you research on the Internet. Enter the title of each site into your search engine to access these sites.

Statistics

FedStats (statistics from more than one hundred government agencies)
U.S. Bureau of Labor Statistics
U.S. Census Bureau

News Organizations

Magazine Directory (links to hundreds of online magazines)
Newspapers.com (access to newspapers from all over the world)
New York Times site for college students

Job Sites

Monster.com
Jobs.org

Academic Research Sites

Encyclopedia.com
Encyclopaedia Britannica
Google Scholar

Evaluate Sources

15.4 Evaluate sources.

Be careful when you use Internet sources. Some sites contain misleading information, and some sites are maintained by people who have very strong and specific biases. Remember that the content of Internet sites is not always verified for accuracy. When you view sites, try to determine who benefits from the publication. What is the site's purpose?

HINT: Evaluating a Source

When you find a source, ask yourself the following questions:

- Will the information support the point that I want to make?
- Is the information current? When was the site last updated? Ask yourself if the date is appropriate for your topic.
- Is the site reliable and highly regarded? Is it a well-known newspaper, journal, or site? Is the English grammatically correct?
- Is the author an expert on the subject? (Many sites provide biographical information about the author.)
- Does the author present a balanced view? Ask yourself if the author has a political or financial interest in the issue.
- Does the author develop key ideas with solid supporting facts and examples? Does the author quote reliable sources?
- Is there advertising on the site? Consider how advertising might influence the site's content.

PRACTICE 1

Imagine that you are writing an essay about the effectiveness of antidepressants. Answer the questions by referring to the list of sites on the next page.

1. Write the letters of the three sites that you should investigate further. Briefly explain how each site could be useful.

_____

_____

_____

2. Write the letters of the three sites that are not useful for your essay. For each site, explain why.

_____

_____

_____

_____

A. **Common antidepressant may change brain differently in depressed and non-depressed people**
http://www.sciencedaily.com/releases/2015/09/150904144456.htm
Sept. 4, 2015—A commonly prescribed antidepressant may alter brain structures in depressed and non-depressed individuals in very different ways.

B. **Buy Antidepressants Online**
antidepressants377 . . . com
Jan 20, 2017—Buy **Antidepressants** online and save money. **Antidepressants** buy Easily online. UK buy **Antidepressants** Purchase order **Antidepressants** . . .

C. **Depression: How effective are antidepressants**
http://www.ncbi.nlm.nih.gov/pubmedhealth/PMH0087089/
Jan 18, 2015—Depression: How effective are antidepressants? Like psychotherapy, antidepressants are a key element in treating depression.

D. **Weight Gain and Antidepressants (Including SSRIs)**
www.webmd.com/depression/features/antidepressants-weight-gain . . .
Up to 25% of people who take **antidepressants** gain weight. Is there anything . . . Depression Myths and Facts. What's Causing Your Depression? Getting Help: . . .

E. **Antidepressants suck.**
forums.massassi.net → . . . → Main Massassi Forums → Discussion Forum
Went to the doctors, with the sole purpose of geting my hands on some happy pills. Its a new university year and I have no wish to have mood . . .

F. **In Defense of Antidepressants — NYTimes.com**
www.nytimes.com/2011/07/10/opinion/ . . . /10antidepressants.html? . . .
Jul 9, 2011—IN terms of perception, these are hard times for antidepressants. A number of articles have suggested that the drugs are no more effective than . . .

PRACTICE 2

1. Go to Google, and type *prison reform* in the search bar. How many hits did you get?

_____

2. Now put *prison reform* in quotation marks. How many hits did you get?

_____

3. Find sites with the following domains.

.edu _____

.org _____

.gov _____

4. On a separate sheet of paper, write a paragraph comparing two sites. Choose one that is not reliable and explain why. Then choose a site that is probably quite reliable and explain why. To evaluate the sites, refer to the questions in the "Evaluating a Source" Hint box on page 221.

Keeping Track of Sources

RESEARCH LINK
To find out more about the MLA and its guidelines, visit *MLA.org*.

Source information is easy to find in most print publications. It is usually on the second or third page of the book, magazine, or newspaper. On many Internet sites, however, finding the source information can take more investigative work. When you research on the Internet, look for the home page to find the site's title, publication date, and so on. Record as much of the following information from the site as possible.

Book, Magazine, Newspaper	**Website**
Author's full name	Author's full name
Title of article	Title of article
Title of book, magazine, or newspaper	Title of site
Publishing information (name of publisher, city, and date of publication)	Publisher of site
	Date of publication or updating
Pages used	Date you accessed the site
	Complete site address

Add a Paraphrase, Summary, or Quotation

15.5 **Add a paraphrase, summary, or quotation.**

To add research to a piece of writing, you can paraphrase it, summarize it, or quote it.

- When you **paraphrase**, use your own words to present someone's ideas. A paraphase is about the same length as the original selection.

- When you **summarize**, briefly state the main ideas of another work. A summary is much shorter than the original selection.

- When you **quote**, either directly state a person's exact words (with quotation marks) or report them (without quotation marks).

All of these are valid ways to incorporate research in your writing, as long as you give credit to the author or speaker.

HINT: Avoid Plagiarism!

Plagiarism is the act of using someone else's words or ideas without giving that person credit. Plagiarism is a very serious offense and can result in expulsion from college or termination from work. The following actions are examples of plagiarism.

- Buying another work and presenting it as your own
- Using another student's work and presenting it as your own
- Failing to use quotation marks or properly set off an author's exact words
- Using ideas from another source without citing that source

- Making slight modifications to an author's sentences but presenting the work as your own
- Copying and pasting text from an Internet source without using quotation marks to set off the author's words

To avoid plagiarism, always cite the source when you borrow words, phrases, or ideas from an author. Include the author's name, the title of the work, and the page number (if it is available).

Paraphrasing and Summarizing

Two ways you can avoid plagiarism are paraphrasing and summarizing. Both paraphrases and summaries present the ideas that you have found in a source. The main difference between a paraphrase and summary is the length. While a paraphrase can be the same length as the original selection, a summary is much shorter.

HOW TO PARAPHRASE

To paraphrase, do the following:

- Highlight the main ideas in the original text.
- Restate the main ideas using your own words. You can keep specialized words, common words, and names of people or places. However, find synonyms for other words and use your own sentence structure.
- Use a dictionary or thesaurus, if necessary, to find synonyms.
- Acknowledge the source in the paraphrase or place the source information in parentheses after the paraphrase.
- Maintain the original author's ideas and intent.
- After you finish writing, proofread your text.
- Your paraphrase should be roughly the same length as the original selection.

HOW TO SUMMARIZE

When you summarize, you condense a message to its basic elements. To summarize, do the following:

- Read the original text carefully because you will need a complete picture before you begin to write.
- Ask yourself *who, what, when, where, why,* and *how* questions to help you identify the central idea of the text.
- Acknowledge the source in your summary, or place the source information in parentheses after the summary.
- Reread your summary. Make sure that you have expressed the essential message in your own words.
- Your summary should be a maximum of 30 percent of the length of the original work.

Review examples of an original selection followed by a paraphrase and summary.

Original Selection

Glass provides valuable evidence because we come in contact with it so often. If we were to analyze a piece or pieces of glass, we would ask certain questions. . . . For instance, when we observe glass in a fire scene, is the soot baked on? If so, it was most likely a slow moving fire. If the soot is readily wiped off the glass, then we have a fast moving fire and should look for an accelerant.

—Wilson T. Sullivan III, *Crime Scene Analysis*, p. 135

Paraphrase

Investigators are able to determine the speed of a fire, according to Wilson T. Sullivan III in his book *Crime Scene Analysis*. When soot is difficult to remove from glass, the fire probably burned slowly. If the soot can be removed with ease, the fire burned quickly and may have been aided with some type of gasoline or other catalyst.

Summary

According William T. Sullivan, in his book *Crime Scene Analysis*, glass at a fire scene can give clues to a fire's speed, with easily removed soot indicating that a fire may have been intentionally started.

PRACTICE 3

Paraphrase and summarize the following selections.

1. Several common events occur after a major lottery win. First comes the shock. As Mary Sanderson, a telephone operator in Dover, New Hampshire, who won $66 million, said, "I was afraid to believe that it was real." Mary never slept worse than her first night as a multimillionaire. Then reporters and TV crews appear on the winner's doorstep. They demand to know how the money will be spent. After that, long forgotten friends and distant relatives—who suddenly have emergencies in their lives—call. The winner even gets calls from strangers who have ailing mothers, terminally ill kids, and sick dogs. The normal becomes abnormal, and for some, life falls apart. For instance, in 1998, New Jersey resident Phyllis Klinebiel sued her son Michael for half of his $2 million lottery winnings. And after Mack Metcalf, a forklift operator, won $34 million, his former wife sued him and his current wife divorced him. Within three years, he had drunk himself to death. Sudden wealth, in other words, poses a threat that has to be guarded against. And I can just hear you say, "I'll take the risk."

—James M. Henslin, *Sociology: A Down to Earth Approach*, p. 265

Paraphrase: _____

_____

_____

_____

_____

_____

_____

Summary: _____

_____

_____

2.   Unfortunately, it turns out that hit men, genocidal maniacs, gang leaders, and violent kids often have high self-esteem, not low self-esteem. A recipe for their violence is a mean streak combined with an unwarranted sense of self-worth. When such a boy comes across a girl or parents or schoolmates who communicate to him that he is not all that worthy, he lashes out.

—Martin Seligman, "The American Way of Blame," *APA Monitor Online*

Paraphrase: _____

_____

_____

_____

_____

_____

Summary: _____

_____

_____

_____

GRAMMAR LINK
To find out more about using quotations, see Chapter 35.

Quoting Sources

A **direct quotation** contains the exact words of a source, and the quotation is set off with quotation marks. Use direct quotations to reveal the opinions of an expert or to include ideas that are particularly memorable and important. Quotations should be integrated into sentences, and the source of the quotation should be mentioned either in the introductory phrase or sentence or in parentheses after the quotation. Details about citing sources in the body of your essay appear later in this chapter.

> **EXAMPLE:** In his book *Sociology*, John E. Farley writes, "Human history abounds with legends of lost or deserted children who were raised by wild animals" (97).

HINT: Words That Introduce Quotations

One common way to introduce a quotation is to write *The author says*. However, there are a variety of other verbs that you can use.

admits	comments	explains	mentions	reports	suggests
claims	concludes	maintains	observes	speculates	warns

PRACTICE 4

Read the following selections, and try to identify examples of plagiarism. The original selection, written by Bill Bryson, appeared in *A Short History of Nearly Everything* on page 24.

Original Selection

    Most schoolroom charts show the planets coming one after the other at neighborly intervals, but this is a necessary deceit to get them all on the same piece of paper. . . . Such are the distances, in fact, that it isn't possible, in any practical terms, to draw the solar system to scale. Even if you added lots of fold-out pages to your textbooks or used a really long sheet of poster paper, you wouldn't come close. On a diagram of the solar system to scale, with Earth reduced to about the diameter of a pea, Jupiter would be over a thousand feet away and Pluto would be a mile and a half distant.

1. **Summary**
According to Bill Bryson, in *A Short History of Nearly Everything*, the solar system's true size is too large to show on a piece of paper, even if you added lots of fold-out pages. If you reduced Earth to the diameter of a pea, Jupiter would be over a thousand feet away.

   Is this plagiarism? _____ Yes _____ No

   Why? _____

   _____

2. **Summary**
Bill Bryson cleverly demonstrates how pictures of the solar system are misleading. In fact, our solar system is so immense that a piece of paper would have to be more than a mile long to show all of the planets (24).

   Is this plagiarism? _____ Yes _____ No

   Why? _____

   _____

3. **Summary**
Drawings of the solar system are misleading. Actually, the solar system is so immense that it is not possible, in practical terms, to draw the solar system to scale. If the Earth were depicted as the size of a pea, Pluto would be over a mile away.

   Is this plagiarism? _____ Yes _____ No

   Why? _____

   _____

Cite Sources Using MLA Style

15.6 Cite sources using MLA style.

Each time you use another writer's words or ideas, you must **cite the source**, giving complete information about the original document from which you borrowed the material. When quoting, paraphrasing, or summarizing, you can set off the source information using parentheses. These **in-text citations**, also known as **parenthetical citations**, allow you to acknowledge where you obtained the information. You must also cite your sources in an alphabetized list at the end of your essay. The Modern Language Association (MLA) refers to the list as Works Cited.

HINT: Choose a Documentation Style

Common styles for documenting sources are the Modern Language Association (MLA) format, *Chicago Manual of Style* (CMS) format, the American Psychological Association (APA), and the Council of Science Editors (CSE) format. Before writing a paper, check with your instructor to see which documentation style you should use and to learn where you can find more information about it.

Citing the Source in the Body of Your Essay

When you paraphrase, summarize, or quote, you must cite the source in the body of the essay. You must also cite the source in a Works Cited page at the end of your essay. See page 229 to view the Works Cited page for the following quotations.

There are two ways to show that you have borrowed an idea or quotation: cite the source in the sentence or cite the source in parentheses.

Source	Source cited in the sentence	Source cited in parentheses
Print	Mention the author's name in the sentence. Include the page number in parentheses.	Put the author's last name and the page number in parentheses.
	In *Critical Issues in Criminal Justice*, Ronald Burns says, "Bike theft may seem like petty street crime, but it's actually a humming illegal industry" (26).	One expert says, "In the wide world of illegal activity, bike thievery seems to occupy a criminal sweet spot" (Burns 27).
Internet	For online sources, just mention the author's name. No page number is necessary.	For online sources, just put the author's last name in parentheses.
	Jane E. Brody discusses the dangers when women smoke: "Today, women who smoke are even more likely than men who smoke to die of lung cancer."	Women should think twice before smoking: "Today, women who smoke are even more likely than men who smoke to die of lung cancer" (Brody).
	If an online source does not provide an author's name, mention the article's title or the site title in the sentence.	If the online source does not provide an author's name, write a short form of the title in parentheses.
	According to "Bipolar Support and Self Help," not all people use medications: "Living well with bipolar disorder requires certain adjustments."	Not all people use medications: "Living well with bipolar disorder requires certain adjustments" ("Bipolar").

GRAMMAR HINT: Quoting from a Secondary Source

Sometimes you may want to quote from an indirect source. If your source material contains a quotation from someone, then put the abbreviation **qtd. in**—which means *quoted in*—in the parentheses.

> Dr. Lauren Streicher says, "There are a lot of profit-motivated physicians out there" (qtd. in Parikh).

See Chapter 35 for more information about using quotations.

Preparing an MLA Works Cited Page

The Works Cited page gives details about each source you have used, and it appears at the end of your essay. To prepare it, follow these basic guidelines.

1. On a new page, write "Works Cited" at the top and center it. Make sure your last name and page number appear in the upper-right corner.
2. List each source alphabetically, using the author's last name. If no author is mentioned, use the title.
3. Indent the second line and all subsequent lines of each reference.
4. Double-space the entire page.

A Works Cited entry generally has the following parts, with the order and punctuation shown below.

1. Author	Complete last name, first name
2. Title of Source:	
-Title of short work	"Article" or "Short Story"
-Title of long work	*Book* or *Magazine* or *Website Name*

3. Container (information to identify the location of the source)

-Title of container where the source can be found	Title of *Book*, *Series*, *Journal*, or *Website*
-Other contributors	Edited by, Translated by, Illustrated by, Adapted by, Directed by, and Narrated by
-Version	2nd ed., 3rd ed., or Updated ed.
-Volume and issue numbers	vol. 8, no. 4
-Publisher	Complete Name of Company or Organization (unless the Website name is essentially the same as the publisher's name)
-Date of publication and	2018
-Time of publication for a webpage	11:15 a.m.
-Page number(s) in print sources	p. 53 or pp. 783–787
-Website URL (omit the http://) or Digital Object Identifier (DOI)	

HINT: Placement and Order of Works Cited

The Works Cited list should be at the end of the research paper. List sources in alphabetical order of the authors' last names. If there is no author, put the title in the alphabetized list. The example is a Works Cited page for the quotations listed on page 228.

Works Cited

"Bipolar Support and Self-Help." *HelpGuide.org*, 15 May 2016, www.helpguide.org/ articles/bipolar-disorder/bipolar-support-and-self-help.htm.

Brody, Jane E., "Smoking Gender Gap Closes." *The New York Times*, 15 May 2013, well.blogs.nytimes.com/2013/02/18/women-smokers-catch-up/?_r=0.

Burns, Ronald G. *Critical Issues in Criminal Justice.* Pearson, 2009. pp. 26–27.

Model Entries

BOOK

comma	period		period	comma		comma	period

Last name, First name. *Title of the Book*. edition, Publisher, Year.

One author

Scupin, Raymond. *Cultural Anthropology*. 9th ed., Pearson, 2016.

Two authors

After the first author's last and first name, put *and* followed by the first and last name of the subsequent author.

Ember, Carol R., and Melvin Ember. *Cultural Anthropology*. 14th ed., Pearson, 2015.

Three or more authors

Put the first author's name followed by *et al.,* which means "and others."

Manza, Jeff, et al. *The Sociology Project 2.0*. Pearson, 2016.

Work in an anthology

For articles or essays taken from an anthology, write "edited by" and the editor's name after the title.

> Budnitz, Judy. "Nadia." *The Best American Nonrequired Reading*, edited by Dave Eggers, Houghton Mifflin, Harcourt, 2006, pp. 89–112.

Encyclopedia or dictionary

It is unnecessary to mention volume and page numbers. Simply list the edition and year of publication.

> "Morocco." *Columbia Encyclopedia.* 6th ed., 2005.

> "Democracy." *The New American Webster Handy College Dictionary.* 3rd ed., 1995.

PERIODICAL

> Last name, First name. "Title of Article." *Title of Magazine, Newspaper, or Journal*, volume, number, date, pages.

Note: If the pages are not consecutive, put the first page number and a plus sign (15+).

Newspaper article

> Freed, Curt. "Why True Marriage Equality Matters to Us." *Seattle Times*, 31 Oct. 2015, A5.

Magazine article

> Thurman, Judith. "Drawn From Life." *The New Yorker*, 23 Apr. 2012, pp. 49–55.

ELECTRONIC (INTERNET) SOURCE

When using a source published on the Internet, include as much of the following information as you can find. Keep in mind that some sites do not contain complete information. **Include the complete Web address but omit "http://".**

> Last name, First name. "Title of Article." *Title of Site or Online Publication, Publisher or Sponsor (if available)*, Date, URL or DOI.

Online newspaper article

> Floyd, Jacquielynn. "Armed and Angry, the Formula for Gun Violence." *The Dallas Morning News*, 28 Aug. 2015, www.dallasnews.com/news/columnists/jacquielynn-floyd/20150827-armed-and-angry-the-formula-for-gun-violence.ece.

Online magazine article

> Poniewozik, James. "Stephen Colbert's Night Vision." *Time*, 27 Aug. 2015, time.com/4012855/stephen-colberts-night-vision/.

Online scholarly journal

> Glendinning, Laura, et. al. "Variability of the Sheep Lung Microbiota." *Applied and Environmental Microbiology*, vol. 82, no. 12, June 2016, American Society for Microbiology, doi: 10.1128/AEM.00540-16.

Online dictionary

"Ubiquitous." *Longman Dictionary of Contemporary English*. Pearson ELT, 2014.

Social Media

Last name, First name (or in a Tweet, the user name). "Entire tweet or first few words of Facebook update." Date posted, Time viewed, URL.

@dottynixon. "For my next writing project, finally got around to reading the Canadian Constitution. Funny what work you put off. #cdnpoli." *Twitter*, 15 Mar. 2016, 7:17 a.m., twitter.com/dottynixon.

Paranjape, Meghana. "Monkeying around in the forest . . . ." *Facebook*, 30 Mar. 2015, 2:18 p.m., www.facebook.com/meghana.paranjape?fref=ts.

E-Book

Format the e-book like the print copy. If possible, include the chapter number.

McKenna, Christina. *The Misremembered Man*. AmazonEncore, 2008, www.amazon.com/Misremembered-Man-Christina-McKenna-ebook/dp/B004ZMWUCU/ref=asap_bc?ie=UTF8.

Web-only article

Doig, Will. "It's Time to Love the Bus." *Salon*, 3 Mar. 2012, www.salon.com/2012/03/03/its_time_to_love_the_bus/.

No listed author

If the site does not list an author's name, begin with the title of the article.

"How to Detect Lies." *Bifaloo.com*, 2012, www.blifaloo.com/info/lies.php.

OTHER SOURCES

Film or DVD

For a film, include the names of the most relevant contributors to the project. For instance, you could include the name of the director and/or main performers. Also mention the studio and the year of release. For an online video, include the website link.

If the video is long, include the exact time of the video that you are referencing in your in-text citation.

The Jungle Book. Directed by Jon Favreau, performance by Idris Elba, Walt Disney Pictures, 2016.

"Vladimir Putin Documentary." *60 Minutes*. Interview by Charlie Rose, CBSnews, 7 Dec. 2015, www.cbsnews.com/news/60-minutes-a-new-direction-on-drugs-2/.

Sound recording

Include the name of the performer or band, the title of the song, the title of the CD, the name of the recording company, and the year of release. If it is a digital source, include the URL.

Charles, Ray. "Fever." *Genius Loves Company*, Hear Music, 2004.

Television or radio program

Include the segment title, the narrator (if applicable), the program name, the station, and the broadcast date.

"Hands Off the Wheel." *60 Minutes*, narrated by Bill Whitaker, CBS, 4 Oct. 2015.

PRACTICE 5

Imagine that you are using the following sources in a research paper. Arrange the sources for a Works Cited list using MLA style. You can type your Works Cited list on a separate piece of paper. Double-space each entry, and indent the second line of each entry.

- You use a definition of "honesty" from the online dictionary *Merriam-Webster*. The publication date is 2016, and the URL is www.merriam-webster.com/dictionary/honesty.

- You use statistics from an article called "Honesty/Ethics in Professions." The website is *Gallup*, and the publication date is Dec. 6, 2015. The URL is www.gallup.com/poll/1654/honesty-ethics-professions.aspx.

- You quote from a book by Dan Ariely called *The (Honest) Truth about Dishonesty*. The publisher is HarperCollins, and the publication date is 2012.

- You quote from page 231 of the textbook *Psychology* by Saundra K. Ciccarelli and J. Noland White. It is the fourth edition. The publisher is Pearson, and the publication date is 2015.

- You quote from the article "The King of Human Error" by Michael Lewis. It appeared in a magazine called *Vanity Fair*, which was published in December 2011. Your quote was from page 153.

- You quote from an online magazine called *Salon*. "I Was a Lying Psychic" was written by Erin Auerbach and published on March 26, 2015. The URL is www.salon.com/2015/03/26/i_was_a_lying_telephone_psychic/.

Works Cited

_____

_____

_____

_____

_____

_____

_____

_____

_____

_____

_____

_____

_____

_____

_____

_____

_____

Sample Research Essay Using MLA Style

15.7   **Analyze a sample research essay that uses MLA style.**

Although MLA does not insist on an outline for a research essay, your instructor may request one.

Outline

Thesis: The virtual office has negative effects on workers, including decreased structure, increased distraction, and lack of human interaction.

I. There is less structure for employees.
   A. Traditional office provides fixed hours and clear tasks.
   B. Virtual offices lack a central meeting place.
   C. My cousin lacked discipline when he worked at home.
II. Furthermore, workers in virtual offices are more prone to being distracted.
   A. Citrix survey shows decreased productivity (Wong).
   B. People play games, nap, and clean the house instead of working.
   C. My cousin played Scrabble during working hours.
III. The most serious issue with virtual offices is the lack of human interaction.
   A. Cornell study shows that virtual workers miss socializing.
   B. Coworkers provide people with an important social group.
   C. People are happier, more loyal, and more productive in regular workplaces.

The Research Essay

Read the complete student essay that follows. Notice how the student integrates paraphrases, summaries, and quotations.

Cahoon 1

Samuel Cahoon

Professor Darrington

Composition 101

25 November 2016

The Virtual Office: Why It's Problematic

Imagine a middle-aged woman rolling out of bed. With a yawn, she walks over to her couch, and she turns on her laptop. Still in her pajamas, the woman groggily checks her email, texts her coworkers, and responds to clients. She has become a dehumanized robot, isolated in her ideas, and stuck in her home with no separation between her career and personal life. In the 21st century, such detrimental routines are an increasing part of society. By the end of

> Put your last name and page number at the top of each page.

> Double-space your name, instructor's name, course title, and date.

> Center the title without underlining, italics, or boldface type.

> Double-space throughout. Use 12 pt. Times New Roman typeface.

Cahoon 2

It is not necessary to document your common knowledge.

Cite the source of a paraphrase.

End your introduction with a thesis statement.

If the author is not known, put the first word of the title in parentheses.

You can integrate a quotation into a sentence.

Place the author's last name in parentheses.

Three spaced periods indicate that part of the quotation has been deleted. The word in square brackets shows an added word.

Include the page number of a print source.

2016, America's virtual office worker population will reach 43 percent of the total workforce, according to Forrester Research (Narayanan). The virtual office has negative effects on workers, including less structure, more distractions, and lack of human interaction.

Although virtual offices may provide economic benefits for businesses, one noticeable disadvantage is decreased structure for employees. In a traditional brick-and-mortar office, workers have an organized and planned day, with fixed hours of operation and clear tasks. Employees interact, share ideas, and meet expectations. Virtual offices lack a central meeting room: "Essentially, there is no home base office for employees to report to or meet with colleagues ("Advantages")." My cousin, for instance, worked at home as an editor for two years. He lost the job because he missed deadlines. He did not have self-discipline, and he procrastinated because nobody was watching him closely. He now admits that he needs the structure and support that an office environment provides.

Furthermore, workers in virtual offices are more prone to being distracted. A new survey by Citrix, a company that designs technology for virtual offices, shows that productivity has decreased as virtual office workers are distracted by day-by-day life. Based on a survey of 1,013 American office workers, conducted in June 2012, "43 percent watch TV or a movie and 20 percent play video games during work hours, and 26 percent say they take naps. Others are distracted by housekeeping" (Wong). My cousin says that he often played Scrabble on his iPad instead of working. Such distractions decrease productivity because workers naturally combine their personal and work lives.

The most serious issue with virtual offices is the lack of human interaction. Many companies have attempted to fulfill this need by using groupware tools and organization programs, but such tools are inadequate. Human beings enjoy and need group interaction. John J. Macionis states, "Almost everyone wants a sense of belonging . . . [and] members of social groups think of themselves as a special 'we'" (180). In an office, staff members bond and form meaningful connections. Ben Waber, owner of Sociometric Solutions in Boston, believes in on-site office

Cahoon 3

collaboration: "If you're surrounded by friends, you're happier, you're more loyal, you're more productive" (qtd. in Stewart). Although technology provides the means for people to connect electronically with one another, it is not a substitute for rich meaningful face-to-face interactions.

> You can introduce a quotation with a complete sentence.

There are workplace models that are more effective than virtual offices. Google, for instance, has an effective business model. Although some Google employees are permitted to work from home, on a case-by-case basis, that is not the norm. The company fosters an environment of togetherness through the sharing of meals, ideas, and on-site recreational activities. Mr. Neville-Manning, Google's engineering director, says, "Google's success depends on innovation and collaboration. Everything we did was geared toward making it easy to talk" (qtd. in Stewart). The most efficient and innovative businesses know that the highest bandwidth network is found between the water fountain and the coffee machine, in the cafeteria line, and across the conference table in face-to-face interaction.

> Use "qtd. in" to show that the quotation appeared in a secondary source.

Cahoon 4

Works Cited

"Advantages and Disadvantages of Virtual Offices." *Telsec*, 14 Jan. 2014, www.telsec.net/blog/advantages-and-disadvantages-of-virtual-offices/.

Macionis, John J. *Sociology*. 15th ed., Pearson, 2014.

Narayanan, Naveen. "The New Workplace Reality: Out Of The Office." *Wired*, Conde Nast, 2013, www.wired.com/insights/2013/06/the-new-workplace-reality-out-of-the-office/.

Stewart, James B. "Looking for a Lesson in Google's Perks." *The New York Times*, 15 Mar. 2013, www.nytimes.com/2013/03/16/business/at-google-a-place-to-work-and-play.html.

Wong, Venessa. "What People Really Do When They're 'Working From Home.'" *Bloomberg Business Week*, 25 June 2012, www.bloomberg.com/news/articles/2012-06-25/what-people-really-do-when-theyre-working-from-home.

> Put the Works Cited list on a separate page.

> Center the "Works Cited" heading.

> Place sources in alphabetical order.

> If the source has no known author, begin with the title.

> Double-space throughout, and indent the second line of each source.

Reflect On It

Think about what you have learned in this chapter. If you do not know an answer, review that topic.

1. What are the differences between a paraphrase and a summary?

Paraphrase	Summary
_____	_____
_____	_____
_____	_____

2. What is a Works Cited page?

_____

_____

_____

The Writer's Room

Writing Activity 1

Choose a paragraph or an essay that you have written, and research your topic to get more detailed information. Then insert at least one paraphrase, one summary, and one quotation into your work. Remember to acknowledge your sources.

Writing Activity 2

Write an essay about one of the following topics. Your essay should include research (find at least three sources). Include a Works Cited page at the end of your assignment.

1. Write about a controversial issue that is in the news. In your essay, give your opinion about the issue.
2. Write about your career choice. You could mention job opportunities in your field, and you could include statistical information.
3. Write about the importance of daily exercise. Find some facts, examples, or statistics to support your view.

Part IV
The Editing Handbook

Why Is Grammar so Important?

When you speak, you have tools such as tone of voice and body language to help express ideas. When you write, however, you have only words and punctuation to get the message across. Naturally, if your writing contains errors in style, grammar, and punctuation, you may distract readers from the message, and they may focus instead on your inability to communicate clearly. You increase the chances of succeeding in your academic and professional life when you write in clear standard English.

The chapters in this Editing Handbook can help you understand important grammar concepts and ensure that your writing is grammatically correct.

16 Subjects and Verbs in Simple Sentences

SECTION THEME: Popular Culture

LEARNING OBJECTIVES

16.1 Identify subjects.

16.2 Identify prepositional phrases.

16.3 Identify verbs.

16.4 Identify helping verbs.

In this chapter, you read about topics related to advertising and consumerism.

The Writer's Journal

What is your cultural background? How would you identify yourself culturally? Write a paragraph about your cultural identity.

Identify Subjects

16.1   Identify subjects.

A **sentence** contains one or more subjects and verbs, and it expresses a complete thought. Although some sentences can have more than one idea, a **simple sentence** expresses one complete thought. The **subject** tells you who or what the sentence is about. The **verb** expresses an action or a state. If a sentence is missing a subject or a verb, it is incomplete.

Singular and Plural Subjects

Subjects may be singular or plural. To determine the subject of a sentence, ask yourself who or what the sentence is about.

A **singular subject** is one person, place, or thing.

> **Kayla Rice** is a marketing consultant.
>
> **Manhattan** has many advertising agencies.

A **plural subject** is more than one person, place, or thing.

> Contemporary **marketers** try to reach a mass audience.
>
> Many **countries** import American products.

Pronouns

A **subject pronoun** (*he, she, it, you, I, we, they*) can act as the subject of a sentence, and it replaces the noun.

> Jeff Bezos sold books. **He** founded Amazon.com.
>
> Consumers have rights. **They** can complain about unethical advertising.

Gerunds (*-ing* words)

Sometimes a gerund (*-ing* form of the verb) is the subject of a sentence.

> **Advertising** surrounds us.
>
> **Business planning** is an ongoing process.

Compound Subjects

Some subjects are made up of more than one noun. *Compound* means "multiple." Therefore, a **compound subject** contains two or more subjects.

> **Men** and **women** evaluate products differently.
>
> The **accountants**, **designers**, and **managers** will meet to discuss the product launch.

HINT: Recognizing Simple and Complete Subjects

In a sentence, the **simple subject** is the noun or pronoun. The complete name of a person, place, or organization is a simple subject.

> he   dancer   Omar Epps   Sony Music Corporation

The **complete subject** is the noun, plus the words that describe the noun. In the next examples, the descriptive words are in italics.

> *new electric* piano   *old, worn-out* shoes   *Anna's green* sofa

In the following sentences, the simple and complete subjects are identified.

> simple subject
> The glossy new **magazine** contained interesting articles.
> complete subject

Practice 1

Underline the complete subject and circle the simple subject(s).

EXAMPLE: Academic (institutions) teach popular culture.

1. Popular music, films, books, and fashions are the sources of our common culture.

2. Marketing is linked to all types of entertainment.

3. You and your friends and family may see hundreds of ads each day.

4. Jack Nevin and Linda Gorchels study consumer behavior.

5. Traditional marketing methods are losing their impact.

6. Restless and cynical citizens are bored with television, radio, billboard, and even pop-up ads.

7. Creative advertisers constantly look for new ways to seduce the public.

8. Social networking sites are now targeted by marketing firms.

9. Other strategies include buzz marketing and guerilla marketing.

10. Expensive advertising does not always produce results.

Special Subject Problems

UNSTATED SUBJECTS (COMMANDS)

In a sentence that expresses a command, the subject is unstated, but it is still understood. The unstated subject is *you*, and "should" is implied.

> Remember to use your coupon.
> Pay the cashier.
> Do not use a credit card.

Here/There

Here and *there* are not subjects. In a sentence that begins with *Here* or *There*, the subject follows the verb.

> There are five **ways** to market a product.
> Here is an interesting **brochure** about cosmetics.

Practice 2

In the following paragraph, circle the simple subject(s). If the subject is unstated, then write the subject (*you*) before the verb.

EXAMPLE: To see the announcement, you (should) watch carefully.

    There are many advertisements on the streets of our cities. Look at any bus shelter, billboard, store window, or newspaper. Certainly, some ads appear in surprising places. There are framed announcements on the doors of hotel bathrooms, for example. Furthermore, there are commercials hidden in the middle of the action in movies and television shows. For instance, soft-drink and car companies advertise during the popular reality show *American Idol*. There are soft drinks on the table in front of the show's judges. The show's performers often sing a tribute to an American automobile company. View advertising with a critical eye.

Identify Prepositional Phrases

16.2 Identify prepositional phrases.

A **preposition** is a word that links nouns, pronouns, or phrases to other words in a sentence. It expresses a relationship based on movement or position. Here are some common prepositions.

Common Prepositions					
about	around	beyond	from	off	to
above	at	by	in	on	toward
across	before	despite	inside	onto	under
after	behind	down	into	out	until
against	below	during	like	outside	up
along	beside	except	near	over	with
among	between	for	of	through	within

A **phrase** is a group of words that is missing a subject, a verb, or both and is not a complete sentence. A **prepositional phrase** is made up of a preposition and its object (a noun or a pronoun). In the following phrases, an object follows the preposition.

Preposition	+	**Object**
in		the morning
among		the shadows
over		the rainbow

HINT: Be Careful

Because the object of a preposition is a noun, it may look like a subject. However, the object in a prepositional phrase is *never* the subject of the sentence. For example, in the next sentence, the subject is *child*, not *cereal box*.

subject

Inside the cereal box, the **child** found the hidden gift.

Sometimes a prepositional phrase appears before or after the subject. For help in identifying the subject of a sentence, you can put parentheses around prepositional phrases or mark them in some other way. In each of the following sentences, the subject is in boldface type and the prepositional phrase is in parentheses.

(With huge sales,) **Amazon** is an amazing success story.

Jeff Bezos, (with very little money,) launched his website.

Sometimes a sentence can contain more than one prepositional phrase.

prepositional phrase   prepositional phrase
(In the mid 1990s,) (inside his Seattle garage,) **Bezos** created his online bookstore.

HINT: According to . . .

When a sentence contains *according to*, the noun that immediately follows is *not* the subject of the sentence. In the following sentence, *Jack Solomon* is not the subject.

subject
(According to Jack Solomon,) **consumers** are easily persuaded.

Practice 3

Circle the simple subject in each sentence. Optional: For help in finding the simple subject, you can place parentheses around prepositional phrase(s).

EXAMPLE: (In a bus), a young (girl) uses her phone (to shop online).

1. In 2014, American businesses sold over $260 billion worth of goods on the Internet .

2. By 2020, Internet retailers will increase their sales to over $400 billion .

3. Consumers between the ages of eighteen and forty years old bought a quarter of their holiday gifts online in 2014 .

4. According to *Millennial Marketing,* young adults are more likely to "impulse shop" online than at a store .

5. Even large stores, like Wal-Mart or Sears, have moved more of their sales online.

6. According to *Forbes* journalist Barbara Thau, many physical retail outlets in North America will close over the next few years .

7. With their flexible business models, new Internet entrepreneurs can build companies for very little money .

8. The American company Bumblebee Linens, with only $630 in startup money, built a million-dollar online business.

9. Despite thousands of existing boutiques and malls, online shopping is here to stay.

Practice 4

Look at the underlined word in each sentence. If it is the subject, write *C* (for "correct") beside the sentence. If the underlined word is not the subject, then circle the correct subject(s).

EXAMPLES: In past eras, bustling (markets) contained consumer goods. _____

Enclosed shopping malls are a fairly recent development. <u>c</u>_____

1. In Edina, Minnesota, the first indoor mall was built. _____

2. The world's largest mall has eight hundred stores. _____

3. For some <u>shopaholics</u>, a sale is a dangerous thing. _____

4. On her twenty-second <u>birthday</u>, Amber Wyatt divulged a secret. _____

5. During the previous four years, <u>she</u> had piled up $60,000 in credit card debts. _____

6. She acknowledges, with a shrug, her shopping <u>addiction</u>. _____

7. Today, with a poor credit <u>rating</u>, Amber is unable to get a lease. _____

8. Her <u>brother</u>, boyfriend, and aunt have lent her money. _____

9. Her <u>parents</u>, with some reluctance, allowed their daughter to move back home. _____

10. Many <u>American</u> men and women, according to a recent survey, have a shopping addiction. _____

Identify Verbs

16.3 **Identify verbs.**

Every sentence must contain a verb. The **verb** either expresses what the subject does or links the subject to other descriptive words.

Action Verbs

An **action verb** describes an action that a subject performs.

> In 2006, China <u>launched</u> an electric car called the ZAP Xebra.

> Engineers <u>designed</u> the car's energy-efficient engine.

Linking Verbs

A **linking verb** connects a subject with words that describe it, and it does not show an action. The most common linking verb is *be*.

> The marketing campaign <u>is</u> expensive.

> Some advertisements <u>are</u> very clever.

Other linking verbs refer to the senses and indicate how something appears, smells, tastes, and so on.

> The advertising photo <u>looks</u> grainy.

> The glossy paper <u>feels</u> smooth.

Common Linking Verbs		
appear	feel	smell
be (am, is, are, was, were, etc.)	look	sound
become	seem	taste

Compound Verbs

When a subject performs more than one action, the sentence has a **compound verb**.

> Good advertising <u>informs</u>, <u>persuades</u>, and <u>convinces</u> consumers.

> Members of the public either <u>loved</u> or <u>hated</u> the logo.

HINT: Infinitives Are Not the Main Verb

Verbs preceded by *to* such as *to fly*, *to speak*, and *to go* are infinitives. An infinitive is never the main verb in a sentence.

          V   infinitive   V   infinitive

Kraft wants **to compete** in Asia. The company hopes **to sell** millions of products.

Practice 5

Underline one or more main verbs in these sentences. Remember that infinitives such as *to sell* are not part of the main verb. Write *L* above two linking verbs.

EXAMPLE: Our consumer culture <u>affects</u> everyone.

1. Before the 1940s, diamonds were not more popular than other stones.

2. During marriage ceremonies, a groom gave a simple gold or silver band to his bride.

3. Then, in 1947, Frances Gerety created the best marketing slogan in history.

4. A diamond is forever.

5. The slogan connected diamonds with love and marriage.

6. De Beers also paid Hollywood stars to pose with diamond engagement rings.

7. The advertising campaign had a huge impact on diamond sales.

8. The emotional appeals changed people's buying habits.

9. Marketers produced an irrational demand for an expensive product.

10. Today, the majority of brides expect to receive a diamond ring.

Identify Helping Verbs

16.4 Identify helping verbs.

A verb can have several different forms, depending on the tense that is used. **Verb tense** indicates whether the action occurred in the past, present, or future. In some tenses, there is a **main verb** that expresses what the subject does or links the subject to descriptive words, but there is also a helping verb.

    The **helping verb** combines with the main verb to indicate tense, negative structure, or question structure. The most common helping verbs are forms of *be*, *have*, and *do*. **Modal auxiliaries** are another type of helping verb; they indicate ability (*can*), obligation (*must*), possibility (*may, might, could*), advice (*should*), and so on. For example, here are different forms of the verb *open*. The helping verbs are underlined.

<u>is</u> opening	<u>had</u> opened	<u>will</u> open	<u>should have</u> opened
<u>was</u> opened	<u>had been</u> opening	<u>can</u> open	<u>might be</u> open
<u>has been</u> opening	<u>would</u> open	<u>could be</u> opening	<u>could have been</u> opened

The **complete verb** consists of the helping verb and the main verb. In the following examples, the helping verbs are indicated with *HV* and the main verbs with *V*.

HV HV   V

American culture has been spreading across the globe for years.

HV HV V

You must have seen the news articles.

In **question forms**, the first helping verb usually appears before the subject.

HV   subject   HV   V

Should the coffee chain have expanded so quickly?

HV   subject   V

Will the coffee and cakes sell in Moscow?

Interrupting words may appear between verbs, but they are *not* part of the verb. Some interrupting words are *easily, actually, not, always, usually, sometimes, frequently, often, never,* and *ever.*

HV   V

Consumers have often complained about product quality.

HV   HV   V

The car maker should not have destroyed its electric cars.

Practice 6

Underline the helping verbs once and the main verbs twice. Be careful because some sentences only have main verbs.

EXAMPLE: In 2008, a global recession affected many people financially.

1. How should the government protect consumers?

2. In 2008, the financial crisis destroyed many businesses and bankrupted thousands of people.

3. That same year, the Consumer Financial Protection Bureau (CFPB) was created.

4. In fact, before the crisis, the idea for the CFPB had been discussed in an article by Harvard professor Elizabeth Warren.

5. According to the CFPB, credit-card companies should not charge such high interest rates.

6. Banks should never deceive people about their mortgage rates.

7. These institutions must also provide consumers with clearer, more accurate information.

8. Some banks and mortgage companies had been criticized for their practices before 2008.

9. Ocwen Financial Services, a mortgage and loan company, was required to reduce the amount of interest on its loans by over $2 billion.

GRAMMAR LINK
For information on the position of mid-sentence adverbs, such as often, sometimes, and never, see page 393 in Chapter 30.

10. Some companies have been sued for racial discrimination in mortgage lending.

11. To protect consumers, the CFPB has implemented rules to address the systemic misconduct of banks and credit-card companies.

12. The organization has continued to fight for new regulations in the financial industry.

Practice 7

Circle the simple subjects and underline the complete verbs. Remember to underline all parts of the verb.

EXAMPLE: Have (you) been lured in by click-bait?

1. In 2006, Jonah Peretti started the website Buzzfeed as a "viral lab" in New York City. He has had great success using the click-bait model. Freelance writers and photographers contribute to the site. Buzzfeed is not trying to be a traditional news organization. Instead of posting investigative or breaking news stories, the site offers the most "shareable" articles and photos on the Web. Many competitors have tried to copy Buzzfeed's style. These media companies use catchy headlines and "Top 10" lists instead of traditional news stories. For example, a clever strategy is to create a "curiosity gap." One popular tactic on sites like Buzzfeed is an open question about something controversial or shocking. Another model of "shareable" articles challenges readers to complete quizzes. These headlines convince people to fill the curiosity gap by clicking on the link. Some critics have complained about the celebrity look-alike quizzes and cute cat, dog, and baby images.

2. Advertisers love the click-bait model. The articles and photos receive millions of page views. Then readers see and buy the advertised products. Each article does not cost a lot. Buzzfeed, for instance, spends very little on its content. Such sites do not need to pay for traditional reporting. Do those sites mislead people? It is easy to dismiss the click-bait model as silly or deceitful. However, with high Web traffic and a lot of advertising dollars, Buzzfeed and other websites deserve to be taken seriously.

Reflect On It

Think about what you have learned in this chapter. If you do not know an answer, review that concept.

1. What is a sentence? _____

_____

2. What does the subject of a sentence do? _____

_____

3. What is a verb? _____

_____

4. Write an example of a linking verb and an action verb.

   Linking _____ Action _____

Circle the best answers.

5. Can the object of a preposition be the subject of a sentence?   No   Yes
6. Can a sentence have more than one subject?   No   Yes
7. Can a sentence have more than one verb?   No   Yes

Final Review

Circle the simple subjects, and underline the complete verbs. Underline *all* parts of the verb. Remember that infinitives such as *to go* or *to run* are not part of the main verb.

EXAMPLE: A good (name) and (logo) are immensely important.

1. In their book *Marketing: Real People, Real Choices*, Michael R. Solomon, Greg Marshall, and Elnora Stuart discuss brands. 2. With a great deal of care, companies must carefully choose the best name for their products. 3. According to the authors, product names should be memorable. 4. Irish Spring, for instance, is a fresh and descriptive name for soap.

5. Occasionally, mistakes are made. 6. The company Toro called its lightweight snow blower "Snow Pup." 7. The product did not sell well. 8. Later, the product was renamed "Snow Master" and then "Snow Commander." 9. The sales have improved tremendously since then.

10. Some brands have become the product name in consumers' minds. 11. Everyone knows popular brands such as Kleenex, Jell-O, Scotch Tape, and Kool-Aid. 12. Without a second thought, many consumers will ask for a Kleenex but not for a tissue with another brand name. 13. Therefore, a great name can be linked to the product indefinitely.

14. According to Solomon, Marshall, and Stuart, there are four important elements in a good brand name. 15. It must be easy to say, easy to spell, easy to read, and easy to remember. 16. Apple, Coke, and Dove are examples of great product names. 17. Good names should also have a positive or functional relationship with the product. 18. Drano is a very functional name. 19. On the other hand, Pampers and Luvs suggest good parenting but have no relation to the function of diapers. 20. Ultimately, large and small businesses put a great deal of care into product branding.

The Writer's Room

Write about one of the following topics. After you finish writing, identify your subjects and verbs.

1. Describe an effective advertising campaign. List the elements that make the campaign so successful.

2. Compare two online shopping sites. Describe the positive and negative features of each site.

17 Compound Sentences

SECTION THEME: Popular Culture

LEARNING OBJECTIVES

17.1 Compare simple and compound sentences.

17.2 Combine sentences using coordinating conjunctions.

17.3 Combine sentences using semicolons.

17.4 Combine sentences using transitional expressions.

In this chapter, you read about topics related to fads and fashions.

The Writer's Journal

Do you have body art, such as tattoos and piercings? In a paragraph, explain why you do or do not have body art.

Compare Simple and Compound Sentences

17.1 Compare simple and compound sentences.

When you use sentences of varying lengths and types, your writing flows more smoothly and appears more interesting. You can vary sentences and create relationships between ideas by combining sentences.

Review the differences between simple and compound sentences.

A **simple sentence** is an independent clause. It expresses one complete idea, and it stands alone. Simple sentences can have more than one subject and more than one verb.

One subject and verb	Tattooing <u>is</u> not a new fashion.
Two subjects	<u>Tattooing</u> and <u>body piercing</u> <u>are</u> not new fashions.
Two verbs	<u>Della McMahon</u> <u>speaks</u> and <u>writes</u> about current trends.

A **compound sentence** contains two or more simple sentences. The two complete ideas can be joined in several ways.

	Vera creates handbags. + She also designs shoes.
Add a coordinator	Vera creates handbags, **and** she also designs shoes.
Add a semicolon	Vera creates handbags**;** she also designs shoes.
Add a semicolon and conjunctive adverb	Vera creates handbags**; moreover,** she designs shoes.

Combine Sentences Using Coordinating Conjunctions

17.2 Combine sentences using coordinating conjunctions.

A **coordinating conjunction** joins two complete ideas and indicates the connection between them. The most common coordinating conjunctions are *for, and, nor, but, or, yet*, and *so*.

Complete idea,	**coordinating conjunction**	complete idea.

Review the following chart showing coordinating conjunctions and their functions.

Coordinating Conjunction	Function	Example
for	to indicate a reason	Henna tattoos are great, **for** they are not permanent.
and	to join two ideas	Jay wants a tattoo, **and** he wants to change his hairstyle.
nor	to indicate a negative idea	Cosmetic surgery is not always successful, **nor** is it particularly safe.
but	to contrast two ideas	Tattoos hurt, **but** people get them anyway.
or	to offer an alternative	Jay will dye his hair, **or** he will shave it off.
yet	to introduce a surprising choice	He is good-looking, **yet** he wants to get cosmetic surgery.
so	to indicate a cause and effect relationship	He saved up his money, **so** he will get a large tattoo.

HINT: Recognizing Compound Sentences

To be sure that a sentence is compound, place your finger over the coordinating conjunction, and then ask yourself whether the two clauses are complete sentences.

Simple	The fashion model was tall **but** also very thin.
Compound	The fashion model was tall, **but** she was also very thin.

Practice 1

Indicate whether the following sentences are simple (S) or compound (C). Underline the coordinating conjunction in each compound sentence.

EXAMPLE: There are many ways to alter your appearance.   _S_

1. Many people permanently alter their bodies, and they do it for a variety of reasons.   _____

2. Body altering is not unique to North America, for people in every culture and in every historical period have found ways to permanently alter their bodies.   _____

3. In past centuries, some young girls in China had their feet painfully bound, and their feet stopped growing any further.   _____

4. In Africa, some men used facial scars to identify their tribe or social position.   _____

5. In the 1700s, wealthy European men wore tight corsets to have a slim figure.   _____

6. Then, in the next century, King George of England wore a tight corset, and he nearly fainted from lack of oxygen.   _____

7. Today, some people want to improve their physical appearance, so they sculpt their bodies with cosmetic surgery.   _____

8. Liposuction surgery is popular for both men and women.   _____

9. Body altering can be painful and very costly, but people do it anyway.   _____

Practice 2

Read the following passages. Insert an appropriate coordinating conjunction in each blank. Choose from the list below, and try to use a variety of coordinating conjunctions.

for   and   nor   but   or   yet   so

EXAMPLE: Fashions usually take a while to be accepted, ____but____ fads appear and vanish quickly.

1.   Have you heard of Harajuku culture? Harajuku is the name of a district

in Tokyo, _____ it is also a teen subculture. Every Sunday afternoon,

hundreds of Japanese teenagers meet on Jinju Bridge, _____ they

engage in "cosplay" (costume play). Some young males dress up, _____

most of the Harajuku kids are female. The girls want to be noticed,

_____ they wear homemade frilly dresses and carry parasols. Their

costumes require a lot of effort. They might dress up as a cute cartoon

character, _____ they can choose to dress in dark gothic costumes.

2.   The pop star Gwen Stefani has a perfume brand called "Harajuku," _____ she loves that subculture. Today, the Harajuku district is famous, _____ many visitors go there. Tourists and professional photographers search for the best-dressed youths. Seventeen-year-old Shoshi lives in Toyko, _____ she visits Jinju Bridge every week. Next Sunday, she might wear a yellow bow in her hair, _____ she may wear a white lace cap. Her costumes are elaborately detailed, _____ she attracts a lot of attention. Tourists stare at her, _____ she is not self-conscious. Shoshi is frequently photographed, _____ she always wears the most eye-catching outfits. She never refuses to pose, _____ do most of her friends.

3.   Curiously, participants love to socialize and make friends, _____ they do not use their real names. The teens choose special names, _____ they use those pseudonyms whenever they dress up in costume. Harajuku culture will probably remain a unique Japanese lifestyle.

HINT: Place a Comma Before the Coordinating Conjunction

Add a comma before a coordinating conjunction if you are certain that it joins two complete sentences. If the conjunction joins two nouns, verbs, or adjectives, then you do not need to add a comma before it.

Comma	The word *fashion* refers to all popular styles, **and** it does not refer only to clothing.
No comma	The word *fashion* refers to all popular styles **and** not only to clothing.

Practice 3

Create compound sentences by adding a coordinating conjunction and another complete sentence to each simple sentence. Remember to add a comma before the conjunction.

EXAMPLE: Many people deny it ___, but they worry about their personal style.___

1. I don't have a tattoo _____

_____

2. Body piercing is common _____

_____

3. Cosmetic surgery is expensive _____

_____

4. She dyed her hair _____

_____

Combine Sentences Using Semicolons

17.3 **Combine sentences using semicolons.**

Another way to form a compound sentence is to join two complete ideas with a semicolon. The semicolon replaces a coordinating conjunction.

Complete idea	;	complete idea.

Advertisers promote new fashions every year; they effectively manipulate consumers.

HINT: Use a Semicolon to Join Related Ideas

Do not use a semicolon to join two unrelated sentences. Remember that a semicolon takes the place of a conjunction.

Incorrect   Some societies have no distinct word for art; people like to dress in bright colors.
(The second idea has no clear relationship with the first idea.)

Correct   Some societies have no distinct word for art; art is an intrinsic part of their cultural fabric.
(The second idea gives further information about the first idea.)

Practice 4

Insert the missing semicolon in each sentence.

EXAMPLE: Bizarre diet trends often become accepted ; many people follow these fads.

1. In recent years, there have been many strange diet trends in *The Guardian*, an article by Ellen Connolly lists these trends.

2. The mono-meal diet is becoming more popular its practitioners only eat one type of fruit or vegetable for each of their meals.

3. Other people subscribe to the "Paleo" diet this diet consists of lots of meat, nuts, and vegetables.

4. More and more food distributors are offering gluten-free options bread and many types of grains or carbohydrates are absent.

5. For those with a taste for hamburgers, the Keto diet is very appealing it advises people to eat a lot of meat, nuts, and cheese.

6. Silicon Valley millionaire Dave Asprey created a weight-loss drink called Bulletproof Coffee it contains two scoops of butter.

7. Many dieters have a hard time avoiding fatty foods the "diet bet" allows them to gamble money on their own weight loss.

8. New diet fads appear all the time there will be strange new fads in the future.

Practice 5

Write compound sentences by adding a semicolon and another complete sentence to each simple sentence. Remember that the two sentences must have related ideas.

EXAMPLE: Last year my sister had her tongue pierced *; she regretted her decision*.

1. Youths rebel in many ways _____

_____

2. Hair dyes can be toxic _____

_____

3. At age thirteen, I dressed like other teens _____

_____

4. Running shoes are comfortable _____

_____

Combine Sentences Using Transitional Expressions

17.4   Combine sentences using transitional expressions.

A third way to combine sentences is to join them with a semicolon and a transitional expression. A **transitional expression** can join two complete ideas together and show how they are related. Most transitional expressions are **conjunctive adverbs** such as *however* or *furthermore*.

Transitional Expressions					
Addition	Alternative	Comparison or Contrast	Time	Example or Emphasis	Result or Consequence
additionally	in fact	equally	eventually	for example	consequently
also	instead	however	finally	for instance	hence
besides	on the contrary	nevertheless	later	namely	therefore
furthermore	on the other hand	nonetheless	meanwhile	of course	thus
in addition	otherwise	similarly	subsequently	undoubtedly	
moreover		still			

If the second part of a sentence begins with a transitional expression, put a semicolon before it and a comma after it.

Complete idea**;**	**transitional expression,**	complete idea.

Yuri is not wealthy
; nevertheless, he always wears the latest fashions.
; however,
; nonetheless,
; still,

Practice 6

Punctuate the following sentences by adding any necessary semicolons and commas.

EXAMPLE: Tattoos are applied with needles ; thus , they are painful.

1. During the era of the Roman Empire, soldiers received tattoos on their hands consequently deserting soldiers could be easily identified.

2. More recently, tattoos represented a person's spirituality or profession for instance sailors commonly had anchors tattooed on their biceps.

3. During World War II, some people were forced to get tattoos for example the Nazis tattooed concentration camp victims.

4. Since the 1990s, tattoos have surged in popularity in fact ordinary citizens of all ages and from all economic classes get them.

5. Some people hate the new fad meanwhile others have become addicted to tattooing.

6. At age sixteen, Rick Genest got a skull and crossbones tattoo on his left shoulder eventually he tattooed his arms, his face, and his skull.

7. He has spent over $17,000 on tattoos hence his hobby is very expensive.

8. These days, tattoos are not always harmless body decorations on the contrary they can symbolize membership in a criminal organization.

9. In Japan, "yakuza" criminals have large colorful tattoos similarly in El Salvador, members of the Mara 18 gang have lip tattoos.

10. Most of my friends have tattoos nevertheless I refuse to get one.

Practice 7

Combine sentences using one of the following transitional expressions. Choose an expression from the following list, and try to use a different expression in each sentence.

in contrast   for example   ~~however~~   of course   thus

in fact   for instance   nevertheless   therefore

EXAMPLE: Today's parents often complain about their children. ~~Young~~ *; however, young* people today are not more violent and rebellious than those of past generations.

1. Youth rebellion is not new. In each era, teenagers have rebelled.

2. Teenagers distinguish themselves in a variety of ways. They listen to new music, create new dance styles, wear odd fashions, and break established social habits.

3. The most visible way to stand out is to wear outrageous fashions. Teenagers try to create original clothing and hairstyles.

4. In the past fifty years, rebellious teens have done almost everything to their hair, including growing it long, buzzing it short, dyeing it, spiking it, shaving it off, and coloring it blue. It is difficult for today's teenagers to create an original hairstyle.

5. Sometimes a certain group popularizes a style. Hip-hop artists wore baggy clothing in the late 1980s.

6. Many parents hated the baggy, oversized pants. Boys wore them.

7. In the past, most people pierced their ears with tiny holes. Many of today's youths stretch their earlobes to create large holes.

8. "Retro" hair and clothing styles will always be popular. People often look to the past for their inspiration.

HINT: Subordinating conjunctions Versus Conjunctive Adverbs

A **subordinating conjunctions** is a term such as *when, because, until,* or *although.* Do not confuse subordinating conjunctions with conjunctive adverbs. When a subordinating conjunction is added to a sentence, the clause becomes incomplete. However, when a conjunctive adverb is added to a sentence, the clause is still complete.

Complete	She wore fur.
Incomplete (with subordinator)	When she wore fur.
Complete (with conjunctive adverb)	Therefore, she wore fur.

When you combine two ideas using a conjunctive adverb, use a semicolon.

No punctuation	She was criticized when she wore fur.
Semicolon	It was very cold; therefore, she wore fur.

Practice 8

Create compound sentences by using the next transitional expressions. Try to use a different expression in each sentence.

in fact   however   ~~therefore~~   furthermore   consequently

EXAMPLE: I have my own style ; therefore, I refuse to spend money following the latest fad.

1. Designer clothing is expensive _____

   _____

2. I cannot sew _____

   _____

3. Some men shave their heads _____

   _____

4. My best friend loves to shop _____

   _____

Reflect On It

Think about what you have learned in this unit. If you do not know an answer, review that concept.

1. a. What is a simple sentence? _____

   _____

   b. Write a simple sentence. _____

   _____

2. a. What is a compound sentence? _____

   _____

   b. Write a compound sentence. _____

   _____

3. What are the seven coordinating conjunctions? _____

   _____

4. When two sentences are joined by a coordinating conjunction such as *but*, should you put a comma before the conjunction?   Yes ☐   No ☐

5. When you join two simple sentences with a transitional expression, how should you punctuate the sentence?

   _____

   _____

Final Review

Read the following essay. Create at least twelve compound sentences by adding semicolons, transitional expressions (*however, therefore,* and so on), or coordinating conjunctions (*for, and, nor, but, or, yet, so*). You may choose to leave some simple sentences.

EXAMPLE: Plastic surgery is becoming more popular for men. ~~The~~ percentage of men getting cosmetic surgery has risen by 272 percent since 1997.

; for example, the

1.　　　We live in a culture where youth and beauty are prized. Most people on television are young, fit, and beautiful. However, in the past, plastic surgery was more popular for women. Now, more and more men are opting for cosmetic surgery. There are two reasons men typically choose this option. They want to look good. They want to stay competitive in the job market.

2.　　　Many men feel they need to look good to get ahead in their careers. Most male plastic surgery patients are trying to climb the corporate ladder. They want a more defined jawline or more defined abs. That is not always possible to achieve through diet or exercise. These procedures are not for people on a limited income. The average price of a surgical procedure is about $5,000. According to plastic surgeon Dr. Douglas Steinbrech, there are different "types" who get plastic surgery. The "male model" type usually wants liposuction or abdominal implants. Young men feel pressured to have perfect six-pack abs. Insecure men of all ages respond to this pressure with six-pack silicon implants. Many men fall under the "body-builder" type. These men want bigger, more defined muscles. They often use liposuction to emphasize the shape of their muscles.

3.　　　Many men admit to having cosmetic surgery. Some go to great lengths to hide it from their friends and family. According to dermatologist Dr. Doris Day, these men hide their appointments from their wives. They secretly save money for their procedures. They fear being stigmatized for having plastic surgery. They still decide to go under the knife. Often, men between the ages of twenty-four and forty-four make this decision. Maybe attitudes about male cosmetic surgery will change in time.

4. Controversy about cosmetic surgery will continue. Many dislike the concept of plastic surgery. However, for others, plastic surgery is a form of art. According to Dr. Day, aesthetic surgery is about optimizing natural features. Critics should reevaluate the goal of this type of surgery. This is an important debate. It may never be resolved.

The Writer's Room

Write about one of the following topics. Include some compound sentences.

1. Think about some fashions over the last one hundred years. Which fashion trends do you love the most? Give examples.
2. List the steps you take when you make a major purchase. For example, what process do you follow when you decide to buy an appliance, car, computer, or house?

18 Complex Sentences

SECTION THEME: Popular Culture

LEARNING OBJECTIVES

18.1 Identify a complex sentence.

18.2 Use subordinating conjunctions.

18.3 Use relative pronouns.

18.4 Use embedded questions.

In this chapter, you read about topics related to sports and activity fads.

The Writer's Journal

How active are you? Write a paragraph about some of the physical activities that you do. Provide specific examples and anecdotes.

What Is a Complex Sentence?

18.1 Identify a complex sentence.

Before you learn about complex sentences, it is important to understand some key terms. A **clause** is a group of words containing a subject and a verb. There are two types of clauses.

An **independent clause** has a subject and a verb and can stand alone because it expresses one complete idea.

> Laban Nkete won the race.

A **dependent clause** has a subject and a verb, but it cannot stand alone. It "depends" on another clause to be complete.

> Although he had injured his heel

A **complex sentence** combines both a dependent and an independent clause.

dependent clause   independent clause
Although he had injured his heel, Laban Nkete won the race.

HINT: More About Complex Sentences

Complex sentences can have more than two clauses.

1
Although women have played organized football for over a century,

2   3
their salaries are not very high because their games are rarely televised.

You can also combine compound and complex sentences. The next example is a **compound-complex sentence**.

complex
Although Kyra is tiny, she plays basketball, and she is a decent player.
compound

Use Subordinating Conjunctions

18.2   Use subordinating conjunctions.

An effective way to create complex sentences is to join clauses with a subordinating conjunction. When you add a **subordinating conjunction** to a clause, you make the clause dependent. *Subordinate* means "secondary," so subordinating conjunctions are words that introduce secondary ideas. Here are some common subordinating conjunctions followed by examples of how to use these types of conjunctions.

Common Subordinating Conjunctions

after	as though	if	though	where
although	because	provided that	unless	whereas
as	before	since	until	wherever
as if	even if	so that	when	whether
as long as	even though	that	whenever	while

Main idea	**subordinating conjunction**	secondary idea.
The fans celebrated	**because**	the team won the game.

Subordinating conjunction	secondary idea,	main idea.
Because	the team won the game,	the fans celebrated.

Practice 1

The following sentences are complex. In each sentence, circle the subordinating conjunction, and then underline the dependent clause.

EXAMPLE: Even if we cannot know for sure, early humans probably played games and sports.

1. When two students from Oxford University visited Egypt in the 1800s, they found the rules for the oldest sport in recorded history.

2. Wrestling was done in many different cultures before any other sport was played.

3. A cave painting from 7000 B.C. depicted two men wrestling each other in a pit while a huge crowd of spectators cheered them on.

4. In ancient China, *shuai-jiao* wrestling was created when soldiers needed a training exercise to practice.

5. Nearly two thousand years ago, a group of wrestlers in Greece wrote a list of rules so that they could teach others how to play the sport.

6. Whenever anthropologists study different societies, they usually find some form of wrestling or combat sport.

Meanings of Subordinating Conjunctions

Subordinating conjunctions create a relationship between the clauses in a sentence.

	Cause or Reason	Condition or Result	Contrast	Place	Time
Conjunctions	as because since so that	as long as even if if only if provided that so that unless	although even though if though whereas unless	where wherever	after before once since until when/whenever while
Example	Eric learned karate **because** he wanted to be physically fit.	He will not fight **unless** he feels threatened.	People learn karate **even though** it is difficult to master.	**Wherever** you travel, you will find karate enthusiasts.	**After** he received his black belt, he became a teacher.

Practice 2

In each of the following sentences, underline the dependent clause. Then, indicate the type of relationship between the two parts of the sentence. Choose one of the following relationships.

condition   contrast   reason   place   time

EXAMPLE: <u>When Kara feels bored</u>, she goes to the park to play basketball.   _time_

1. After James Naismith invented basketball, the sport grew in popularity quickly.   _____

2. Basketball is the fastest growing sport in the world because people can play the game with very little space or equipment.   _____

3. Millions of teenagers run to a basketball court whenever they have spare time.   _____

4. Worldwide, the older generation prefers soccer whereas young people prefer basketball.   _____

5. Wherever Kara travels, she brings a basketball with her.   _____

6. Basketball will continue to be popular unless a different game replaces it.   _____

HINT: Punctuating Complex Sentences

If you use a subordinator at the beginning of a sentence, put a comma after the dependent clause. Generally, if you use a subordinator after the main clause and end the sentences with its subordinate clause, you do not need to use a comma.

Comma   **Even though** she is afraid of heights, Melanie tried skydiving.

No comma   Melanie tried skydiving **even though** she is afraid of heights.

Practice 3

Underline the subordinating conjunction in each sentence. Then add eight missing commas.

EXAMPLE: Although most sports are quite safe, some sports are extremely hazardous.

1. Each year, many people are killed or maimed when they practice a sport. Although skydiving and bungee jumping are hazardous extreme sports like base jumping, free diving, and rodeo events are even more dangerous.

2. Even though they may get arrested many people try base jumping. Wherever there are tall structures there may also be base jumpers. The jumpers wear parachutes and dive off buildings and bridges so that they can feel an adrenaline rush. Because the parachute can get tangled on the structure base jumping is an extremely risky sport.

3. Free divers hold their breath until they are as deep as possible underwater. So that they can break existing records some free divers have dived almost 400 feet. If their brains lack oxygen they have to be resuscitated.

4. Although most rodeo sports can be safe bull riding is dangerous. Many bull riders are injured or even killed because the bull throws them off and tramples them.

5. Surprisingly, most sports-related injuries occur when people ride bicycles. If anyone rides a bike he or she should wear a protective helmet.

Practice 4

Add a missing subordinating conjunction to each sentence. Use each subordinating conjunction once.

although	even though	~~when~~	whereas
because	unless	whenever	

EXAMPLE: ___**When**___ you refer to a "football" in Europe, Africa, or Asia, most people assume you are talking about a round black-and-white ball.

1.   British people will assume you are speaking about soccer _____ you specifically say "American football."

2.   Soccer is the world's most popular sport _____ it is inexpensive to play. _____ someone decides to join a soccer team, he or she does not require expensive padding or equipment.

3.   _____ a lot of Americans love to play soccer, there are not many professional teams in the United States. Sports such as basketball, baseball, and football have professional teams and are shown on network television _____ soccer is not widely viewed.

4.   _____ soccer has yet to become as popular as other sports in the United States, it is America's fastest-growing sport, according to the American Soccer Federation.

HINT: Put a Subject After the Subordinator

When you form complex sentences, always remember to put a subject after the subordinator.

Wrestling is like theater because _it_ involves choreographed maneuvers.

Boxers do not know who will win the round when _they_ enter the ring.

Practice 5

Combine each pair of sentences into a single sentence. Add one of the following subordinating conjunctions. Use each conjunction once.

~~although~~   even   because   after   when   if
                 though

EXAMPLE: I am not athletic. I love football.
Although I am not athletic, I love football.

1. Professional football players can achieve fame and fortune. Many students want to play the sport.

_____

_____

2. Football is a great sport. It has some drawbacks.

_____

_____

3. Linebackers hit other players. They can develop head injuries.

_____

_____

4. Players have concussions. They should receive proper medical care.

_____

_____

5. Professional football players retire. Some have long-term health problems.

_____

_____

Use Relative Pronouns

18.3   **Use relative pronouns.**

A **relative pronoun** describes a noun or pronoun. You can form complex sentences by using relative pronouns to introduce dependent clauses. Review the most common relative pronouns.

who   whom   whomever   whose   which   that

That

Use *that* to add information about a thing. Do not use commas to set off clauses that begin with *that*.

> In 1947, Jackie Robinson joined a baseball team **that** <u>was located in Brooklyn</u>.

Which

Use *which* to add nonessential information about a thing. Generally, use commas to set off clauses that begin with *which*.

> Football, **which** <u>had been segregated</u>, began to include African American players in 1946.

Who

Use *who* (*whom, whomever, whose*) to add information about a person. When a clause begins with *who*, you may or may not need a comma. Put commas around the clause if it adds nonessential information. If the clause is essential to the meaning of the sentence, do not add commas. To decide if a clause is essential or not, ask yourself if the sentence still makes sense without the *who* clause. If it does, the clause is not essential.

> Most women **who** <u>play sports</u> do not earn as much money as their male counterparts.
> (The clause is essential. The sentence would not make sense without the *who* clause.)

> Tennis player Serena Williams, **who** <u>has won many tournaments</u>, earns millions of dollars in endorsement deals.
> (The clause is not essential.)

HINT: Using *That* or *Which*

Both *which* and *that* refer to things, but *which* refers to nonessential ideas. Also, *which* can imply that you are referring to the complete subject and not just a part of it. Compare the next two sentences.

> Local baseball teams **that** have very little funding can still succeed.
>
> (This sentence suggests that some teams have good funding, but others don't.)
>
> Local baseball teams, **which** have very little funding, can still succeed.
>
> (This sentence suggests that all of the teams have poor funding.)

GRAMMAR LINK
For more information about punctuating relative clauses, refer to Chapter 34, "Commas."

Practice 6

Using a relative pronoun, combine each pair of sentences to form a complex sentence.

EXAMPLE: Rock climbers go on many adventures. Their adventures lead to injuries. <u>Rock climbers go on many adventures that can lead to injuries.</u>

1. Rock climbing is a complex sport. It requires strength and agility.

_____

_____

2. Rock climbing is a subcategory of mountain climbing. Rock climbing involves scaling cliffs.

_____

_____

3. Men and women try the sport. They must be very well trained.

_____

_____

4. Some people climb without ropes. They cling to rocks with their fingertips.

_____

_____

5. Alex takes great risks. He scaled cliffs in Yosemite National Park.

_____

_____

Practice 7

Add a dependent clause to each sentence. Begin each clause with a relative pronoun (*who, which,* or *that*). Add any necessary commas.

EXAMPLE: Teams <u>that have good leadership</u> often win tournaments.

1. The player _____ might be hired to promote running shoes.

2. An athlete _____ should
be suspended for at least one game.

3. Bungee jumping is an activity _____

4. Skydiving _____ is a sport
I would like to try.

5. Athletes _____
should be warned about the dangers of steroids.

Use Embedded Questions

18.4 Use embedded questions.

It is possible to combine a question with a statement or to combine two questions. An **embedded question** is a question that is set within a larger sentence.

Question	How old are the Olympic Games?
Embedded question	The sprinter wonders <u>how old the Olympic Games are</u>.

Embedded questions do not require the usual question word order, added helping verbs, or in some cases, even question marks. As you read the following examples, pay attention to the word order in the embedded questions.

Combine two questions.

Separate	Do you know the answer? Why **do** they like bullfighting? (The second question includes the helping verb *do*.)
Combined	Do you know <u>why they like bullfighting</u>? (The helping verb *do* is removed from the embedded question.)

Combine a question and a statement.

Separate	I wonder about it. When **should** we go to the arena? (In the question, the helping verb *should* appears before the subject.)
Combined	I wonder <u>when we should go to the arena</u>. (In the embedded question, *should* is placed after the subject.)

HINT: Use the Correct Word Order

When you edit your writing, make sure that you have formed your embedded questions properly. Remove question form structures from the embedded questions.

He wonders why ~~do~~ people like bullfighting. I asked him what ~~did he think~~ ^{he thought} about the sport.

Practice 8

Correct eight embedded question errors, and modify verbs when necessary.

EXAMPLE: Have you seen what ~~is~~ the latest sport? ^{is}

1. In 1998, J.K. Rowling released the first Harry Potter novel. In the book, young wizards play a game. Do you know what is the sport? It is called Quidditch. Wizards fly on broomsticks and attempt to score points by putting a "Quaffle" ball through hoops. In 2007, reporters were amazed to learn what have some students done. College students on more than two hundred American campuses have replicated the fictional sport.

2. Of course, many people wonder how can humans play Quidditch. Real-life players run holding a broomstick. Do you know what does a Quidditch "pitch" look like? On college campuses, Quidditch matches are played on grass fields, and there are three hooped goal posts on both ends of the field. In the Harry Potter novels, a "Snitch" is a golden ball with wings. Guess what do human Quidditch players do. At each game, a neutral player dresses in gold and tries to evade capture. Fans love to see how do players catch the snitch.

3. There have been Quidditch matches in countries around the world. There is even a Quidditch World Cup. Do you know where was last year's Quidditch World Cup? Last year, Randall, New York, hosted about one hundred Quidditch teams from around the world. I wonder when will I see a Quidditch game.

Reflect On It

Think about what you have learned in this chapter. If you do not know an answer, then review that concept.

1. Write six subordinating conjunctions. _____

   _____

2. Write a complex sentence. _____

   _____

3. List six relative pronouns. _____

4. Correct the error in the following sentence.

5. Clayton wonders why should he wear a helmet when he goes skateboarding.

Final Review

The following paragraphs contain only simple sentences. To give the paragraphs more variety, form at least ten complex sentences by combining pairs of sentences. You will have to add some words and delete others.

When people   , they
EXAMPLE: ~~People~~ pierce their tongues. ~~They~~ risk getting an infection.

1.   Many activity fads come and go. Many of these fads are ridiculous. Why do fads become so popular? Nobody knows the answer. There were some unusual fads in the 1960s. Hula hoops hit the market. Millions of people bought and used the circular plastic tubes. The hula hoop fad did not last long. It briefly provided people with an innovative way to exercise. People put the hoops around their waists. They would gyrate to keep the hoops spinning. In the spring of 1974, a streaking fad began. It occurred on college campuses in Florida and California. Young people stripped naked. They may have felt embarrassed. They ran through public places such as football stadiums and malls.

2.   Fads are not always the same around the world. Some Japanese parks and spas have amusement baths. People wear bathing suits. They jump into a large round tub filled with noodles. The bathtub looks like a giant soup bowl. New Zealanders have a zorbing craze. A zorb looks like a giant hamster ball. It is very safe. Someone climbs inside the transparent ball. He or she rolls down a hill.

3.   Today, many people want to exercise. They do not want to leave their homes. Luckily, video games no longer encourage lethargy. Companies have produced active games. The games force participants to move vigorously. Children play Dance Dance Revolution. They burn three times more calories than those who use traditional hand-held games. Even adults buy the games. They can play tennis or football in their living rooms. Do you know the answer to the following question? Why do adults love active video games? The reasons are simple. The games are entertaining and provide some exercise.

The Writer's Room

Write about one of the following topics. Include some complex sentences.

1. Think about a sport that you really enjoy and a sport that you dislike. Compare and contrast the two sports.

2. What causes children to love or hate gym class in grade school?

19 Sentence Variety

SECTION THEME: Popular Culture

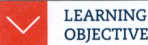

In this chapter, you will read about topics related to cultural icons and issues in popular culture.

The Writer's Journal

Would you like to be famous? What are some problems that could be associated with fame? Write a paragraph about fame.

What Is Sentence Variety?

19.1 Define sentence variety.

In Chapters 17 and 18, you learned how to write different types of sentences. This chapter focuses on sentence variety. **Sentence variety** means that your sentences have assorted patterns and lengths. In this chapter, you will learn to vary your sentences by consciously considering the length of sentences, by altering the opening words, and by joining sentences using different methods.

Combine Sentences

19.2 Combine sentences.

A passage filled with simple, short sentences can sound choppy. When you vary the lengths of your sentences, the same passage becomes easier to read and flows more smoothly. For example, read the following two passages about social networking and relationships. In the first paragraph, most of the sentences are short, and the style is repetitive and boring. In the second paragraph, there is a mixture of simple, compound, and complex sentences.

GRAMMAR LINK
If you forget what compound and complex sentences are, refer to Chapters 17 and 18.

Simple Sentences

Many people are becoming disillusioned with social networking. They feel frustrated about the time wasted online. They may have hundreds of cyber contacts. Most are not real friends. For instance, Hal Niedzviecki is a writer. He invited his six hundred Facebook "friends" to a gathering. About thirty responded. Only one person came. He was quite upset. At the same time, the incident was revealing. People want connections with others. They don't want to work at those relationships.

Simple, Compound, and Complex Sentences

Feeling frustrated about the time wasted online, many people are becoming disillusioned with social networking. They may have hundreds of cyber contacts, but most are not real friends. For instance, Hal Niedzviecki, a writer, invited his six hundred Facebook "friends" to a gathering; about thirty responded. Only one person came, so he was quite upset. At the same time, the incident was revealing. Although people want connections with others, they don't want to work at those relationships.

HINT: Be Careful with Long Sentences

If a sentence is too long, it may be difficult for the reader to understand. If you have any doubts, break up a longer sentence into shorter ones.

Long and complicated	Elvis Presley is a cultural icon who achieved the American dream by using his musical skills to transform himself from a truck driver into a rock-and-roll legend, yet he did not handle his fame very well, and by the end of his life, he was unhappy and addicted to painkillers.
Better	Elvis Presley is a cultural icon who achieved the American dream. Using his musical skills, he transformed himself from a truck driver into a rock-and-roll legend. However, he did not handle his fame very well. By the end of his life, he was unhappy and addicted to painkillers.

Practice 1

Modify the following paragraph so that it has both long and short sentences. Make sure you write some compound and complex sentences.

A cultural icon can be an object, a person, or a place. Cultural icons symbolize a belief or a way of life. Each country has its own icons. They become part of the country's history. For example, Mickey Mouse is more than eighty years old. The cartoon character symbolizes American optimism. The Statue of Liberty is also a potent symbol. It represents America's willingness to welcome immigrants. People can be icons, too. Benito Juarez is celebrated in Mexico. Martin Luther King Jr. is idolized in the United States. These icons reflect shared cultural experiences.

Include a Question, a Quotation, or an Exclamation

19.3 Include a question, a quotation, or an exclamation.

The most common type of sentence is a statement. A simple but effective way to achieve sentence variety is to do the following:

- Ask and answer a **question**. You could also insert a **rhetorical question**, which does not require an answer but is used for effect.

  Did Elvis really do anything shocking**?**

- Include the occasional **exclamation** to express surprise. However, do not overuse exclamations, especially in academic writing.

  Elvis's swinging hips were considered obscene!

- Add a **direct quotation**, which includes the exact words that somebody said.

  Elvis said, "I didn't copy my style from anybody."

In the next passage, a question, an exclamation, and a quotation add variety.

Some divorce attorneys are pleased with the massive expansion of Facebook. **Why are they so happy?** Social networking sites have contributed to marital breakups. **According to Tom Johansmeyer, in an article for *Daily Finance*, "More and more divorce petitions are mentioning Facebook and similar tools as contributing factors."** In the past, people could spend weeks or months tracking down old flames, and communication was difficult, with long-distance phone bills leaving telltale evidence. **These days, with a click of the mouse, a man can find his high school sweetheart in minutes!** Those flirty exchanges, however, can provide clear evidence in a court of law.

`Question` →

`Quotation` →

`Exclamation` →

HINT: Punctuating Quotations

If you introduce your quotation with a phrase like "he said," put a comma after the phrase and before the opening quotation marks. Put the final period inside the closing quotation marks.

Marilyn Monroe once complained, **"**Everybody is always tugging at you.**"**

If the end of the quotation is not the end of the sentence, place a comma inside the final quotation mark.

"They were terribly strict,**"** she once said.

GRAMMAR LINK
For more information about punctuating quotations, refer to Chapter 35.

Practice 2

Read the following passage. Change one sentence to a question and one to an exclamation.

EXAMPLE: <del>Many</del> <ins>Why do many</ins> young men want to be star athletes<del>.</del> **?**

Some of the most famous people in the world are professional athletes. Many ordinary teenagers view athletes as the ultimate role models. Athletes appear powerful and exciting, which is intoxicating for some teens. In an article for *Psychology Today*, Matt Beardmore describes how this hero worship can be damaging. It can lead to anxiety and depression. In some cases, youths even fantasize about having personal bonds with the hero. Such worship can hinder a teen's social development. Parents should speak to their children about unhealthy attachments to star athletes.

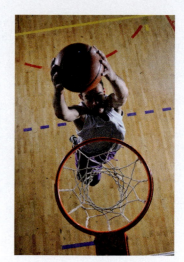

Vary the Opening Words

19.4 Vary the opening words.

An effective way to make your sentences more vivid is to vary the opening words. Instead of beginning each sentence with the subject, you could try the following strategies.

Begin with an Adverb

An **adverb** is a word that modifies a verb, and it often (but not always) ends in *-ly*. *Slowly*, *usually*, and *suddenly* are adverbs. Other adverbs include words such as *sometimes*, *never*, *however*, and *often*.

<u>Generally</u>, a cultural icon arouses strong feelings in members of that culture.

<u>Often</u>, an extremely gifted and famous person becomes an icon.

Begin with a Prepositional Phrase

A **prepositional phrase** is a group of words made up of a preposition and its object. *Under the chair, in the beginning*, and *after the fall* are prepositional phrases.

<u>In New York's harbor</u>, the Statue of Liberty welcomes visitors.

<u>At dawn</u>, we photographed the statue.

HINT: Comma Tip

Generally, when a sentence begins with an adverb or a prepositional phrase, place a comma after the opening word or phrase.

Cautiously, the reporter asked another question to the volatile star.

Without any warning, she stood up and left the room.

Practice 3

Rewrite the following sentences by placing an adverb or prepositional phrase at the beginning. First, strike out any word or phrase that could be moved. Then, rewrite that word or phrase at the beginning of the sentence. Finally, correctly punctuate your new sentence.

EXAMPLE: ___In the United States, few___ ~~Few~~ technological advances ~~in the United States~~ have been as revolutionary as the Internet.

1. _____ The United States' fastest growing industry is actually located in California.

2. _____ The term "Silicon Valley" first appeared in a series of articles for *Electronic News* in 1971.

3. _____ The area around San Francisco quickly became a beacon for the brightest minds in the IT sector.

4. _____ Silicon Valley's population exploded for that reason.

5. _____ You can find the headquarters for Facebook, Netflix, and Google during a visit to Silicon Valley.

Practice 4

Add an opening word or phrase to each sentence. Use the type of opening that is indicated in parentheses. Remember to punctuate the sentence properly.

EXAMPLE: (Adverb) _____Surprisingly,_____ the playwright Naomi Iizuka loves the 50-foot Hollywood sign.

1. (Adverb) _____ the sign is more than just white letters that spell "Hollywood."

2. (Prepositional phrase) _____ the sign is like a beacon to aspiring actors.

3. (Prepositional phrase) _____ thousands of people arrive with dreams of stardom.

4. (Adverb) _____ some people find acting jobs, but many do not.

5. (Prepositional phrase) _____ the sign is an important American symbol.

Combine Sentences with a Present Participle

19.5 Combine sentences with a present participle.

You can combine two sentences with a present participle. A **present participle** is a verb that ends in *-ing*, such as *believing, having*, and *using*. Combine sentences using an *-ing* modifier only when the two actions happen at the same time and the sentences have the same subject.

Separate sentences	He looked across the harbor. He saw the Statue of Liberty.
Combined sentences	<u>Looking</u> across the harbor, he saw the Statue of Liberty.

Practice 5

Combine the next sentences by converting one of the verbs into an *-ing* modifier.

EXAMPLE: Pop artists focused on familiar images. They painted comic strips and supermarket products.

Focusing on familiar images, pop artists painted comic strips

and supermarket products.

1. Andy Warhol worked as an illustrator. He drew footwear for a shoe company.

_____

_____

2. He desired respect. He wanted his work to be in art galleries.

_____

_____

3. One gallery owner rejected Warhol's art. She wanted original ideas.

_____

_____

4. Warhol felt inspired. He decided to create pop art.

_____

_____

5. Warhol needed an original idea. He focused on his favorite brands.

_____

_____

6. He reproduced soup cans and Coke bottles. He attracted a lot of attention.

_____

_____

Combine Sentences with a Past Participle

19.6 Combine sentences with a past participle.

Another way to combine sentences is to use a past participle. A **past participle** is a verb that has an *-ed* ending (although there are many irregular past participles, such as *gone, seen, broken,* and *known*).

You can begin a sentence with a past participle. To do this, you must combine two sentences that have the same subject, and one of the sentences must contain a past participle.

> **GRAMMAR LINK**
> For a complete list of irregular past participles, see Appendix 2.

Separate sentences	Roma is influenced by Kim Kardashian. Roma desires luxurious items.
Combined sentences	<u>Influenced by Kim Kardashian</u>, Roma desires luxurious items.

Practice 6

Combine each pair of sentences into one sentence beginning with a past participle.

EXAMPLE: Kim Kardashian was encouraged by Paris Hilton in 2007. Kim decided to star in a reality show.

Encouraged by Paris Hilton in 2007, Kim Kardashian decided to star in a reality show.

1. The Kardashians have been followed by cameras since 2007. They have exposed their lavish lifestyle.

   _____

   _____

2. The show is condemned by many critics. The show glamorizes greed.

   _____

   _____

3. The Kardashian sisters are also criticized for their weight and curves. They respond with laughter.

   _____

   _____

4. The sisters were frustrated by the negative comments. They express disinterest in being size zeros.

   _____

   _____

5. Roma Winters is surprised by the criticism of the show. She looks up to the Kardashians.

   _____

   _____

6. Women are held to impossible weight standards. Some women feel better about having curves after seeing the show.

   _____

   _____

Combine Sentences with an Appositive

19.7 Combine sentences with an appositive.

An **appositive** is a word or phrase that gives further information about a noun or pronoun. You can combine two sentences by using an appositive. In the example, the italicized phrase could become an appositive because it describes the noun *Bob Marley*.

Two sentences   Bob Marley was *a founding member of The Wailers*. He went on to have a solo career.

You can place the appositive directly before the word that it refers to or directly after that word. Notice that the appositives are set off with commas.

appositive

Combined A founding member of The Wailers, **Bob Marley** went on to have a successful solo career.

appositive

Combined **Bob Marley**, a founding member of The Wailers, went on to have a successful solo career.

HINT: Finding an Appositive

To find an appositive, look for a word or phrase that describes or renames a noun. The noun could be anywhere in the sentence.

Bob Marley popularized a new fashion trend. He wore dreadlocks.

In the preceding sentences, "dreadlocks" describes the new fashion trend. You could combine the sentences as follows:

appositive

Bob Marley popularized **a new fashion trend**, dreadlocks.

Practice 7

Combine the following pairs of sentences. In each pair, make one of the sentences an appositive. Try to vary the position of the appositive. In some sentences, you could put the appositive at the beginning of the sentence, and in others, you could put the appositive after the word that it describes.

EXAMPLE: Bob Marley was a Jamaican. He greatly popularized reggae music.

Bob Marley, a Jamaican, greatly popularized reggae music.

_____

1. Bob Marley brought international attention to reggae music. He was a great musician.

   _____

   _____

2. Marley was biracial. He was born in 1945 in Jamaica.

   _____

   _____

3. Marley's father was a sailor. His father died when Marley was young.

   _____

   _____

4. At the age of 14, Marley jammed with Joe Higgs. Higgs was a Rastafarian and reggae musician.

   _____

   _____

5. Jamaicans loved the reggae sound of Bob Marley and The Wailers. The group was one of the most famous bands in the country.

_____

_____

6. Bob Marley has had a profound influence on contemporary music. Marley is a music icon.

_____

_____

Reflect On It

Think about what you have learned in this unit. If you do not know an answer, review that topic.

1. Why is sentence variety important? _____

_____

2. Write a sentence that begins with an adverb. _____

_____

3. Write a sentence that begins with a present participle. _____

_____

4. Write a sentence that begins with a past participle. _____

_____

5. Write a sentence that begins with an appositive. _____

_____

Final Review

The next essay lacks sentence variety. Use the strategies that you have learned in this and in previous chapters to create up to fifteen varied sentences.

EXAMPLE: People are obsessed with fame. ~~Perhaps they believe~~ _, believing_ that fame will make them immortal.

1. In 2008, Hal Niedzviecki was a writer. He was fascinated with online blogs, videos, and social media networks. He wondered why so many people share their private thoughts with strangers. To find the answers, he did a lot of research. He wrote a book called *The Peep Diaries*. His book was about the shocking amount of oversharing online. Millions of people use Twitter, YouTube, Facebook, and personal blogs. They become stars in their own lives. The book made Niedzviecki a minor celebrity after it was selected by Oprah Winfrey's magazine *O* as a "must-read" book in 2009.

2.   Filmmakers Sally Blake and Jeannette Loakman heard about the book. They approached Neidzviecki about a documentary project. He agreed to embark on an interesting experiment. He allowed cameras to film him 24 hours a day. During the documentary, he met with some colorful characters. For example, he met Cork. Cork was a man in his early thirties. Cork lived alone. Cork's home was filled with cameras. Cork's home was like a studio. His every move was watched by thousands of followers. Neidzviecki also met with a pilot and with a gastric bypass patient.

3.   At first, Niedzviecki felt uncomfortable with the cameras in his home. He hid upstairs. He quickly began to love the attention from the followers of his video blog. Sometimes he said or did embarrassing things. Then he would run to his computer to see how his online audience reacted. He was treated like a mini celebrity. He felt intoxicated with power.

4.   Niedzviecki ultimately sees a downside to peep culture. He is concerned about possible abuses. He warns parents to teach their children about proper boundaries. If we have an audience, it does not make our lives better or more valuable. According to Niedzviecki, the life lived in privacy is just as important as the one lived in front of millions.

The Writer's Room

Choose one of the following topics, and write a paragraph or an essay. When you write, remember to follow the writing process.

1.   Define *hero*. What makes a person a hero?
2.   Why do so many people crave fame? How does celebrity status affect people? Write about the causes or effects of fame.

READING LINK

To learn more about popular culture and identity, read the following essays:

"Comics as a Social Commentary" (p. 178)
"Chicken Hips" (p. 189)
"Just Say No" (p. 207)
"Being a Hyphenated American" (p. 487)
"This Boat Is My Boat" (p. 494)
"Emojis" (p. 492)

The Writer's Circle: Collaborative Activity

Get into a group of three or four students. Then think about songs that you really love. Each person in your team should contribute five song titles to the list.

Using the titles as inspiration, write a paragraph. Add words and sentences to make your paragraph complete. Your paragraph should have at least one simple sentence, one compound sentence, and one complex sentence. Also, vary the beginnings of sentences, ensuring that one sentence begins with a present participle and one begins with a past participle.

20 Fragments

SECTION THEME: Psychology

20.1 Identify and correct fragments.

In this chapter, you will read about topics related to psychological profiles.

The Writer's Journal

How do men and women deal with personal problems? Do they use different strategies? Write about problem-solving techniques that men and women use.

Fragments

20.1 Identify and correct fragments.

A **sentence** must have a subject and a verb, and it must express a complete thought. A **fragment** is an incomplete sentence. Either it lacks a subject or a verb, or it fails to express a complete thought. You may see fragments in newspaper headlines and advertisements (*Wrinkle-free skin in one month*). However, in college writing, it is unacceptable to write fragments.

Sentence	Sigmund Freud was a famous psychologist.
Fragment	Considered to be the founder of psychoanalysis.

Phrase Fragments

A phrase fragment is missing a subject or a verb. In the following examples, the fragments are underlined.

No verb	First, B. F. Skinner. He did research on human behavior.
No subject	B. F. Skinner wrote a novel about human behavior. Called *Walden Two*.

HOW TO CORRECT PHRASE FRAGMENTS

To correct a phrase fragment, either add the missing subject or verb, or join the fragment to another sentence. Here are two ways you can correct the phrase fragments in the previous examples.

Join sentences	First, B. F. Skinner did research on human behavior.
Add words	B. F. Skinner wrote a novel about human behavior. **It was** called *Walden Two*.

HINT: Incomplete Verbs

A sentence must have a subject and a complete verb. If a sentence has an incomplete verb, it is a phrase fragment. The following example contains a subject and part of a verb. However, it is missing a helping verb; therefore, the sentence is incomplete.

Fragment   Many books about psychology written by Carl Jung.

To make this sentence complete, you must add the helping verb.

Sentence   Many books about psychology **were** written by Carl Jung.

Practice 1

Underline and correct six phrase fragments.

EXAMPLE: Studies show that people can be more productive. ~~By~~ ^{by} focusing on the present.

1.   Mindfulness. It means different things to different people. Most individuals don't know when they are focused. Or unfocused. Many people are constantly distracted by their worries. And anxieties about the future. They are often unable to appreciate the present moment. Therefore, psychologists, spiritualists, and weight-loss specialists use the term "mindfulness" regularly when advising their clients. Some psychologists give advice. On how to practice mindfulness. But what does it mean?

2.   Mindfulness is both a practice and a state of mind. Studies. They show that students perform better on standardized tests after practicing mindfulness exercises. These exercises include focused meditation, attention-building games, and controlled breathing exercises. Mindfulness helps people understand. And control their thoughts.

Fragments with *-ing* and *to*

A fragment may begin with a **present participle**, which is the form of the verb that ends in *-ing* (*running, talking*). It may also begin with an **infinitive**, which is *to* plus the base form of the verb (*to run, to talk*). These fragments generally appear before or after another sentence that contains the subject. In the examples, the fragments are underlined.

-ing fragment	<u>Thinking about positive outcomes</u>. It helps people cope with stress.
to fragment	Oprah Winfrey has developed a resilient attitude. <u>To overcome her childhood traumas.</u>

HOW TO CORRECT *-ING* AND *TO* FRAGMENTS

To correct an *-ing* or *to* fragment, either add the missing words or join the fragment to another sentence. Here are two ways to correct the previous examples.

Join sentences	Thinking about positive outcomes helps people cope with stress.
Add words	Oprah Winfrey has developed a resilient attitude **because she had to** overcome her childhood traumas.

HINT: When the *-ing* Word Is the Subject

Sometimes a gerund (*-ing* form of the verb) is the subject of a sentence. In the next example, *listening* is the subject of the sentence.

Correct	Listening is an important skill.

A sentence fragment occurs when the *-ing* word is part of an incomplete verb string or when the subject was mentioned in a previous sentence.

Fragment	Dr. Phil has achieved success. <u>Listening to people's problems.</u>

Practice 2

Underline and correct six *-ing* and *to* fragments.

EXAMPLE: Many schools help students. <u>~~To~~ deal with bullies.</u> *(to)*

    Bullying is getting a lot of attention in society. Bullying is abusive behavior. To acquire power over someone. Using methods of intimidation. Bullies can control their victims. Psychologists study cases of bullying. To discover the causes and effects of such conduct. Studying the link between bullying and school violence. Researchers have found that two-thirds of students say they have been victims of bullies. Furthermore, studies have shown that 60 percent of identified male student bullies were convicted of a crime by age twenty-four. Recognizing the harmful effects of bullying. School administrators and teachers are implementing anti-bullying programs. People need to make great efforts. To reduce bullying in all areas of society.

Explanatory Fragments

An **explanatory fragment** provides an explanation about a previous sentence and is missing a subject, a complete verb, or both. Such fragments are sometimes expressed as an afterthought. These types of fragments begin with one of the following words.

also	especially	for example	including	particularly
as well as	except	for instance	like	such as

In each example, the explanatory fragment is underlined.

Fragment   Carl Jung studied with many prominent psychologists. <u>For instance, Sigmund Freud.</u>

Fragment   Psychologists analyze behavior. <u>Particularly through methods of observation.</u>

HOW TO CORRECT EXPLANATORY FRAGMENTS

To correct explanatory fragments, add the missing words, or join the explanation or example to another sentence. Here are two ways to correct the fragments in the previous examples.

Add words   Carl Jung studied with many prominent psychologists. For instance, **he worked with** Sigmund Freud.

Join sentences   Psychologists analyze behavior, particularly through methods of observation.

Practice 3

Underline and correct six explanatory fragments. You may need to add or remove words.

EXAMPLE: Some fans are very loyal. ~~Especially~~ *, especially* Red Sox fans.

Stephen Dubner wrote *Confessions of a Hero-Worshipper*. He describes the personality of sports fans, and his book has interesting anecdotes. For example, the 1994 World Cup. The saliva of male soccer fans was tested before and after an important match. The chosen fans were from Brazil. As well as Italy. The testosterone levels in the fans of the winning team rose quickly. Particularly during the final minutes of the game. The losing fans' testosterone levels decreased. Researcher Paul Bernhardt was surprised. Especially by the percentages. The fans of the winning team, with a 20 percent increase, had the same level of testosterone as the athletes. The findings may explain aggressive episodes. Such as soccer hooliganism. Immediately after a testosterone surge, some males may act more aggressively. Especially when provoked.

Dependent-Clause Fragments

A **dependent clause** has a subject and a verb, but it cannot stand alone. It *depends* on another clause to be a complete sentence. Dependent clauses may begin with subordinating conjunctions (subordinators) or relative pronouns. The following are some of the most common words that begin dependent clauses.

Common Subordinating Conjunctions				Relative Pronouns
after	before	though	whenever	that
although	even though	unless	where	which
as	if	until	whereas	who(m)
because	since	what	whether	whose

The next two examples contain dependent-clause fragments. In each example, the fragment is underlined.

Fragment	<u>Although I cross my fingers for luck</u>. I know that it is a silly superstition.
Fragment	I will not walk under a ladder. <u>That is leaning against a wall</u>.

HOW TO CORRECT DEPENDENT-CLAUSE FRAGMENTS

To correct dependent-clause fragments, either join the fragment to a complete sentence or add the necessary words to make it a complete idea. You could also delete the subordinating conjunction. Here are two ways to correct the fragments in the previous examples.

Delete the subordinator	I cross my fingers for luck. I know that it is a silly superstition.
Join sentences	Although I cross my fingers for luck, I know that it is a silly superstition.
	I will not walk under a ladder that is leaning against a wall.

Practice 4

Underline and correct five dependent-clause fragments.

EXAMPLE: <u>Whenever they blame themselves,</u> ^{, negative} ~~Negative~~ thinkers make their problems larger.

1. Jane Elliott is an American teacher and activist. Who created the Blue Eyes / Brown Eyes experiment. For the exercise, she taught her second-grade class. That the children with blue eyes were superior to those with brown eyes. Children with blue eyes received advantages such as more playtime during recess. After they participated in this exercise for a few days. The children in the brown-eyed group started to behave differently. They performed worse on their tests and lost their self-confidence.

2.   Elliot then reversed the roles of the students. The brown-eyed students now started to act arrogantly toward the blue-eyed students. Even though they had received the same treatment the week before. The program taught the students. That being discriminated against is deeply unpleasant.

Reflect On It

Think about what you have learned in this unit. If you do not know an answer, review that concept.

1. What is a sentence fragment? _____

   _____

2. What are the types of fragments?

   _____

   _____

3. Correct the next fragment.

   According to Freud, people unintentionally repress certain memories. Because they are painful or threatening.

Final Review

Correct fifteen fragment errors.

EXAMPLE: Humans rely on memory. ~~To~~ ^{to} perform any action.

1.   Have you ever forgotten a telephone number? That you have just looked up. Forgetting an item of information. It happens to all of us. Memory is an intriguing process. Psychologists identify three types of memory. First, sensory memory. It refers to the initial perception of information. The second kind of memory is short-term memory. By rehearsing, we can transfer information from our sensory memory to our short-term memory. Researchers have discovered that we can hold about seven pieces of information in our short-term memory. But only for about 30 seconds. We store information in our long-term memory. Through chemical changes in our brain.

2.   As we age, our memory declines. However, there are techniques that we can attempt. To help our memory. We can remember information more easily. Using mnemonics. One mnemonic device employs rhymes. A familiar example

is the rule *i* before *e* except after *c*. Which helps us with our spelling. Another mnemonic technique is the acronym. An acronym uses the first letters of a series of words. Such as FBI (Federal Bureau of Investigation). A third type of mnemonic device is called the peg system. Alphabet books. They generally use the peg system when they teach *A for apple, B for ball*, and so on.

3. A very effective memory device is called the SQ4R. According to psychologists. SQ4R (pronounced "square") is an acronym for a study strategy: Survey, Question, Read, Reflect, Recite, and Review. Researchers believe that this system is very useful for students. Who need to remember large amounts of information. By following the SQ4R method, students may have more success at retaining information. Especially when they study for exams.

4. Finally, we must practice organizing and rehearsing information. Because we cannot develop a good memory by being passive. We should use mnemonic devices. When we need to remember a phone number or another item of information.

The Writer's Room

Write about one of the following topics. Check that there are no sentence fragments.

1. Explain why people are superstitious, and give examples to support your point of view.
2. Look again at Practice 2. Have you ever been bullied, bullied someone else, or witnessed bullying? Describe your experience.

SECTION THEME: Psychology

In this chapter, you read about the brain and personality differences.

LEARNING OBJECTIVE

21.1 Identify and correct run-ons.

The Writer's Journal

Do you have any good habits? In a paragraph, describe your good habits. Why do you think they are positive?

Avoiding Run Ons

21.1 Identify and correct run-ons.

A **run-on sentence** occurs when two or more complete sentences are incorrectly joined. In other words, the sentence runs on without stopping. There are two types of run-on sentences.

- A **fused sentence** has no punctuation to mark the break between ideas.

Incorrect	Psychologists study human behavior they use observational methods.
Correct	Psychologists study human behavior. They use observational methods.

• A **comma splice** uses a comma incorrectly to connect two complete ideas.

Incorrect	Wilhelm Wundt was born in 1832, he is often called the founder of modern psychology.
Correct	Wilhelm Wundt was born in 1832. He is often called the founder of modern psychology.

Practice 1

Read the following sentences. Write *C* beside correct sentences and *RO* beside run-ons.

EXAMPLE: Sigmund Freud and Carl Jung were two famous psychologists they profoundly influenced the field of psychology.   *RO*

1. Carl Jung was a famous psychiatrist he developed theories about human personalities.   _____

2. Jung studied medicine at the University of Basel, he later worked with Sigmund Freud.   _____

3. Jung developed the theory that each person fits into a general personality model.   _____

4. Jung's archetypes were based on four different categories, his theories became very popular.   _____

5. Jung developed eight different personality types other psychologists later added to his findings.   _____

6. Katherine Cook Briggs and her daughter Isabel Meyers studied Jung's personality categories the researchers developed a personality profile chart.   _____

7. The Meyers-Briggs theory identified 16 personality types, they used the data to create a personality test.   _____

8. The Performer is one personality type who loves to bring joy to others and be the center of attention.   _____

9. The Visionary is creative, resourceful, and intelligent people in this category typically make great leaders.   _____

10. Human personalities vary greatly it is difficult to categorize them.   _____

How to Correct Run-Ons

You can correct run-on sentences in a variety of ways. Read the following run-on sentence, and then review the four ways to correct it.

Run-On	His parents were Jewish, Freud didn't believe in God.

1. **Make two separate sentences.**   His parents were Jewish. **Freud** didn't believe in God.

2. **Add a semicolon.**   His parents were Jewish**;** Freud didn't believe in God.

3. **Add a comma and a coordinating conjunction.** *(for, and, nor, but, or, yet, so)*   His parents were Jewish, **but** Freud didn't believe in God.

4. **Add a subordinating conjunction.**
    (*after, although, as, because, before, since, when, while*)

Although his parents were Jewish, Freud didn't believe in God.

Practice 2

A. Correct each run-on sentence by making two complete sentences.

EXAMPLE: Psychologists study children's behavior, ~~they~~ `. They` write articles about their findings.

1. Carolyn Weisz was a little girl, she attended the Bing Nursery School.

2. Carolyn went to the daycare everyday it was on the campus of Stanford University.

3. One day, Carolyn was asked to play in a small room it had a desk and a chair.

B. Correct each run-on by joining the two sentences with a semicolon.

EXAMPLE: Some children need few rules `;` others need more boundaries.

4. A young man told Carolyn to sit at the desk, there was a plate full of marshmallows on it.

5. He told Carolyn that she could have one treat right away if she waited while the man was out of the room, Carolyn could have two treats when he returned.

6. Carolyn does not remember her reaction her mom thinks that Carolyn waited for the man's return.

C. Correct the next run-ons by joining the two sentences with a comma and a coordinating conjunction (*for, and, nor, but, or, yet,* or *so*).

EXAMPLE: Most children want to be independent `, but` they also need specific rules.

7. The Stanford marshmallow experiment was initially meant to demonstrate how people delayed gratification the experiment showed some other surprising results.

8. Psychologist Walter Mischel became curious about the children in the study he asked his daughters, who knew and grew up with the test subjects, how their Bing Nursery School friends were doing.

9. Dr. Mischel noticed that those who waited to get two treats did well in life those who could not wait did less well.

D. Correct the next run-ons by joining the two sentences with a subordinating conjunction (*although, even though, because, where, when,* and so on).

When children
EXAMPLE: ~~Children~~ receive praise, they are more cooperative.

10. Psychologist Terrie Moffitt did the same study in New Zealand she wanted to see if the marshmallow experiment could be replicated.

11. The children in both experiments wanted to eat the treat, the patient children could distract themselves in order to wait for two goodies.

12. Those two experiments have astonishing results more self-control studies should be done to reach accurate conclusions.

Practice 3

Some sentences are correct and some are run-ons. Write *C* beside each correct sentence and *RO* beside the run-ons. Using a variety of methods, correct each run-on error.

EXAMPLE: People have studied the link between emotions and physical health , and some researchers have found clear scientific links between the two. RO

1. Our emotions can be more powerful than we previously thought, they can affect everything from allergy symptoms to the body's ability to heal. _____

2. Chronic stress can impair memory, it can cause depression and general fatigue. _____

3. However, short-term stress can boost our immune system it also increases cancer-fighting molecules. _____

4. Dr. Lee Berk devised a study on the effects of laughter he found that laughter boosted a certain mood-enhancing brain chemical by 27 percent. _____

5. The study was successful, many other researchers have created similar experiments. _____

6. Love, the most cherished of the emotions, also has a positive impact on physical health. _____

7. Nerve growth and memory improves for about a year a person falls in love. _____

8. Most of us don't enjoy crying, it can sometimes be good for both our psychological and physical health.   _____

9. Not all emotions can be beneficial; jealousy has been proven to cause weakened immunity and impaired memory.   _____

Practice 4

Correct twelve run-on errors.

EXAMPLE: About 3 percent of births in the United States are twins *, but* the percentage is increasing.

1.   Thomas Bouchard Jr. and some colleagues at the University of Minnesota began studying twins in 1979. Bouchard had read about twins who had been raised apart, he contacted them to study their similarities and differences. By 1990, Bouchard's team had studied seventy-seven sets of identical twins.

2.   Most of the separated twins had astounding similarities. For example, two men named Jim had been separated at birth. They met in 1979 they found that they were similar in many ways. They both married women named Linda, they were both volunteer firefighters. The Jims also enjoyed carpentry, they built similar white benches.

Jim Lewis and Jim Springer

3.   In the study, one set of twins was unusual. Japanese-born twins were adopted by different families in California. They shared some similarities researchers were puzzled by their differences. One twin had 20/20 vision, the other wore glasses. One was afraid to travel by airplane the other had no such fear. One twin was quite timid, the other was easygoing and friendly.

4.   Researchers suspect that the environment may play a role in twin differences. For example, one twin could be malnourished, the other could have a healthy diet. The differences in diet could affect the development of the twins' brains and bodies. Birthing problems may also result in differences between twins one twin might receive less oxygen during delivery.

5.   The separated-twin studies suggest certain possibilities, for example, twins raised separately may be more similar than twins raised together. Twins raised together may emphasize their differences twins raised apart would have no need to search for their individuality. More research is needed to know how genes influence behavior.

Reflect On It

Think about what you have learned in this unit. If you do not know an answer, review that concept.

1. What is a run-on? _____

_____

2. Define a comma splice. _____

_____

3. Define a fused sentence. _____

_____

4. Explain the four ways to correct a run-on sentence.

a. _____

b. _____

c. _____

d. _____

Final Review

Correct fifteen run-on errors.

EXAMPLE: The brain is an extremely complex organ, it is the center of the human nervous system.

1. The basis of human behavior is the human brain, if it malfunctions, people experience problems. Yet, researchers still have a lot to learn about the human brain.

2. In 1985, Dr. Oliver Sacks wrote a book called *The Man Who Mistook His Wife for a Hat*, he analyzed some interesting cases of patients who had exhibited puzzling behavior. One of Dr. Sacks's patients was a music teacher he had lost his ability to identify objects or people. This condition is known as agnosia, it has many possible causes. For example, Anita Kaye was in a car accident. She was hurled out of the car, she experienced brain trauma. Now she no longer recognizes people, shapes, and objects. She can see a plate placed before her she cannot name it. If she wants something, she describes the object to a family member.

3.   Another interesting case concerned Mrs. O'C. She was old, she started to hear Irish music. She became Dr. Sacks's patient she wanted to stop hearing the music. Apparently, she was experiencing small epileptic seizures they triggered her brain to recall music from her childhood. Mrs. O'C was an orphan, the seizures may have released a desire to relive her childhood before her parents' death.

4.   According to some accounts, a Russian composer had a similar experience. During World War II, a bomb exploded near Dmitri Shostakovich a small piece of metal lodged in his head. Years later, he consulted a Chinese neurologist, the composer wanted to know if the metal should be removed. Whenever he moved his head, the piece of metal shifted, and he would hear music. Shostakovich decided to leave the metal in place, he enjoyed his brain's private concerts.

5.   The brain is a mysterious organ researchers are trying to understand it. According to neurologist Wilder Penfield, the brain is the organ of destiny, it holds secrets that will determine the future of the human race.

The Writer's Room

Write about one of the following topics. Make sure that you have not written any run-ons.

1. Narrate a story about one of your earliest memories.
2. Compare and contrast twins by looking at their similarities and differences. If you don't know any twins, then describe the similarities and differences between siblings (brothers and sisters).

LEARNING OBJECTIVES

22.1 Define parallel structure.

22.2 Identify faulty parallel structure.

In this chapter, you read about topics related to psychological experiments.

The Writer's Journal

Write a short paragraph comparing your personality to that of a family member or friend. Describe how your personalities are similar and different.

What Is Parallel Structure?

22.1 Define parallel structure.

Parallel structure occurs when pairs or groups of items in a sentence are balanced. In each of the following sentences, the underlined phrases use the same grammatical structure for equivalent ideas.

Each sentence is balanced or parallel in structure. <u>Internet sites</u>, <u>magazines</u>, and <u>newspapers</u> published the results of the experiment.
(The nouns are parallel.)

Psychologists <u>observe</u> and <u>predict</u> human behavior.
(The present tense verbs are parallel.)

The experiment was <u>fascinating</u>, <u>groundbreaking</u>, and <u>revolutionary</u>.
(The adjectives are parallel.)

To get to the psychology department, go <u>across the street</u>, <u>into the building</u>, and <u>up the stairs</u>.
(The prepositional phrases are parallel.)

There are some test subjects <u>who develop a rash</u> and some <u>who have no reactions</u>.
(The "who" clauses are parallel.)

Practice 1

All of the following sentences have parallel structures. Underline the parallel items.

EXAMPLE: Students in my psychology class <u>listened to the instructor</u>, <u>took notes</u>, and <u>asked questions</u>.

1. Professor Stanley Milgram taught at Yale, conducted a famous experiment, and wrote a book about his research.

2. Milgram's experiment was controversial, provocative, and surprising.

3. His experiment tried to understand how humans reacted to authority, how they obeyed authority, and how they felt about authority.

4. For his experiment, Milgram used one actor in a lab coat, one actor with glasses, and one unsuspecting subject in street clothes.

5. The psychologist told the subject to sit at the desk, to watch the "patient" behind the glass, and to listen to the experiment "leader."

6. The leader told the subject when to start electric shocks, when to increase the level of shocks, and when to stop the experiment.

7. Milgram's experiment raised important questions, ended in astonishing results, and gave valuable insight into human behavior.

8. Psychologists continue to perform experiments, give lectures, and debate issues.

Identify Faulty Parallel Structure

22.2 Identify faulty parallel structure.

It is important to use parallel structure for a series of words or phrases, paired clauses, a comparison, and a two-part construction.

Series of Words or Phrases

Use parallel structure when words or phrases are joined in a series.

Not parallel	Students, administrators, and people who teach sometimes volunteer for psychology experiments.
Parallel	<u>Students</u>, <u>administrators</u>, and <u>teachers</u> sometimes volunteer for psychology experiments. (The nouns are parallel.)
Not parallel	I plan to study for tests, to attend all classes, and listening to the instructor.
Parallel	I plan <u>to study</u> for tests, <u>to attend</u> all classes, and <u>to listen</u> to the instructor. (The verbs are parallel.)

Paired Clauses

Use parallel structure when independent clauses are joined by *and, but*, or *or*.

Not parallel	He was surprised by the results, but he did not have a feeling of pleasure.
Parallel	He <u>was surprised</u> by the results, but he <u>was not pleased</u>. (The adjectives are parallel.)
Not parallel	She felt dizzy, and she also had a feeling of fright.
Parallel	She felt <u>dizzy</u>, and she also felt <u>frightened</u>. (The adjectives are parallel.)

GRAMMAR LINK
To learn more about active and passive voice, see pages 324–325 in Chapter 24.

HINT: Use Consistent Voice

When a sentence has two independent clauses and is joined by a coordinating conjunction, use a consistent voice. In other words, if one part of the sentence is active, the other should also be active.

Not parallel	The researcher conducted the experiment, and then a report was written by him.
Parallel	The researcher <u>conducted the experiment</u>, and then <u>he wrote a report</u>. (Both parts use the active voice.)

Practice 2

Correct the faulty parallel structure in each sentence.

EXAMPLE: Some psychology experiments are bold, pioneering, and ~~show their originality~~. ^{original}

1. Sociologists, social workers, and people who study psychology conduct experiments about human behavior.

2. An Orlando journalist performed an experiment on bystander apathy, and the effectiveness of "Missing Persons" posters also interested him.

3. He posted a "missing person's" photo on a store wall, asked the girl in the photo to sit beside the poster, and was watching the reactions of customers.

4. He filmed customers as they walked through a parking lot, up some stairs, and a store is where they entered.

5. The journalist wanted to see if customers walking past the "missing" girl would be oblivious, interested, or they would try to help.

6. Most people didn't notice the girl, a few people became puzzled about her, and mall security was called by only two people.

7. People were honest, and they were full of insight about their behavior.

8. They did not want to look stupid, confused, or be seen as foolish if they were wrong about the situation.

9. The findings of the experiment were interesting, disturbing, and thought to be important.

Comparisons

Use parallel structure in comparisons containing *than* or *as*.

Not parallel	Creating new experiments is more difficult than to re-create an earlier experiment.
Parallel	<u>Creating a new experiment</u> is more difficult than <u>re-creating an earlier experiment</u>. (The *-ing* forms are parallel.)
Not parallel	His home was as messy as the way he kept his laboratory.
Parallel	His <u>home</u> was as messy as his <u>laboratory</u>. (The nouns are parallel.)

Two-Part Constructions

Use parallel structure for the following paired items.

either . . . or	not . . . but	both . . . and
neither . . . nor	not only . . . but also	rather . . . than

Not parallel	My psychology class was both informative and a challenge.
Parallel	My psychology class was both <u>informative</u> and <u>challenging</u>. (The adjectives are parallel.)
Not parallel	I would rather finish my experiment than leaving early.
Parallel	I would rather <u>finish</u> my experiment than <u>leave</u> early. (The verbs are parallel.)

Practice 3

Correct twelve errors in parallel construction.

EXAMPLE: Philip Zimbardo is creative and ~~an interesting person.~~ interesting

1. Philip Zimbardo created an experiment that was both unique and startled others. The Stanford Prison Experiment examined how ordinary people react when placed in positions of power or helplessness. He chose twenty-four students who were healthy, stable, and they abided by the law. Each subject would be either a guard or a prisoner for a two-week period.

2.   On the first day of the experiment, each guard was told to wear a uniform, carry a baton, and sunglasses were put on. Ordinary people who had committed no crime, who had broken no laws, and had been honest were placed in a cold room. The prisoners were not only arrested but the guards also deloused them.

3.   Immediately, the experimenters observed shocking behavior. Some of the guards started to act controlling, sadistic, and they abused the prisoners. On the second day, the prisoners rioted, and the guards attacked. Some prisoners decided that they would rather leave than continuing with the experiment.

4.   During the next few days, officials, priests, and teachers observed the experiment. Nobody questioned the morality of the proceedings. Then, on the sixth day, Zimbardo's girlfriend visited the lab, and her shock was expressed. At first, Zimbardo's response was neither receptive nor did he encourage her.

5.   Later that day, Zimbardo agreed that the actors were taking the experiment too seriously. Both the prisoners and the students playing the guards could experience long-term effects. They might be seriously hurt, distressed, and suffer from depression. Zimbardo terminated the planned two-week experiment after six days. He decided it was safer to end the experiment than completing it.

Practice 4

Correct ten errors in parallel construction.

EXAMPLE: Information about the best way to nurture children is surprising and ~~of interest~~ *interesting*.

1.   Harry Harlow was both a famous American psychologist and a researcher who was controversial. Harlow became known for his studies with rhesus monkeys. He started to collect data, to investigate behaviors, and proposing theories about the relationship between infants and their mothers. One of his studies was the Surrogate Mother experiment. Harlow's colleagues considered the experiment to be ground-breaking, astounding, and of significance.

2.   In 1932, Harlow established a breeding colony of rhesus monkeys. He set up the colony not only quickly but also he was careful. Harlow's experiment involved separating the monkeys from their mothers at birth. Maternal deprivation affected monkeys as much psychologically as in a physical way.

3.　　In the experiment, some monkeys had a cloth mother with no food, and a wire mother with food was given to some of them. Surprisingly, the monkeys with the wire mother showed more signs of stress than the cloth mother monkeys. According to the results of the study, when faced with a loud noise, the monkeys with the cloth surrogate went to their mothers, rubbed against them, and they became calmed down. However, the monkeys with a wire surrogate felt anxious, and they also had a feeling of terror.

4.　　One variation on Harlow's study produced an interesting conclusion: Baby monkeys who don't have any contact at all with other primates may develop crippling phobias, may be unable to socialize with other primates, and permanent psychological damage may be developed. When raising children, many parents do not want to appear too distant, vigilant, or be seen as being overprotective. However, it is clear young children need a lot of attention from their parents. Many experts believe this is a strong argument in favor of adoption versus institutionalized childcare for orphans.

Practice 5

Write sentences using parallel structure with the following grammatical items.

1. Parallel nouns: _____

    _____

2. Parallel verbs: _____

    _____

3. Parallel adjectives: _____

    _____

4. Parallel *who* clauses: _____

    _____

Reflect On It

Think about what you have learned in this chapter. If you do not know an answer, review that concept.

1. What is parallel structure? _____

    _____

2. Why is parallel structure important? _____

    _____

Fill in the blanks of the following sentences. Make sure the grammatical structures are parallel.

3. The college I attend is both _____ and

_____.

4. In my spare time, I _____, _____, and

_____.

Final Review

Correct fifteen errors in parallel construction.

EXAMPLE: Psychiatrists, psychologists, and ~~other people who are counselors~~ counselors
help patients deal with their mental health problems.

1. Have you ever been in a group discussion where you wanted to offer a different point of view but did not? Psychologist Irving Janis was ambitious, intelligent, and worked hard. In 1972, he studied group dynamics and then a book was written by him. He called his book *Groupthink*.

2. Groupthink occurs when members of a group feel a strong need to agree with others. These are people who do not criticize a prevailing position, who do not offer alternative strategies, and do not voice any disagreement. Group participants not only suppress common sense, but unpopular opinions are also avoided.

3. Janis presented an interesting example of groupthink in his book. In 1961, CIA operatives, military leaders, and people in American politics wanted to overthrow Fidel Castro. When President John F. Kennedy heard about the plan to invade Cuba, he was both agreeable and enthusiasm was felt by him. Kennedy's group of advisors wanted to be both cooperative and acting patriotic. Consequently, all of Kennedy's counselors agreed with the proposal. The invasion was planned blindly, quickly, and without care. As a result, the Bay of Pigs invasion was a failure.

4. In October 1962, the Soviet Union placed nuclear warheads in Cuba. When Kennedy heard about the missiles, he wanted to react immediately rather than delaying his response. He walked rapidly through the garden, along the corridor, and he went into the Oval Office. At the meeting with his advisors, Kennedy employed strategies to avoid groupthink. His advisors were encouraged to discuss, to debate, and they could disagree. Therefore, the men could either challenge bad ideas or good ideas could be analyzed. Using diplomacy, the president solved the crisis. The Soviets removed the nuclear weapons from Cuba immediately and with speed.

5.   Janis's book has shown how groupthink can have negative consequences in government, in academics, and for people who work in business. Many executives ignore groupthink rather than to learn about it. It is a phenomenon that can lead to very bad decision making.

The Writer's Room

Choose one of the following topics and write a paragraph or an essay. When you write, remember to follow the writing process.

1. What makes you happy? Describe some situations or events that make you happy.
2. What are some different ways that people deal with their fears? Classify their responses to fear into three categories.

READING LINK
Readings on Psychological Issues:

"What Is Luck?" (p. 198)
"Don't Worry, Act Happy" (p. 211)
"The Catcher of Ghosts" (p. 502)
"The Sanctuary of School" (p. 505)
"Planting False Memories" (p. 508)

The Writers' Circle: Collaborative Activity

When you apply for a job, the employer often asks about your strengths and weaknesses. Work with a team of students to do the following activity.

STEP 1   Think of a successful person. You could choose a person from any of the next categories.

A business tycoon	A politician	A movie star
A musician	An athlete	A writer or artist

STEP 2   Brainstorm one list of that person's strengths and another list of that person's weaknesses.

STEP 3   Write a short paragraph about that successful person, discussing the person's strengths and weaknesses.

STEP 4   Exchange paragraphs with another team. Proofread the other team's paragraph, checking especially for fragments, run-ons, and parallel structure.

23 Present and Past Tenses

SECTION THEME: Spies and Hackers

LEARNING OBJECTIVES

23.1 Define verb tense.

23.2 Identify simple present tense.

23.3 Identify simple past tense.

23.4 Avoid double negatives.

In this chapter, you read about spy tools and communication technology.

The Writer's Journal

Write a short paragraph describing the last spy or suspense movie that you have seen. Describe what happened in the movie.

What Is Verb Tense?

23.1 Define verb tense.

A verb shows an action or a state of being. A **verb tense** indicates when an action occurred. Review the various tenses of the verb *work*.

Present	She <u>works</u> alone.
Past	The agent <u>worked</u> in Monaco last summer.
Future	She <u>will work</u> in the Middle East next year.

Use Standard Verb Forms

Nonstandard English is used in everyday conversation, and it may differ according to the region in which you live. **Standard English** is the common language generally used and expected in schools, businesses, and government institutions in North America. Most of your instructors will want you to write using Standard English.

Nonstandard	He <u>don't</u> have <u>no</u> time.	She <u>be</u> busy.
Standard	He **does not** have **any** time.	She **is** busy.

The Simple Present Tense

23.2 **Identify simple present tense.**

In English there are two forms of the present tense. The **simple present tense** indicates that an action is a general fact or habitual activity. Note that the present progressive form is explained in the Hint box and in Chapter 25.

Fact	The Spy Museum <u>contains</u> many interesting spy artifacts.
Habitual activity	The computer hacker <u>goes</u> online every day.
	The undercover agent <u>meets</u> her superiors once a month.

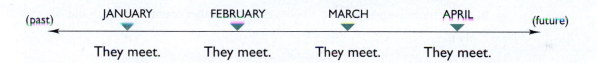

GRAMMAR LINK
For more information about progressive forms, see pages 329-331 in Chapter 25.

HINT: The Present Progressive

The **present progressive tense** indicates that an action is in progress at this moment. In this chapter, you focus on the simple present form.

present progressive tense

Right now, the agent **is taking** photos with her spy camera.

Forms of the Simple Present Tense

Simple present tense verbs (except *be*) have two forms. *Be* has three forms: *is, am, are*.

- **Base form:** When the subject is *I, you, we,* or *they,* or the equivalent (*women, the Rocky Mountains*), do not add an ending to the verb.

  Nations **rely** on spies to gather secret information.

- **Third-person singular form:** When the subject is *he, she, it,* or the equivalent (*Mark, Carol, Miami*), add an *-s* or *-es* ending to the verb. Remember that *have* is an irregular verb. The third-person singular form is *has*.

  That woman **works** as a spy.

  Look at the singular and plural forms of the verb *work*.

Present Tense of *Work*		
	Singular	**Plural**
First person	I work.	We work.
Second person	You work.	You work.
Third person	He work**s**. She work**s**. It work**s**.	They work.

Practice 1

Circle the correct present tense form of the verbs in parentheses.

EXAMPLE: Spying (seem / (seems)) like an exciting job.

1. According to Christopher Andrew, coauthor of *The Sword and the Shield*, the acronym *MICE* (sum / sums) up the reasons why a person may become a traitor.

2. *MICE* (stand / stands) for "money, ideology, compromise, and ego."

3. According to Andrew, the most popular reason (is / are) money.

4. Some agents (receive / receives) millions in cash, jewelry, and so on.

5. Another reason (is / are) ideology.

6. Sometimes people (believe / believes) that another country's way of life is better.

7. Some men and women (become / becomes) spies because they are ashamed of something that they have done.

8. For example, if a government bureaucrat (steal / steals) money and another person (find / finds) out, the bureaucrat can be blackmailed to become a spy.

9. Finally, many people (think / thinks) that spying (is / are) an exciting profession.

10. Andrew (say / says) that "an interesting minority want to be secret celebrities" in their own little world of espionage.

The Simple Past Tense

23.3 Identify simple past tense.

The **simple past tense** indicates that an action occurred at a specific past time. In the past tense, there are regular and irregular verbs. **Regular verbs** end in *-d* or *-ed* (*talked, ended, watched*). **Irregular verbs** do not follow a regular pattern and do not end in any specific letter (*knew, saw, met*).

Yesterday morning, the drone **passed** over my home.
Last month, someone **stole** my computer.

YESTERDAY MORNING   TODAY

The drone **passed** over my home.

HINT: The Past Progressive

The **past progressive tense** indicates that an action was in progress at a particular past moment. In this chapter, you focus on the simple past.

past progressive tense

While the detectives **were watching** the house, the suspect escaped.

GRAMMAR LINK
See Chapter 25, "Other Verb Forms," for more information about progressive verb forms.

Regular Past Tense Verbs

Regular past tense verbs have a standard -d or -ed ending. Use the same form for both singular and plural subjects.

Singular subject	The agent **learned** to speak six languages.
Plural subject	During the war, spies **used** code names.

SPELL REGULAR PAST TENSE VERBS CORRECTLY

Most regular past tense verbs are formed by adding -ed to the base form of the verb.

walk**ed**   question**ed**

However, there are some exceptions.

• When the regular verb ends in -e, just add -d.

realiz**ed**   appreciat**ed**

• When the regular verb ends in consonant + -y, change the y to i and add -ed.

reply–repl**ied**   try–tr**ied**

• When the regular verb ends in the vowel + -y, just add -ed.

play**ed**   employ**ed**

• When the regular verb ends in a consonant–vowel–consonant combination, double the last consonant and add -ed.

tap–tap**ped**   plan–plan**ned**

• When verbs of two or more syllables end in a stressed consonant–vowel–consonant combination, double the last letter and add -ed. But if the final syllable is not stressed, just add -ed.

Final stressed syllable	refer–refer**red**	omit–omit**ted**
Final unstressed syllable	open–open**ed**	develop–develop**ed**

GRAMMAR LINK
See Chapter 33, "Spelling and Commonly Confused Words," for information about spelling verbs.

HINT: Do Not Confuse *Past* and *Passed*

Some people confuse *past* and *passed*. *Past* is a noun that means "in a previous time" or "before now."

>   She has many secrets in her <u>past</u>.

Passed is the past tense of the verb *pass*, which has many meanings.

>   Many days <u>passed</u> as we waited for her arrival.
>   (*Passed* means "went by.")

>   I <u>passed</u> you the butter a moment ago.
>   (*Passed* means "took something and gave it to someone.")

>   He <u>passed</u> the entrance exam.
>   (*Passed* means "successfully completed.")

Practice 2

Write the simple past form of each verb in parentheses. Make sure you spell the past tense verb correctly.

EXAMPLE: The United States (launch) _____<u>launched</u>_____ a spy satellite in 1960.

1.   The Central Intelligence Agency (use) _____ a series of spy

satellites during the 1960s and 1970s. Officials (name) _____

each satellite with a code word. They (call) _____ the operation

"Corona." The satellites (pass) _____ over sensitive locations in the

former Soviet Union.

2.   Each Corona spy satellite (contain) _____ a powerful

camera and regular film. When the camera (finish) _____

filming, it ejected from the satellite inside a special capsule. Then back on

Earth, experts (study) _____ the images and (learn) _____

about the military secrets of other nations. During the 1960s, the Corona

satellites (drop) _____ at least three hundred capsules. Parachutes

(open) _____ and the capsules (float) _____ down. Then Air

Force pilots (recover) _____ the capsules.

3.   In the 1970s, the numbers of satellites (multiply) _____

dramatically. Last year, thousands of satellites (provide) _____

nations with high-resolution images of everything from shifting ice masses to

traffic conditions in Los Angeles.

GRAMMAR LINK
See Appendix 2, for a list of irregular verbs.

Irregular Past Tense Verbs

Irregular verbs change internally. Because their spellings change from the present to the past tense, these verbs can be challenging to remember.

The prisoner **wrote** with invisible ink.
(wrote = past tense of *write*)

The guards **sent** the letter.
(sent = past tense of *send*)

Practice 3

Write the correct past form of each verb in parentheses. Some verbs are regular, and some are irregular. If you do not know the past form of an irregular verb, consult Appendix 2.

EXAMPLE: The 2009 virus (have) _____ had _____ peculiar properties.

1.   What is the difference between a computer virus and a worm? A virus requires action, such as clicking on an email attachment, to infect a computer. A worm spreads without any human action. Last year, Internet security systems (find) _____ over a million viruses and worms!

2.   In 2009, clever experts (write) _____ a computer program called Stuxnet. They (send) _____ the sophisticated worm around the world. For several months, Stuxnet (make) _____ targeted hits on controllers, which regulate the machinery in factories and power plants. The worm (have) _____ no impact on ordinary computers and on most controllers. But when the worm (spread) _____ to nuclear reactors in Iran, it attacked the machinery. At that time, people in many governments (feel) _____ concerned about Iran's nuclear capabilities. According to experts, an unidentified nation (build) _____ the complicated worm to sabotage Iran's nuclear plants.

3.   The worm worked by spinning the centrifuges of the nuclear facility at extreme speeds so that they would self-destruct. At the same time, the worm (show) _____ fake readings to Iranian scientists. They (see) _____ regular measurements. While the reactor was quietly destroying itself, Iranian scientists (think) _____ it was functioning normally.

4.   In 2010, Stuxnet (come) _____ under intense scrutiny. What nation initially (run) _____ the program? Some suspect that Israel, the United States, and Germany (take) _____ part in the worm's development. Clearly, cyberwarfare is now possible.

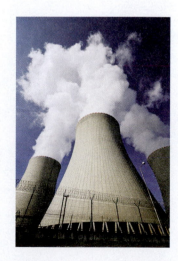

BE (WAS OR WERE)

Past tense verbs generally have one form that you can use with all subjects. However, the verb *be* has two past forms: *was* and *were*.

Past Tense of *Be*		
	Singular	**Plural**
First person	I was	We were
Second person	You were	You were
Third person	He **was**	They were
	She **was**	
	It **was**	

Practice 4

Write *was* or *were* in each space provided.

EXAMPLE: Donald Ewen Cameron _____was_____ not an ordinary psychiatrist.

1. During the early 1950s, Dr. Ewen Cameron worked for the U.S. Central Intelligence Agency (CIA). He _____ an eccentric psychiatrist, and he was involved in a mind-control program known as MKUltra. The research project _____ bizarre and controversial. Its goal _____ to create mind-altering drugs that the CIA could administer to suspected Soviet spies. The CIA _____ curious about the drugs' effects during interrogations. In a Montreal hospital, some psychiatric patients _____ not aware that they had received LSD and other powerful psychedelic drugs. Researchers also conducted studies on college campuses and in prisons.

2. Eventually, the research program included CIA agents. In one study, the CIA gave an agent a dose of LSD in his coffee, and the agent _____ psychotic for the rest of the day. He claimed to see monsters inside passing cars. Other CIA agents _____ unhappy to learn they had also been dosed with LSD. The study expanded to include army personnel, prisoners, and even prostitutes at certain brothels. The CIA researchers _____ experts at extracting information and confessions. When MKUltra became public, many people _____ furious because they believed that the program was unethical.

PROBLEMS WITH *BE*, *HAVE*, AND *DO*

Some students find it particularly difficult to remember how to use the irregular verbs *be*, *have*, and *do* in the past tense. Here are some helpful guidelines.

Avoiding Common Errors with *be*

•   Use *were* in the past tense when the subject is plural. Do not use *was*.

>   were
>   The spies ~~was~~ arrested in 1995.

- Use the standard form of the verb (*is* or *was*), not *be*.

  is
  The camera ~~be~~ small enough to fit in a pen.

Avoiding Common Errors with *have*

- Use the past form of the verb (*had*), not the present form (*have* or *has*), when speaking about a past event.

  had
  During the war, the agent ~~has~~ several passports.

Avoiding Common Errors with *do*

- Use *done* only when it is preceded by a helping verb (*was done, is done,* and so on).

  did
  In 2002, Valerie Plame ~~done~~ undercover work.

Practice 5

Underline and correct ten verb errors. If the verb is incorrectly formed, or if the verb is in the wrong tense, write the correct form above it.

have
EXAMPLE: Some people <u>has</u> a lot of concerns about espionage programs.

1.   Many citizens believes that wiretapping—secretly monitoring a telephone

conversation—is a recent spying strategy. In fact, in the early 1900s, wiretapping

been common. A 1928 Supreme Court ruling gived law enforcement officials

the constitutional right to intercept phone communications. Police forces was

able to tap the phones of Prohibition-era bootleggers, and they haved great

success with that tactic. American military intelligence officers be also able to

intercept phone communications of foreign governments.

2.   According to an article on *PBS.org*, Operation Shamrock was the first large-

scale domestic espionage program. From 1945 to 1975, NSA agents kept

copies of international telegrams sent across the United States. They also

choosed to monitor over 600 "dangerous" Americans, including Dr. Martin

Luther King Jr. and many other prominent civil rights leaders. In the early

1970s, when citizens first learned about the program, some felt angry. At

that time, many people thought that the government should not spy on its own

citizens. The issue of spying on citizens remains controversial.

Negative and Question Forms

In the present and past tenses, you must add a helping verb (*do, does,* or *did*) to question and negative forms. In the present tense, use the helping verb *do*, or use *does* when the subject is third-person singular. Use *did* in the past tense.

Questions	**Do** you know about the Spy Museum in Washington?
	Does the museum open on weekends?
	Did you visit the spy museum last summer?

Negatives	We **do not** live in Washington.
	The museum **does not** open on holidays.
	We **did not** visit the spy museum last summer.

When the main verb is *be* (*is, am, are*), no additional helping verb is necessary.

| Questions | **Is** the spy story suspenseful? |
| | **Were** foreign spies in New York during the event? |

| Negatives | The story **is not** suspenseful. |
| | Foreign spies **were not** in New York during the event. |

A NOTE ABOUT CONTRACTIONS

In informal writing, it is acceptable to contract negative verb forms. However, you should avoid using contractions in your academic writing.

>   does not
> The CIA ~~doesn't~~ have enough multilingual interpreters.

HINT: Use the Correct Question and Negative Forms

In question and negative forms, always use the base form of the main verb, even when the subject is third-person singular.

>   have
> Why does the Spy Museum ~~has~~ so many spy gadgets?

>   discuss
> In 1914, Mata Hari did not ~~discussed~~ her identity.

Practice 6

Write questions for each answer. Remember to add a helping verb (*do, does,* or *did*) when necessary.

EXAMPLES: Where is the International Spy Museum?

     The International Spy Museum is in Washington, D.C.

     What does it contain?

     It contains hundreds of spy gadgets.

1. _____

The Spy Museum opened in 2002.

2. _____

The spy gadgets are from nations around the world.

3. _____

Yes, the museum is open on Sundays.

4. _____

Yes, the camera has a powerful lens.

5. _____

Yes, many tourists visit the museum each year.

Practice 7

Combine the words in parentheses to form negatives. Remember to add a helping verb (*do*, *does*, or *did*) when necessary.

EXAMPLE: Washington's Spy Museum has hundreds of spy gadgets, but it (have, not) _____does not have_____ paintings.

1.   Washington's International Spy Museum contains many interesting gadgets. For example, on display is a tube of lipstick called "The Kiss of Death." The tube (have, not) _____ an obvious function. It (add, not) _____ color to a person's lips. Instead, the lipstick tube conceals a tiny pistol. In 1965, a female Russian spy carried the pistol in her purse, and others (know, not) _____ about her hidden weapon.

2.   The museum also has interesting listening devices. Some of them (be, not) _____ very large. In 1960, Hal Lipset (work, not) _____ for the government. He was a private detective, and he created an "olive" microphone. The olive (look, not) _____ fake when it was placed inside a martini. The toothpick acted as an antenna. It (have, not) _____ a very wide range and could only pick up nearby sounds. In the 1960s, recording devices (be, not) _____ very sensitive. Nowadays, microphones (have, not) _____ to be in a particular room to pick up a conversation.

3.   Clearly, the Spy Museum is an extremely interesting place. Tourists (have, not) _____ to spend the entire day at the museum because it (be, not) _____ a very large place.

HINT: Use the Base Form After *To*

Remember to use the base form of verbs that follow *to* (infinitive form).

Greenstein wanted to ~~studied~~ study the postcard.

Practice 8

The next selection contains verb tense, spelling, and *past* versus *passed* errors. Underline and correct fifteen errors.

                                      worked
EXAMPLE: In 2011, Wael Ghonim <u>work</u> for Google.

1.   In 1981, Hosni Mubarak becomed the president of Egypt. Thirty years past by, and Egyptians did not mobilized against their dictator. Mubarak thinked that he would rule for the rest of his life. But in 2010, something be different in the world. New online tools and websites helped disillusioned citizens organize a revolution.

2.   In 2010, Wael Ghonim, the head of marketing for Google in the Middle East, maked a Facebook page in memory of an anti-government protestor. In retaliation, Mubarak's regime putted Ghonim in prison. Ghonim's family telled the international media about his disappearance. Many bloggers writed about the case. Eleven days later, the government gived in to public pressure and released Ghonim. During an emotional interview on Egyptian television, Ghonim said that the regime did not deserved support.

3.   During the following weeks, Egyptians used cell phone messages, Twitter, and Facebook to organized. On February 11, 2011, the Egyptian government fallen. Unfortunately, life in Egypt did not improved significantly afterward. Many Egyptians are still unhappy with their leaders. According to many observers, YouTube, blogs, Facebook, and Twitter was essential tools for the movement known as Arab Spring.

Avoid Double Negatives

23.4 Avoid double negatives.

A double negative occurs when a negative word such as *no, nothing, nobody,* or *nowhere* is combined with a negative adverb such as *not, never, rarely,* or *seldom*. The result is a sentence that has a double negative. Such sentences can be confusing because the negative words cancel each other.

The agent <u>didn't</u> accept <u>no</u> money.
(According to this sentence, the agent accepted money.)

How to Correct Double Negatives

There are several ways to correct double negatives.

- Completely remove one of the negative forms.

  accepted no or didn't accept
  The agent ~~didn't accept no~~ money.

- Change *no* to *any* (*anybody, anything, anywhere*).

  any
  The agent didn't accept ~~no~~ money.

Practice 9

Underline and correct the six errors with double negatives. There is more than one way to correct each error.

had no (or didn't have any)
EXAMPLE: The spy <u>didn't have no</u> money.

1.   Every year, intelligence agencies develop highly sophisticated spy tools.

   Today, spy planes are lightweight and fly at extremely high altitudes. They

   don't have no pilots. Instead, ground teams direct the planes using remote

   control technology. For example, during a 2005 flight over Iraq, the Predator

   spy drone provided about fifteen hours of surveillance. It didn't make no

   noise, so people on the ground didn't see or hear nothing. The plane took

   high-resolution videos. More recently, the Global Hawk flew from the United

   States to Afghanistan and collected data from a height of about 65,000 feet.

   The Global Hawk did not need no refueling during the long journey.

2.   Scientists are trying to shrink the size of flying robots. According

   to the *Washington Post*, federally funded teams are working on remote

   control insects. However, the CIA did not confirm nothing to the reporters.

   Intelligence agents do not want nobody to know exactly what they are doing.

Reflect On It

Think about what you have learned in this chapter. If you do not know an answer, review that concept.

1. What are the present and past forms of the verb *be*?

	Present	Past
I	_____	_____
he, she, it	_____	_____
you, we, they	_____	_____

2. Write two regular past tense verbs. _____

3. Write two irregular past tense verbs. _____

4. Correct one verb tense error in each of the following sentences.

   a. In 1954, a Russian agent surrender to the United States.

   b. Khokhlov defected because he did not wanted to kill another Russian agent.

   c. Khokhlov past many days and nights hiding in a forest.

   d. The agent owned a cigarette case that be a secret weapon.

   e. The cigarette case fired bullets that was poisonous.

Final Review

Underline and correct errors in present and past tense verbs. Also look for one double negative. There are fifteen errors.

EXAMPLE: When people talk about espionage, they generally ~~thinks~~ *think* about secret agents who work for governments.

1. A nation's economic survival depend on its ability to be innovative.

   Countries try to protect secret technologies. For example, in the 1970s,

   DuPont created Kevlar, a synthetic fiber that be five times stronger than steel.

   It appears in products such as bulletproof vests. When DuPont developed

   Kevlar, the company didn't wanted competitors to learn its trade secrets.

   However, in 2006, an angry employee revealed information about Kevlar to a

   foreign company.

2.   In 2006, Michael David Mitchell losed his job at DuPont after twenty-five years of employment. Immediately, he done some unethical acts. First, he brung home private documents. Then he told DuPont officials that he didn't have no sensitive files. Two weeks later, he goed to work as a consultant for a Korean firm called Kolon, Inc. While there, he past secret information about Kevlar to his new employers. He also tried to got additional secret information from some of his former DuPont colleagues.

3.   In 2007, DuPont officials finded out that Mitchell was contacting former colleagues looking for information. Of course, DuPont executives be furious, and they contacted the FBI. In 2008, federal agents searched Mitchell's home. To save himself, Mitchell agree to cooperate with the government.

4.   Governments around the world take industrial espionage seriously. In the past, unhappy employees selled private documents to competitors. These days, secrets travel around the world electronically within seconds, so businesses are more vulnerable than ever.

The Writer's Room

Write about one of the following topics. Check your verb tenses carefully.

1. In the past, did you spy on someone, or did someone spy on you? For example, did you read somebody's diary, emails, or text messages, or eavesdrop on private conversations? Describe what happened.

2. Describe an emotional moment from your past. Include details that appeal to the five senses: taste, touch, sight, smell, sound.

24 Past Participles

SECTION THEME: Spies and Hackers

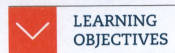
24.1 Identify past participles.

24.2 Define the present perfect tense.

24.3 Define the past perfect tense.

24.4 Identify the passive voice.

24.5 Use the past participle as an adjective.

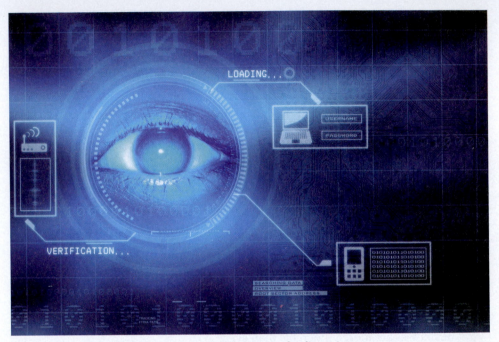

In this chapter, you read about some spying techniques and online privacy.

The Writer's Journal
Do you regularly use a social networking site such as Facebook or Twitter? Why or why not?

Past Participles

24.1 Identify past participles.

A **past participle** is a verb form, not a verb tense. You cannot use a past participle as the only verb in a sentence; instead, you must use it with a helping verb such as *have, has, had, is, was,* or *were.*

	helping verbs	past participles
Ian Fleming	was	raised in England.
His novels	have	become very popular.

Regular Verbs

GRAMMAR LINK
For a list of irregular past participles, see Appendix 2, on pages 000–000.

The past tense and the past participle of regular verbs are the same.

Base Form	Past Tense	Past Participle
walk	walked	walked
try	tried	tried

Irregular Verbs

The past tense and the past participle of irregular verbs may be different. For a complete list of irregular past participles, see Appendix 2.

Base Form	Past Tense	Past Participle
begin	began	begun
speak	spoke	spoken

Practice 1

Each group of verbs contains one error. Underline the error, and write the correct verb form in the space provided.

EXAMPLE:

	Base Form	Past Tense	Past Participle	
	lose	<u>losed</u>	lost	*lost*
1.	cost	cost	costed	_____
2.	come	came	came	_____
3.	build	builded	built	_____
4.	sing	sang	sang	_____
5.	bring	brang	brought	_____
6.	think	thank	thought	_____
7.	choose	choosed	chosen	_____
8.	fall	felt	fallen	_____
9.	feel	felt	fell	_____
10.	blow	blew	blowed	_____
11.	tear	tore	tore	_____
12.	take	taked	taken	_____
13.	bite	bited	bitten	_____
14.	sit	sat	sitten	_____
15.	grow	grew	growed	_____

Practice 2

In the following selection, the past participles are underlined. Correct ten past participle errors. Write *C* over five correct past participles.

EXAMPLE: Prominent activists have <u>meeted</u> many times to discuss the issue.
                                      met

1.   Consumer groups have <u>express</u> concerns about the lack of privacy for social

    media users. Particularly, the social networking site Facebook has <u>came</u> under

    attack. Since its inception, Facebook has <u>use</u> a "real-name" policy. Accounts

    of people using fake names can be <u>deleted</u> from the site without warning.

2.　　In 2014, a stricter version of the "real-name" policy was <u>introduced</u>. In the past, Facebook removed an account if it was <u>flag</u> by another user or if an account was <u>maked</u> with a bizarre name. However, in 2014, Facebook deleted many people's accounts because their Facebook names did not match the names on their government identification. For example, music journalist Legs McNeil was <u>tell</u> that he had to use his real name on Facebook. In 2015, an article that was <u>writed</u> by a Native American author, Dana Lynn Lone Elk, argued that Facebook doesn't believe in Indian names. Her account was <u>suspended</u> when she used her father's last name "Elk." According to Facebook, the policy has <u>protected</u> many people, especially women, from potential harassment. Victims can see the names of their abusers and refuse to add them as friends. However, one woman was <u>find</u> online by her abusive ex-boyfriend because she *couldn't* use a fake name. In another example, an Ethiopian LGBT activist was <u>forced</u> to either abandon his Facebook activism or use his real name and risk imprisonment.

3.　　Facebook's real-name policy has always <u>being</u> controversial. Perhaps the company could be <u>convince</u> to rethink its policy.

The Present Perfect Tense: *have/has* + Past Participle

24.2 Define the present perfect tense.

Combine *have* or *has* and a past participle to form the **present perfect tense**. You can use this tense in two different circumstances.

- Use the present perfect to show that an action began in the past and continues to the present time. You will often use *since* and *for* with this tense.

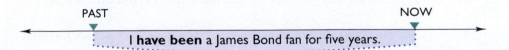
PAST ─── I **have been** a James Bond fan for five years. ─── NOW

- Use the present perfect to show that one or more completed actions occurred at unspecified past times.

PAST (unspecified past times)   NOW

I **have watched** at least four James Bond movies.

HINT: Use Time Markers

Time markers are words that indicate when an action occurred.

Simple Past Tense

To refer to a completed incident that occurred at a specific past time, use the following time markers.

yesterday	ago	when I was . . .	last (week, month, year . . .)
in the past	in 2005	during the 1970s	in the early days of . . .

Ian Fleming **wrote** his first novel <u>in 1953</u>.

Present Perfect Tense

- To refer to an action that began in the past and is still continuing, use the following time markers.

since	for (a period of time up to now)	ever
up to now	so far	not . . . yet

Spy films **have been** popular <u>since the 1930s</u>.

- To refer to an action that occurred at unspecified past times, use the following types of time markers

once	twice	several times	lately	recently	many

I **have seen** *Skyfall* <u>once</u> and *Spectre* <u>twice</u>.

Look at the difference between the past and the present perfect tenses.

Simple past	In 1962, Sean Connery **appeared** in the first James Bond film, *Dr. No*. (This event occurred at a known past time.)
Present perfect	Many different actors **have played** James Bond. (We do not really know when the actors played James Bond.) James Bond movies **have been** popular for more than forty years. (The action began in the past and continues to the present.)

Practice 3

Write the simple past or present perfect form of each verb in parentheses.

EXAMPLE: We (meet) _____ *have met* _____ many times to discuss the problem.

1.   Spying on employees is not new; in fact, companies (do) _____ it for many years. Since 2000, some employers (scan) _____ their staff's computer usage. Over the years, employer spying (become) _____ more and more prevalent.

2.   Raymond Croft, the CEO of a small company, (buy) _____ _____ several types of spying software over the years. Two years ago, he (purchase) _____ SpectorSoft monitoring software. Since then, he (use) _____ the software to do spot checks on employees. For example, last January, a young female member of the staff (take) _____ her laptop to a coffee shop. She (tell) _____ her boss that she was going to work from home. Instead, she (spend) _____ the afternoon sending out résumés and reading tabloid gossip. She (realize, not) _____ that her computer was being monitored. Since then, Croft (fire) _____ that employee.

3.   Over the years, many critics (complain) _____ that spy software leads to a hostile work atmosphere. Since 2005, too many employees (lose) _____ their jobs simply for being human and going online during breaks. On the other hand, many employers (catch) _____ staff doing illegal activities such as selling trade secrets. Certainly, workers should remember that their bosses can spy on them.

The Past Perfect Tense: *had* + Past Participle

24.3 Define the past perfect tense.

The **past perfect tense** indicates that one or more past actions happened before another past action. It is formed with *had* and the past participle.

PAST PERFECT ▼   PAST ▼   NOW ▼

The robbers **had left** when the police arrived.

Notice the differences between the simple past, the present perfect, and the past perfect tenses.

Simple past	Last night I **watched** a documentary on double agents. (The action occurred at a known past time.)
Present perfect	I **have read** many articles about spying. (The actions occurred at unspecified past times.)
Past perfect	Government officials **had suspected** the agent for a long time before they arrested him as a spy. (All of the actions happened in the past, but one action happened before another.)

Practice 4

Underline the correct verb form. You may choose the simple past, the present perfect, or the past perfect tense.

EXAMPLE: Chen Lee (was / <u>has been</u>) a security expert since 2001.

1.   Chen and Ryan (are / were / have been) friends since they were children. By the age of twenty-one, Ryan (had made / have made) several online mistakes that compromised his security. In March 2014, Ryan clicked on the link to a smartphone ad. He did not realize that a hacker (put / had put) a malicious virus into the ad. The virus infected Ryan's computer. Unfortunately, Ryan (already used / had already used) the same password for all of his online accounts.

2.   At that time, Ryan claimed that he (never saw / had never seen) warnings about the importance of using different passwords. He also admitted that he (has told / had told) his Facebook password to an ex-girlfriend. Because of these lapses in judgment, on April 2, 2014, hackers (stole / had stolen) his credit-card number. By the end of April, all of his Facebook friends and email contacts (received / had received) messages from him that contained viruses.

3.   Chen is much more careful than Ryan. Chen's security system (never failed / has never failed) in his entire life. He uses the most advanced malware technology. By the time he was eighteen years old, Chen (has already learned / had already learned) that using non-alpha-numeric characters greatly helps password security. For example, he puts a punctuation mark or underscore at the beginning and ending of his passwords. Since 2012, he (changed / has changed) his passwords several times. Over the years, Chen (taken / has taken) several other steps to protect his online security.

4.   Chen and Ryan met in 2014, at the time of the hack. At that time, Chen told Ryan that he (never saw / had never seen) such shoddy online protection. Since then, Ryan (changed / has changed) all of his passwords, and he (had bought / has bought) new antivirus software.

The Passive Voice: *be* + Past Participle

24.4 Identify the passive voice.

In sentences with the **passive voice**, the subject receives the action and does not perform the action. Look carefully at the next two sentences.

Active   The diplomat **gave** secret documents to an undercover agent.
          (This is active because the subject, *diplomat*, performed the action.)

Passive   Secret documents **were given** to an undercover agent.
          (This is passive because the subject, *documents*, was affected by the action and did not perform the action.)

To form the passive voice, use the appropriate tense of the verb *be* plus the past participle.

Verb Tenses	Active Voice (The subject performs the action.)	Passive Voice: *be* + Past Participle (The subject receives the action.)
Simple present	She writes spy stories.	Spy stories are written (by her).
Present progressive	is writing	are being written
Simple past	wrote	were written
Present perfect	has written	have been written
Future	will write	will be written
Modals	can write	can be written
	could write	could be written
	should write	should be written
	would have written	would have been written

Practice 5

Underline the appropriate verb in parentheses. Then decide if it is active or passive. Write *A* for "active" or *P* for "passive" above each verb.

                                                    P
EXAMPLE: The software (designed / <u>was designed</u>) to spy on users of infected computers.

1.   During times of war, nations (have used / have been used) soldiers, tanks, and airplanes to fight each other. Today, another type of war (is fighting / is being fought) online. In 2012, for *Vanity Fair* magazine, Michael Joseph Gross (wrote / was written) the article "World War 3.0." He says that battle lines (have drawn / have been drawn) between some regimes and their technologically savvy opponents. Nations (can use / can be used) stealthy computer worms to spy.

2.   In 2012, a type of malware called "Flame" (discovered / was discovered) in Iran. Flame (targeted / was targeted) Windows operating systems. It (could not detect / could not be detected) by antivirus software. With Flame, computer experts (could access / could be accessed) the private messages of government officials in the Middle East. Even audio files and conversations on Skype (could record / could be recorded) by the spy program. At the time, Flame (considered / was considered) the most sophisticated spying software in the world.

HINT: The *by . . .* Phrase

In many passive sentences, it is not necessary to write the *by . . .* phrase because the noun performing the action is understood.

> CIA agents **are selected** according to their abilities.

> (Adding "by CIA recruiters" after "selected" is not necessary.)

Practice 6

Complete the following sentences by changing each italicized verb to the passive form. Do not alter the verb tense. Note: You do not have to include the *by . . .* phrase.

EXAMPLE: Intelligence organizations *spy* on many different people.

> Many different people _are spied on (by intelligence organizations)._

1. Government agencies *track* the online activity of criminals.

The online activity of criminals _____

_____

2. A National Security Agency (NSA) program *captures* photos sent by smartphone or email.

Photos sent by smartphone or email _____

3. Last year, the government *created* new laws to limit spying.

Last year, new laws to limit spying _____

4. Several news organizations *have released* stories about government spying practices.

Stories about government spying practices _____

_____

5. Citizens *will debate* this issue.

This issue _____

HINT: Avoid Overusing the Passive Voice

Generally, use the active voice instead of the passive voice. The active voice is more direct and less wordy than the passive voice. For example, read the next two versions of the same message.

Passive voice   The problem has been rectified by us, and a new order is being prepared for you. You will be contacted by our sales department.

Active voice   We have corrected the problem and are preparing a new order for you. Our sales department will contact you.

In rare cases when you do not know who did the action, the passive voice may be more appropriate.

> James Bond's miniature camera was made in Italy.

> (You do not know who made the camera.)

Practice 7

Underline examples of the passive voice in the following letter. Then rewrite the letter using the active voice.

Dear Parents,

Security cameras have been installed in our school for several reasons. First, intruders have been seen by students. Also, if fighting is done by students, the scenes will be recorded and the culprits will be caught. In addition, any vandalism to school property can be viewed by our staff. For further information, we can be contacted at any time during school hours.

Sincerely,
Tony Romano, Principal, Rosedale High School

_____

_____

_____

_____

_____

_____

_____

_____

_____

_____

_____

The Past Participle as an Adjective

24.5 **Use the past participle as an adjective.**

A past participle can function as an adjective when it appears after a linking verb such as *be* or *feel*. In the example, *excited* modifies *agent*.

The young <u>agent</u> was **excited**.

A past participle can also function as an adjective when it describes or modifies the noun that follows it. In the example, *broken* modifies *promises*.

She was angry about the **broken** <u>promises</u>.

GRAMMAR LINK
For more information about linking verbs, see page in Chapter 16.

HINT: Be Careful!

In the passive voice, sometimes the verb *be* is suggested but not written. The following sentence contains the passive voice.

Many activities _^ done in the 1920s are still common today.

that were

Practice 8

Underline and correct fifteen past participle errors.

EXAMPLE: The scandal has <u>result</u> in the closing of the newspaper.
resulted

1. In the early 2000s, cell phone messages that belonged to Prince William, Jude Law, and other celebrities were hack. The information was gave to tabloid journalists. At first, the public was not very interest in the issue. After all, celebrities are expect to have no privacy.

2. Privacy issues affect non-celebrities as well. In 2011, information was leak to the media about the phone hacking of ordinary citizens. Allegedly, back in 2002, a tabloid call *News of the World* paid a private investigator to investigate the disappearance of thirteen-year-old Milly Dowler. Later it was discover that some of Dowler's voicemail messages were delete. Dowler's parents were thrilled because they thought that their cherish daughter had remove the messages herself. Their hopes were dash when the phone hacking was reveal.

3. An article, wrote by *The Guardian* newspaper, gave details about the scandal. Members of the public were shock, and they demanded action. In the summer of 2011, the celebrated *News of the World* newspaper was close.

Reflect On It

Think about what you have learned in this chapter. If you do not know an answer, review that concept.

1. Give two circumstances in which you would use the present perfect tense.

   _____

   _____

2. When do you use the past perfect tense? _____

   _____

3. How do you form the passive voice? _____

   _____

4. Identify and correct the errors in the following sentences.

   a. Robert Ludlum's first book was publish in 1971.

   b. By 2000, he had wrote twenty-one spy novels.

   c. Millions of people have buyed his novel *The Bourne Identity*.

   d. Have you ever saw a movie that was based on a book by Ludlum?

Final Review

Part A: Fill in each blank with the appropriate verb tense. The sentence may require the active or passive voice.

EXAMPLE: Closed-circuit cameras (be) _____<u>have been</u>_____ common for many years.

1.   Since the 1990s, many ordinary citizens (install) _____ security cameras outside their homes. For example, in 2009, a camera (place) _____ outside a home in Coventry, England. In August 2010, a forty-five-year-old woman named Mary Bale (film) _____ by the security camera as she picked up Darryl Mann's cat and threw it into a large blue trash container. The cat, Lola, (discover) _____ fifteen hours later by the owners.

2.   The next day, Mann released the video on his Facebook page. It quickly became viral, and the culprit, Mary Bale, (identify) _____ by a member of the public. She couldn't deny her action because she (catch) _____ red-handed. A few days later, she said, "It was just a cat," and her life (threaten) _____ by angry animal lovers. Since then, Bale (have) _____ to move to another city.

3.   Although Bale (break) _____ the law before that incident, she became the most hated woman in Britain. Many times since then, the gray-haired woman (apologize) _____. Do people deserve to be named and shamed when they make mistakes?

Part B: Underline and correct five past participle errors.

EXAMPLE: The video was <u>use</u> in court.
used

4.   Over the years, personal privacy has diminish. For example, the 2010 footage that was took and put online helped capture Bale. She was not gave the opportunity to apologize to the family and to deal with the incident privately. Instead, over a million people have viewed the "Cat in Bin in Coventry" video on YouTube, and Bale has losed her good reputation. These days, many people are shame when they act improperly in public.

The Writer's Room

Write about one of the following topics. Make sure that verb forms are correct.

1. Define an ideal politician. What characteristics should a great politician have?

2. Why do some parents spy on their children? What are the effects of such spying? Write about the causes and effects of spying on children.

25   Other Verb Forms

SECTION THEME: Spies and Hackers

In this chapter, you read about political and computer hacking scandals.

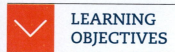

LEARNING OBJECTIVES

25.1 Identify problems with progressive forms (-*ing* verbs).

25.2 Avoid nonstandard forms: *gonna, gotta, wanna*.

25.3 Use gerunds and infinitives.

25.4 Use conditional forms.

25.5 Avoid nonstandard forms: *would of, could of, should of*.

The Writer's Journal

In your opinion, is it ethical to use cameras to spy on nannies, babysitters, or other caregivers? Write a paragraph about the issue.

Problems with Progressive Forms (-*ing* Verbs)

25.1 Identify problems with progressive forms (-*ing* verbs).

Most verbs have progressive tenses. The **progressive tense** indicates that an action is, was, or will be in progress. For example, the present progressive indicates that an action is happening right now or for a temporary period of time.

> **Simple present**   Every day, Detective Jonkala **spies** on cheating spouses.
>
> **Present progressive**   Today, he **is following** Ms. Wang.

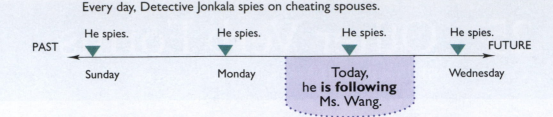

Every day, Detective Jonkala spies on cheating spouses.

To form the progressive, use the appropriate tense of the verb *be* with the *-ing* verb.

Present progressive	Right now, Detective Jonkala is **watching** the suspect.
Past progressive	He **was taking** notes when the suspect left the hotel.
Future progressive	Tomorrow, at 6:00 A.M., Natasha **will be following** the suspect.
Present perfect progressive	Detective Jonkala **has been working** for the police since 1994.
Past perfect progressive	He **had been waiting** in his car when his partner arrived.

Common Errors with the Progressive Form

- Do not use the progressive form when an action happens regularly.

  complains
  Every day, he ~~is complaining~~ about his job.

- In the progressive form, use the correct form of the verb *be*.

  is
  Right now, the nanny ~~be~~ playing with the children.

- In the progressive form, always include the complete helping verb.

  are   *have*
  Right now, the agents examining the photos. They been working for hours.

HINT: Nonprogressive Verbs

Some verbs do not take the progressive form because they indicate an ongoing state or a perception rather than a temporary action. Here are some examples of nonprogressive verbs.

Perception Verbs	Preference Verbs	State Verbs	Possession
admire	care*	believe	belong
feel*	desire	know	have*
hear	doubt	mean	own
look*	hate	realize	possess
see	like	recognize	
seem	love	suppose	
smell*	prefer	think*	
taste*	want	understand	

*The verbs marked with an asterisk have more than one meaning and can also be used in the progressive tense. Compare the next pairs of sentences.

Nonprogressive

He **has** a video camera. (Expresses ownership)

I **think** it is unethical. (Expresses an opinion)

Progressive

He **is having** a bad day.

I **am thinking** about you.

Practice 1

Each sentence has errors with progressive forms. Underline and correct each error.

have been
EXAMPLE: I <u>been</u> shopping online for years.

1. Generally, I am loving social media, but recently something happened that disturbed me.

2. Yesterday morning, I be browsing the Internet, and I visited a social networking site.

3. I was looking at my personal page when I was noticing an ad for my favorite restaurant.

4. I be upset because the social networking site knew my dining habits.

5. Many different corporations been tracking my online activity.

6. Even Google been scanning the emails and search history of its users for information to sell to advertisers.

7. I like to shop online, and every day I am using my phone for searches and transactions.

8. It's weird that others been tracking the businesses I visit.

Nonstandard Forms: *Gonna, Gotta, Wanna*

25.2 Avoid nonstandard forms: *gonna, gotta, wanna.*

Some people commonly say *I'm gonna, I gotta,* or *I wanna.* These are nonstandard forms, and you should not use them in written communication.

- Write *going to* instead of *gonna.*

  going to
  The nanny is <del>gonna</del> sue her employer.

- Write *have* or *had to* instead of *gotta.*

  have to
  The Smiths <del>gotta</del> go to court to fight the lawsuit.

- Write *want to* instead of *wanna.*

  want to
  They <del>wanna</del> win their case.

Practice 2

Underline and correct eight incorrect verb tenses or nonstandard verbs.

EXAMPLE: Some traitors just <u>wanna</u> earn extra money.
want to

1. From 1976 to 2001, Robert Hanssen worked for the Federal Bureau of Investigation. For fifteen years, while he be doing his day job, he also spying for the Russian government. He regularly passed documents to Russian agents. In 2000, FBI agents realized that Hanssen was a spy.

2. Usually, if agents are gonna arrest someone, they gotta have solid evidence. To get that evidence, the FBI promoted Hanssen and placed him under surveillance. Hanssen did not wanna accept the promotion because he would lose access to useful information. However, he had no choice, so he moved to FBI Headquarters. He soon became suspicious. He noticed that his new assistant was watch him closely.

3. By January 2001, Hanssen realized that he was gonna be arrested. Still, he continued working as a spy. On February 18, he placed a white piece of tape on a sign, which was a signal to his Russian contact. Then, while he was attach a package of documents to the bottom of a wooden footbridge, he was arrested. As agents were handcuffing him, Hanssen asked, "What took you so long?"

Using Gerunds and Infinitives

25.3 Use gerunds and infinitives.

Sometimes a main verb is followed by another verb. The second verb can be a gerund or an infinitive. A **gerund** is a verb with an *-ing* ending. An **infinitive** consists of *to* and the base form of the verb.

verb + gerund

Gerund Hanssen <u>considered</u> **joining** the FBI.

verb + infinitive

Infinitive He <u>wanted</u> **to have** a long career.

Do not confuse gerunds with progressive verb forms. Compare the following sentences.

Maria is writing.	(The action of writing is in progress right now.)
Some people <u>enjoy</u> **writing**.	(*Writing* is a gerund that follows *enjoy*.)

Some Common Verbs Followed by Gerunds			
acknowledge	deny	keep	recall
adore	detest	loathe	recollect
appreciate	discuss	mention	recommend
avoid	dislike	mind	regret
can't help	enjoy	miss	resent
complete	finish	postpone	resist
consider	imagine	practice	risk
delay	involve	quit	tolerate

EXAMPLES: She would <u>consider</u> **working** for us.

She <u>risks</u> **losing** her job.

Some Common Verbs Followed by Infinitives			
afford	decide	manage	refuse
agree	demand	mean	seem
appear	deserve	need	swear
arrange	expect	offer	threaten
ask	fail	plan	volunteer
claim	hesitate	prepare	want
compete	hope	pretend	wish
consent	learn	promise	would like

EXAMPLES: He <u>expected</u> **to keep** his job.

He <u>promised</u> **to be** honest.

Some Common Verbs Followed by Gerunds or Infinitives				
Some verbs can be followed by either a gerund or infinitive.				
begin	continue	like	love	start

EXAMPLES: Marcus <u>loves</u> **to spy**.

Marcus <u>loves</u> **spying**.

HINT: Using *Stop*

You can follow *stop* with a gerund or infinitive, but there is a difference in meaning.

Stop **+ gerund** means "to permanently stop doing something."

Hanssen <u>stopped</u> **selling** information to the Soviets.

Stop **+ infinitive** means "to stop an activity to do something else."

The agent was leaving when he <u>stopped</u> **to talk** to an old friend.

Practice 3

Underline the appropriate verb form. Choose the gerund or the infinitive.

EXAMPLE: The spy's job involved (<u>passing</u> / to pass) information to the Russians.

1.   Robert Hanssen, like many double agents, was a very good liar. Most people can't help (lying / to lie) at one time or another. Psychologist Robert Feldman enjoys (studying / to study) human deception. He says that human beings need (lying / to lie) sometimes. Lying seems (being / to be) a part of human nature.

2.   Feldman conducts experiments to learn how people lie. In one test, he places two strangers in a small room. He asks (videotaping / to videotape) the participants. After ten minutes, he stops (taping / to tape), and then he questions the two people. Usually, the subjects deny (to lie / lying). Then, while watching the video, they stop (fooling / to fool) themselves, and they admit that they have made many inaccurate statements. For instance, in one trial, the male participant falsely claimed (being / to be) a musician, and the female pretended (to like / liking) the same music as the male. They justified (being / to be) inaccurate by saying that their lies were not harmful. It appears that humans simply cannot avoid (lying / to lie) sometimes.

Using Conditional Forms

25.4 Use conditional forms.

In **conditional sentences**, there is a condition and a result. There are three types of conditional sentences, and each type has two parts, or clauses. The main clause depends on the condition set in the *if* clause.

First Form: Possible Present or Future

The condition is true or very possible.

If + present tense, ————————► present or future tense

Condition (*if* clause)	**Result**
If you **buy** the book,	you **will learn** about satellites.

Second Form: Unlikely Present

The condition is not likely and will probably not happen.

If + past tense, ————————► *would* (expresses a condition)

If + past tense, ————————► *could* (expresses a possibility)

Condition (*if* clause)	**Result**
If he **had** the chance,	he **would work** for the CIA.

Note: In formal writing, when the condition contains the verb *be*, always use *were* in the *if* clause.

If Amanda **were** older, she **would become** a spy.

Third Form: Impossible Past

The condition cannot happen because the event is over.

If + past perfect tense, ———————➤ *would have* (+ past participle)

Condition (*if* clause)	**Result**
If Amanda **had known** him,	she **would have been** more careful.

HINT: Be Careful with the Past Conditional

In the third type of conditional sentence, the impossible past, the writer expresses regret about a past event or expresses the wish that a past event had worked out differently. In the *if* part of the sentence, remember to use the past perfect tense.

If + past perfect tense,   . . . *would have* (past participle) . . .

                                    had listened
If CIA agents ~~would have listened~~ to the tape, they **would have discovered** the agent's identity.

Practice 4

Fill in the blanks with the past conditional tense.

EXAMPLE: If the police (make) _____had made_____ an investigation, the
case would have been solved.

1.   Is hacking ethical? In "A Brief History of Hacking," Mark Ward says that

    in the 1960s, "hackers were benign creatures." A "hack" was "an inspired

    solution to a problem." If you (live) _____ in

    1986, you (admire) _____ the hackers. Most

    early hackers just wanted to find the flaws in computer systems. Some of

    them did silly pranks, but others hacked for personal gain. For instance,

    Steve Jobs hacked telephone systems to make free phone calls. Perhaps if the

    police (arrest) _____ Jobs back in the 1980s, he

    (form, not) _____ Apple Computers.

2.   Another early hacker went by the name Dark Dante. He took over the phone

    lines of radio shows and won major prizes. For instance, in 1990, he was the

    102nd caller to a Los Angeles radio show, and he won a Porsche. If those radio

    stations (know) _____ about the hacking, they

    (change) _____ the contest rules. After exploits such

    as Dark Dante's became well known, new anti-hacking laws were introduced.

Nonstandard Forms: *Would of, Could of, Should of*

25.5 **Avoid nonstandard forms:** *would of, could of, should of.*

Some people commonly say *would of, could of,* or *should of.* They may also say *woulda, coulda,* or *shoulda.* These are nonstandard forms, and you should avoid using them in written communication. When you use the past forms of *should, would,* and *could,* always include *have* + the past participle.

> **could have**
> Those thieves ~~coulda~~ been more careful. They should ~~of~~ noticed the bank's
> **have**
> security cameras.

Practice 5

Underline and correct twelve errors in conditional forms or in the past forms of *could* and *should.*

should have
EXAMPLE: The banks ~~shoulda~~ been more careful.

James Thew

1.   On a winter day in early 2015, a Kiev bank's security cameras recorded something strange. An ATM machine was spitting out money that "lucky" customers were scooping up. The bank hired a Russian security firm, Kaspersky Lab, to investigate. If the bank would have ignored the cash machine problem, nobody would of discovered a shocking plot. International cybercriminals had infiltrated the internal computer systems of more than a hundred banks in thirty nations. According to Kaspersky Lab, the organized crime figures coulda stolen nearly a billion dollars.

2.   The hack began with infected emails sent to bank employees. Those employees shoulda been more careful because the emails carried malicious code. Some argue that if the banks would have known about the malware, they coulda bolstered their computer security. But police suggest that the hackers could of infiltrated any type of banking software. Certainly, the bank should have discover the heist sooner. The hackers had lurked in the banking system for almost two years! Those banks could of been the target of many other cyberattacks in the past. However, banks don't like to publicize such attacks because they don't want consumers to worry about the safety of banking systems.

3.   In 2015, *New York Times* journalists wondered if banks would continuing to be susceptible to computer viruses. If that faulty cash machine in the Ukraine hadn't become part of a larger investigation, the press would not of learned of the theft so quickly. The cybercriminals should have went to prison. However, they used sophisticated computer software and have not been caught. This heist could be the largest cybercrime ever.

Reflect On It

Think about what you have learned in this chapter. If you do not know an answer, review that concept.

1. When do you use the progressive form of verbs? _____
   _____

2. Write your own examples of the three types of conditional sentences.

   First form: _____
   _____

   Second form: _____
   _____

   Third form: _____
   _____

3. Correct the following sentences by writing the standard form of each nonstandard verb.

   a. If you wanna succeed, you gotta work hard.

   b. J. Rowen been investigating UFOs since 1978.

   c. If Kennedy would have taken another route, maybe he woulda lived.

   d. Maybe one day somebody is gonna tell the truth about the Kennedy case.

   e. I enjoyed to read a book about the trial.

Final Review

Underline and correct twenty errors with verbs. Look for nonstandard verbs and errors with conditionals, gerunds, and progressive forms.

EXAMPLE: Monsegur should <u>of</u> found a computer security job.
                              have

1.   In early February 2011, Aaron Barr, the CEO of a security firm, did an

   interview with the *Financial Times*. He boasted that he was gonna expose core

   leaders in the hacker collective Anonymous. Many people read the interview,

   including some hackers. A few days later, on February 6, Barr be watching

   the Super Bowl. When he finished to drink his coffee, he tried unsuccessfully

   to access his email account. At that moment, hackers annihilating Barr's

   website, changing his passwords, and posting thousands of his emails on

   Pirate Bay. Barr panicked and realized that he should not of threatened

   Anonymous. He called his computer technician, pleading, "You gotta do

   something." It was too late. If Barr would have kept quiet, he would have

   avoided a major headache.

2.   Feeling bold after the Barr attack, the Anonymous members promised hacking the CIA and the FBI. They felt sure that nobody was gonna catch them. But those hackers should not of been so cocky. On June 7, 2011, two FBI agents put on their bulletproof vests and went to a housing complex in New York's Lower East side. That day was very hot, so the agents be sweating profusely. Hector Xavier Monsegur, a twenty-eight-year-old unemployed father of two, be cooking for his children when someone knocked on the door. Monsegur, who used the online name "Sabu," couldn't believe it when he saw the agents. At first, he denied to be a hacker, but his computers provided the evidence the agents needed. Soon after, Sabu agreed working undercover for the FBI. Of course, he woulda felt really guilty about snitching on his friends, but he didn't wanna lose his children and spend his life in prison.

3.   In March 2012, based on Sabu's information, police arrested Ryan Ackroyd, a twenty-five-year-old British citizen. Maybe if Ackroyd woulda been more suspicious of Sabu, he could have saved himself. A few days later, Jake Davis, an eighteen-year-old hacker, must of been shocked when the police turned up at his door. Many argue that the hackers should not of attacked government and corporate websites and that their arrests were justified. Since then, other hackers have filled the void left by the arrests. Clearly, computer hacking is gonna continue in the future.

The Writer's Room

Write about one of the following topics. Review your verb forms carefully.

1. How would your life have been different if you had lived one hundred years ago? List some ways.
2. Should journalists report on the private lives of politicians? For example, is it important to know if a candidate has committed adultery or has had an addiction to drugs or alcohol? Explain your views.

READING LINK
To learn more about spies and hackers, read the next essays.
"How Spies Are Caught" (p. 533)

The Writers' Circle: Collaborative Activity

Work with a group of two or three other students. Choose a scandal that was in the news. It can be a scandal that happened to a celebrity, politician, sports figure, or business person. Discuss what happened. First, as a team, write a short paragraph about the scandal. Use the simple past tense. Then, in a second paragraph, write about what you would have done. Explain why, and give some details.

26 Subject–Verb Agreement

SECTION THEME: College Life

In this chapter, you read about topics related to college issues.

LEARNING OBJECTIVES

26.1 Identify basic subject–verb agreement rules.

26.2 Maintain subject–verb agreement when there is more than one subject.

26.3 Identify special subject forms.

26.4 Maintain subject–verb agreement when the verb is before the subject.

26.5 Identify interrupting words and phrases.

The Writer's Journal

In a short paragraph, express your opinion about the extracurricular activities on your campus.

Basic Subject–Verb Agreement Rules

26.1 Identify basic subject–verb agreement rules.

Subject–verb agreement simply means that a subject and verb agree in number. A singular subject needs a singular verb, and a plural subject needs a plural verb.

Singular subject Mr. Connor **teaches** in a community college.

Plural subject The students **appreciate** his approach.

Simple Present Tense Agreement

Writers use the **simple present tense** to indicate that an action is habitual or factual. Review the following rules for simple present tense agreement.

- When the subject is *he, she, it*, or the equivalent (*Adam, Maria, Florida*), add an *-s* or *-es* ending to the verb. This is also called the **third-person singular form**.

  Singular   Michael **works** in the college bookstore. (one person)

  This neighborhood **needs** a medical clinic. (one place)

  The trophy **belongs** to the best athlete in the college. (one thing)

- When the subject is *I, you, we, they*, or the equivalent (*the Zorns, the mountains, Amber and Tom*), do not add an ending to the verb.

  Plural   College students **have** many options. (more than one person)

  Many colleges **host** political debates. (more than one place)

  The benefits **include** a higher standard of living.
  (more than one thing)

For example, review the present tense forms of the verb *help*.

Present Tense of *Help*		
	Singular	Plural
First person	I help	We help
Second person	You help	You help
Third person	He **helps**	They help
	She **helps**	
	It **helps**	

Practice 1

Write the present tense form of each verb in parentheses.

EXAMPLE: Counselors (encourage) _____encourage_____ students to seek help for problems.

1. A freshman, Alex Snow (study) _____ at a college four hours away from his hometown.

2. He (rent) _____ a small room near the college, but he (try) _____ to go home as often as possible.

3. Alex (realize) _____ that he sometimes (get) _____ lonely.

4. He (miss) _____ his family and friends.

5. Many students (find) _____ that they (become) _____ homesick in their first months at college.

6. Alex's college (offer) _____ a counseling service for students experiencing difficulties, such as homesickness, depression, and so on.

7. Alex (know) _____ that it is important to get help, so he (see) _____ a counselor once a week.

Troublesome Present Tense Verbs: *Be, Have, Do*

Some present tense verbs are formed in special ways. Review the verbs *be, have,* and *do.*

	Be	Have	Do
Singular Forms			
First person	I am	I have	I do
Second person	You are	You have	You do
Third person	He **is** She **is** It **is**	He **has** She **has** It **has**	He **does** She **does** It **does**
Plural Forms			
First person	We are	We have	We do
Second person	You are	You have	You do
Third person	They are	They have	They do

HINT: Use Standard Forms of *Be*

Some people use sentences such as *He be ready* or *She ain't happy.* However, those are nonstandard forms and should not be used in written conversation. Review the following corrections.

>   is   is not
> That man ~~be~~ cool, but he ~~ain't~~ a good candidate for Student Council president.

Practice 2

Look at the underlined verbs, and correct fifteen errors in subject–verb agreement or the incorrect use of *ain't*. Write C above five correct verbs.

                        learn
EXAMPLE: Successful students <u>learns</u> good study skills.

1. College applicants <u>need</u> to have a solid transcript if they <u>wants</u> to get accepted to a good college. Every college <u>have</u> its own rules for acceptance, but a good SAT score <u>be</u> one of the most important requirements. The SAT <u>is</u> a standardized test. The question portion <u>take</u> about three hours to complete. It <u>have</u> questions about a wide range of topics. The test also <u>include</u> an essay section. It <u>ain't</u> easy to do well on the test.

2. Nakala <u>be</u> a typical student. She <u>have</u> a very busy schedule. Often, she <u>wait</u> until the last minute to finish assignments, and she <u>do</u> the least amount of studying possible. Nakala and her friends <u>worries</u> about the SAT test. They <u>hope</u> to receive high scores on the test.

3.   Many organizations <u>offers</u> instructional videos about the SAT. Students

<u>prepares</u> for the SAT by trying the sample questions on websites. Some

students also <u>write</u> practice essays to prepare for the written portion of the

SAT. Nakala <u>have</u> to do the test this spring, so she <u>plans</u> to practice online.

Simple Past Tense Agreement

In the past tense, all verbs except *be* have one past form.

Regular	I called.	He called.	You called.	We called.	They called.
Irregular	I slept.	He slept.	You slept.	We slept.	They slept.

EXCEPTION: *BE*

In the past tense, the only verb requiring subject–verb agreement is the verb *be*, which has two past forms: *was* and *were*.

Was	**Were**
I was	We were
He was	You were
She was	They were
It was	

Present Perfect Tense Agreement

When writing in the present perfect tense, which is formed with *have* or *has* and the past participle, use *has* when the subject is third-person singular.

My college **has** raised tuition fees. Other colleges **have** not raised their fees.

Agreement in Other Tenses

GRAMMAR LINK
For more information about using the present perfect tense, see Chapter 24.

When writing in most other verb tenses, and in modal forms (*can, could, would, may, might,* and so on), use the same form of the verb with every subject.

Future	I will **work**; she will **work**; they will **work**; you will **work**; we will **work**
Past perfect	I had **met**; she had **met**; they had **met**; you had **met**; we had **met**
Modals	I can **talk**; she should **talk**; they could **talk**; you might **talk**; we would **talk**

Practice 3

Correct twelve subject–verb agreement errors among the underlined verbs, and write C above five correct verbs.

EXAMPLE: A problem <u>exist</u> in many colleges and universities. *(exists)*

1.   Credit card debt <u>be</u> common on American campuses. Card companies <u>mail</u>

applications to students. Today, the average undergraduate <u>have</u> more than

$2,000 in credit card debt. Of course, the longer a student <u>takes</u> to pay off a

debt, the higher the debt <u>become</u>.

2.   Jeremy <u>be</u> a thirty-year-old man who is still paying for the pizza that he ate in college. Ten years ago, Jeremy and his friends <u>was</u> not careful. They <u>were</u> happy to buy food, video games, and clothing with their credit cards. Since then, Jeremy <u>have never managed</u> to pay off the debt. In fact, he still <u>use</u> his Visa card regularly. He <u>want</u> to pay $42, which is the minimum payment. He <u>don't</u> realize that only 89 cents will be applied to his debt. The rest of the money <u>will goes</u> toward late fees and interest fees.

3.   Credit card companies <u>charge</u> extremely high fees. When you <u>receives</u> a credit card, you <u>should pays</u> the balance every month. You <u>can avoid</u> interest rates of about 20 percent.

More Than One Subject

26.2   **Maintain subject–verb agreement when there is more than one subject.**

Special agreement rules apply when there is more than one subject.

and

When subjects are joined by *and*, use the plural form of the verb.

> <u>Colleges</u> and <u>universities</u> **prepare** students for the job market.

or, nor

When two subjects are joined by *or* or *nor*, the verb agrees with the subject that is closer to it.

> plural
> Neither Amanda Jackson nor her <u>students</u> **use** the computer lab.

> singular
> Either the teacher or <u>Amanda</u> **uses** the department's portable laptop computer.

HINT: *As Well As* and *Along With*

The phrases *as well as* and *along with* are not the same as *and*. They do not form a compound subject. The real subject is before the interrupting expression.

> <u>Joe</u>, as well as Carlos and Peter, **works** in a career college.

> <u>Joe</u>, along with Carlos and Peter, **teaches** business classes.

Practice 4

Underline the correct verb in each sentence. Make sure the verb agrees with the subject.

EXAMPLE: College administrators (<u>make</u> / makes) rules to discourage underage drinking.

1. College administrators, student counselors, and parents (worry / worries) about a major problem on college campuses.

2. College students and young workers (abuse / abuses) alcohol.

3. Beer, as well as hard liquor, (is / are) common on college campuses.

4. Dorian and Alfredo (drink / drinks) because of peer pressure.

5. Keshia, along with her friends, (go / goes) to bars on weekends.

6. Either Keshia or her boyfriend (buy / buys) alcohol to take to parties.

7. Underage drinkers sometimes (miss / misses) classes, (engage / engages) in unplanned sexual activities, or (injure / injures) themselves.

8. Either the police or an administrator (punish / punishes) students who are caught drinking.

9. Sometimes a male or female student (get / gets) expelled from college due to underage drinking.

Special Subject Forms

26.3 Identify special subject forms.

Some subjects are not easy to identify as singular or plural. Two common types are indefinite pronouns and collective nouns.

Indefinite Pronouns

Indefinite pronouns refer to a general person, place, or thing. Carefully review the following list of indefinite pronouns.

Indefinite Pronouns				
Singular	another	each	nobody	other
	anybody	everybody	no one	somebody
	anyone	everyone	nothing	someone
	anything	everything	one	something
Plural	all, both, few, many, others, several, some			

SINGULAR INDEFINITE PRONOUNS

In the following sentences, the verbs require the third-person singular form because the subjects are singular.

<u>Everyone</u> **knows** that career colleges offer practical, career-oriented courses.

<u>Nothing</u> **stops** people from applying to a career college.

You can put one or more singular nouns (joined by *and*) after *each* and *every*. The verb is still singular.

<u>Each</u> man and woman **knows** the stories about secret societies.

PLURAL INDEFINITE PRONOUNS

Both, few, many, others, and *several* are all plural subjects. The verb is always plural.

> Many **apply** to high-tech programs.

> Others **prefer** to study in the field of health care.

Practice 5

Underline the subjects and circle the correct verbs.

EXAMPLE: Many <u>Americans</u> (is / (are)) English instructors in Korea.

1. Angel Chen (live / lives) in Taichung, Taiwan. She (is / are) a Chinese American. Angel, along with her friend Robin, (teach / teaches) English at a high school in Taiwan. Both (consider / considers) their jobs to be very satisfying.

2. Generally, Taiwanese students (want / wants) to speak English. Many (enroll / enrolls) in language classes while attending high school. Most parents (value / values) education, so they (pressure / pressures) their children to do extra classes. Students often (have / has) very little free time. Therefore, Angel (work / works) with extremely busy students. All of them (desire / desires) high grades. However, some (lack / lacks) the ability to "think outside the box." They typically (learn / learns) by repetition and memorization. Angel sometimes (have / has) problems convincing her students to speak and debate issues.

3. Most Taiwanese students (is / are) very respectful. When Angel (walk / walks) into a class, everyone (bow / bows) to her. Although Angel is a young woman, each student (address / addresses) her formally as "Teacher Angel." In class, everybody always (listen / listens) to her. Almost nobody (argue / argues) with the instructor.

4. Neither Angel nor Robin (want / wants) to return to the United States yet. Both still (have / has) one more year on their teaching contract. They (is / are) happy with their lives in Taichung.

Collective Nouns

Collective nouns refer to a group of people or things. These are common collective nouns.

Some Common Collective Nouns				
army	class	crowd	group	population
association	club	family	jury	public
audience	committee	gang	military	society
band	company	government	organization	team

Generally, each group acts as a unit, so you must use the singular form of the verb.

The <u>committee</u> **supports** the new policies.

If the members of the group act individually, use the plural form of the verb. It is a good idea to use a phrase such as *members of*.

Acceptable	The <u>committee</u> **are** not able to come to an agreement.
Better	The <u>members of the committee</u> **are** not able to come to an agreement.

HINT: *Police* Is Plural

The word *police* is always thought of as a plural noun because the word *officers* is implied but not stated.

The police **have** arrested the senator.

The police **are** patrolling the neighborhood.

Practice 6

In each sentence, underline the subject and circle the correct verb.

EXAMPLE: The <u>government</u> (offer / (offers)) financial aid for some students.

1. A career college (is / are) a sensible choice for many students wanting practical work skills. Such institutions (offer / offers) a variety of career-related programs. For example, my college (have / has) programs in high-tech, health care, business, and hospitality.

2. My friend Santosh (studies / study) in the hospitality program. Santosh (was / were) a cook in the army, but now he (want / wants) a career in adventure tourism. The army (provide / provides) financial help to Santosh for his studies. In fact, the military (encourage / encourages) its soldiers to continue their education and training. Santosh's family also (give / gives) him encouragement.

3. People (need / needs) social, math, communication, and organizational skills in the hospitality business. Everyone (enter / enters) this field knowing that he or she must be able to get along with people during stressful situations. The industry (is / are) growing, but it (is / are) very important to have the right education. Career colleges (give / gives) students an advantage in this highly competitive market.

Verb Before the Subject

26.4 **Maintain subject–verb agreement when the verb is before the subject.**

Usually the verb comes after the subject, but in some sentences, the verb comes before the subject. In such cases, you must still ensure that the subject and verb agree.

there or *here*

When a sentence begins with *there* or *here*, the subject always follows the verb. *There* and *here* are not subjects.

>   V   S   V   S
>
> Here **is** the college course <u>list</u>. There **are** many night <u>courses</u>.

Questions

In questions, word order is usually reversed, and the main or helping verb is placed before the subject. In the following example, the main verb is *be*.

>   V   S   V   S
>
> Where **is** the <u>cafeteria</u>? **Is** the <u>food</u> good?

In questions in which the main verb isn't *be*, the subject usually agrees with the helping verb.

>   HV   S   V   HV   S   V
>
> When **does** the <u>library</u> **close**? **Do** <u>students</u> **work** there?

Practice 7

Correct any subject–verb agreement errors. If the sentence is correct, write *C* in the blank.

EXAMPLE: ~~Has~~ you ever gotten a scholarship?   <u> Have </u>

1. Does students from various backgrounds have the same opportunities?   <u>   </u>

2. There is many student loans available for college students.   <u>   </u>

3. Does the American government provide enough PELL grants for college students?   <u>   </u>

4. There is many pressures on students with limited incomes.   <u>   </u>

5. Do each low-income student receive enough help?   <u>   </u>

6. Why do many students fail to qualify for student aid?   <u>   </u>

7. Has many students benefited from the scholarships?   <u>   </u>

8. Is there a reason to cut back on such grants?   <u>   </u>

9. Perhaps there be more ways to make college accessible to poor and middle-class students.   <u>   </u>

10. Often, there is creative solutions for funding problems.   <u>   </u>

Interrupting Words and Phrases

26.5 **Identify interrupting words and phrases.**

Words that come between the subject and the verb may confuse you. In these cases, look for the subject and make sure that the verb agrees with the subject.

S   interrupting phrase   V

Some <u>rules</u> regarding admission to this college **are** controversial.

S   prepositional phrase   V

A <u>student</u> in two of my classes **writes** for the college newspaper.

HINT: Identify Interrupting Phrases

When you revise your paragraphs, add parentheses around words that separate the subject and the verb. Then you can check to see whether your subjects and verbs agree.

S   prepositional phrase   V

The single <u>mother</u> (in my literature class) also **works** part time.

When interrupting phrases contain *of the* or similar words, the subject appears before the phrase.

S   prepositional phrase   V

<u>One</u> (of my biggest problems) **is** my lack of organization.

Practice 8

Underline the subject in each sentence. Add parentheses around any words that come between each subject and verb. Then circle the correct form of the verb that is in bold.

EXAMPLE: <u>One</u> (of the most controversial issues on campus) **(is)**/ **are** affirmative action.

1.   Some colleges in this country **have / has** more relaxed admission standards for students from ethnic minority groups. Such colleges, with good reason, **want / wants** to have a vibrant and diverse student population. However, arguing that they have been discriminated against, students from across the nation **have / has** sued their colleges. Judges in many jurisdictions **have / has** had to consider whether affirmative action is unfair.

2.   People in favor of affirmative action **have / has** compelling arguments. Historically, some ethnic groups in the United States **has / have** not had access to higher education. Many factors, such as poverty, **contribute / contributes** to the problem. University of California professor Norman Matloff, in an article for *Asian Week*, **suggest / suggests** that society suffers when there is a large, poorly educated underclass. Additionally, affirmative action **help / helps** create a diverse student body.

3.   Opponents of affirmative action **feel / feels** that admissions should be based purely on test scores. Barbara Grutter, a white businesswoman, **was / were** thinking of changing careers. Her application to the University of Michigan's law school **was / were** refused. She **argues / argue** that affirmative action is reverse discrimination. One of her best arguments **is / are** compelling: Grutter, as a forty-year-old single mother, **add / adds** to the university's diversity. On June 23, 2003, a decision about Grutter's affirmative action case **was / were** made. Although justices in the U.S. Supreme Court **were / was** divided, the Court ruled that race can be used as one of the factors in college admissions.

4.   For some people, regulations to safeguard affirmative action **help / helps** equalize opportunities in our society. For others, such regulations **is / are** unfair to certain groups. What is your opinion?

Interrupting Words: *who, which, that*

Some sentences include a relative clause beginnning wih the pronoun *who, which,* or *that*. In the relative clause, the verb must agree with the antecedent of *who, which,* or *that*.

In the first example below, the antecedent of *who* is *woman*. In the second example, the antecedent of *that* is *newspapers*. And in the third example, the *antecedent* of which is *article*.

There is a <u>woman</u> in my neighborhood *who* **counsels** students.

Here are some old <u>newspapers</u> *that* **discuss** steroid abuse.

One <u>article</u>, *which* **contains** stories about corruption, is very interesting.

Practice 9

Underline and correct nine subject–verb agreement errors.

EXAMPLE: The candidate who <u>support</u> tax increases is unlikely to win.
supports

1.   Students who hope to become politicians usually becomes active in college politics. The experience that they gain help them advance politically. For instance, Chandra Wang, who is in a community college, have a position on the student council. About once a month, she go to council meetings. The council discusses issues that affects students. In the future, Wang hopes to become a senator.

2. There is many people who wants to enter the political arena. Generally, nobody start at the top. Almost every leader who is successful have a lot of experience.

Reflect On It

Think about what you have learned in this unit. If you do not know an answer, review that concept.

1. When should you add -s or -es to verbs? _____

   _____

2. Look at the following nouns. Circle all the collective nouns.

family	people	army	committee
judge	crowd	brothers	audience

3. When do you use *was* and *were*?

   Use *was* _____

   Use *were* _____

4. Circle and correct any subject–verb agreement errors in the following sentences.

   a. There is many colleges in Florida.

   b. Yale is a university that have several secret societies.

   c. Either the Edwards sisters or Simon have been initiated.

   d. One of our cousins go to Yale.

   e. There is no hazing rituals on our campus.

Final Review

Underline and correct twenty errors in subject–verb agreement.

                                                    does
EXAMPLE: A Federal PELL grant, unlike a loan, do not need to be repaid.

1.   Every Saturday at 9 A.M., Derek Brown volunteer at a seniors' residence. He

   helps the staff entertain residents. He, along with another classmate, read

   to some of the seniors. Derek enjoys the work, but he also have another

motive. In fact, almost every high school student who volunteer also hopes to be eligible for a scholarship. According to *U.S News & World Report*, there be many scholarships available for any student who do volunteer work. However, the numbers of scholarships have decreased in recent years. Most institutions offer scholarships based on performance rather than financial need. These days, there is relatively few scholarships for low-income students. Almost everyone who attend college in the United States graduate with a lot of student debt.

2.　　Many parents find the expense of college prohibitive. Neither Derek nor his parents has a lot of money. Derek, as well as many of his classmates, work part time to save money for college. Derek cooks at a fast-food restaurant that stay open all night. At the restaurant, nobody like to do the late shift, so Derek often has to do it. One of his most difficult challenges are to get enough sleep. Of course, his grades suffers because often he is tired. Derek really hopes to receives a scholarship to a good school. Otherwise, he may not be able to afford college.

3.　　According to a *New York Times* article by Jason DeParle, costs associated with attending public universities has increased "by 60 percent in the last two decades." How do a country thrive? One of the best ways are to have an educated population. Governments at all levels needs to provide more help for low-income students.

The Writer's Room

Write about one of the following topics. Make sure that your subjects and verbs agree.

1. Examine this photo. Define a term that relates to the photo. Some ideas might be *debt, interest rates, reckless spender, cheapskate, spendthift,* or *credit card junkie.*
2. Should college be free? What are the advantages or disadvantages of free college?

27   Tense Consistency

SECTION THEME: College Life

In this chapter, you will read about people who have made difficult choices.

The Writer's Journal

How do images in the media influence the way that people judge their own bodies? Write a short paragraph about the media and body image.

Consistent Verb Tense

27.1   Use consistent verb tense.

When you write, the verb tense you use gives the reader an idea about the time when the event occurred. A **faulty tense shift** occurs when you shift from one tense to another for no logical reason.

Faulty tense shift	College reporter Erica Santiago interviewed a protester and <u>asks</u> about his political philosophy.
Correct	College reporter Erica Santiago interviewed a protester and <u>asked</u> about his political philosophy.

Sometimes the time frame in a text really does change. In those circumstances, you would change the verb tense. The following example accurately shows two different time periods. Notice that certain key words (*during my childhood, today*) indicate what tense the writer should use.

past   present

During my childhood, I <u>ate</u> a lot of fast food. Today, I <u>try</u> to eat a healthy diet.

Practice 1

Identify and correct each faulty tense shift. If the sentence is correct, write *C* in the space.

EXAMPLE: Generally, many college students study and ~~worked~~ **work**   in unpaid internships.

1. College is a very difficult experience for many students because they studied and gain work experience for their future careers. _____

2. Last September, Jorge Fonseca was a student in communications when a television station offered him an unpaid internship. _____

3. Soon after he received the offer, Jorge met with a career counselor; she advises Jorge to accept the internship. _____

4. After their meeting, Jorge researched unpaid internships, and he discovers that many companies abuse this practice. _____

5. Last year, from February to July, Jorge has to balance his coursework and the internship, so he felt anxious. _____

6. During that time, Jorge was frustrated because the television station expected him to work long hours. _____

7. Nowadays, Jorge wants a paying job because he had to pay for his tuition fees. _____

HINT: *Would* and *Could*

When you tell a story about a past event, use *would* instead of *will*, and use *could* instead of *can*.

could

In 1996, college wrestler Robert Burzak knew that he <u>can</u> bulk up if he used

would

steriods, but he promised his coach that he <u>will</u> not.

Practice 2

Underline and correct ten faulty tense shifts.

EXAMPLE: Kendra went to career college after she <u>finishes</u> high school.
finished

1.   According to historians, America's first institution of higher education was founded in 1636. Harvard University opened only sixteen years after the

Mayflower lands at Cape Cod. The university was named after John Harvard, who leaves his money to the institution after his death. He also gives Harvard about four hundred books.

2.   One of Harvard's earliest donors was a woman. Anne Radcliff Moulson, along with her husband, Thomas Moulson, operated an inn. After her husband's death, "Lady Anne" built up the family business, and she decides to create a scholarship at Harvard. Throughout her lifetime, however, the university excludes women. In fact, for the first 147 years of its existence, women can't go to Harvard. They can complain, but the school won't change its policies.

3.   Eventually, in 1873, builders created an annex for women, and the university names it after Radcliff. Finally, in 1999, Harvard and Radcliff joined, and women can study alongside men. These days, females outnumber males at Harvard and at many other major universities.

Reflect On It

Think about what you have learned in this unit. If you do not know an answer, review that concept.

1. What is a faulty tense shift? _____

   _____

2. If you are writing a paragraph about a past event, what word should you use instead of these two?

   a. will: _____   b. can: _____

3. Read the following paragraphs, and find five faulty tense shifts. Correct the errors.

   EXAMPLE: Kaitlin diets because she wants ~~wanted~~ to look thinner.

   In 2010, college student Amy Heller became severely malnourished. In an attempt to lose weight, Heller ingested diet pills, and she severely restricts her intake of food. When others suggested that she had a problem, Heller will deny it. By July 2011, she weighs only 88 pounds. Heller finally sought treatment, and soon she can eat regular meals.

   In 2013, Heller decided to speak about her condition. She went to a treatment center and offers her services. Today, she works with patients who suffer from eating disorders.

Final Review

Underline and correct fifteen faulty tense shifts.

EXAMPLE: Last year, there was an election, and many people ~~vote~~. *voted*

1.   During America's last election, a low percentage of eligible citizens registered and vote. The turnout was lower than in recent years. According to CNN, the lowest turnout is in Hawaii, where only 43 percent bothered to visit their polling stations. During the last election, Hawaiian citizens Michael and Donna Ellison don't vote because they disliked the candidates.

2.   In the United States, voting is not compulsory. However, about thirty nations have a voting law. In Greece, Thailand, and Italy, everybody of legal age must vote, but the laws are not strict. During typical elections, officials did not arrest nonvoters. Additionally, Mexico and Panama do not enforce their compulsory voting laws, so voter turnout remained low.

3.   Many other nations, including Turkey, Uruguay, and Argentina, have very strict voting laws. Officials sometimes punish nonvoters with fines or even imprisonment. For example, during Argentina's 2003 election, Ileana Guerera decided that she will not vote in the election because she disapproved of the candidates. She receives a fine, and she had to pay it. Her brother also stayed home on October 25, 2015, but he has a doctor's note. He knew he will not receive a fine. He had a legitimate excuse, so he can stay home that day.

4.   In the early 1920s, many Australian citizens were apathetic, and close to 50 percent do not participate in elections. Then in 1924, government officials passed a law making voting compulsory. In the election of 1925, people rushed to the polling stations and vote. They worried that they can be arrested if they refused to vote. Today, the voter turnout in Australia is about 95 percent.

5.   There are many people who support compulsory voting. They believe that voting was a civic duty. However, others consider voting a civil right rather than a duty. They regarded compulsory voting laws as an infringement on personal rights. Do you support compulsory voting?

READING LINK
To learn more about college issues, read the following essays.
"The Wonders of PowerPoint" (p. 193)
"Homophobia" (p. 197)
"Cuban Schools and American Schools" (p. 205)
"The Importance of Music" (p. 214)
"It's Class, Stupid!" (page 497)
"Why Diversity on Campus Matters" (p. 500)

The Writer's Room

Write about one of the following topics. Ensure that you have no faulty tense shifts.

1. Describe your college campus. You might describe an interesting building or area of the campus.

2. What is your opinion of compulsory voting? Should everybody have to vote in elections? Explain why or why not.

The Writer's Circle: Collaborative Activity

Work with a team of students, and create a short survey. Form at least five interesting questions about college life. For example, you can ask about food services, course selection, transportation, student fees, extracurricular activities, fashions, student study habits, or any other topic that you can think of.

For each question that you create, include a list of possible choices. It will be much easier to compile your results if all students choose from a selection. Do not give open-ended questions. Finally, if a question asks about student knowledge, give an "I don't know" choice. Otherwise, students may simply guess, and that would skew your results.

After you have completed your survey questions, one team member should remain seated, and the other team members should split up and sit with other groups in the class to ask the questions. After each member has gathered information, the original group should get together and write a summary of the results.

28 Nouns, Determiners, and Prepositions

SECTION THEME: Our Environment

LEARNING OBJECTIVES

28.1 Identify singular and plural nouns.

28.2 Identify count nouns and noncount nouns.

28.3 Define determiners.

28.4 Define prepositions.

In this chapter, you read about topics related to the environment and about environmental movers and shakers.

The Writer's Journal

Think about our world. Many things seem wrong in it, yet other things give us hope. Write about what is going well in the world.

Singular and Plural Nouns

28.1 **Identify singular and plural nouns.**

Nouns are words that refer to people, places, or things. Nouns are divided into common nouns and proper nouns.

- **Common nouns** refer to general people, places, or things and begin with a lowercase letter. For example, *books*, *computer*, and *city* are common nouns.

- **Proper nouns** refer to particular people, places, or things and begin with a capital letter. For example, *Rachel Carson*, *Greenpeace*, and *Love Canal* are proper nouns.

Nouns are either singular or plural. A **singular noun** refers to one of something, while a **plural noun** refers to more than one of something. Regular plural nouns end in *-s* or *-es*.

	Singular	**Plural**
People	inventor	inventors
	writer	writers
Places	town	towns
	village	villages
Things	computer	computers
	box	boxes

HINT: Adding -es

When a noun ends in *s*, *x*, *ch*, *sh*, or *z*, add *-es* to form the plural.

business/business**es**   tax/tax**es**   church/church**es**

Irregular Plural Nouns

Nouns that do not use *-s* or *-es* in their plural forms are called **irregular nouns**. Here are some common irregular nouns.

Singular	**Plural**	**Singular**	**Plural**
person	people	woman	women
child	children	tooth	teeth
man	men	foot	feet

Some nouns use other rules to form the plural. It is a good idea to memorize both the rules and the exceptions.

- For nouns ending in *f* or *fe*, change the *f* to *v* and add *-es*.

Singular	**Plural**	**Singular**	**Plural**
knife	kni**ves**	thief	thie**ves**
wife	wi**ves**	leaf	lea**ves**

Some exceptions: belief, beliefs; roof, roofs; safe, safes

- For nouns ending in a consonant + *y*, change the *y* to *i* and add *-es*.

Singular	**Plural**	**Singular**	**Plural**
lady	lad**ies**	berry	berr**ies**
baby	bab**ies**	lottery	lotter**ies**

If a vowel comes before the final *y*, then the word retains the regular plural form.

Singular	**Plural**	**Singular**	**Plural**
day	day**s**	key	key**s**

- Some nouns remain the same in both singular and plural forms.

Singular	**Plural**	**Singular**	**Plural**
fish	fish	deer	deer
moose	moose	sheep	sheep

- Some nouns are thought of as being only plural and therefore have no singular form.

Plural Form with a Plural Verb

clothes	goods	pants	scissors
eyeglasses	proceeds	savings	shorts

Plural Form with a Singular Verb

news	economics	politics	physics

- Some nouns are **compound nouns**, which means that they are made up of two or more words. To form the plural of compound nouns, add -s or -es to the most important word of the compound, which is usually the last.

Singular	Plural	Singular	Plural
bus stop	bus stops	artificial heart	artificial hearts
air conditioner	air conditioners	jet airplane	jet airplanes

In hyphenated compound nouns, if the first word is a noun, add -s to the noun.

Singular	Plural	Singular	Plural
senator-elect	senators-elect	runner-up	runners-up
sister-in-law	sisters-in-law	husband-to-be	husbands-to-be

- Some nouns that are borrowed from Latin or Greek keep the plural form of the original language.

Singular	Plural	Singular	Plural
millennium	millennia	paparazzo	paparazzi
datum	data	phenomenon	phenomena

HINT: *Persons* versus *People*

There are two plural forms of *person*. *People* is the most common plural form.

Some people take the bus to work. Many people ride their bikes to work.

Persons is used in a legal or official context.

The crime was committed by persons unknown.

Practice 1

Fill in the blanks with either the singular or the plural form of the noun. If the noun does not change, put an X in the space.

EXAMPLES:

Singular	Plural
man	men
X	goggles
1. person	_____
2. _____	teeth
3. brother-in-law	_____
4. lady	_____
5. _____	jeans
6. sheep	_____
7. _____	binoculars
8. _____	shelves
9. _____	sunglasses
10. alarm clock	_____

Practice 2

Underline and correct ten errors in singular or plural noun forms.

EXAMPLE: Rachel Carson started writing about wildlife in her early
twentys.
twenties

1.   After World War II, Americans became aware of the need to protect
nature. Many persons turned their attention to environmental issues. One
of the most important womans in the early green movement was Rachel
Carson.

2.   Carson was born in Pennsylvania in 1907. She trained as a marine
biologist and wrote many articles about wildlife such as deer, wolfs, and
fishes. In the 1950s, Carson became concerned about the use of pesticides.
In the late 1940s, the government had started spraying pesticide with DDT
to halt the progress of fire ants. The pesticide turned tree and shrub leafs
brown. It also killed birds because they ate berrys that were covered with
chemicals.

3.   Carson collected a lot of datas on the harmful effects of pesticides.
She wrote to all politicians, from the president to senator-elects, about
the negative effects of DDT. She also wrote a book, *Silent Spring*, about
her discoverys. The book became an international best-seller, and the
environmental movement became a global phenomena.

Key Words for Singular and Plural Nouns

Some key words will help you determine whether a noun is singular or plural.

- Use a singular noun after words such as *a, an, another, each, every,* and *one*.

  As **a** young mother, Dorothy Gerber prepared homemade baby food for her
  daughter.

  Gerber tried to sell her product to **every** grocery store in her town.

- Use a plural noun after words such as *all, both, few, many, several, some,* and *two*.

  Very **few** companies produced food targeted to children.

  Today, **many** babies eat Gerber's baby food.

HINT: Using Plural Nouns After *of the*

Use a plural noun after the expressions *one (all, two, each, few, lots, many, most,
several) of the* . . .

  One of the easiest **methods** to reduce pollution is recycling.

Practice 3

Underline the correct noun in each set of parentheses.

EXAMPLE: Many (visitor / <u>visitors</u>) are astounded by the extraordinary beauty of national (park / <u>parks</u>).

1. Every (year / years), millions of (person / people) visit national parks. During the late 1700s, George Catlin was one of the first (artist / artists) to travel the American wilderness. He painted lots of (landscape / landscapes) in the Dakotas and Montana. At that time, many (settler / settlers) were moving westward. Catlin believed that new (settlement / settlements) would have a negative (impact / impacts) on American Indian culture and on the environment. In the nineteenth century, few (American / Americans) worried about protecting nature. In the 1830s, Catlin lobbied the government to preserve some (area / areas) of the wilderness.

2. Several (decade / decades) later, Congress made the Yosemite Valley into a state (park / parks). Then, in 1872, the government passed a (law / laws) that allowed land to be preserved for the enjoyment of the public. The Yellowstone (sector / sectors) became one of the first national (park / parks) in the United States. Today, there are over 187 (region / regions) designated as national parks. Each national (park / parks) is unique. The (area / areas) have great natural beauty. So for your next (vacation / vacations), why not visit a national (park / parks)? But be sure to make a reservation if you want to stay overnight!

Count Nouns and Noncount Nouns

28.2   Identify count nouns and noncount nouns.

In English, nouns are grouped into two types: count nouns and noncount nouns. **Count nouns** refer to people or things that you can count, such as *engine, paper*, or *girl*. Count nouns usually can have both a singular and plural form.

> She read a <u>book</u> by Rachel Carson. She read five <u>books</u> about water management.

Noncount nouns refer to people or things that you cannot count because you cannot divide them, such as *electricity* and *music*. Noncount nouns usually have only the singular form.

> Michael uses new <u>software</u> to track global weather patterns.

> Biologists take samples of <u>air</u> to monitor pollution levels.

To express a noncount noun as a count noun, refer to it in terms of types, varieties, or amounts.

> Environmentalists use **a variety of** <u>equipment</u> for their research.

> Dr. Morgan Schule examines **four test tubes of** <u>water</u> for each experiment.

Here are some common noncount nouns.

Common Noncount Nouns					
Categories of Objects		**Food**	**Nature**	**Substances**	
clothing	machinery	bread	air	chalk	paint
equipment	mail	fish	earth	charcoal	paper
furniture	money	honey	electricity	coal	
homework	music	meat	energy	fur	
jewelry	postage	milk	radiation	hair	
luggage	software	rice	water	ink	
Abstract Nouns					
advice	effort	information	progress		
attention	evidence	knowledge	proof		
behavior	health	luck	research		
education	help	peace	violence		

Practice 4

Change the italicized words to the plural form, if necessary. If the word ends in *y*, you may have to change the *y* to *i* for the plural form. Write X in the space if the word does not have a plural form.

EXAMPLE: Greenpeace *member*___s___ distribute environmental
information ___X___ to the *public*___X___.

1. In 1971, the United States was planning to conduct underground nuclear *test*_____ in Amchitka, Alaska. The *island*_____ is on the West Coast. It is home to many *type*_____ of sea *otter*_____ , *eagle*_____ , *fish*_____, and other *animal*_____.

2. Environmental *activist*_____ from Vancouver, Canada, decided to protest peacefully. They rented a *ship*_____ , bought some camera *equipment*_____, and stocked up on enough *rice*_____ , *meat*_____ , and *vegetable*_____ for their long *journey*_____. Their *boat*_____ was intercepted by the U.S. Navy, but their *luck*_____ held out. They took *photo*_____ and gathered *evidence*_____ of Amchitka's fragile *ecosystem*_____. Since the *protestor*_____ did not use *violence*_____ , their *activity*_____ received favorable international *attention*_____ , and the United States abandoned nuclear testing on the island.

3. Within a few *year*_____ , the environmental *movement*_____ had spread, and several *country*_____ started their own Greenpeace *branch*_____. These *day*_____ , Greenpeace is one of the largest environmental action *group*_____ in the *world*_____.

Determiners

28.3   Define determiners.

Determiners are words that help a reader figure out whether a noun is specific or general.

> Arthur Scott used **his** imagination and created **a** new invention, **the** paper towel.

You can use many words from different parts of speech as determiners.

Articles	a, an, the
Demonstratives	this, that, these, those, such
Indefinite pronouns	all, any, both, each, every, either, few, little, many, some, several
Numbers	one, two, three
Possessive nouns	Jack's, the teacher's, a man's
Possessive adjectives	my, your, his, her, its, our, their, whose

A, An, The

Some determiners can be confusing because you can use them only in specific circumstances. *A* and *an* are general determiners, and *the* is a specific determiner.

general   specific

> I need to find <u>a</u> new **car**. <u>The</u> **cars** that I looked at were electric.

- Use *a* and *an* before singular count nouns but not before plural or noncount nouns. Use *a* before words that begin with a consonant (*a man*), and use *an* before words that begin with a vowel (*an invention*).

  > <u>An</u> extraordinary **woman** created <u>a</u> very profound **documentary** on nature.

  Exceptions:

  > When *u* sounds like *you*, put *a* before it (*a unicycle*, *a university*).
  >
  > When *h* is silent, put *an* before it (*an hour*, *an honest man*).

- Use *the* before nouns that refer to a specific person, place, or thing. Do not use *the* before languages (*he studies Greek*), sports (*we played football*), and most city and country names (*Biro was born in Hungary*).

  > Forests cover one-third of <u>the</u> **world's surface**.

Many, Few, Much, Little

- Use *many* and *few* with count nouns.

  > <u>Many</u> **environmentalists** lobby the government, but <u>few</u> **politicians** are open to suggestions.

- Use *much* and *little* with noncount nouns.

  > Manu Joshi spent too <u>much</u> **money** on very <u>little</u> **research**.

This, That, These, Those

- Use *this* and *these* to refer to things that are physically close to the speaker or at the present time. Use *this* before singular nouns and *these* before plural nouns.

  <u>This</u> **tablet** in my purse measures three by five inches. <u>These</u> **days**, electronic devices are very small.

- Use *that* and *those* to refer to things that are physically distant from the speaker or in the past or future. Use *that* before singular nouns and *those* before plural nouns.

  In the 1950s, computers were invented. In <u>those</u> **years**, computers were very large. In <u>that</u> **building**, there is a very old computer.

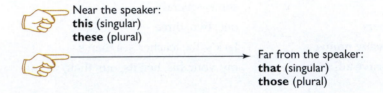

Near the speaker:
this (singular)
these (plural)

Far from the speaker:
that (singular)
those (plural)

Practice 5

Write *a*, *an*, or *the* in the space before each noun. If no determiner is necessary, write X in the space.

EXAMPLE: I read __*an*__ interesting biography on Francisco "Chico" Mendes.

1.   Chico Mendes was born in 1944 in _____ Brazil. After working in _____ rubber plantations in the Amazon rainforest, he became _____ prominent activist in the fight to preserve the Amazon. While working as _____ rubber-tapper, Mendes, like most other plantation workers, was not allowed to get _____ education. Eventually, he left _____ plantations and accepted _____ position at _____ newly formed Rubber Tappers' Union, which sought to gain certain rights for workers in _____ Brazil. Mendes organized _____ meeting of union members in 1985, which took place in _____ Brasilia, Brazil's capital. The union decided to strike and blocked access to _____ rubber reserves. _____ charismatic Mendes also convinced environmentalists and Marxists to share _____ single vision for _____ progress in Brazil.

2.   Mendes won several _____ awards for his work in protecting the Amazon rainforest. He fought against politicians, _____ rubber plantation owners, and other powerful groups. Mendes was particularly upset by _____ sale of a large rubber reserve to notorious land baron Darly Alves Da Silva. Environmental groups supported _____ outspoken activist when he fought against Da Silva's plan to raze _____ forest in the area. However,

they could not protect Mendes from his more powerful enemies. Mendes was murdered in 1988 by Da Silva's son, Darci. The murder drew _____ worldwide attention. Today, _____ other environmentalists still fight against deforestation in the Amazon.

Practice 6

Underline the appropriate determiner in parentheses. If the noun does not require a determiner, underline X.

EXAMPLE: Climate change is (X / <u>a</u> / the) very important issue.

1.   (A / The) weather is (a / the) common topic of discussion for (many / much) people. According to meteorologists, global warming affects weather patterns. For example, (the / X) snowstorms are becoming more powerful in (the / X) North America. (A / The) snowstorm in Boston is not uncommon. However, in 2015, there was a record-setting storm in (the / X) New England and other parts of the American Northeast. In (this / that) year, over 100 inches of snow blanketed (much / many) cities and caused (much / many) damage. (Few / Little) people link increased snow to global warming, but according to the Environmental Protection Agency, powerful snowstorms are indeed a consequence of climate change.

2.   (Many / Much) people are fascinated by hurricanes and other tropical storms. During hurricanes, (the / X) people should stay away from windows and glass doors and spend as (few / little) time as possible outside. (A / The) tropical storm in 2012, named Hurricane Sandy, caused over $60 billion worth of damage. (An / A) interesting fact about (the / X) hurricane is that 7.5 million people were without power for parts of it.

3.   (The / X) surface temperature of the ocean was five degrees cooler in 1970. In (these / those) days, storms were not as powerful. Today, (much / many) research about climate change shows that extreme precipitation will only increase. (These / this) days, the more (a / an / X) information we get about these weather patterns, the more we worry about future storms.

Practice 7

Correct fifteen errors in singular nouns, plural nouns, and determiners.

EXAMPLE: Biologists do a lot of ~~researches~~ ^{research} to develop better conservation methods.

1.   Conservationists refer to the passenger pigeon as a example of nature's fragility. In past centuries, the passenger pigeon was one of the most common bird in the North America. Until the twentieth century, the birds were seen all over a Western Hemisphere. Unfortunately, the species is now extinct.

2.   When the first Europeans started to colonize the New World, there were little hunting regulations. In these days, settlers would often hunt passenger pigeons for their feathers. Ladyes wanted to wear feathers in their hairs. In 1878, in Petoskey, Michigan, fifty thousand passenger pigeons were killed each days. Furthermore, as farmers cleared much forests for agriculture, many passenger pigeons lost their nesting grounds. Citizens had very few information about the decline of the species.

3.   Conservationists noticed the decline of the bird population, and they made a lot of attempts to limit the slaughter. At this time, politicians did not pay much attentions to conservation. By the 1890s, almost all of the passenger pigeon had been hunted. Martha, the last passenger pigeon, died in the Cincinnati Zoo in 1914. The only positive outcome of the passenger pigeon's extinction was that peoples became interested in creating conservation laws.

Prepositions

28.4 Define prepositions.

Prepositions are words that show concepts such as time, place, direction, and manner. They show connections or relationships between ideas.

The public protested the use of DDT <u>during</u> the 1960s.

I saw an interesting book on the Amazon River <u>in</u> the bookstore.

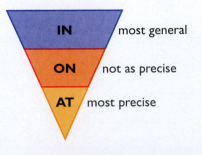

IN   most general

ON   not as precise

AT   most precise

Prepositions	Prepositions of Time	Prepositions of Place
at	at a specific time of day (at 8:30 P.M.) at night at breakfast, lunch, dinner	at an address (at 15 Maple Street) at a specific building (at the hospital)

on	on a day of the week (on Monday)
	on a specific date (on June 16)
	on a specific holiday (on Martin Luther
	   King Day)
	on time (meaning "punctual")
	on my birthday
		on a specific street (on 17th Avenue)
		on technological devices (on TV, on the
		   radio, on the phone, on the computer)
		on a planet (on Earth)
		on top

in	in a year (in 2018) in a month (in July) in the morning, afternoon, evening in the spring, fall, summer, winter	in a city (in Boston) in a country (in Spain) in a continent (in Africa)

from . . . to	from one time to another (from 6 A.M.
	   to 8 P.M.)
		from one place to another (from Las
		   Vegas to Miami)

for	for a period of time (for six hours)	for a distance (for ten miles)

Commonly Confused Prepositions

TO **AND** *AT*

Use *to* after verbs that indicate movement from one place to another.

> Each morning, Albert <u>walks</u> **to** the library, he <u>goes</u> **to** the coffee shop, and he <u>returns</u> **to** his office.

Exception: Do not put *to* directly before *home*.

> Albert returned ~~to~~ home after he won his prize. He didn't go to his friend's home.

Use *at* after verbs that indicate being or remaining in one place (and not moving from one place to another).

> In the afternoon, he <u>stays</u> **at** home. He <u>sits</u> **at** his desk and <u>looks</u> **at** his books on the environment.

FOR, DURING, **AND** *SINCE*

Use *during* to explain when something happens. Use *for* to explain how long it takes to happen. Use *since* to show when an activity started.

> **During** <u>the month of August</u>, the animal protection society office closes **for** <u>two weeks</u>.

> The government sprayed pesticides in fields and forests **for** <u>many years</u> **during** <u>World War II</u>.

> **Since** <u>World War II</u>, many countries have experienced environmental problems.

Practice 8

Write the correct preposition in each blank. Choose *in, on, at, to, for, during, since,* or *from*. If no preposition is necessary, write *X* in the space.

EXAMPLE: The International Year of Forests was ___*in*___ 2011.

1. _____ the beginning of the twentieth century, many parts of the world have experienced deforestation. Kenya has been experiencing deforestation _____ many years.

2.   Wangari Muta Maathai was born _____ April 1, 1940 _____

Ihithe village, Kenya. _____ school, she was a good student.

_____ 1960 _____ 1966, she studied _____ the United States.

_____ her studies, she became aware of Kenya's environmental

problems. When she returned _____ home, she started working for the

United Nations. She organized the Green Belt Movement _____ 1977,

which encouraged community-based organizers to plant millions of trees

_____ rural areas of Kenya.

3.   Professor Maathai never thought her idea would become so successful.

_____ 2004, one morning _____ October, she received a phone call

_____ 9 A.M. A voice _____ the phone said that she had received

the Nobel Peace Prize for environmental activism. She became the first

African woman to win the prize. _____ the start of the program, Green

Belt Movement supporters have planted over 40 million trees. Professor

Maathai died _____ September 25, 2011, of ovarian cancer.

Practice 9

Underline the correct preposition in the parentheses.

EXAMPLE: (During / <u>Since</u>) the end of the last century, global warming has
become an important environmental issue.

1.   (In / On / At) 2006, the documentary film *An Inconvenient Truth* received
good reviews (in / on / at) the Sundance Film Festival. The film also opened
(in / on / at) May 24, 2006 (in / on / at) New York City. (For / During /
Since) its release, the film has earned around $49 million.

2.   Al Gore has been a champion of environmental causes (for / during /
since) many years. (On / From / In) 1993 (to / in / on) 2001, Al Gore was
vice president of the United States. (For / During / Since) the Clinton
administration, Gore encouraged a carbon tax on energy sources.

3.   (In / On) the film, Gore, the narrator, argues that global warming is
a serious threat to life (in / on) Earth. (For / During) the film's premiere,
audiences were captivated by the film's message. Gore's other idea, The
Climate Reality Project, was launched (on / at) the same time as the film.
(For / During / Since) that time, both projects have inspired people to take
climate change seriously.

Common Prepositional Expressions

Many common expressions contain prepositions. These types of expressions usually convey a particular meaning.

verb preposition

EXAMPLE: The company <u>complied with</u> the regulations.

Some Common Prepositional Expressions		
accuse (somebody) of	escape from	prevent (someone) from
acquainted with	excited about	protect (someone) from
add to	familiar with	proud of
afraid of	feel like	provide (someone) with
agree with	fond of	qualify for
angry about	forget about	realistic about
angry with	forgive (someone) for	refer to
apologize for	friendly with	related to
apply for	good for	rely on
approve of	grateful for	rescue from
argue with	happy about	responsible for
ask for	hear about	sad about
associate with	hope for	satisfied with
aware of	hopeful about	scared of
believe in	innocent of	search for
belong to	insist on	similar to
capable of	insulted by	specialize in
care about	interested in	stop (something) from
care for	introduce to	succeed in
commit to	jealous of	take advantage of
comply with	keep from	take care of
concern about	located in	thank (someone) for
confronted with	long for	think about
consist of	look forward to	think of
count on	opposed to	tired of
deal with	participate in	upset about
decide on	patient with	upset with
decide to	pay attention to	willing to
depend on	pay for	wish for
be disappointed about	pray for	worry about
be disappointed with	prepared for	
dream of	prepared to	

Practice 10

Write the correct preposition in each blank. Use the preceding list of prepositional expressions to help you.

EXAMPLE: Dr. Singh succeeded _____in_____ helping the villagers conserve water.

1. In 1984, Dr. Rajendra Singh traveled from New Delhi to the district of

    Alwar. Alwar is located _____ Rajasthan, a desert state in India. Dr.

Singh was looking forward _____ starting a health clinic for villagers in the district. When he arrived there, he was confronted _____ a difficult problem. The water supply in the area had dried up. The villagers had to walk for miles to search _____ water. Eventually, Dr. Singh was responsible _____ changing people's attitudes about water usage.

2. Dr. Singh thought _____ how to help the villagers. He realized that the villagers no longer relied _____ traditional methods to store water. He decided _____ convince them to go back to ancient practices of collecting water. He showed the villagers how to build small dams or *johads* to collect rainwater.

3. In seven months, the johads were full of water, and the rivers were flowing. The villagers were grateful _____ Singh's ideas. The district has also benefitted from the water collection system. The water table has risen; forests have regrown; and antelopes, leopards, and birds have returned to the region to take advantage _____ the water. Other drought-ravaged areas also depend _____ Dr. Singh's system of water management to increase their water supply.

Reflect On It

Think about what you have learned in this chapter. If you do not know an answer, review that concept.

1. Make the following nouns plural.
    a. tooth   _____
    b. backseat driver   _____
    c. bride-to-be   _____
    d. kiss   _____
    e. homework   _____
    f. loaf   _____

2. Correct the errors in the following sentences.

                          much
EXAMPLE: John Muir spent ~~many~~ time in the wilderness.

    a. He had much ideas for environmental conservation.

    b. On 1892, he helped to found the Sierra Club.

    c. He was one of the most dedicated environmentalist in the United States.

    d. Few peoples were as passionate about conservation as Muir was.

Final Review

Correct twenty errors in singular or plural forms, determiners, or prepositions.

EXAMPLE: California faced one of the longest ~~drought~~ ^{droughts} in American history.

1.   The central valley of California is one of the most important source of
food in the United States. The region is also vital to a world's food supply.
Farms in California grow avocados, kiwis, lemons, and strawberrys. In the
past century, California had plenty of rain. In these days, farmers spent few
time worrying about how much water they were using. Currently, California
is experiencing drought. Environmentalists and politicians are confronted
about a complicated problem to solve.

2.   The water shortage has several negative effect. Because of low rainfall,
farmers are using too many groundwater for certain cash crops like almonds.
Forest fires are burning in the drought regions. Many environmental agencys
are collecting a lot of datas about the wildfires, which are responsible at the
destruction of thousands of acres of forests and billions of dollars of property
damage.

3.   On 2015, California Governor Jerry Brown imposed strict new laws
to limit water use. Each households was limited to just over 100 gallons
of water per day. Violators of the law paid fines of about $10,000. Even so,
famous persons were caught stealing water from public sources, such as fire
hydrants. The California is not the only place in Earth suffering from extreme
drought conditions. Each years, more and more countries suffer water
shortages, including China, Colombia, Australia, and Kenya.

4.   Those days, many people are deeply concerned for the water shortages
facing California and other parts of the country. Politicians must commit on
policies that will preserve the water supply.

The Writer's Room

Write about one of the following topics. Then review your nouns, determiners, and prepositions.

1. Are you concerned about the environment? Why or why not?
2. Describe at least three actions you can take to reduce your carbon footprint. To find out what your carbon footprint is, you can search "carbon footprint calculator" online.

GRAMMAR LINK
For more information about apostrophes, see Chapter 35.

Some possessive adjectives sound like certain contractions. When using the possessive adjectives *their*, *your*, and *its*, be careful that you do not confuse them with *they're*, *you're*, and *it's*.

Their is the possessive adjective.	<u>Their</u> flight to Mexico City was late.
They're is the contraction of *they are*.	<u>They're</u> looking forward to going to Cancun.
Your is the possessive adjective.	<u>Your</u> tour guide has a map of the conference center.
You're is the contraction of *you are*.	<u>You're</u> going to lecture on carbon emissions.
Its is the possessive adjective.	The documentary will be shown, and <u>its</u> director will give an interview.
It's is the contraction of *it is*.	<u>It's</u> going to win first prize.

HINT: Choosing *His* or *Her*

To choose the correct possessive adjective, think about the possessor (not the object that is possessed).

- If something belongs to a female, use *her* + noun.

    Cecilia read <u>her</u> report.

- If something belongs to a male, use *his* + noun.

    Tony booked <u>his</u> flight.

Practice 1

Underline the correct possessive adjective or possessive pronoun in each set of parentheses.

EXAMPLE: Some of the rescue workers had (<u>their</u> / theirs / they're) own equipment.

1.   On March 24, 1989, the oil tanker *Exxon Valdez* and (it's / its / their) captain became infamous when the ship hit a reef in Prince William Sound, Alaska. The tanker leaked crude oil because (it's / its / their) holding tanks were damaged. The oil spill was the second largest in U.S. history. The oil leaked in a very remote location. The area and (its / it's / her) ecosystem were destroyed. According to reporters, Captain Joe Hazelwood and (her / his) crew made some critical errors. The ship was not using the shipping lanes due to icebergs. Moreover, the third mate, Gregory Cousins, did not carry out (her / its / his) orders to move the ship back into the shipping lane near the reef.

2.   From March to June 2010, oil spilled into the Gulf of Mexico because of an explosion during deepwater drilling by British Petroleum. The spill and (it's / its / his) consequences were grim for the environment. Thousands of workers were needed to clean up the oil. The people of the region used

all of (their / theirs) resources for the cleanup. The fishers still talk about the destruction of (their / they're / theirs) livelihood because the oil spill destroyed the commercial fishing industry.

3.   Fiona Phillips, a journalist, has written about (her / his) research into the accident. Fiona has posted (his / her / hers) photos of oil spills on a website, and other photojournalists have posted (their / they're / theirs). Many people have visited the site. They post (their / theirs) comments, and Fiona adds (her / hers). We should create (our / ours) own website about the 2010 BP oil disaster. You can write (your / you're / yours) opinions, and I will post (my / mine).

Pronouns in Comparisons with *than* or *as*

Avoid making errors in pronoun case when the pronoun follows *than* or *as*. If the pronoun is a subject, use the subjective case, and if the pronoun is an object, use the objective case.

If you use the incorrect case, your sentence may have a meaning that you do not intend it to have. For example, people often follow *than* or *as* with an objective pronoun when they mean to follow it with a subjective pronoun. Look at the difference in the meaning between the next sentences.

objective case

I like environmental studies as much as **him**.
(I like environmental studies as much as I like him.)

subjective case

I like environmental studies as much as **he**.
(I like environmental studies as much as he likes environmental studies.)

HINT: Complete the Thought

If you are unsure which pronoun case to use, test yourself by completing the thought. Look at the following examples.

He likes to watch documentaries more than **I** (like to watch documentaries).

He likes to watch documentaries more than (he likes to watch) **me**.

Pronouns in Prepositional Phrases

In a prepositional phrase, the noun or pronoun that follows the preposition is the object of the preposition. Therefore, always use the objective case of the pronoun after a preposition.

To **them**, learning about the environment is not important.

Between **you** and **me**, our environmental ethics class is very interesting.

Pronouns with *and* or *or*

Use the correct case when pronouns are joined by *and* or *or*. If the pronouns are the subject, use the subjective case. If the pronouns are the object, use the objective case.

Subjective	<u>He and I</u> H̶i̶m̶ ̶a̶n̶d̶ ̶m̶e̶ had to do a presentation on icebergs.
Objective	<u>him and me</u> The instructor asked h̶e̶ ̶a̶n̶d̶ ̶I̶ to present first.

HINT: Finding the Correct Case

An easy way to determine whether your case is correct is to say the sentence with just one pronoun.

The librarian asked her and (I, me) to speak quietly.

Choices	The librarian asked I . . . *or* The librarian asked me . . .
Correct	The librarian asked her and <u>me</u> to speak quietly.

Practice 2

Correct any errors with pronoun case. Write C in the space if the sentence is correct.

EXAMPLE: Last summer, my friend and m̶e̶ attended an environmental
conference. _____I_____

1. Recently, my friend Cindy Huang and me toured Chernobyl. _____

2. She wanted to see Chernobyl more than me but convinced
me to go along. _____

3. She and I are interested in environmental issues. _____

4. Between you and I, I was a bit concerned about being so close to a
radioactive site. _____

5. The guide, Ivana, told we visitors that the explosion at
Chernobyl in 1986 was more powerful than 90 atomic bombs. _____

6. Ivana took photos of Cindy and me near the dam. _____

7. We didn't have our camera, so we used her's. _____

8. Cindy is as aware as me of how the devastating the effects
of the meltdown were. _____

9. Cindy or me will give a presentation on our experience
at Chernobyl, and the ways to prevent another nuclear disaster. _____

10. Cindy said goodbye to Ivana because her and me had
to catch our train. _____

Relative Pronouns (*Who, Whom, Which, That, Whose*)

29.2   **Identify relative pronouns.**

Relative pronouns can join two separate sentences. The individual sentences are called clauses, and a relative pronoun can be either the subject or the object of its own clause. Here is a list of relative pronouns.

who	whom	which	that	whose
whoever	whomever			

- *Who* (or *whoever*) and *whom* (or *whomever*) always refer to people. *Who* is the subject of the clause, and *whom* is the object of the clause.

  Subject   The lawyer **who** specializes in environmental law is speaking today.

  Object   The lawyer **whom** you met is my mother.

- *Which* always refers to things.

  The ancient city of Machu Picchu, **which** receives two thousand visitors every year, is being slowly eroded by tourists' feet.

- *That* refers to things.

  Elizabeth Cartwright's book **that** is on pesticides received a prize.

- *Whose* always shows that something belongs to or is connected with someone or something. It usually replaces possessive pronouns such as *his*, *her*, or *their*. Do not confuse *whose* with *who's*, which means "who is."

  The geographer traced the route. His maps were on the table.

  The geographer, **whose** maps were on the table**,** traced the route.

> **GRAMMAR LINK**
> Clauses with *which* are set off with commas. For more information, see Chapter 34, "Commas."

HINT: Choosing *Who* or *Whom*

If you are unsure whether to use *who* or *whom*, test yourself in the following way. Replace *who* or *whom* with another pronoun. If the replacement is a subjective pronoun such as *he* or *she*, use *who*. If the replacement is an objective pronoun such as *her* or *him*, use *whom*.

I know a man **who** works at the Environmental Protection Agency.

(He works at the Environmental Protection Agency.)

The man to **whom** you gave your portfolio is the director of the Environmental Protection Agency.

(You gave your portfolio to him.)

Practice 3

Write the correct relative pronoun in each blank. Choose *who, whom, which, whose,* or *that.*

EXAMPLE: The Love Canal story, _____*which*_____ has been made into a film, is very tragic.

1.   William T. Love, for _____ the Love Canal community was named, wanted to build a canal joining the Niagara River with Lake Ontario. The project, _____ was started in the 1890s, was abandoned due to many zoning obstacles. In the 1940s, the Hooker Electrochemical Company, _____ owned the Love Canal land, dumped toxic chemicals on the site.

2.   In the early 1970s, some Niagara Falls town councilors _____ wanted to build housing on the site offered to buy the land from the Hooker Company. Company managers refused to sell the land because of toxic chemicals. The owners, _____ knowledge about the site was important, told city officials about the toxic chemicals. But some city officials _____ were members of the planning committee ignored the warning. The soil _____ the houses and school stood on was polluted.

3.   The school _____ all the local children attended shut down because its water supply contained toxic chemicals. Children _____ had been healthy before started to become ill. Two journalists _____ investigated the situation were shocked. The mothers _____ the journalists interviewed told them about a high number of birth defects in newborn babies. A local resident _____ son developed epilepsy became the spokesperson for the community.

4.   It took a long time for the government to deal with the tragedy of Love Canal. Residents _____ lives were destroyed eventually received compensation from the government. The law _____ Congress passed requires polluters to be responsible for any damage.

Reflexive Pronouns (*-self* or *-selves*)

29.3   Identify reflexive pronouns.

Use **reflexive pronouns** when you want to emphasize that the subject does an action to him- or herself.

I asked **myself** many questions.

History often repeats **itself**.

Do not use reflexive pronouns with the verbs *wash*, *dress*, *feed*, and *shave*. However, you can use reflexive pronouns to draw attention to a surprising or an unusual action.

The little <u>boy</u> fed **himself**.

(The boy probably could not feed himself at a previous time.)

The next chart gives subjective pronouns and the reflexive pronouns that relate to them.

Pronouns That End with *-self* or *-selves*

	Antecedent	Reflexive Pronoun
Singular		
1st person	I	myself
2nd person	you	yourself
3rd person	he, she, it	himself, herself, itself
Plural		
1st person	we	ourselves
2nd person	you	yourselves
3rd person	they	themselves

HINT: Common Errors with Reflexive Pronouns

Hisself and *theirselves* are not accepted in standard English. These are incorrect ways to say *himself* or *themselves*.

                                          themselves
The children made the recycling video by ~~theirselves~~.

                                       himself.
Franklin wrote about solar energy by ~~hisself~~.

Practice 4

Fill in the blanks with the correct reflexive pronouns.

EXAMPLE: I introduced _____*myself*_____ to the famous climatologist, Dr. Saleem Khan.

1.   Dr. Saleem Khan attended the meeting on climate change in Cancun, Mexico, by _____. His colleague Radhika Ketkar was supposed to attend but had to cancel. The day before, she had fallen and hurt _____.

2.   The agenda of the meeting was to develop policy on reducing greenhouse gas emissions. The international members could not agree among _____ on the details of the policy. Some nations criticized the United States for not taking a stronger stand on reducing carbon emissions. The government was quick to defend _____.

3. I was at the meeting with a group of other journalists. We attended the talks and saw for _____ that governments could not agree on many issues. I told my colleagues that I was going to go by _____ to interview some of the protesters. "Don't go by _____," they advised. So we went together to talk to the activists.

Pronoun–Antecedent Agreement

29.4 Maintain pronoun–antecedent agreement.

Antecedents are words that pronouns have replaced, and they always come before the pronoun. A pronoun must agree with its antecedent, which is the word to which the pronoun refers. Pronouns must agree in person and number with their antecedents.

My instructor took us on a field trip to the wetlands. **He** took **his** family with **him**.
(*My instructor* is the antecedent of *he*, *his*, and *him*.)

China has many dust storms. **They** originate in the Gobi Desert.
(*Dust storms* is the antecedent of *they*.)

Compound Antecedents

Compound antecedents consist of two or more nouns joined by *and* or *or*. When the nouns are joined by *and*, use a plural pronoun to refer to them.

The scholar and her husband brought **their** son to the bird sanctuary.

When the nouns are joined by *or*, you may need a singular or a plural pronoun. If the antecedents are plural, use a plural pronoun. If both nouns are singular, use a singular pronoun.

Either the men or women completed **their** research first.
Does England or France have **its** own environmental policy?

Collective Noun Antecedents

GRAMMAR LINK
For a list of collective nouns, see page 345 in Chapter 26.

Collective nouns refer to a group of people or things. When the noun acts as a unit, it is singular.

The government tried to implement **its** policies.

Practice 5

Fill in the blank spaces with the appropriate pronouns or possessive adjectives.

EXAMPLE: Oil companies want to increase ____*their*____ profits.

1. Does Saudi Arabia or Canada export more of _____ oil to the United States? The United States imports more oil from _____

neighbor Canada than from any other country in the world. Canada has the third largest proven oil reserve in the world. However, acquiring Canadian oil is problematic and expensive because _____ is found in sandy deposits in Alberta. Extracting oil from sand greatly pollutes the environment. Therefore, either Canadian government ministries or Canadian oil companies send _____ lobbyists to promote Canadian oil exports to the United States.

2.   Bobby Hinds and _____ sister Beth work in the Canadian tar sands industry. _____ are engineers, and _____ employer is one of the largest oil companies in the world. Sometimes managers ask Beth or _____ brother to solve public relations problems for the company.

3.   Each month, either environmentalists or oilmen send _____ representatives to meet with Bobby and Beth to inform _____ about the environmental issues. The oil company and _____ supporters meet with politicians to discuss the economic importance of the oil industry. Janice Cole is an environmentalist. She and _____ colleagues also lobby the government. The government says that _____ mandate is to provide jobs for citizens. The government, the oil companies, and the environmentalists stick to _____ own points of view. _____ all know that there is a tradeoff—economic progress versus environmental responsibility.

Indefinite Pronouns

29.5   **Identify indefinite pronouns.**

Use **indefinite pronouns** when you refer to people or things whose identity is not known or is unimportant. The next chart shows some common singular and plural indefinite pronouns.

Indefinite Pronouns				
Singular	another	each	nobody	other
	anybody	everybody	no one	somebody
	anyone	everyone	nothing	someone
	anything	everything	one	something
Plural	both, few, many, others, several			
Either singular or plural	all, any, none, more, most, half (and other fractions), some			

SINGULAR

When you use a singular indefinite antecedent, also use a singular pronoun to refer to it.

Everybody feels shocked when **he or she** sees China's air pollution.

Nobody should forget to visit China's northern forests in **his or her** lifetime.

PLURAL

When you use a plural indefinite antecedent, also use a plural pronoun to refer to it.

> The two documentaries are new, and <u>both</u> have **their** own point of view.

> The world has many illegal logging sites; there are <u>several</u> operating in China, but **they** cannot be controlled.

EITHER SINGULAR OR PLURAL

Some indefinite pronouns can be either singular or plural, depending on the noun to which they refer.

> Many geologists came to the site. <u>All</u> were experts in **their** field.

> (*All* refers to geologists; therefore, the pronoun is plural.)

> We excavated <u>all</u> of the site and **its** surrounding area.

> (*All* refers to the site; therefore, the pronoun is singular.)

HINT: Using *one of the* and *each of the* Expressions

In sentences containing the expression *one of the* . . . or *each of the* . . . , the subject is the indefinite pronoun *one* or *each*. Therefore, any pronoun referring to that phrase must be singular.

> <u>One</u> of the reports is missing **its** appendix.

> <u>Each</u> of the men has **his** own map.

Practice 6

Identify and correct eight errors in pronoun–antecedent agreement. You may change either the antecedent or the pronoun. If you change any antecedents, make sure that your subjects and verbs agree.

EXAMPLE: Everybody was worried about his or her ~~their~~ children.

1. One of the worst industrial accidents happened in April 2013 in West, Texas. West Fertilizer Company supplied farmers in the area with fertilizer for his crops. The factory exploded on April 17, destroying a large chunk of the small town. The cause of the explosion is still unclear, but the damage was catastrophic. Over 150 buildings were destroyed. Nobody in the small town could have predicted that their life was in danger.

2. However, there had been warning signs. Several years before the explosion, one of the government inspectors visiting the site tried to warn their boss that the factory was storing ammonia improperly. When investigators from the EPA visited the factory in 2006, he fined the factory for failing to submit a proper safety plan. Someone at the Department of Homeland Security said that their department had not been informed about 270 tons of highly explosive ammonium nitrate stored at the factory.

3. Several reports about the accident indicate that it was preventable. The public blamed West Fertilizer Company and the government for the catastrophe. Both had not done its job well. Fifteen people lost their lives in the tragedy, and hundreds more were injured. Others lost his homes due to the powerful explosion. Each of the town's citizens had their life disastrously altered.

HINT: Avoid Sexist Language

Terms like *anybody, somebody, nobody,* and *each* are singular antecedents, so the pronouns that follow those words must be singular. At one time, it was acceptable to use *he* as a general term meaning "all people." However, today it is more acceptable to use *he or she*.

Sexist	Everyone had to leave his home.
Solution	Everyone had to leave his or her home.
Better solution	The citizens had to leave their homes.

Exception: If you know for certain that the subject is male or female, then use only *he* or only *she*.

Practice 7

Underline the correct pronouns in the following paragraphs.

EXAMPLE: Many people have lost (his or her / <u>their</u>) homes because of wildfires.

1. In 2012, more wildfires raged across the southern United States than in past years. Almost everybody in the path of the fires had (his or her / their) home destroyed. Police and firefighters had to use all of (they're / their) training to fight the blazes. The army sent (its / his / their) water bombers to help put out the fires. Katrina Hobbart and (his / her / their) husband fled minutes before flames engulfed the road. Others also had to save (theirselves / themselves). Ronald, (who / whom) is a reporter, stated that he had never seen wildfires burn with such speed.

2. My friend Petra and (I / me) volunteered to help rebuild communities that were destroyed. I directed traffic in my part of town, and Petra directed traffic in (her's / hers). I also collected donations. Petra's boss, to (who / whom) I sent the money, gave it to community organizers. Between you and (I / me), other volunteers were just as committed to rebuilding as (I / me).

3. Climate change and (its / their / it's) consequences are severe. For example, a rise in temperature might cause drought or wildfires. Nature is often more powerful than (us / we) are.

Vague Pronouns

29.6   Identify and correct vague pronouns.

Avoid using pronouns that could refer to more than one antecedent.

Vague	Frank asked his friend where <u>his</u> book on environmental statistics was. (Whose book is it: Frank's or his friend's?)
Clearer	**Frank** wondered where **his** book on environmental statistics was, so he asked his friend about it.

Avoid using confusing pronouns such as *it* and *they* that have no clear antecedent.

Vague	<u>They</u> say that people should get vaccines before traveling to certain countries. (Who are *they*?)
Clearer	**Health authorities** say that people should get vaccines before traveling to certain countries.
Vague	<u>It</u> stated in the magazine that scientists were collaborating on research. (Who or what is *it*?)
Clearer	**The magazine article** stated that scientists were collaborating on research.

This, that, and *which* should refer to a specific antecedent.

Vague	The teacher told us that we should study hard for our ecology exams because they were going to be difficult. <u>This</u> caused all of us to panic. (What is *this*? The word(s) that *this* refers to is not explicitly stated; it is only implied.)
Clearer	The teacher told us that we should study hard for our ecology exams because they were going to be difficult. **This information** caused all of us to panic.

HINT: Avoid Repeating the Subject

When you clearly mention a subject, do not repeat the subject in pronoun form.

The Sahara Desert **it** is growing.

The book **it** is really interesting.

Practice 8

Each sentence has either a vague pronoun or a repeated subject. Correct the errors. You may need to rewrite some sentences.

EXAMPLE: ~~They~~ Politicians say that we have to develop a precise policy on nuclear power.

1. It said on the news that nuclear power generates about 14 percent of the world's electricity.

2. Professor Tate told his student Michael that his paper on nuclear energy will be published.

3. It stated in the textbook that nuclear energy is a controversial topic.

4. Proponents they believe that using nuclear energy is better for the environment than burning fossil fuels.

5. Critics they say that relying on nuclear power may have dangerous effects, such as radiation poisoning, on humans.

6. In Japan, the Fukushima Daiichi nuclear plant it was destroyed by an earthquake and tsunami.

7. They claimed that the disaster was caused by poor enforcement of safety standards.

8. Politicians and the public passionately debate this.

Pronoun Shifts

29.7   Identify and correct pronoun shifts.

If your writing contains unnecessary shifts in person or number, you may confuse your readers. Carefully edit your writing to ensure that your pronouns are consistent in number and person.

Making Pronouns Consistent in Number

Pronouns and antecedents must agree in **number**. If the antecedent is singular, then the pronoun must be singular. If the antecedent is plural, then the pronoun must be plural.

The **director** of the laboratory encouraged ~~their~~ *her* employees to be on time.

When the **activitists** protested, ~~he~~ *they* carried signs.

Making Pronouns Consistent in Person

Person is the writer's perspective. In some writing assignments, you may use first person (*I, we*). For other assignments, especially most college and workplace writing, you may use second person (*you*) or third person (*he, she, it, they*).

When you shift your point of view for no reason, your writing may become unclear, and you may confuse your readers. If you begin writing from one point of view, do not shift unnecessarily to another point of view.

If ~~one~~ *we* considered the expenses involved in visiting another country, **we** would probably never travel.

We visited the dam, but ~~you~~ *we* could not enter it.

HINT: Avoiding Pronoun Shifts in Paragraphs

Sometimes it is easier to use pronouns consistently in individual sentences than it is in larger paragraphs or essays. When you write paragraphs and essays, always check that your pronouns agree with your antecedents in person and in number. In the next example, the pronouns are consistent in the first two sentences; however, they shift in person in the third sentence.

We went to Mexico City last year. **We** traveled around on the subway.

Sometimes the subway was so crowded that ~~you~~ ^{we} could barely move.

Practice 9

Correct six pronoun shift errors.

EXAMPLE: When scientists study climate change, ~~you~~ ^{they} have to consider natural causes as well as human causes.

1.   There are two clear sources that cause climate change: natural and human. Climatologists often state that you have limited historical data on weather patterns. Scientists know that one must take natural forces into account. For instance, in the past, climate changes have caused many ice ages.

2.   We are working on computer models of weather systems. We collect data on environmental events. For example, we study volcanic eruptions, and you can see that ash affects global temperatures. We need to have complete statistics before you can make predictions about climate change. We analyze the statistics very carefully because one must be accurate.

3.   Politicians need to craft a clear policy to tackle climate change because if one does not, the problem will become more critical.

Reflect On It

Think about what you have learned in this chapter. If you do not know an answer, review that concept.

1. Write a sentence that includes an objective pronoun. _____

    _____

2. When do you use possessive pronouns (*my, mine, his, hers,* etc.)? _____

    _____

3. Circle the best answer: In a sentence, *whom* replaces

    a. the subject.   b. the object

4. What is an antecedent? _____

    _____

5. Circle the best answer: Pronouns must agree with their antecedents

    a. only in number.   b. only in person.

    c. both in number and in person.   d. neither in number nor in person.

FINAL REVIEW

Correct fifteen errors with pronouns in the next paragraphs.

EXAMPLE: Susan wants to heat ~~his~~ ^{her} home with geothermal energy.

1.	Our society has depended economically on oil for the past two hundred years. We know that oil is a nonrenewable energy source and that you must reduce our dependence on it. Politicians and they're advisors react badly to suggestions on reducing oil consumption. They're concerned about economic progress. Yet environmentalists they believe that burning fossil fuels is causing temperatures around the world to become warmer. Scientists whom are interested in climate change are trying to develop alternative energy sources.

2.	Nuclear energy is one alternative source of energy. This is a cause for concern. Many environmentalists with who I have spoken talk about a need for caution when discussing nuclear power. Dr. Cynthia Malick and his students are studying the effects of nuclear disasters. There have been many, such as Chernobyl and Three Mile Island. The worst was the Fukushima nuclear accident caused by the 2011 tsunami in Japan. Everybody has their own opinions about nuclear energy.

3.	Another source of alternative energy is geothermal. The United States produces the greatest amount of geothermal electricity in the world. Either the Philippines or Indonesia is also developing their geothermal production.

4.	My professor, Dr. Lam Ping, and me are researching wind energy. Currently, turbines who use wind power produce about 2.5 percent of the world's electricity. Between you and I, Dr. Ping knows more about wind-generated electricity than me. Dr. Ping does much of the research on wind energy by hisself. However, the university asked both him and I to give a presentation on the subject. Our government needs to develop and promote energy alternatives.

READING LINK
To learn about environmental issues, read the following essays.

"Roaring Waves of Fire" (p. 188)
"The Purpose of Pets" (p. 202)
"Mother Nature's Melting Pot" (p. 512)
"The Beeps" (p. 519)

The Writer's Room

Choose one of the following topics. Make sure that pronoun case and pronoun–antecedent agreement are correct.

1. What are the different types of pollution? Divide types of pollution into different categories.

2. How would you organize an environmental awareness event?

The Writers' Circle: Collaborative Activity

Work with a group of three to five students.

Imagine that you are having a dinner party. You can invite any five people that you want. The guests can be historical figures or living people. As a team, write three sentences about each person and explain who the person is and what he or she will contribute to the party. After you finish, underline the pronouns in your sentences and verify that they have been used correctly.

30 Adjectives and Adverbs

SECTION THEME: Health Care

In this chapter, you read about topics related to health care.

The Writer's Journal

Write a short paragraph describing how people can best protect their health. List several examples in your paragraph.

Adjectives

30.1 Define adjectives.

Adjectives describe nouns (people, places, or things) and pronouns (words that replace nouns). They add information explaining how many, what kind, or which one. They also help you appeal to the senses by describing how things look, smell, feel, taste, and sound.

The **dynamic** <u>doctor</u>, Christiaan Barnard, completed a **complicated** <u>surgery</u>.

He performed the **first heart transplant** <u>operation</u> in 1967.

Placement of Adjectives

You can place adjectives either before a noun or after a linking verb such as *be*, *look*, *appear*, *smell*, or *become*.

Before the noun	The **young unemployed** man received a scholarship for **medical** school.
After the linking verb	He was **shocked**, but he was **happy**.

In the "After the linking verb" example, LV appears above "was" in both clauses.

Practice 1

Underline the adjectives in the next sentences.

EXAMPLE: American politicians debate the soaring cost of medical school.

1. Unemployed students and young graduates struggle to get adequate health care.

2. Certain groups of university students cannot afford sufficient, useful medical training.

3. Student loan debt is higher for medical students than for law students or business students.

4. Students graduating from health-care programs generally owe over one-hundred thousand dollars.

5. The Association of American Medical Colleges estimates that the United States will face a serious shortage of specialized doctors due to an aging population.

6. Some politicians argue that more doctors are needed in rural areas.

7. In 2013, politicians passed what they hope is decent and fair legislation to reduce student debt for health-care professionals who work in places with a shortage of doctors.

Problems with Adjectives

You can recognize many adjectives by their endings. Be particularly careful when you use the following adjective forms.

ADJECTIVES ENDING IN *-FUL* OR *-LESS*

Some adjectives end in *-ful* or *-less*. Remember that *-ful* ends in one *l* and *-less* ends in double *s*.

> Alexander Fleming, a **skillful** scientist, conducted many **useful** experiments. His work appeared in **countless** publications.

ADJECTIVES ENDING IN *-ED* AND *-ING*

Some adjectives look like verbs because they end in *-ing* or *-ed*.

- When the adjective ends in *-ed*, it describes the person's or animal's expression or feeling.

    > The **overworked** scientist presented her findings to the public.

- When the adjective ends in *-ing*, it describes the quality of the person or thing.

    > Her **compelling** and **promising** discovery pleased the public.

HINT: Keep Adjectives in the Singular Form

Always make an adjective singular, even if the noun following the adjective is plural. In the next example, "year" acts as an adjective.

Paul was a nine-~~years~~-old boy when he broke his arm while playing with
year

~~others~~ children.
other

Practice 2

Underline and correct eight adjective errors. The adjectives may have the wrong form, or they may be misspelled.

EXAMPLE: Many ~~surprised~~ medical findings happen by accident.
surprising

1. One of the world's amazed scientifics discoveries happened by pure chance. Born in 1881, Alexander Fleming was a tireles medical doctor. He worked in his small London clinic, where he treated famous people for venereal disease. He also conducted many biologicals experiments.

2. One day in 1928, he put some *Staphylococcus* bacteria in a culture dish. Two weeks later, Fleming, who was a carefull researcher, discovered that a clear ring encircled the yellow-green mold on the dish. A mold spore had flown into the dish from a laboratory on the floor below. At that point, Fleming made an insightfull observation. He had an astounded revelation. He realized that the mold somehow stopped the growth of bacteria in the culture dish.

3. Fleming named the new product penicillin. During World War II, the drug saved millions of lives, and it continues to be used today to treat differents infections.

Adverbs

30.2 Define adverbs.

Adverbs add information to adjectives, verbs, or other adverbs. They give more specific information about how, when, where, and to what extent an action or event occurred.

verb   adverb

Doctors in ancient Rome <u>performed</u> surgeries **skillfully**.

adverb   adverb

These surgeons could remove cataracts **quite** <u>quickly</u>.

adverb   adjective

The ancient Romans were **highly** <u>innovative</u>.

Forms of Adverbs

Adverbs often end in *-ly*. In fact, you can change many adjectives into adverbs by adding *-ly* endings.

- If you add *-ly* to a word that ends in *l*, then your new word will have a double *l*.

  scornful + ly

  Many ancient Romans viewed surgeons **scornfully**.

- If you add *-ly* to a word that ends in *e*, keep the *e*. Exceptions to this rule are *truly* and *duly*.

  extreme + ly

  Doctors were **extremely** careful when they operated on patients.

HINT: Some Adverbs and Adjectives Have the Same Form

Some adverbs look exactly like adjectives. The only way to distinguish them from adjectives is to see what they are modifying or describing. The following words can be either adjectives or adverbs.

early	fast	high	often	right
far	hard	late	past	soon

adjective   adverb

Dr. Greenbay has a **hard** job. She works **hard**.

Practice 3

Underline the correct adjectives or adverbs in each sentence.

EXAMPLE: In 1980, the World Health Organization (official / <u>officially</u>) stated that it had eradicated smallpox.

1. The worldwide eradication of smallpox was one of the most important

    accomplishments in modern medicine. Smallpox was a (high / highly)

    contagious global disease. Throughout history, smallpox epidemics were a

    (frequent / frequently) occurrence. People who contracted the disease had

    (painful / painfully) sores. Around 30 percent of smallpox victims suffered

    (horrible / horribly) deaths. In the Americas, smallpox (severe / severely)

    weakened native populations.

2. In the mid-twentieth century, in North America and Europe, smallpox

    outbreaks were (rapid / rapidly) controlled with the use of vaccinations.

    However, in other parts of the world, the illness occurred (regular /

    regularly). In the early 1960s, the former Soviet Union proposed a (global /

    globally) initiative to eliminate smallpox. Health-care workers knew they would have to work (careful / carefully) to help identify regions where the disease still occurred. They (patient / patiently) educated people about the malady and inoculated those at risk. With great effort, the World Health Organization eradicated the (terrible / terribly) disease. Since 1977, there has been no (natural / naturally) recurrence of smallpox anywhere in the world.

Placement of Frequency Adverbs

Frequency adverbs are words that indicate how often someone performs an action or when an event occurs. Common frequency adverbs are *always, ever, never, often, sometimes,* and *usually.* They can appear at the beginning of sentences, or they can appear in the following mid-sentence locations.

- Place frequency adverbs before regular present tense and past tense verbs.

  Medical doctors **always** <u>recite</u> the Hippocratic oath.

- Place frequency adverbs after all forms of the verb *be (am, is, are, was, were).*

  My patients <u>are</u> **usually** punctual for appointments.

- Place frequency adverbs after helping verbs.

  I <u>have</u> **never** broken any bone in my body.

Practice 4

Correct eight errors in the placement of mid-sentence frequency adverbs.

                    often
EXAMPLE: Chronic pain is treated ~~often~~ with narcotics.
                    ^

1.   Almost two million Americans are prescribed painkillers every year. Patients fail often to recognize that they are addicted to painkillers. Doctors label sometimes this problem the "silent addiction."

2.   Many patients usually have started taking painkillers after an accident. For example, Emma was suffering from chronic back pain. She took painkillers to reduce her pain but found soon that she needed a stronger dose. So she doubled quickly the dose of her prescription. Her personality started to change, and she found that she was critical often of people around her. She realized that she was addicted to painkillers and spoke to her doctor about her problem. Now, she reads always bottle labels and she takes never pain medication.

Problems with Adverbs

USE THE CORRECT FORM

Many times, people use an adjective instead of an adverb after a verb. Make sure that you always modify your verbs using an adverb.

really quickly
Ancient Greek medicine advanced ~~real quick~~ after the time of Homer.

slowly
However, patients recovered very ~~slow~~.

Practice 5

Underline and correct eight errors in adjective and adverb forms.

really
EXAMPLE: Mental illness is a <u>realy</u> important issue.

1. Mental illness is a disorder that slow inhibits a person's ability to cope with the ordinary demands of life. When a person has severely mental illness, he or she has trouble dealing with day-to-day activities. Mental illness can affect anybody, but young people are particular affected. Some people may feel acute depressed, while others may show signs of anxiety, bipolar disorder, phobias, and so on. Sometimes, the mentally ill are stigmatized very quick.

2. Mental illness should be taken real seriously. The World Health Organization states that four out of ten causes of disability in the United States are due to mental illness, and around 46 percent of the population will suffer from some form of mental illness. If mental illness is left untreated, people can suffer tragically consequences, such as unemployment, homelessness, and imprisonment. Doctors can use different types of treatment on their patients. For example, doctors may treat patients with medication or talk therapy very successful.

USING *GOOD* AND *WELL*, *BAD* AND *BADLY*

Good is an adjective, and *well* is an adverb.

Adjective	Louis Pasteur had a **good** reputation.
Adverb	He explained his theories **well**.

Exception: Use *well* to describe a person's health: I do not feel **well**.

Bad is an adjective, and *badly* is an adverb.

Adjective	My father has a **bad** cold.
Adverb	His throat hurts **badly**.

Practice 6

Underline the correct adjectives or adverbs.

EXAMPLE: Check the label (good / <u>well</u>) before you buy food.

1. Tainted food can damage the (good / well) reputations of food companies.

2. Some customers reacted (bad / badly) when they found bits of metal in their Kraft Macaroni & Cheese boxes.

3. Fortunately, health inspectors investigated the case really (good / well) and recalled over 200,000 boxes immediately.

4. The makers of Sabra Hummus and Blue Bell Ice Cream received some (bad / badly) news when they found out their products had been infected with Listeriosis.

5. Listeriosis causes a (bad / badly) case of indigestion, and food that is inspected (good / well) should be tested for Listeria bacteria.

6. Some companies do not take (good / well) care when handling their food.

7. Chinese inspectors discovered that some Chinese McDonald's and KFC franchises served (bad / badly) meat.

8. Some employees did not wash their hands (good / well) before handling the food, and even used meat that had been on the ground.

Comparative and Superlative Forms

30.3   Identify comparative and superlative forms.

Use the **comparative form** to show how two persons, things, or items are different.

Adjectives	Dr. Jonas Salk was a <u>better</u> researcher than his colleague.
	Dr. Sabin is <u>more famous</u> for his research on the polio virus than Dr. Enders.
Adverbs	Dr. Salk published his results <u>more quickly</u> than Dr. Drake.
	Dr. Salk debated the issue <u>more passionately</u> than his colleague.

Use the **superlative form** to compare three or more items.

Adjectives	Dr. Salk was the <u>youngest</u> scientist to receive funding for polio research at the University of Michigan.
	Polio was one of the <u>most destructive</u> diseases of the twentieth century.
Adverbs	Dr. Parekh talked the <u>most rapidly</u> of all the doctors at the conference.
	She spoke the <u>most effectively</u> of all of the participants.

How to Write Comparative and Superlative Forms

You can write comparative and superlative forms by remembering a few simple guidelines.

USING -*ER* AND -*EST* ENDINGS

Add -*er* and -*est* endings to one-syllable adjectives and adverbs.

Adjective or Adverb	Comparative	Superlative
tall	tall**er** than	the tall**est**
hard	hard**er** than	the hard**est**
fast	fast**er** than	the fast**est**

Double the last letter when the adjective ends in one vowel + one consonant.

Adjective or Adverb	Comparative	Superlative
hot	hot**ter** than	the hot**test**

USING *MORE* AND *THE MOST*

Add *more* and *the most* to adjectives and adverbs of two or more syllables.

Adjective or Adverb	Comparative	Superlative
dangerous	**more** dangerous than	**the most** dangerous
effectively	**more** effectively than	**the most** effectively
nervous	**more** nervous than	**the most** nervous

When a two-syllable adjective ends in *y*, change the *y* to *i* and add -*er* or -*est*.

Adjective	Comparative	Superlative
happy	happ**ier** than	the happ**iest**

USING IRREGULAR COMPARATIVE AND SUPERLATIVE FORMS

Some adjectives and adverbs have unique comparative and superlative forms. Study this list to remember how to form some of the most common ones.

Adjective or Adverb	Comparative	Superlative
good, well	better than	the best
bad, badly	worse than	the worst
some, much, many	more than	the most
little (a small amount)	less than	the least
far	farther, further	the farthest, the furthest

> **GRAMMAR LINK**
> Farther indicates a physical distance. Further means "additional." For more commonly confused words, see Chapter 33.

Practice 7

Underline the appropriate comparative or superlative form of the words in parentheses.

EXAMPLE: Some vaccination programs are (<u>more</u> / most) effective than others.

1. Polio causes paralysis and sometimes death in infected people. Although

    the virus has menaced human beings for thousands of years, it became

    (more / most) dangerous in the twentieth century than in previous centuries.

    The 1910s had the (worse / worst) epidemics of all time. Until scientists developed a polio vaccine in the 1950s, the disease was one of the (more / most) frightening of all human diseases.

2. In 1962, Czechoslovakia and Cuba began the two (earlier / earliest) immunization programs in the developed world. Most countries in the Americas were polio free by the late 1980s. Peru was the (further / furthest) behind in its vaccination program in the Americas, but in 1991, it reported the last case of polio.

3. Since 1988, the World Health Organization (WHO) has been implementing one of the (greater / greatest) global health campaigns in history. It aims to eradicate the polio virus. The (bigger / biggest) hurdle for eradication is the lack of basic health care in the (poorer / poorest) countries in the world, such as India, Nigeria, and Pakistan. As another obstacle, certain minority groups in developing countries oppose taking the vaccine. These groups are (less / least) knowledgeable about the positive aspects of immunization than other sectors of society. Therefore, they are suspicious of the polio vaccine program.

4. Since the eradication initiative, doctors have reported (fewer / fewest) cases of polio than in previous years. In 2015, the (less / least) amount of polio outbreaks was reported since the eradication campaign began. Currently, only Afghanistan, Pakistan, and Nigeria report polio cases among their citizens.

Practice 8

Complete the sentences by writing either the comparative or superlative form of the word in parentheses.

EXAMPLE: Some drugs produce (good) _____better_____ results than others.

1. Our bodies need small amounts of vitamins and minerals to keep us healthy. Micronutrients are the (less) _____ exciting of all health-care topics. But the (small) _____ deficiency in micronutrients can lead to some of the (bad) _____ problems in human health.

2. Many people in Africa and Asia lack iodine in their diets. The shortfall can cause one of the (serious) _____ birth defects— brain damage. Countries that have the (great) _____ number of hungry people have the (high) _____ rates of infant mental

slowness. Mental deficiency is (common) _____ in

smaller villages in remote areas than in (large) _____ cities

because villagers lack a varied diet.

3.　The Micronutrient Initiative is one of the (important)

_____ but (little-known) _____

health-care organizations in the world. Based out of Ottawa, Canada, it

delivers micronutrients to the (vulnerable) _____

citizens of the world—the malnourished. It costs (little) _____

than any other health-care program. The Micronutrient Initiative started

to deliver iodized salt in the early 1990s. Initially, doctors were (frustrated)

_____ than they had expected to be because

villagers thought that putting iodine in salt would make people sterile. But

the benefits became (clear) _____ after people started adding

iodized salt to their food.

Problems with Comparative and Superlative Forms

USING *MORE* AND *-ER*

In the comparative form, never use *more* and *-er* to modify the same word. In the superlative form, never use *most* and *-est* to modify the same word.

> Some people thought that Salk's vaccine was better ~~more better~~ than Sabin's vaccine.
>
> The polio vaccine was one of the best ~~most best~~ discoveries of our times.

USING *FEWER* AND *LESS*

In the comparative form, never use *less* to compare two count nouns. Use *less* to compare two noncount nouns. (Noncount nouns are nouns that cannot be divided, such as *information* and *music*.) Use *fewer* to compare two count nouns.

> Today, fewer ~~less~~ people get vaccinated than in previous decades because some question the safety of certain vaccinations. Less ~~Fewer~~ information about vaccines was available in the 1950s than is available today.

GRAMMAR LINK
For a list of noncount nouns, refer to page 362 in Chapter 28.

HINT: Using *the* in the Comparative Form

Although you would usually use *the* in superlative forms, you can use it in some two-part comparatives. In these expressions, the second part is the result of the first part.

> action　　　　　result
> <u>The more</u> you exercise, <u>the better</u> your health will be.

Practice 9

Underline and correct fifteen adjective and adverb errors.

EXAMPLE: Some people are <u>real</u> concerned about diseases like the Ebola virus.

really

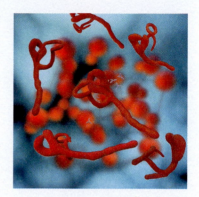

1.   Vaccines have let most people worldwide live more better lives than ever before. However, some diseases, like Ebola, don't yet have an effective vaccine to combat them. In 2014, West Africa saw one of the worse outbreaks of Ebola ever recorded.

2.   The outbreak started in Guinea, and devastated the most poorest communities in countries like Sierra Leone and Liberia. The initial response to the outbreak was real slow. Two other problems produced obstacles to containing the disease quick. First, the infrastructure of the war-torn region was heavy damaged, making the efforts of aid workers very difficult. Furthermore, the virus spread rapid to countries like the United States, Spain, and England because people exposed to the virus traveled between countries. According to the charity organization Doctors Without Borders, the international community reacted real poorly to the initial crisis.

3.   However, the outbreak has forced health-care workers and governments to pay more attention to preventing disease. The less equipment and training workers in the field have, the worst their ability to avoid being infected themselves. The awareness of how to safely transport and care for health-care workers is more higher nowadays than it was in the past. One company has even invented a specialized container to safely transport aid workers from infected regions.

4.   While the Ebola outbreak has been controlled, the possibility of another epidemic still lingers. Less people in certain war-torn parts of western Africa have access to proper medical care than ever before. The richest a country is, the best its chances of resisting a future episode. Contracting a disease like Ebola is one of the worse experiences anyone can go through. Hopefully, future governments and medical professionals will be most prepared to deal with a similar epidemic than they were during past epidemics.

Reflect On It

Think about what you have learned in this unit. If you do not know an answer, review that concept.

1. What is an adjective? _____

   _____

2. What is an adverb? _____

   _____

3. Underline the correct word in parentheses.

   a. My doctor treats her patients (good / well). She is one of the (better / best) eye surgeons in Berlin.

   b. My brother has (less / fewer) work experience than I do, but he also has (less / fewer) responsibilities.

4. The following sentences contain adjective or adverb errors. Correct each mistake.

   a. We had a real nice time at the medical conference.

   b. Everyone was dressed casual.

   c. My sister changes often her mind about her career.

   d. The advancing medical textbook is my sister's.

Final Review

Underline and correct twenty errors in adjectives and adverbs.

1. Health care is one of the most fastest growing fields in the world. In our nation, the aging population is making the demand for nurses more and more intenser. According to *Health Affairs*, an online magazine, there is an acute nursing shortage. Less people enter the nursing profession than in the past. In fact, the number of people in their early twenties entering the nursing profession is at its lower point in forty years. The shortage is worldwide. Canada, England, and many other nations have a more greater shortage than the United States has. As a possible career, more people should consider the nursing profession.

2. First, nurses have greater responsibility and a more diversely role than most people realize. In states such as California, nurses can write prescriptions and nurse midwives can deliver babies. Forensic nurses treat traumatizing victims of violent crime. Furthermore, hospitals are not the only places

where nurses can work. Nursing jobs are available in walk-in clinics, schools, vacation resorts, and medical equipment firms. Even film studios hire sometimes on-set nurses.

3.   Also, nursing can be an extreme rewarding career. Joan Bowes, a nurse in Oregon, says that she feels as if she is doing something usefull each day. Occasionally, her actions help to save lives. Last month, a young patient who had been injured really bad was admitted to the hospital where Joan works. A few days later, Joan noticed that the patient was unable to move his head as easy as before. She quick alerted a specialist who then diagnosed a meningitis infection. Joan's observation helped to save the patient's life. Joan's husband, Keith, is a home-care nurse. He is compassionate, and he interacts good with his patients. As one of a growing number of men in the profession, Keith feels that entering nursing was the better decision he has ever made.

4.   Nurses are more better compensated than in the past. In the 1970s, salaries for nurses were much worst than they are today. In fact, nurses were paid the less among health-care professionals. Nowadays, because nurses are in such high demand, many hospitals give signing bonuses, decent schedules, and real good salaries.

5.   Potential nurses should enjoy helping people. For those who want to have a rewarding career with decent benefits, nursing is an excellent career choice. The more society appreciates nurses, the best health care will be.

The Writer's Room

Write about one of the following topics. Underline adjectives and adverbs.

1. What steps can parents take to ensure that their children maintain a healthy weight?

2. Prescription drugs are very expensive. How do the high prices affect ordinary people? List some effects of the high drug prices, and provide specific examples to support your point.

31 Mistakes with Modifiers

SECTION THEME: Health Care

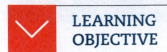

LEARNING OBJECTIVE

31.1 Identify and correct misplaced modifiers.

31.2 Identify and correct dangling modifiers.

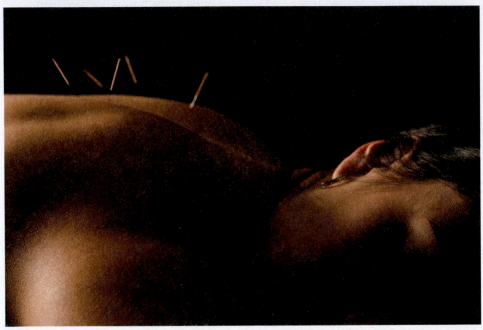

In this chapter, you read about topics related to alternative medicine.

The Writer's Journal
Have you ever hurt yourself or had an accident? What happened?

Misplaced Modifiers

31.1 Identify and correct misplaced modifiers.

A **modifier** is a word, phrase, or clause that describes or modifies nouns or verbs in a sentence. For example, *holding the patient's hand* is a modifier. To use a modifier correctly, place it next to the word(s) that you want to modify.

<u>Holding the patient's hand</u>, **the doctor** explained the procedure.

modifier   words that are modified

A **misplaced modifier** is a word, phrase, or clause that is not placed next to the word it modifies. When a modifier is too far from the word that it is describing, then the meaning of the sentence can become confusing or unintentionally funny.

I saw a pamphlet about acupuncture sitting in the doctor's office.

(How could a pamphlet sit in a doctor's office?)

Commonly Misplaced Modifiers

As you read the sample sentences for each type of modifier, notice how the meaning of the sentence changes depending on where the modifier is placed. In the examples, the modifiers are underlined.

PREPOSITIONAL PHRASE MODIFIERS

A prepositional phrase is made of a preposition and its object. The phrase can act like an adjective or adverb.

Confusing	Cora read an article on acupuncture written by reporter James Reston <u>in a café</u>. (Who was in the café, James or Cora?)
Clear	<u>In a café</u>, Cora read an article on acupuncture written by reporter James Reston.

PRESENT PARTICIPLE MODIFIERS

A present participle modifier is a phrase that begins with an *-ing* verb.

Confusing	James Reston learned about acupuncture <u>touring China</u>. (Can acupuncture tour China?)
Clear	While <u>touring China</u>, James Reston learned about acupuncture.

PAST PARTICIPLE MODIFIERS

A past participle modifier is a phrase that begins with a past participle (*walked, gone, known,* and so on).

Confusing	<u>Called meridians</u>, acupuncturists claim there are two thousand pathways on the body. (What are called meridians, the acupuncturists or the pathways?)
Clear	Acupuncturists claim there are two thousand pathways <u>called meridians</u> on the body.

LIMITING MODIFIERS

Limiting modifiers are words such as *almost, nearly, only, merely, just,* and *even*. In the examples, notice how the placement of *almost* changes the meaning.

Almost all of the doctors went to the lecture that disproved acupuncture.
(Some of the doctors did not attend, but most did.)

All of the doctors **almost** went to the lecture that disproved acupuncture.
(The doctors did not go.)

All of the doctors went to the lecture that **almost** disproved acupuncture.
(The lecture did not disprove acupuncture.)

HINT: Other Types of Modifiers

There are many other types of modifiers. For example, some modifiers begin with relative clauses and some are appositives. Ensure that your modifier is near the word it is describing.

Relative Clause

Confusing	The treatments involved acupuncture needles <u>that were expensive</u>. (What was expensive, the treatment or the needles?)
Clear	The treatments <u>that were expensive</u> involved acupuncture needles.

Appositive

Confusing	<u>A very sick man</u>, Monica helped her uncle find a doctor. (How could Monica be a very sick man?)
Clear	Monica helped her uncle, <u>a very sick man</u>, find a doctor.

Practice 1

Circle the letter of the correct sentence in each pair. Underline the misplaced modifier in each incorrect sentence.

EXAMPLE: (a.)   With interest, Lara noticed students meditating.

           b.   Lara noticed students meditating <u>with interest</u>.

1. a. Lara does an exercise called meditation to focus her mind.
   b. Called meditation, Lara does an exercise to focus her mind.

2. a. Based on ancient practices, Lara's teacher explains meditation techniques.
   b. Lara's teacher explains meditation techniques based on ancient practices.

3. a. Lara became curious about meditation vacationing in Korea.
   b. While vacationing in Korea, Lara became curious about meditation.

4. a. Lara spent a weekend in silence at a Buddhist temple.
   b. Lara spent a weekend at a Buddhist temple in silence.

5. a. A recent survey showed that nearly twenty million Americans practice meditation.
   b. A recent survey showed that twenty million Americans nearly practice meditation.

6. a. Scientists found a connection between meditation and a change in people's blood pressure who were doing clinical studies.
   b. Scientists who were doing clinical studies found a connection between meditation and a change in people's blood pressure.

7. a. Dr. Grey will study Lara, an expert on meditation research.
   b. Dr. Grey, an expert on meditation research, will study Lara.

HINT: Correcting Misplaced Modifiers

To correct misplaced modifiers, do the following:

- Identify the modifier.

    The volunteer pushed the wheelchair <u>in sneakers</u>.

- Identify the word or words that are being modified.

    Who wore sneakers? **The volunteer**

- Move the modifier next to the word(s) being modified.

    <u>In sneakers</u>, **the volunteer** pushed the wheelchair.

Practice 2

Underline the misplaced modifiers in the following sentences. Then, rewrite the sentences. You may have to add or remove words to give the sentence a logical meaning.

EXAMPLE: Lucia, a holistic medicine provider, suggested that Alex think about his health <u>with a smile</u>.

<u>With a smile, Lucia, a holistic medicine provider, suggested Alex think</u>

<u>about his health.</u>

1. Holistic medicine is considered to be ineffective for patients in scientific literature.

    _____

    _____

2. However, researchers have found that some people respond positively to natural therapies who study holistic medicine.

    _____

    _____

3. Vincent Pagano tried many different methods to cure his anxiety having concerns.

    _____

    _____

4. Misdiagnosing the problem, medication was suggested by Vincent's previous doctor.

    _____

    _____

5. Feeling scared, Dr. Lucia Alvarez explained a more holistic approach to Vincent.

    _____

    _____

6. Dr. Alvarez has almost had success with 90 percent of her patients by treating them holistically.

    _____

    _____

Dangling Modifiers

31.2 **Identify and correct dangling modifiers.**

A **dangling modifier** opens a sentence but does not modify any words in the sentence. It "dangles" or hangs loosely because it is not connected to any other part of the sentence.

To avoid having a dangling modifier, make sure that the modifier and the first noun that follows it have a logical connection.

Confusing	While talking on a cell phone, the ambulance drove off the road. (Can an ambulance talk on a cell phone?)
Clear	While talking on a cell phone, the ambulance **technician** drove off the road.
Confusing	To get into medical school, high grades are necessary. (Can high grades get into a school?)
Clear	To get into medical school, **students** need high grades.

Practice 3

Circle the letter of the correct sentence in each pair. Underline the dangling modifier in each incorrect sentence.

EXAMPLE: a. Having taken a pill, the results were surprising.

        (b.) Having taken a pill, I was surprised by the results.

1. a. With the patient's budget in mind, the least expensive drugs were prescribed.

   b. With the patient's budget in mind, the doctor prescribed the least expensive drugs.

2. a. Believing in their effects, placebos are often given to patients.

   b. Believing in their effects, Dr. Zimboro sometimes gives placebos to patients.

3. a. After taking a sugar pill, patients often feel relieved.

   b. After taking a sugar pill, there is often a feeling of relief.

4. a. Surprised, the word *placebo* means "to please."

   b. Surprised, I read that the word *placebo* means "to please."

5. a. Thinking about the mind–body relationship, scientist Esther Sternberg conducted an experiment.

   b. Thinking about the mind–body relationship, an experiment was conducted.

6. a. Frustrated, Sternberg's temptation was to give up.

   b. Frustrated, Sternberg was tempted to give up.

7. a. Using laboratory rats, Sternberg discovered a link between the mind and body.

   b. Using laboratory rats, a link was discovered between the mind and body.

8. a. Given an antidepressant, the arthritis disappeared.

b. Given an antidepressant, some rats no longer had arthritis.

9. a. Excited about her discovery, Sternberg wrote an article for a medical journal.

b. Excited about her discovery, an article was written for a medical journal.

HINT: Correcting Dangling Modifiers

To correct dangling modifiers, do the following:

• Identify the modifier.

> To teach yoga, a flexible body is needed.

• Identify the word or words that are being modified.

> Who needs a flexible body? **The yoga instructor**

• Add the missing subject and, in some cases, also add or remove words so that the sentence makes sense.

> To teach yoga, **the instructor** needs a flexible body.

Practice 4

In each sentence, underline the dangling modifier. Then rewrite each sentence, adding or removing words to provide a logical meaning.

EXAMPLE: Worried about their health, laughter yoga is practiced.
> Worried about their health, people practice laughter yoga.

1. When exercising, getting bored is common.

_____

_____

2. Gathering in a park in Mumbai, India, laughter yoga was practiced.

_____

_____

3. Muscles are gently stretched while chanting "Haha hoho" in unison.

_____

_____

4. To take a laughter yoga class, $20 is needed.

_____

_____

5. Doing laughter yoga, stress is reduced.

_____

_____

6. When experimenting with laughter yoga, the advice of a professional is helpful.

_____

_____

Practice 5

Some sentences in this practice have dangling or misplaced modifiers. Write *M* next to misplaced modifiers, *D* next to dangling modifiers, and *C* next to correct sentences. If the modifier is misplaced, move it. If the modifier is dangling, add words to make the sentence complete.

EXAMPLE: Hoping to live a long life, ~~different therapies are tried.~~ people try different therapies   _D___

1. Called acupuncture, ancient Chinese developed a form of alternative medicine. _____

2. Made of silver and gold, archaeologists discovered 2,000-year-old acupuncture needles. _____

3. Relieving chronic pain, effective results were obtained with acupuncture. _____

4. Acupuncture has been used throughout Asia for centuries. _____

5. Studying ancient Chinese philosophy, essential parts of this therapy are learned. _____

6. Called The Yellow Emperor's Classic of Internal Medicine, **R**eaders can find information on acupuncture in an ancient Chinese text _____

7. Later, an emperor in the Ming Dynasty made acupuncture a state-sponsored medical practice wearing traditional robes. _____

8. In the early 1900s, acupuncture became popular in the United States. _____

9. Feeling skeptical, the merits of acupuncture are questioned. _____

10. In fact, many conventionally trained doctors believe acupuncture has no therapeutic value. _____

Reflect On It

Think about what you have learned in this unit. If you do not know an answer, review that concept.

1. What is a misplaced modifier? _____

   _____

2. What is a dangling modifier? _____

   _____

3. What type of modifier error is in each sentence? Write *M* for "misplaced" and *D* for "dangling." Then correct the sentence.

   a. Overeating, a weight problem was developed.

   _____

   b. The doctor examined the X-ray in the lab coat.

   _____

Final Review

Underline ten dangling or misplaced modifier errors in the next selection. Then, correct each error. You may need to add or remove words to ensure that the sentence makes sense.

EXAMPLE: Underline: Manipulating her neck, ~~a surprising result occurred~~.
the chiropractor had a surprising result.

1.   There are many fraudulent claims in alternative medicine. In fact, feeling desperate, fortunes are spent on suspect therapies. It is difficult for members of the public to determine which therapies are valid and which are pure quackery. At an important medical conference, some doctors discussed chiropractic neck treatments eating lunch together.

2.   Based on spinal adjustments, Dr. Daniel Palmer developed a new healing technique. Born in Canada, Palmer did his first treatment in 1895. A janitor complained that he had lost his hearing after straining his back. Manipulating the janitor's neck, the man's hearing was restored. Using the therapy all over America, neck manipulations are actively promoted.

3.   In 2006, a young mother went to see a chiropractor with severe headaches. Misdiagnosing the patient's illness, a mistake was made. Pierrette Parisien died following her neck treatment. The coroner recommended a review of chiropractic procedures speaking to the media.

4.   Many medical doctors have questioned the safety of neck manipulations. Chiropractors refute the criticism feeling angry. According to Dr. Rick Morris, chiropractors pay low malpractice insurance rates because injuries are so rare. Having confidence in chiropractors, neck manipulations continue to be popular.

The Writer's Room

Write about one of the following topics. Include some modifiers and make sure that your sentences are formed correctly.
1. Have you ever been to an acupuncturist, a massage therapist, a naturopath, a homeopath, or any other alternative healing practitioner? Describe the treatment that you received.
2. Give your opinion about alternative therapies.

READING LINK
Readings on health issues:
"Chicken Hips" (p. 189)
"How I Overcame my Panic Attacks" (p. 194)
"Don't Worry, Act Happy" (p. 211)
"Planting False Memories" (p. 508)

The Writers' Circle: Collaborative Activity

Work with a group of students and create an advertisement for an alternative medical treatment. You can even invent a new one. For example, you can make an advertisement to cure warts, reduce acne, or help back pain.

In your ad, include some adjectives and adverbs. In some of your sentences, include phrases that begin with who, that, and which. When you finish, exchange advertisements with another team. Check that the other team's advertisement contains correct adjectives, adverbs, and modifiers.

LEARNING OBJECTIVES

32.1 Use specific and detailed vocabulary.

32.2 Recognize and correct wordiness and redundancy.

32.3 Recognize and correct clichés.

32.4 Identify standard English versus slang.

In this chapter, you read about topics related to property crimes.

The Writer's Journal

Write a paragraph that summarizes the events of a well-known crime. Describe what happened.

Use Specific and Detailed Vocabulary

32.1   **Use specific and detailed vocabulary.**

Great writing evokes an emotional response from the reader. Skilled writers not only use correct grammatical structures, but they also infuse their writing with precise and vivid details that make their work come alive.

When you proofread your work, revise **vague words**, which lack precision and detail. For example, the words *nice* and *bad* are vague. Readers cannot get a clear picture from them. Compare the following sets of sentences.

Vague	The movie was bad.
Precise	The predictable film included violent, gory scenes.
Vague	Thieves stole a nice Rembrandt painting.
Precise	Hooded thieves stole Rembrandt's somber artwork of a boat rocked by towering waves.

Creating Vivid Language

When you choose the precise word, you convey your meaning exactly. Moreover, you can make your writing clearer and more impressive by using specific and detailed vocabulary. To create vivid language, try the following strategies.

- **Modify your nouns.** If your noun is vague, make it more specific by adding one or more adjectives. You could also replace the noun with a more specific term.

  | **Vague** | the man |
  | **Vivid** | the taxi driver   the thin, nervous soldier |

- **Modify your verbs.** Use more vivid and precise verbs. You could also add adverbs.

  | **Vague** | walk |
  | **Vivid** | saunter   stroll   march briskly |

- **Include more details.** Add detailed information to make the sentence more complete.

  | **Vague** | Several signs foretold Caesar's death. |
  | **Precise** | Several ominous signs, such as Caesar's horses getting loose and a soothsayer's warning, foretold Caesar's impending murder. |

HINT: Use Imagery

You can make your writing come alive by using **imagery**, which is description using the five senses: sight, sound, smell, touch, and taste. In the examples, the underlined words add details to the sentence and contribute to a more exact description.

> Wearing a blond wig, the armed robber smashed the glass display case and pocketed the luxury watches.

WRITING LINK
You can find more information about appealing to the five senses in Chapter 6, "Description."

Practice 1

Replace the familiar words in parentheses with more vivid words or phrases, and add more specific details. Use your dictionary or thesaurus if you need help.

EXAMPLE: Graffiti artists (write) _____*scrawl words and pictures*_____ on walls.

1. Many cities spend a lot of money (cleaning graffiti) _____
   _____

2. (Youths) _____ spray-paint on many (places)
   _____

3. They worry about getting caught by (someone) _____
   _____

4. Some cities permit graffiti artists to mark up specific (locations) _____
   _____

5. Sometimes graffiti artists write (bad words) _____
   _____

6. Governments could combat the problem (with many solutions) _____

_____

7. Some people think graffiti artists should be (treated harshly) _____

_____

Practice 2

Underline all of the words in the paragraph that add vivid details to the description.

EXAMPLE: Paul bounded upstairs, <u>scrubbed the greasy odor of the dishwater from his hands</u> with the <u>ill-smelling soap</u> he hated, and then <u>shook over his fingers a few drops of violet water</u> from the bottle he kept hidden in his drawer.

The east-bound train was plowing through a January snowstorm; the dull dawn was beginning to show grey when the engine whistled a mile out of Newark. Paul started up from the seat where he had lain curled in uneasy slumber, rubbed the breath-misted window-glass with his hand, and peered out. The snow was whirling in curling eddies above the white bottom lands, and the drifts lay already deep in the fields and along the fences while here and there the tall dead grass and dried weed-stalks protruded black above it. Lights shone from the scattered houses, and a gang of laborers who stood beside the track waved their lanterns.

—Willa Cather, "Paul's Case"

HINT: Adding Appositives

An appositive is a word or phrase that gives further information about a noun or pronoun. You can write sentences that are more exact and detailed by adding appositives.

appositive
Sherlock Holmes, <u>the famous detective</u>, was helped by his friend,

appositive
<u>Dr. Watson.</u>

Avoid Wordiness and Redundancy

32.2   Recognize and correct wordiness and redundancy.

Sometimes students fill their writing assignments with extra words to meet length requirements. However, good ideas can easily get lost in work that is too wordy. Also, if the explanations are unnecessarily long, then writing becomes boring. To improve your writing style, use only as many words or phrases as you need to fully explain your ideas.

The police department was ~~a distance of~~ two blocks from the municipal library.
(A block is a measure of a distance, so it is unnecessary to repeat that information.)

Correcting Wordiness

You can cut the number of words needed to express an idea by substituting a wordy phrase with a single word. You could also remove the wordy phrase completely.

Because ~~of the fact that~~ the security guard was alone, the thieves easily overwhelmed him.

Some Common Wordy Expressions and Substitutions

Wordy	Better	Wordy	Better
at that point in time	then, at that time	great, few in number	great, few
big, small in size	big, small	in order to	to
in close proximity	close *or* in proximity	in spite of the fact	although, even though
a difficult dilemma	a dilemma	in the final analysis	finally, lastly
due to the fact	because	past history	past *or* history
equally as good as	as good as	period of time	period
exactly the same	the same	personal opinion	opinion
exceptions to the rule	exceptions	reason why is that	because
final completion	end	return again	return
for the purpose of	for	still remain	remain
gave the appearance of	looked like	a true fact	a fact

Practice 3

In the next sentences, cross out all unnecessary words or phrases, or modify any repeated words or ideas.

EXAMPLE: Many ~~A great number of~~ thefts have been committed by the Pink Panthers crime syndicate.

1. In December 2008, four men entered a Harry Winston jewelry shop in Paris for the purpose of stealing diamonds and other expensive jewelry.

2. In spite of the fact that there were security guards, the thieves were able to avoid suspicion.

3. In order to fool the security guards, the robbers disguised themselves as women.

4. It is a true fact that these thieves were members of the infamous Pink Panther crime group.

5. The whole entire value of diamonds stolen from Parisien shops was over $100 million.

6. Police were unaware at that period of time that the group was responsible for a heist at the same jewelry store a year earlier.

7. At the first robbery, the thieves were not found due to the fact that they were dressed as construction workers.

8. Some of the estimated two hundred members of the group have been arrested, but many still remain at large.

9. The FBI estimates that, on a yearly basis, the Pink Panthers commit fifteen to twenty robberies annually.

Avoid Clichés

32.3 Recognize and correct clichés.

Clichés are overused expressions. Because they are used too often, they lose their power and become boring. You should avoid using clichés in formal writing. In each example, the underlined cliche has been replaced with more direct words.

remain positive
The suspect tried to <u>keep her chin up</u> when the officer handcuffed her.

extremely upset
The lawyer was <u>fit to be tied</u> when the client fled before the trial.

Some Common Clichés		
a drop in the bucket	break the ice	jump in with both feet
as light as a feather	butter someone up	keep your eyes peeled
as luck would have it	cost an arm and a leg	top dog
axe to grind	drop the ball	under the weather
between a rock and a hard place	easier said than done	work like a dog

Correcting Clichés

When you modify a cliché, you can change it into a direct term. You might also try playing with language to come up with a more interesting description.

Cliché	She was as busy as a bee.
Direct language	She was extremely busy.
Interesting description	She was as busy as an emergency room nurse.

Practice 4

Underline twelve clichéd expressions, and then replace them with fresh or direct language.

stay alert
EXAMPLE: Jack Garcia had to <u>keep his eyes peeled</u>.

1. Cuban-born Jack Garcia is recognized as the best undercover agent in the FBI's history. During his career, he was a mover and shaker in more than a hundred different operations. For instance, some of Florida's largest drug smugglers are now in the big house thanks to Garcia. The agent's work also led to the arrest of some corrupt Florida police officers. Playing the role of "Big Frankie" or "Big Tony," Garcia would bribe officers. The officers were bent out of shape when they were arrested.

2. Garcia was able to infiltrate New York's Gambino crime family by pretending to be "Jack Falcone." To prepare for his role, Garcia had to jump into Sicilian culture with both feet. For example, he learned about Italian food. He knew he was playing with fire whenever he sat with the crime boss Greg DePalma, and he had to be convincing. If he dropped the ball, he could find himself six feet under.

3. Garcia played DePalma like a fiddle. He constantly buttered up the boss. Also, Garcia provided DePalma with the finer things in life such as jewelry, iPods, and televisions. The FBI agent was so convincing in his role as "Big Jack" that the crime boss offered to promote Garcia in the crime family.

4. Jack Garcia's job was no piece of cake. One day, when Mafia members became suspicious of Garcia, the FBI pulled the plug on the operation. Today, thirty-one members of the Gambino crime family are in jail, and Garcia has retired from the FBI.

Standard English Versus Slang

32.4 Identify standard English versus slang.

Most of your instructors will want you to write using standard **English**. The word *standard* does not imply "better." Standard English is the common language generally used and expected in schools, businesses, and government institutions in North America.

Slang is nonstandard language. It is used in informal situations to communicate common cultural knowledge. In any academic or professional context, do not use slang.

Slang	My friends and I <u>hang</u> together. Last weekend, we watched a show that was <u>kinda weird but also pretty cool</u>. It was called *True Detective*.
Standard English	My friends and I <u>spend a lot of time</u> together. Last weekend, we watched a show that was <u>unusual but fascinating</u>. It was called *True Detective*.

HINT: Do Not Use Slang in Academic Writing

Slang is very informal and should be avoided in academic writing. Keep in mind that slang changes depending on generational, regional, cultural, and historical influences. For example, rather than saying "I have to *leave*," people in one group might say *scram* or *split* while those in another group might say *bail* or *bounce*. Avoid using slang expressions in your writing because they can change very quickly—so quickly, in fact, that you might remark that this textbook's examples of slang are "lame."

Practice 5

Substitute the underlined slang expressions with the best possible choice in standard English.

EXAMPLE: Every day, <u>the cops</u> deal with drug dealers.   <u>police officers</u>

1. Drug dealers can be <u>guys or chicks</u>.   _____

2. Some young people think that dealing drugs is <u>cool</u>.   _____

3. Most people deal drugs because they want to earn <u>lots of dough</u>   _____

4. However, most of them are forced to work for
   <u>chump change</u>. _____

5. Drug dealers are always on the lookout for <u>narcs</u>. _____

6. It's <u>dicey</u> to sell drugs. _____

7. In addition to the police, rival dealers often <u>beef</u> over
   territory. _____

8. Many communities feel <u>on edge</u> because of the violence. _____

9. According to some experts, too many drug dealers
   and drug users are in <u>the joint</u> _____

10. Some people believe nonviolent drug offenders
    should receive <u>a slap on the wrist</u>. _____

Reflect On It

Think about what you have learned in this unit. If you do not know an answer, review that concept.

1. What is vivid language? _____

   _____

2. Edit the following sentences for wordiness, clichés, and overused expressions. Modify them to make them more concise.

   a. The suspect lived in close proximity to the bank that he had robbed.

   b. Peter will be in for a rude awakening if he does not study for his law-enforcement exams.

   c. Peter is feeling under the weather today.

3. Edit the following sentences for slang. Replace the slang words with standard English.

   a. Replacing the contents of a stolen wallet is such a drag.

   b. I read a cool biography about Al Capone.

Final Review

Edit the following paragraphs for slang, clichés, and vague language.

PART A

In the next paragraph, four vague words are underlined. Replace these words with specific details to make the paragraph more interesting. Also correct four wordy expressions.

cash and belongings

EXAMPLE: The Bling Ring managed to steal about $3 million worth of <u>stuff</u>.

At the end of 2008, Rachel Lee was rebellious. Small in size, she was the

daughter of successful business owners. Perhaps, as a result of the fact that celebrity

culture is so strong, Lee wanted to dress like a movie star. In order to feed her cravings, Lee convinced her shy friend, Nick Prugo, to help her rob the home of Paris Hilton. For the next eleven months, Lee led a group of teen house burglars. They managed to steal clothing and money from rich <u>people</u> in Hollywood. They wanted to have a <u>good</u> life. But in 2009, the police captured the gang. At this point in time, <u>the girl</u> has finished her four-year prison sentence. Filmmaker Sofia Coppola directed a movie about the <u>interesting story</u>.

PART B

Underline and replace twelve slang or clichéd expressions.

EXAMPLE: Nick Prugo was a nervous <u>dude</u>. young man

1. Rachel Lee was able to mess with people's heads and get them to follow her. For their first robbery, Lee and Prugo wondered who would leave the front door unlocked and some dough lying around. They targeted Paris Hilton because they thought the celebrity was as dumb as a bag of rocks. Sure enough, Hilton's house was unlocked. They robbed Hilton several times before the celebrity realized that something was missing. They also ripped off Audrina Patridge, Rachel Bilson, and Lindsay Lohan. Of course, the gang's victims were bummed after realizing that they had been robbed.

2. Nick Prugo claimed that he was a bit of a wimp, and he would sometimes freak out during the robberies. Rachel Lee, on the other hand, was super chill, even stopping to use a celebrity's bathroom during one burglary. As the gang expanded, the female members especially targeted the designer clothing of their celebrity victims. Lee and the others often dressed to the hilt and wore a lots of stolen bling.

3. Eventually, a schoolmate told authorities that Lee and Prugo had robbed Lindsay Lohan. The police had a surveillance camera photo of Prugo.

    A whiz cop had the idea of searching Prugo's Facebook page, where he found Rachel Lee's name. Police noticed the designer clothing that the thieves wore in their Facebook photos. Quickly, the gang's sweet gig came to an end.

The Writer's Room

Write about one of the following topics. Make sure that you use exact and concise language.

1. List some steps that parents can take to prevent their children from joining gangs or breaking laws.
2. Classify crimes into three different types.

33 Spelling and Commonly Confused Words

SECTION THEME: The Legal World

In this chapter, you read about topics related to crimes and criminals.

The Writer's Journal:

What are some reasons that people commit crimes?

Spelling Rules

33.1 Identify and correct spelling errors.

Spelling mistakes can detract from good ideas in your work. To improve your spelling skills, always proofread your written work and check a dictionary for the meaning and spelling of words about which you are unsure. The guidelines in this chapter can also help you build stronger skills.

HINT: Using a Dictionary

If you are unsure about the spelling of a word, consult a print or digital dictionary. Also, your word processing program has a built-in dictionary that can help as you write.

Writing *ie* or *ei*

Remember the following rule so that you know when to use *ie* or *ei*. Write *i* before *e*, except after *c* or when *ei* is pronounced *ay*, as in *neighbor* and *weigh*.

i before e	niece	field	grief
ei **after** *c*	ceiling	conceive	perceive
ei **pronounced** *ay*	beige	vein	weigh
Exceptions:	efficient	either	foreigner	height
	leisure	neither	science	seize
	society	species	their	weird

Practice 1

Underline the correct spelling of each word.

EXAMPLE: recieve / <u>receive</u>

1. decieve / deceive
2. foreigner / foriegner
3. friend / freind
4. hieght / height
5. vien / vein

6. science / sceince
7. efficient / efficeint
8. theif / thief
9. deciet / deceit
10. chief / cheif

READING LINK
For more information about using a dictionary, see page 482 in Part V, "Reading Strategies and Selections" (Chapter 38).

Adding Prefixes and Suffixes

A **prefix** is added to the beginning of a word, and it changes the word's meaning. For example, *con-*, *dis-*, *pre-*, *un-*, and *il-* are prefixes. A **suffix** is added to the ending of a word, and it changes the word's tense, meaning, or function in the sentence. For example, *-ly*, *-ment*, *-ed*, and *-ing* are suffixes.

When you add a prefix to a word, keep the last letter of the prefix and the first letter of the main word.

un + **n**atural = un**n**atural   dis + **s**atisfaction = dis**s**atisfaction

When you add the suffix *-ly* to words that end in *l*, keep the *l* of the root word. The new word will have two *l*'s.

personal + ly = personally   actual + ly = actually

HINT: Words Ending in *-ful*

Although the word *full* ends in two *l*'s, when *-ful* is added to another word as a suffix, it ends in one *l*.

care<u>ful</u>   success<u>ful</u>   hope<u>ful</u>

Notice, however, the unusual spelling when *full* and *fill* are combined: fulfill.

Practice 2

Read the following words and decide if they are correctly spelled. If the word is correct, write C in the space provided. If the word is incorrect, write the correct word in the space.

EXAMPLES: factualy _____*factually*_____   untrue _____*c*_____

1. ilogical _____   6. beautifull _____
2. continually _____   7. iresponsible _____
3. imoral _____   8. unusual _____
4. unecessary _____   9. carefuly _____
5. mispell _____   10. fulfilled _____

Adding -s or -es

Add -s to nouns and to present tense verbs that are third-person singular. However, add -es to words in the following situations.

- When words end in s, sh, ss, ch, or x, add -es.

    Noun: church–churches   **Verb:** fix–fixes

- When words end with the consonant y, change the y to i and add -es.

    Noun: berry–berries   **Verb:** marry–marries

- When words end in o, add -es in most cases.

    Noun: hero–heroes   **Verb:** do–does

    Exceptions: piano–pianos; radio–radios; logo–logos; patio–patios

- When words end in f or fe, change the f to v and add -es.

    leaf–leaves   knife–knives

    Exceptions: belief–beliefs; roof–roofs

Practice 3

Add -s or -es to each word, and adjust the spelling if necessary. Write the new word in the space provided.

EXAMPLE: reach _____*reaches*_____

1. hero _____   7. potato _____
2. crutch _____   8. miss _____
3. fix _____   9. fly _____
4. echo _____   10. teach _____
5. carry _____   11. scarf _____
6. tomato _____   12. candy _____

Adding Suffixes to Words Ending in *-e*

When you add a suffix to a word ending in *e*, make sure that you follow the next rules.

- If the suffix begins with a vowel, drop the *e* on the main word. Some common suffixes beginning with vowels are *-ed*, *-er*, *-est*, *-ing*, *-able*, *-ent*, and *-ist*.

    hope–hop**ing**   encourage–encourag**ing**   sue–su**ing**

    Exceptions: For some words that end in *ge*, keep the *e* and add the suffix.

    courage–courage**ous**   change–change**able**

- If the suffix begins with a consonant, keep the *e*. Some common suffixes beginning with consonants are *-ly*, *-ment*, *-less*, and *-ful*.

    sure–sure**ly**   like–like**ness**   hope–hope**ful**

    Exceptions: Some words lose their final *e* when a suffix is added.

    argue–argu**ment**   true–tru**ly**   judge–judg**ment**

HINT: American and British Spelling

Some global regions use variations of English spellings. Generally, these fall into two categories: British English and American English. Canadians, Australians, Indians, and New Zealanders generally follow British spelling conventions.

American English			British English		
color	center	realize	colour	centre	realise

Practice 4

Rewrite each word with the suggested ending.

EXAMPLE: use + ed _____*used*_____

1. achieve + ment _____
2. strange + est _____
3. argue + ment _____
4. love + ing _____
5. true + ly _____
6. endorse + ment _____
7. argue + ing _____
8. nine + ty _____
9. write + ing _____
10. change + able _____

Adding Suffixes to Words Ending in *-y*

When you add a suffix to a word ending in *y*, make sure that you follow the next rules.

- If the word has a consonant before the final *y*, change the *y* to an *i* before adding the suffix.

    beauty–beautiful   supply–supplied

- If the word has a vowel before the final *y*, if the word is a proper name, or if the suffix is *-ing*, do not change the *y* to an *i*.

    day–days   try–trying   the Vronsky family–the Vronskys

Exceptions: Some words do not follow the previous rule.

day–daily   lay–laid   say–said   pay–paid

Practice 5

Rewrite each word with the suggested ending.

EXAMPLE: try + ed _____tried_____

1. happy + est	_____	7. envy + able	_____
2. play + er	_____	8. angry + ly	_____
3. pretty + er	_____	9. day + ly	_____
4. Connolly + s	_____	10. say + ing	_____
5. lonely + ness	_____	11. dirty + est	_____
6. lazy + er	_____	12. stay + ed	_____

Doubling the Final Consonant

Sometimes when you add a suffix to a word, you must double the final consonant. Remember the next tips.

ONE-SYLLABLE WORDS

- Double the final consonant of one-syllable words ending in a consonant–vowel–consonant pattern.

    jog–jogger   plan–planned   prod–prodded

- Do not double the final consonant if the word ends in a vowel and two consonants or if it ends with two vowels and a consonant.

    cool–coolest   park–parking   clean–cleaner

WORDS OF TWO OR MORE SYLLABLES

- Double the final consonant of words ending in a stressed consonant–vowel–consonant pattern.

    prefer–preferred   occur–occurred

- If the word ends in a syllable that is not stressed, then do not double the last letter of the word.

    happen–happened   visit–visiting

Practice 6

Rewrite each word with the suggested ending.

EXAMPLES:	**Add -ed**		**Add -ing**
stop	_____stopped_____	try	_____trying_____
1. slip	_____	6. smile	_____
2. load	_____	7. stay	_____
3. mention	_____	8. enter	_____
4. plan	_____	9. begin	_____
5. commit	_____	10. refer	_____

Practice 7

Underline and correct twelve spelling mistakes in the next selection.

EXAMPLE: Andre's friend <u>happyly</u> told a story about a funny botched crime.
                  happily

1. Committing a succesfull theft is not always as easy as it appears. Some
    robbers have failled in humorous ways. Unfortunatly for some would-be
    master criminals, their brains did not match their ambition.

2. For example, Matthew McNelly and Joey Miller decided to rob someone's
    home. To disguise themselfs, they unwisely used permanent marker and
    drew all over their faces. A woman called the police when she spotted the
    young men attempting to enter her nieghbor's home. Moments later, police
    easily caught the thieves because they could not remove their disguises!

3. Anthony Lescowitch robed a man in front of a bank, and cameras captured
    the robber's face. The police put Lescowitch's mugshot on the departmental
    Facebook page, and developped a strategy to apprehend him. Their efforts,
    however, were unecessary. Lescowitch saw the mugshot, and it occured to
    him that it would be hilarious to repost the image on his own Facebook wall.
    Useing a fake Facebook account, the police convinced Lescowitch that an
    attractive woman was asking him to go for a drink. After chating with police
    for an hour, he agreed to the "date." Hours later, Lescowitch was arrested by
    police at a prearranged coffee-shop meeting.

Spelling Two-Part Words

Some one-word indefinite pronouns sound as if they should be two separate words, but
they are not. Here are some examples of one-word indefinite pronouns.

Words with *any*	anything, anyone, anybody, anywhere
Words with *every*	everything, everyone, everybody, everywhere
Words with *some*	something, someone, somebody, somewhere

HINT: Spelling *another* and *a lot*

Another is always one word.	Bonnie apprehended **another** criminal.
A lot is always two words.	She catches **a lot** of thieves.

Practice 8

Underline and correct twelve spelling errors in the next paragraphs.

               Another
EXAMPLE: <u>An other</u> scandal occurred last year.

1.   Alot of politicians have been involved in scandals. Some times a public figure takes bribes. For instance, Representative William J. Jefferson was convicted after police found $90,000 in his freezer. A few years later, Governor Rod Blagojevich tried to sell a senate seat to some one. Senator John Edwards is an other politician who made imoral choices. At first, no body knew about the married politician's girlfriend. When a tabloid published a photo of Edwards with his mistress, he denyied the rumors, but eventualy he had to tell the truth.

2.   When politicians act in an unnethical manner, they hurt their families, and they usualy destroy their own careers. Often, citizens discover that their heros, especially in the political world, are capable of just about any thing.

120 Commonly Misspelled Words

33.2 **Recognize 120 commonly misspelled words.**

The next list contains some of the most commonly misspelled words in English.

Some Commonly Misspelled Words			
absence	campaign	environment	loneliness
absorption	careful	especially	maintenance
accommodate	ceiling	exaggerate	mathematics
acquaintance	cemetery	exercise	medicine
address	clientele	extraordinarily	millennium
aggressive	committee	familiar	minuscule
already	comparison	February	mischievous
aluminum	competent	foreign	mortgage
analyze	conscience	government	necessary
appointment	conscientious	harassment	ninety
approximate	convenient	height	noticeable
argument	curriculum	immediately	occasion
athlete	definite	independent	occurrence
bargain	definitely	jewelry	opposite
beginning	desperate	judgment	outrageous
behavior	developed	laboratory	parallel
believable	dilemma	lawyer	performance
benefit	disappoint	ledge	perseverance
business	embarrass	leisure	personality
calendar	encouragement	license	physically

possess	responsible	technique	vacuum
precious	rhythm	thorough	Wednesday
prejudice	schedule	tomato	weird
privilege	scientific	tomatoes	woman
professor	separate	tomorrow	women
psychology	sincerely	traditional	wreckage
questionnaire	spaghetti	truly	writer
receive	strength	Tuesday	writing
recommend	success	until	written
reference	surprise	usually	zealous

HINT: Spelling Strategies

Here are some useful strategies to improve your spelling.

- Keep a record of words that you commonly misspell in your spelling log, which could be in a journal or binder. Ask a friend to quiz you using your list of misspelled words. See Appendix 7 for more information about spelling logs.
- Use memory cards or flash cards to help you memorize the spelling of difficult words.
- Write down the spelling of difficult words at least ten times to help you remember how to spell them.

Practice 9

Underline the correctly spelled word in each pair.

EXAMPLE: <u>foreigner</u> / foriegner

1. noticable / noticeable
2. echos / echoes
3. writting / writing
4. accommodate / accomodate
5. definitely / definitly
6. running / runing
7. appealled / appealed
8. comittee / committee
9. recommend / recommand

10. absence / absense
11. niece / neice
12. personallity / personality
13. exaggerate / exagerate
14. butterflys / butterflies
15. responsible / responsable
16. efficeint / efficient
17. independent / independant
18. appointment / apointment

Practice 10

Underline and correct twenty spelling mistakes in the next selection.

EXAMPLE: Many inmates are not <u>agressive</u>. aggressive

1.   In the last thirty years, the prison population in the United States has

exploded. The United States incarcerates a larger percentage of its own

people than any other nation in the world. Even foriegn countries known to

be repressive, such as China and Russia, have fewer people in jails. Experts have analized the situation. They propose that tougher sentencing guidelines largely account for rising incarceration rates. The United States definitly needs prison reform.

2.   The costs associated with housing nonviolent offenders is very high. Approximatively $74 billion is currently spent on the federal prison system in the United States. Many people who used ilegal drugs are in prison cells. Some politicians acknowlege that putting so many drug offenders in prison is unecessary. They sincerly want to change existing laws. However, they face a dilema. If they release many people from prison, they risk being labelled as "soft on crime."

3.   Mandatory minimum sentences are largely responsable for the increase in prison populations. These sentences do not rely on the jugment of the presiding judge. Instead, there is a predetermined prison sentence. Iowa Judge Mark W. Bennet is familar with the issue. In an article for *The Nation*, he admited, "I have sentenced a staggering number of low-level drug addicts to long prison terms." He beleives that many of the offenders benifit from the wake-up call of a prison sentence, but they do not need to spend ten years in jail. He thinks that the goverment should modify sentencing guidelines. Many of his peers also recommand abolishing mandatory minimum sentences. For example, prominent civil rights lawyir Michelle Alexander argues that people of color are disproportionately affected by drug laws because of institutionalized prejedice. Clearly, the criminal justice system should be throughly overhauled.

HINT: Using a Spelling Checker

Digital spelling checkers (sometimes called "autocorrect") will highlight most misspelled words and provide suggested corrections. However, be aware that these tools' abilities are limited; often they cannot verify that you have used commonly confused words like *your* and *you're* accurately.

Because a spelling checker is not 100 percent reliable, remember to proofread for spelling errors before you submit your final work.

Look-Alike and Sound-Alike Words

33.3 **Distinguish look-alike and sound-alike words.**

Sometimes two English words can sound very much alike but have different spellings and different meanings. For example, two commonly confused words are *defiantly*, which means "to resist or challenge something," and *definitely*, which means "finally" or "decisively." Dictionaries will give you the exact meaning of unfamiliar words. Read the next list to get familiar with many commonly confused words.

Some Commonly Confused Words		
Word	**Meaning**	**Example**
accept	to receive; to admit	The police sergeant accepted an award for outstanding work.
except	excluding; other than	None of his colleagues, except his wife, knew about the award.
affect	to influence	Writer's block affects a person's ability to write.
effect	the result of something	Writer's block can have bad effects on a person's ability to write.
been	past participle of the verb *to be*	Patrick Fitzgerald has been a prosecutor for many years.
being	present progressive form (the *-ing* form) of the verb *to be*	He was being very nice when he signed autographs.
by	preposition meaning *next to*, *on*, or *before*	The defendant sat by her lawyer. By 10 A.M., the jury was getting restless. Everyone hoped the case would be over by the weekend.
buy	to purchase	The lawyer will buy a new car with her fees from this case.
complement	to add to; to complete	The car will be a nice complement to her other possessions.
compliment	to say something nice about someone	Chicago's mayor complimented the detectives.
conscience	a personal sense of right and wrong	The robber had no conscience.
conscious	being aware or awake	The robber was conscious of his terrible crime.
disinterested	to be impartial	The trial judge was disinterested, favoring neither side.
uninterested	to lack interest in something	The robber looked uninterested when told of his sentence.
elicit	to get or draw out	The police tried to elicit a confession from the gang member.
illicit	illegal; unlawful	The police found evidence of the gang's illicit activities.
everyday	ordinary; common	Crime is an everyday occurrence.
every day	during a single day; each day	The police watch the gang members every day.
imminent	soon to happen	The police stated that an arrest was imminent.
eminent	distinguished; superior	Patrick Fitzgerald is an eminent prosecutor.
imply	to suggest	The reporter implied that the police need more time to investigate.
infer	to conclude	The police inferred from the clues the gang's whereabouts.
its	possessive case of the pronoun *it*	The judge's desk is large, and its legs are ornate.
it's	contraction for *it is*	It's generally known that he is very good at solving crimes.
knew	past tense of *know*	Fitzgerald knew that the newspaper executive was guilty.
new	recent; unused	He had new evidence to present to the court.

Word	Meaning	Example
know	to have knowledge of	Many people know about Fitzgerald's work.
no	a negative	The police made no arrests.
lose	to misplace or forfeit something	The police did not want to lose track of the stolen money.
loose	too big or baggy; not fixed	Detectives sometimes wear loose clothing as part of their disguises.
loss	a decrease in an amount	The company experienced a serious loss when the money was stolen.
peace	calm sensation; a lack of violence	The two rival gangs finally made peace. They felt a sense of peace when hostilities stopped.
piece	a part of something else; one item in a group of items	The forensic team examined a piece of broken glass.
personal	private	The criminal has a lot of personal problems.
personnel	employees; staff	The police must hire new personnel.
principal	primary (adj.); director of a school (n.)	The principal detective talked to the principal of our school.
principle	a rule or standard	The police try to follow the principle of law.
quiet	silent	The thieves remained quiet when arrested.
quite	very	The public is becoming quite angry at the increase in crime.
quit	to stop doing something	The detective sometimes wants to quit the force.
taught	past tense of *teach*	Drake taught a class on criminology.
thought	past tense of *think*	He thought his students were intelligent.
than	word used in comparisons	Fitzgerald is more determined than other prosecutors.
then	at a particular time; after a specific time	Cornwell investigated the case, and then she wrote about it.
that	word used to introduce a clause	She wrote that Walter Sickert was Jack the Ripper.
their	possessive form of *they*	The police officers went to their favorite restaurant.
there	a place	They went there by police van.
they're	contraction of *they are*	They're both interesting people.
through	in one side and out the other; finished	The police cruiser passed through a tunnel. Then they were through for the day.
threw	past tense of *throw*	Somebody threw a rock at the officer's car.
thorough	complete	They did a thorough investigation of the crime scene.
to	indicates direction or movement; part of an infinitive	I want to go to the film.
too	also; very	The purse snatcher was too young to be given a prison sentence. Her friend was, too.
two	the number after one	There were two witnesses to the holdup.
where	question word indicating location	The police knew where the diamonds were hidden.
were	past tense of *be*	The diamonds were in a safe place.
we're	contraction of *we are*	We're going to meet the detectives.
who's	contraction of *who is*	The police sergeant, who's very well known, spoke to reporters.
whose	pronoun showing ownership	Criminals, whose crimes hurt society, must be punished.
write	to draw symbols that represent words	Patricia Cornwell will write about the crime.
right	correct; the opposite of the direction left	The police arrested the right criminal. They found the diamonds in her right pocket.

Practice 11

Underline the correct words.

EXAMPLE: The Securities and Exchange Commission (personal / <u>personnel</u>) were shocked to hear about the Ponzi scheme.

1. In December 2008, many wealthy Americans suffered a serious financial (lose / loss).

2. They had (been / being) investing for many years with Bernard Madoff, a well-known financier.

3. Madoff was considered to be an (eminent / imminent) investor.

4. However, he was investing his clients' money in an (elicit / illicit) racket called a Ponzi scheme.

5. Madoff, (who's / whose) reputation is ruined, had used money from later investors to pay off earlier investors, creating an illusion of profit.

6. Madoff's investment scheme ended when his clients pulled money out of investment portfolios in an effort (to / too) reduce financial risk.

7. The clients did not (no / know) that he had cheated them out of (their / there) money until they heard the news in the media.

8. Madoff's Ponzi scheme created (quit / quite) a stir when authorities claimed it was the largest fraud in the history of Wall Street.

Practice 12

Underline and correct fifteen errors in the following passages. Look for the commonly confused words that are indicated in parentheses.

EXAMPLE: He is <u>to</u> busy these days.
too

1. (affect, effect; then, that, than)

Many celebrities get into trouble with the law. A few years ago, former football player Michael Vick was involved in an activity than was illegal. He promoted and funded dog fighting on his property. Many of the dogs fought viciously and than died afterward. When images of mangled dogs appeared online, Vick's reputation was effected. Vick received a prison sentence, but some believe his sentence was lighter then others who engaged in similar activities. The affect of the verdict on Vick was enormous. His stature is more tarnished that before.

2. (threw, through, thorough)

In 2014, Justin Bieber was arrested for dangerous driving. He was allegedly drag racing threw the streets of Miami when he was arrested. After a through investigation, Bieber pleaded guilty to careless driving and resisting arrest. He was also detained after he reportedly through eggs at his neighbor's house. Bieber has apologized both thorough spokespeople and in many different interviews, and he is trying to rehabilitate his reputation.

3. (lose, loose, loss)

Will Bieber loose the respect of his most loyal fans? Despite his problems, he has not seen a significant lose of business opportunities. To his critics, Bieber has been a beneficiary of the lose standards that seem to apply to celebrities. They argue that many noncelebrities would be in prison for similar crimes.

4. (who's, whose)

Many people believe that celebrities get preferential treatment. Should a person whose famous be held to the same standards as anybody else? Should anyone who's profession is in the public spotlight feel pressured to be a role model?

Reflect On It

Think about what you have learned in this unit. If you do not know an answer, review that concept.

1. a. In a word containing *ie*, when does *i* come before *e?*

   _____

   b. When does *e* come before *i* in a word?

   c. _____

4. Circle the correctly spelled words. Correct each misspelled word.

   realy   finally   unatural   illogical   plentifull

5. Correct eight mistakes in the next passage.

   Crimes are quiet a common occurrence in my nieghborhood. The police are planing to increase there surveillance in this area. The public, to, can help. Its important to report any unnusual events. Eventualy, such actions will help lower the crime rate.

Final Review

Underline and correct twenty-five spelling errors and mistakes with commonly confused words.

EXAMPLE: The judge is <u>to</u> busy these days.
      too

1.   In past centuries, shaming justice was quiet common. Judges often recommanded shaming penaltyes. Guilty citizens could be placed in a stockade, and the wooden structure could lock a person's hands and head in place. The goal was to humiliate the offender. Often, even the nicest citizens in town would try spiting on the criminal. Is public shaming preferable to traditionnal prison sentences? Some experts beleive it has a place in the criminal justice system.

2.   Today, shaming penalties are more common then in the 1900s. For example, a judge in Wisconsin orders shoplifters to stand in front of the stores they robed holding an "I am a shoplifter" sign. In Cleveland, resident Shena Hardin drove her SUV on a sidewalk. She excepted responsability for her action and had to stand on a street corner with a sign that read, "Only an idiot would drive on the sidewalk to avoid a school bus."

3.   Some cities have developped interesting ways to deal with those who do elicit activities. For example, in some places, its common to see billboards with the names of deadbeat dads, drug dealers, and public urinators. In Kansas City, men who visit prostitutes may hear there names been broadcast on public television. Since that penalty was introduced, the number of men doing such illegal activities definitly has droped. Nobody likes to be embarased in public.

4.   There are advantages to public shaming instead of incarceration. First, prisons are overcrowded, and it's costly to house each inmate. Also, many offenders would rather loose a day or two of work and be humiliated than spend weeks or months in prison. Raymond Garrid of Virginia stole pants. His loyier, who's reputation was quite good, suggested that Garrid accept the public penalty. Garrid wore the pants around his neck as he was restrained in public stocks. He thought that his lose of reputation was acceptable. He claims that his penalty has not effected his life in a negative way.

READING LINK
Readings on legal issues:

"My Prison Story" (p. 183)
"Robot Ethics" from *The Economist* (p. 215)
"The Criminal Justice Process" (p. 529)
"How Spies Are Caught" (p. 533)
"The Real Reason Crime is Falling" (p. 535)
"My Father Taught Me to Love Guns" (p. 524)

5. Some people object to the principle of public shaming. Others see the punishment as valid, argueing that it costs less for the criminal justice system. What is your opinion about public shaming?

The Writer's Room

Write about one of the following topics. Check for spelling errors, and verify that you have used the correct word.

1. What is your opinion about public shaming? Should shaming sentences be given more frequently?
2. Should juveniles who commit serious crimes be treated as harshly as adults?

The Writers' Circle: Collaborative Activity

Work with a partner or a small group of students and compose a paragraph about the qualities of a good comic book hero. In your paragraph, tell a story about one of the character's heroic actions. Use slang words and clichés. Make sure that your paragraph is double-spaced and that the writing is clear.

When you have finished writing your paragraph, exchange sheets with another team of students. Edit the other team's paragraph and imagine that the audience is a college instructor. Change all clichés and slang expressions into standard English.

34 Commas

SECTION THEME: The Workplace

In this chapter, you read about business etiquette and business decisions.

 LEARNING OBJECTIVES

34.1 Define a comma and what it does.

34.2 Use a comma in a series.

34.3 Use commas after introductory words and phrases.

34.4 Use commas around interrupting words and phrases.

34.5 Use commas correctly in compound sentences.

34.6 Use commas correctly in complex sentences.

34.7 Identify where to use commas in a business letter.

The Writer's Journal

Have you ever thought about having your own business? What type of business would you like to have? Write a paragraph about owning a business.

What Is a Comma?

34.1 **Define a comma and what it does.**

A **comma** (,) is a punctuation mark that helps keep distinct ideas separate. There are many ways to use a comma. In this chapter, you learn some helpful rules about comma usage.

Notice how comma placement changes the meaning of the following sentences. Discuss which animal is having a nap.

The dog bites, the cat runs, and then she has a nap.

The dog bites the cat, runs, and then she has a nap.

Commas in a Series

34.2 Use a comma in a series.

Use a comma to separate items in a series of three or more items. Remember to put a comma before the final *and* or *or*.

unit 1	,	unit 2	,	and	unit 3
				or	

Houston, Dallas, and Austin have vibrant design industries.

The job search requires courage, perseverance, and energy.

You can network, contact employers directly, or use a placement service.

HINT: Punctuating a Series

In a series of three or more items, do not place a comma after the last item in the series (unless the series is part of an interrupting phrase).

Her poise, simplicity, and kindness impressed us.

Do not use commas to separate items if each item is joined by *and* or *or*.

It is not possible to study <u>and</u> listen to music <u>and</u> have a conversation at the same time.

Practice 1

Underline series of items in the next selection. Then add sixteen missing commas where necessary.

EXAMPLE: Frequent business travelers can experience <u>physical fatigue, marital strain, and mental stress.</u>

1. Manfred Durbar travels constantly on company business. He flies mainly to Houston Orlando and Chicago. While he thinks these cities have a lot to offer, Manfred hates the travel time. He is not alone. Pollsters surveyed people who needed to travel a lot for business, such as company executives travel agents and salesmen. According to the survey results, over 92 percent of respondents stated that they do not like to travel.

2. Business travelers gave different reasons for their lack of enthusiasm. Manfred dislikes the hassles of airport security the uncomfortable seats and the usual flight delays. He also dreads sitting next to a crying baby an overly amorous couple or a sick passenger. Businesspeople also stated concerns over hotels. They were anxious about bed bugs noisy guests and uncomfortable beds. Furthermore, respondents worried about falling behind in their work attending boring presentations and being away from their families.

3. Senior company managers acknowledge that travel can be problematic. Many managers are trying to find ways to reduce business travel. One such solution is virtual communication. Many employees prefer sharing ideas through teleconferencing video chats or live Internet radio rather than through traditional face-to-face meetings. Also, virtual conferencing eliminates logistical problems. Employees can participate from any location such as their work station home office or any other room. They need only a laptop or a mobile device.

Commas After Introductory Words and Phrases

34.3 **Use commas after introductory words and phrases.**

Use a comma after an **introductory word**. The introductory word could be an interjection such as *yes, no,* or *well,* it could be an adverb such as *usually* or *generally,* or it could be a transitional word such as *however* or *therefore.*

Introductory word(s)	,	sentence.

Yes, I will help you complete the order.

Frankly, you should reconsider your customer service promise.

However, the job includes a lot of overtime.

Use a comma to set off **introductory phrases** of two or more words. The phrase could be a transitional expression such as *of course* or *on the contrary,* or it could be a prepositional phrase such as *on a warm summer evening.* The introductory phrase could also be a modifier such as *running out of fuel* or *born in France.*

On the other hand, his career was not going well.

In the middle of the meeting, I received a phone call.

Speaking to the crowd, the manager explained the stock's performance.

Practice 2

Underline each introductory word or phrase. Then add ten missing commas.

EXAMPLE: In today's job market, people must remain flexible.

1. For the first time over a third of American adults have a college degree. Furthermore that number continues to grow steadily. For example 68 percent of high school graduates attended college in 2011.

2.   Of course the ability to earn a high salary is not the only reason that people attend a college or university. Still many students want to know which degrees have the highest earning potential. According to a study of over 1,000 universities the ten best-paying college degrees are related to engineering.

3.   In fact almost all of the highest-paid university graduates come from STEM programs. As a result many students are counseled to enter programs in science, technology, engineering, and mathematics. However liberal arts programs also have their benefits. Working in a volatile job market the critical-thinking and problem-solving skills obtained in a liberal arts program are valuable.

Commas Around Interrupting Words and Phrases

34.4 **Use commas around interrupting words and phrases.**

Interrupting words or phrases appear in the middle of sentences. Such interrupters are often asides that interrupt the sentence's flow but do not affect its overall meaning. Some interrupters are *by the way*, *as a matter of fact*, and *for example*. Prepositional phrases can also interrupt sentences.

| Opening phrase | , | interrupting words | , | rest of sentence. |

My sister, for example, has never invested in stocks.

The market, by the way, has been down recently.

My manager, admittedly, decided to go to a movie!

HINT: Using Commas with Appositives

An appositive gives further information about a noun or pronoun. The appositive can appear at the beginning, in the middle, or at the end of a sentence. Set off appositives with commas.

beginning
A large city in Florida, Miami has a variety of public learning centers.

middle
Dr. Anex, a senior surgeon, recommends the transplant.

end
The office is next to Graham's, a local eatery.

Practice 3

The next sentences contain introductory words and phrases, interrupters, and series items. Add the missing commas. If the sentence is correct, write C in the space provided.

EXAMPLE: For some employees, the open office concept offers no privacy, less
personal space, and more stress.   _____c_____

1. Lindsey Kaufman an ad executive in Brooklyn, complains
about the problems in an open office.   _____

2. In open-concept workplaces there are no walls, partitions
or personal offices for employees.   _____

3. Many employees in her opinion do not respect the personal
space of others.   _____

4. She gets annoyed, for example when her co-workers talk
or laugh loudly when she's trying to work.   _____

5. Venting her frustration, she wrote an article for the *Washington
Post* detailing her objections to this style of workplace.   _____

6. Some people, however are proponents of this model and
think more businesses should adopt it.   _____

7. For example, some proponents argue that employees
collaborate more when doors and walls are not separating them.   _____

8. Michael Bloomberg, the long-time mayor of New York City
used an open-style workplace during his time in office.   _____

9. In the early 2000s, many Silicon Valley firms also shifted to
a partition-less environment.   _____

10. Unfortunately Kaufman feels that her performance and
enjoyment of her job have deteriorated significantly since
her agency switched to an open office.   _____

Commas in Compound Sentences

34.5 **Use commas correctly in compound sentences.**

A **compound sentence** contains two or more complete sentences joined by a coordinating conjunction (*for, and, nor, but, or, yet, so*).

| Sentence | , | and | sentence. |

I want a job, **so** I will look in the classified ads.

Some interesting companies are nearby, **and** maybe they are hiring.

Practice 4

Add six commas that are missing from this letter.

EXAMPLE: I am punctual, and I am hardworking.

Dear Mr. Ruzinka,

On Craigslist, I read that you are looking for a computer technician. I am interested in the job so I have enclosed a résumé highlighting my skills and experience.

I have taken computer technology courses at El Camino College and I completed my program with distinction. I also plan to receive Microsoft certification but I have not done the final exams. Furthermore, I have worked at a bank and I have experience repairing computers at a local clinic.

I am available for an interview at any time so please do not hesitate to contact me. Thank you for your consideration and I look forward to hearing from you.

Yours sincerely,

Darius George

Darius George

Commas in Complex Sentences

34.6 **Use commas correctly in complex sentences.**

A **complex sentence** contains one or more dependent clauses (or incomplete ideas). When you add a **subordinating conjunction**—a word such as *because, although,* or *unless*—to a clause, you make the clause dependent.

dependent clause   independent clause

When the stock market opened, he sold his shares.

Use a Comma After a Dependent Clause

If a sentence begins with a dependent clause, place a comma after the clause. Remember that a dependent clause has a subject and a verb, but it cannot stand alone. When the subordinating conjunction comes in the middle of a sentence, it is not necessary to use a comma.

	Dependent clause , main clause.
Comma	After the meeting ends⌃ we will go to lunch.

	Main clause dependent clause.
No comma	We will go to lunch after the meeting ends.

Use Commas to Set Off Nonrestrictive Clauses

Clauses beginning with *who, that,* and *which* can be restrictive or nonrestrictive. A **restrictive clause** contains essential information about the subject. Do not place commas around restrictive clauses.

No commas	The only local company that does computer graphics has no job openings.
	(The underlined clause is essential to understand the meaning of the sentence.)

A **nonrestrictive clause** gives nonessential information. In such sentences, the clause gives additional information about the noun but does not restrict or define the noun. Place commas around nonrestrictive clauses.

Commas	Her book⌃ which is in bookstores ⌃ is about successful entrepreneurs.
	(The underlined clause contains extra information, but if you removed that clause, the sentence would still have a clear meaning.)

HINT: *Which, That, Who*

which

Use commas to set off clauses that begin with *which*.

> ImClone, **which** was founded in 1983, creates pharmaceutical products.

that

Do not use commas to set off clauses begining with *that*.

> The company **that** Sam Waksal founded creates pharmaceutical products.

who

When a clause begins with *who*, you may or may not need a comma. If the clause contains nonessential information, put commas around it. If the clause is essential to the meaning of the sentence, it does not require commas.

Essential	Many people **who** buy stocks think that they will earn a profit.
Not essential	Domestic guru Martha Stewart, **who** became a multimillionaire, was convicted of obstructing justice in 2004.

Practice 5

Edit the following sentences by adding eighteen missing commas.

EXAMPLE: The manager who seems quite nice, asks very probing questions.

1. When people look for jobs they may encounter several types of interviews. The structured interview which occurs during the screening stage helps a company have a uniform hiring process. The employer, who asks a specific set of questions compares the answers of the candidates.

2. The open-ended interview which is more relaxed and unstructured allows job seekers to talk freely. If people reveal too much or ramble on they may not be hired. Anyone who wants a job should remember to maintain a business-like demeanor.

3. During panel interviews a team questions the job-seekers. For instance the supervisor the human resources manager and a co-worker may all interact with the candidates. Some companies even have group interviews which are useful for judging people's communication skills.

4. The worst type of interview is the stress interview. The intense boss, who asks difficult and strange questions often unnerves the candidate. The goal which is not always apparent is to see how people handle demanding situations. Eliza Marcum for example, was asked what type of animal she would like to be. She did not understand the relevance of the question and she responded impatiently. During stress interviews, people who act upset overly nervous, or angry will probably not be hired.

Commas in Business Letters

34.7 Identify where to use commas in a business letter.

When you write or type a formal letter, ensure that you use commas correctly.

Addresses

In the address at the top of the letter, insert a comma between the following elements.

- The street name and apartment number
- The city and state or country

Do not put a comma before the zip code.

Dr. Brent Patterson

312 Appleby Road, Suite 112

Cleveland, OH 45678

If you include an address inside a complete sentence, use commas to separate the street address from the city and the city from the state or country. If you just write the street address, do not put a comma after it.

Commas	The building at 11 Wall Street, New York, contains the Stock Exchange.
No comma	The building at 11 Wall Street contains the New York Stock Exchange.

Dates

In the date at the top of the letter, add a comma between the full date and the year. If you just write the month and the year, then no comma is necessary.

May 21, 2017   January 2017

If you include a date inside a complete sentence, separate the elements of the date with commas.

We visited Washington on Monday, July 26, 2016.

HINT: Writing Numbers

When writing a date in a letter, it is not necessary to write ordinal numbers such as *first* (1st), *second* (2nd), *third* (3rd), or *fourth* (4th). Instead, just write the number: 1, 2, 3, 4, and so on.

February 24, 2001   October 11, 1966

Salutations

Salutations are formal letter greetings. The form "To Whom It May Concern" is no longer used regularly by North American businesses. The best way to address someone is to use his or her name followed by a comma or a colon. The colon is preferred in business letters.

Dear Ms. Lewin: Dear Sir or Madam: Dear Sarah,

Complimentary Closings

Place a comma after the complimentary closing. Notice that the first word of the closing is capitalized.

Respectfully,   Yours sincerely,   Yours truly,

SAMPLE LETTER OF APPLICATION
You send a sample letter of application to an employer when you apply for a job. Review the parts of the following letter.

Sender's address (name, phone, and possibly an e-mail address)
Seamus O'Brien
10 Santa Fe Boulevard
Seattle, WA 90001
(661) 234-5678

Date
September 12, 2016

Recipient's address
Avant Garde Computers
Adelaide and Sinclair Corporation
6116 Greenway Avenue
Seattle, WA 98711

Subject line
Subject: Position of junior programmer

Salutation
Dear Ms. Roebok:

I saw an ad in Saturday's *Seattle Times* stating that you need a junior programmer. I have enclosed a résumé highlighting my skills in this field. I have an aptitude for computers, and, when I was fourteen years old, I created my first game.

I have just graduated with a diploma in computer programming at Marshall College. I took courses in several computer languages. Also, I have completed six weeks of training, and I am enclosing a letter of reference from the owner of the company that offered the program.

If you require further information, please contact me. I am available for an interview at any time and could start work immediately. Thank you for your consideration.

Sincerely,

S. O'Brien

Seamus O'Brien

Closing (After the closing, put your handwritten signature followed by your typed name.)

Enclosures: résumé
            letter of reference

List any documents you have included.

Practice 6

The next letter contains ten errors. Add seven missing commas and remove three unnecessary commas.

Good Food Solutions
2256, Kildare Avenue
Orlando, FL 32818
June 24 2015

Sylvia Hubert

The Harvest Moon Café

1000 International Drive

Orlando, FL, 32819

Dear Ms. Hubert:

As the new owners of the Harvest Moon Café we would like to offer you our best wishes for your success.

Our company Good Food Solutions, has been providing restaurant service training for many years to fine cafés and restaurants in the Orlando area. In fact we have had a very close, and profitable business relationship with the previous owners of the Harvest Moon Café and we hope to continue doing business with you in the very near future.

Our sales representative, Melissa Fung, would be pleased to discuss our products and services at your convenience. Ms. Fung who has been with our company for many years, is very knowledgeable about our operation. Our phone number is (407) 555-9988. We look forward to meeting with you.

Yours truly

Alwyn Scott

Alwyn Scott

Reflect On It

Think about what you have learned in this unit. If you do not know an answer, review that concept.

1. Explain the rules of comma usage in the following situations.

   a. Series of items: _____

   _____

   b. Introductory words or phrases: _____

   _____

   c. Interrupting phrases: _____

   _____

   d. Compound sentences: _____

   _____

2. What is a nonrestrictive clause? _____

   _____

3. Should you place commas around nonrestrictive clauses?

   _____ Yes _____ No

4. Write three common closings for a business letter.

   _____

   _____

   _____

Final Review

Edit the next essay by adding seventeen missing commas and removing three unnecessary commas.

EXAMPLE: Many successful entrepreneurs, such as Bill Gates and Warren Buffet, have valuable advice on how to start a business.

1. America's economy which is the largest in the world is home to many of the world's most successful start-up companies. Facebook, Google, Amazon and Twitter were all created in America. Starting a new business involves many obstacles and dangers. Martin Zwilling a prominent mentor to aspiring entrepreneurs, suggests new business owners should be passionate open to learning new things and realistic.

2. Entrepreneurs, who expect to get rich quickly are likely to be disappointed. On July 1 2014, Justin and Sarah Walsh started the June Lake Brewing Company in June Lake, California. For the first six months they worked eighteen-hour days and relied on help from volunteers in the community. Justin who had some experience as a contractor, also did the electrical work on their warehouse. The company also set up their own newsletter Facebook account, and Twitter account. Sales were modest in the beginning. The business however continued to grow steadily. The brewery set a new company record for sales in January, 2015. Because the Walsh family kept their overhead costs low and did much of the start-up work themselves their small company was set up to succeed.

3. Any business, that wants to have long-term success should start off small. According to Martin Zwilling it is now easier than ever before to start your own business. Incorporation fees and marketing costs are now lower but it is still difficult to raise the capital needed to start a business. This is why Zwilling suggests starting with a small, low-risk business rather than a larger enterprise.

4. After the economic recession of 2008 it was very difficult for small businesses to survive. Of course, the economy will always be volatile and unpredictable. However those who work hard and plan carefully can still start successful companies on their own.

The Writer's Room

Write about one of the following topics. Verify that you have used commas correctly.

1. What was your first job? Describe how you spent your day at your first job.
2. Categorize spenders into different types. Give examples for each type.

35 The Apostrophe, Quotation Marks, and Titles

SECTION THEME: The Workplace

In this chapter, you read about topics related to interesting business stories and controversies.

The Writer's Journal

Write about a successful singer. What are some of the person's best songs? Why do you like that singer?

The Apostrophe (')

35.1 Use apostrophes correctly.

An **apostrophe** is a punctuation mark showing a contraction or ownership.

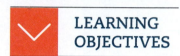

ownership   contraction

Daymond John's business is very successful, and **it's** still growing.

Using Apostrophes in Contractions

To form a **contraction**, join two words into one and add an apostrophe to replace the omitted letter(s).

Apostrophe replaces *o*   is + **not** = isn't

Apostrophe replaces *a*   I + **am** = I'm

COMMON CONTRACTIONS

The following are examples of the most common contractions.

- **Join a verb with *not*.** The apostrophe replaces the letter *o* in *not*.

are + not = aren't	have + not = haven't
could + not = couldn't	is + not = isn't
did + not = didn't	should + not = shouldn't
do + not = don't	was + not = wasn't
does + not = doesn't	were + not = weren't
has + not = hasn't	would + not = wouldn't

Exceptions: will + not = won't, can + not = can't

- **Join a subject and a verb.** Sometimes you must remove several letters to form the contraction.

I + will = I'll	she + will = she'll
I + would = I'd	Tina + is = Tina's
he + is = he's	they + are = they're
he + will = he'll	we + will = we'll
Joe + is = Joe's	who + is = who's
she + has = she's	who + would = who'd

Exception: Do not contract a subject with the past tense of *be*. For example, do not contract *he + was* or *they + were*.

HINT: Contractions with Two Meanings

Sometimes one contraction can have two different meanings.

   I'd = I had or I would   *he's* = he is or he has

When you read, you should be able to figure out the meaning of the contraction by looking at the words in context.

She is
She's hiring new personnel.

She has
She's seen several interesting candidates.

Practice 1

Add nine missing apostrophes to the next selection.

                  hadn't
EXAMPLE: Many Americans hadnt expected investment banks to collapse in 2008.

1.   In 1850, three German brothers immigrated to America and invested

in cotton in Montgomery, Alabama. After the Civil War, the brothers

couldve stayed in Montgomery, but they took their enterprise to New

York. They werent just cotton traders. Theyd also buy and sell other items.

Their company got on the New York Stock Exchange and was a successful institution for more than a hundred years. The brothers couldnt have predicted that Lehman Brothers Holdings would be bankrupt by the start of the 21st century.

2. The company finances didnt remain healthy. In 2007, its stock price started to fall. Investors lost confidence in the firm because it had invested in lending mortgages to risky clients. Managers shouldve been more careful. In the summer of 2008, the firm posted huge losses. The American government wasnt willing to lend the corporation money, so the company failed.

3. Politicians criticized the company. Members of Congress felt that the top executives of Lehman Brothers shouldnt have received millions of dollars in bonuses just before the business filed for bankruptcy. When questioned about his performance, CEO Richard Fuld said that hed made the best decisions he could for the company.

Practice 2

Look at each underlined contraction, and then write out the complete word.

EXAMPLE: They <u>weren't</u> ready to start a business.   **were not**

1. Maria <u>Gomez's</u> extremely pleased with her online clothing company.   _____

2. <u>She's</u> run the company for three years.   _____

3. <u>She's</u> an extremely driven, intelligent woman.   _____

4. Many entrepreneurs wish <u>they'd</u> thought of a service that delivers personalized clothing monthly to members.   _____

5. <u>I'd</u> like to create an Internet start-up, too.   _____

Using Apostrophes to Show Ownership

You can also use apostrophes to show ownership. Review the next rules.

POSSESSIVE FORM OF SINGULAR NOUNS
Add -'s to a singular noun to indicate ownership, even if the noun ends in s.

Daymond's best friends joined his company.

Somebody's house became a factory.

Ross's dad has his own business.

POSSESSIVE FORM OF PLURAL NOUNS
When a plural noun ends in s, just add an apostrophe to indicate ownership. Add -'s to irregular plural nouns.

Many **companies'** websites crash.

The four **friends'** business is very successful.

The **children's** clothing company is expanding.

POSSESSIVE FORM OF COMPOUND NOUNS

When two people have joint ownership, add -'s to the second name. When two people have separate ownership, add -'s to both names.

Joint ownership	Daymond and **Carl's** company is successful.
Separate ownership	**Daymond's** and **Carl's** offices are in different buildings.

Practice 3

Write the singular and plural possessive forms.

EXAMPLE:

	Singular Possessive	Plural Possessive
Mr. Cohen	Mr. Cohen's	the Cohens'
1. client	_____	_____
2. boss	_____	_____
3. secretary	_____	_____
4. Mr. Ness	_____	_____
5. woman	_____	_____
6. salesperson	_____	_____

Practice 4

Write the possessive forms of the following phrases.

EXAMPLE: the sister of the doctor _____the doctor's sister_____

1. the hat of the witch _____

2. the wands of the witches _____

3. the profits of the company _____

4. the directors of the companies _____

5. the house of Jan and Ted _____

6. the car of Omar and the car of Roy _____

Using Apostrophes in Expressions of Time

When an expression of time (*day, week, month, year*) appears to possess something, use the possessive form of that word.

Singular	The customer won a **year's** supply of paper.
Plural	Mike Roy gave two **weeks'** notice before he left the company.

When writing the numerals of a decade or century, do not put an apostrophe before the final -*s*.

In the **1800s**, many immigrants arrived at Ellis Island.
Many "dot com" companies failed in the **1990s**.

HINT: Common Apostrophe Errors

Do not use apostrophes before the final *s* of a verb.

         wants
Simon ~~want's~~ to open a franchise.

Do not confuse contractions with possessive pronouns that have a similar sound. For example, the contraction *you're* sounds like the pronoun *your*. Remember that possessive pronouns never have apostrophes.

                    Its
The company is growing. ~~It's~~ slogan is catchy.

                   theirs.
That is my idea. It is not ~~their's~~.

Practice 5

Correct twelve errors with apostrophes. You may need to add, move, or remove apostrophes.

            Don't   *aren't*
EXAMPLE: ~~Dont~~ be surprised if some products ~~arent~~ as green as they claim to be.

1. Since the 1970's, many companies' have added eco labels to products.

Manufacturers say that customers wont buy products that are'nt

environmentally friendly. Therefore, a company will often attach a green

label to it's popular products.

2. However, theres been controversy with green-product certification.

There are over three hundred green label programs in the world. Some

are fraudulent. In addition, some businesses haven't used an independent

company to verify that products are actually green. For example, S. C.

Johnsons house cleaning products, Shout and Windex, were labeled green by

the company. Some consumers are suing the company for mislabeling. The

corporations lawyers deny any wrongdoing.

3. Most consumers are willing to pay extra for green products. But they

dont want to buy items that make false claims. For example, Jeanette and

Charles local grocery store sell's items with the green label. Recently,

the couple discovered that the items theyd been buying were not really

environmentally friendly. Now they research any product's green claim

before they buy it.

Quotation Marks (" ")

35.2 **Use quotation marks correctly.**

Use **quotation marks** to set off the exact words of a speaker or writer. If the quotation is a complete sentence, there are some standard ways that it should be punctuated.

- Capitalize the first word of the quotation.
- Place quotation marks around the complete quotation.
- Place the end punctuation inside the closing quotation marks.

. . . declared	,	"Complete sentence."

Poet William Butler Yeats declared, "Education is not the filling of a pail but the lighting of a fire."

Generally, when using quotations, attach the name of the speaker or writer to the quotation in some way.

INTRODUCTORY PHRASE

Place a comma after a phrase introducing a quotation.

. . . says	,	"_____."

Malcolm Forbes jokes, "It is unfortunate we can't buy many business executives for what they are worth and sell them for what they think they are worth."

INTERRUPTING PHRASE

When a quotation is interrupted, do the following:

- Place a comma after the first part of the quotation.
- Place a comma after the interrupting phrase.

"_____,"	. . . says,	"_____."

"I've worked hard all of my life," said my grandfather, "and I don't regret a single job I've had."

ENDING PHRASE

When you place a phrase at the end of a quotation, end the quotation with a comma instead of a period.

"_____,"	says _____.

"We'll have to let you go," said her manager.

If your quotation ends with other punctuation, put it before the final quotation mark.

"_____?"	says _____.

"Why are you firing me?" she asked.

"You arrive late every single day!" he groaned.

INTRODUCTORY SENTENCE

You can introduce a quotation with a complete sentence. Simply place a colon (:) after the introductory sentence.

He explains his views:	"_____."

Albert Highfield explains why businesses fail: "They try to grow too quickly."

INSIDE A QUOTATION

If one quotation is inside another quotation, use single quotation marks (' ') around the inside quotation.

> "Main quotation,   'Inside quotation.' "

According to my co-worker, "Bosses usually say, 'I need it done yesterday.' "

HINT: When the Quotation Is an Incomplete Sentence

If the quotation is not a complete sentence, and you simply integrate it into your sentence, do not capitalize the first word of the quotation.

> Sir Francis Bacon once said that an artist's job is to **"d**eepen the mystery.**"**

Practice 6

The next excerpt was adapted from a short story, "The Model Millionaire" by Oscar Wilde. The quotations are in bold. Add quotation marks and commas or colons. Also capitalize the first word of the quotation if necessary.

EXAMPLE: Hughie Erskine wanted to marry Laura Merton. Laura's father gave Hughie his opinion on the engagement :" **Come to me when you have ten thousand dollars of your own**." Hughie was disappointed.

The next morning, he went to see his friend Alan Trevor, an artist. Trevor was painting a beggar. **What an amazing model** whispered Hughie to Trevor.

An amazing model shouted Trevor. **such a beggar as he is not seen every day**

Hughie replied **the poor old guy looks miserable**

Trevor just laughed, but Hughie felt sorry for the beggar model. And although Hughie didn't have much money, he gave the beggar all the coins in his pocket.

The following day, Hughie met Trevor. Trevor had told the beggar all about Hughie and his wish to marry Laura. **He knows all about the lovely Laura** Trevor informed Hughie, **and he knows about the ten thousand dollars**

You told that old beggar all my private affairs cried Hughie, looking angry.

Trevor informed Hughie about the beggar's identity **the old beggar is one of the richest men in the country** Hughie felt very embarrassed that he had given a rich man a few coins.

A few days later, Hughie received a letter from the old beggar. The envelope was addressed to: *A wedding present to Hugh Erskine and Laura Merton from an old beggar.* Inside the envelope, there was a cheque for ten thousand dollars.

When Hughie and Laura married, the "old beggar" gave a speech at the wedding. Trevor remarked **My father used to say**, **millionaire models are rare enough, but model millionaires are rarer still**

Punctuation of Titles

35.3 Punctuate titles correctly.

When using a title within a sentence, place quotation marks around the title of a short work and italicize the title of a longer work. If your text is handwritten, then underline the titles of long works. Here are some guidelines for both.

Short Works	Long Works
Short story: "The Lottery"	**Music album:** *The Chronic*
Web article: "Music Artists Lose Out"	**Novel:** *The Grapes of Wrath*
Chapter: Chapter 1, "Exploring"	**Website:** *CNET News*
Newspaper article: "Missing in Action"	**Book:** *The Writer's World*
Magazine article: "Young Entrepreneurs"	**Newspaper:** *New York Times*
Essay: "Downsizing"	**Magazine:** *Forbes*
TV episode: "The Election"	**Textbook:** *Writing Guidelines*
Song: "Don't Panic"	**TV series:** *Prison Break*
Poem: "Howl"	**CD:** *Parachutes*
	Anthology: *Collected Poems of Beat Writers*
	Movie: *Avatar*
	Blog: *Gizmodo*
	Radio Program: *Morning Edition*

Capitalizing Titles

When you write a title, capitalize the first letter of the first and last words and all the major words.

The Catcher in the Rye   *War and Peace*   "Stairway to Heaven"

Do not capitalize *.com* in a Web address. Also do not capitalize the following words except as the first or last word in a title.

Articles	a, an, the
Coordinators	for, and, nor, but, or, yet, so
Prepositions	by, in, of, off, out, to, up . . .

HINT: Your Own Essay Titles

When writing the title of your own essay, do not put quotation marks around the title. However, you should capitalize key terms.

A Cultural Icon Is Born

Practice 7

A. Add sixteen missing capital letters to the titles in the next paragraphs.

EXAMPLE: Adele contributed to a charity album called *chimes of freedom* for Amnesty International.

<small>C</small> over *chimes*, <small>F</small> over *freedom*

1.   British singer and songwriter Adele has gained a tremendous reputation in the music industry. Her 2008 debut album, *19,* was a huge success in the United Kingdom. In that year, she appeared on the television show *saturday night live* in the United States. With her performance of her song "Someone like you," she gained instant popularity. In fact, Adele has become so successful that she is mentioned in the *guinness book of world records*.

2.   Adele Laurie Blue Adkins was born in 1988 in Tottenham, England. When she was in high school, she saw the singer Pink perform from her album *missundaztood*. Since that time, Adele has wanted to write and sing songs. After she graduated from high school, she published two of her songs on the online magazine *platforms Magazine*. Later, Adele's friend posted the singer's songs on *MySpace*, and a star was born.

3.   In 2011, Adele released her second album, *21*. In an interview in *spin,* Adele stated that her hit single "rolling in the deep" was about a former boyfriend. In a 2011 interview with *rolling stone*, the singer says she is taking her success in stride. Adele's star continues to rise with a third album called *25*.

B. Add quotation marks or underline any titles that should be italicized. There are nine titles.

EXAMPLE: Former *American Idol* contestant Jennifer Hudson won an Academy Award for her role in the movie <u>Dreamgirls</u>.

4.   Recently, televised American talent shows have become very popular. The most famous show is American Idol. But other shows such as Dancing with the Stars and The Voice have also gained fans. Such shows show ordinary people having an extraordinary moment. Indeed, finalists of these talent shows have become very successful. For example, Carrie Underwood's debut album, Some Hearts, went platinum. Her first single, Inside Your Heaven, was an instant hit.

5.   Influenced by the success of the music talent show, a new genre of television shows has developed. These are musical series like Glee. In an article called The Glee Effect, journalist Christopher Loudon writes that the TV show has had an amazing impact on the entertainment industry. Fans

have bought millions of copies of the show's albums. In addition, the show has also led to the development of other similar series. For instance, Smash portrays the lives of characters producing a Broadway musical. Katharine McPhee, a former American Idol contestant, plays one of the leading characters.

Practice 8

Correct twelve errors. First, correctly set off four titles by adding quotation marks or by underling titles that should be in italics. Then look for eight more errors with punctuating quotations, capital letters, and apostrophes.

EXAMPLE: One of electronic band Daft ~~Punks~~ **Punk's** most popular songs is called "Get Lucky."

1. Few people know French musician Thomas Bangalters alter-ego. In fact, he makes up half of the famous French electronic duo Daft Punk. He and his friend, Guy Manuel de Homem Christo, formed Daft Punk in the 1990's. Their style mixe's electronic sounds created with computers and synthesizers and guitar hooks. Their name comes from a negative review in music magazine Melody Maker in which a music critic said their music sounded like "daft punk." Daft Punk's most recent album, Random Access Memories, had hugely successful singles with artists like Pharell Williams and Kanye West.

2. In the past, producing music was an expensive ordeal that required a lot of specialized equipment, so many young people were'nt able to do it. However, recording technology has changed rapidly and gotten much less expensive. For example, Bangalter and Homem de Christo recorded their first album, Homework, on a computer in their bedroom. The first single on the album, Da Funk, was an instant hit.

3. Both members of Daft Punk prefer to keep their identities a secret. The groups signature look is a full-body robot costume, which they wear in videos and during live performances. In a rare interview with Canoe.com, Bangalter explained the band's desire for anonymity within celebrity culture "we don't believe in the star system," Bangalter says. "We want to be the focus of our music, and if we create an image, it must be an artificial image".

Reflect On It

Think about what you have learned in this unit. If you do not know an answer, review that concept.

1. In contractions, which letter does the apostrophe replace in the word *not*? _____

2. Write the possessive forms of the following phrases.

   EXAMPLE: the wife of my brother: <u>my brother's wife</u>

   a. the music of Jennifer Lopez: _____

   b. the books of the professor: _____

   c. the house of Rob and Ann: _____

   d. the cases of the lawyers: _____

3. When a sentence ends with a quotation, the period should be

   a. inside the final quotation marks.

   b. outside the final quotation marks.

4. The titles of short works such as essays, articles, and poems should be

   a. underlined or italicized.

   b. set off with quotation marks.

5. The titles of longer works such as magazines, newspapers, and movies should be

   a. underlined or italicized.

   b. set off with quotation marks.

Final Review

Edit the following paragraphs for fifteen errors with apostrophes, quotations, capitalization, and titles. Underline any titles to indicate that they should be italicized. Any title set off with quotation marks counts as one error.

EXAMPLE: I downloaded Taylor <s>Swifts</s> ^{Swift's} song "Bad Blood" for only 99 cents.

1.   File sharing of music and films has become common in recent year's. A reporter for Fox news writes "An estimated 60 million people participate in file-sharing networks." Opinions about file sharing differ greatly.

2.   David Charles works in the film industry. He says that video sharing is becoming as common as music downloading. Charles' friend, Melissa Peng, often downloads songs. She says, "students don't want to buy a CD for twenty dollars when there are only one or two songs they like".

3.   The Recording Industry Association of America states its position "If you make unauthorized copies of copyrighted music recordings, you're stealing." Television distributers such as HBO have also aggressively pursued those who download popular shows like Game of Thrones. James Hibberd wrote an article in Entertainment Weekly detailing how the shows fifth season premier was illegally downloaded over 30 million times. In his article "*Game of Thrones* Piracy Hits Record Highs, Hibberd writes, "By one estimate, the piracy resulted in $44 million in lost revenue for that one episode alone."

4.   The music and film industries know that consumers will continue to share files. Consequently, they have developed new schemes to increase profits. Apple, along with Google and many others, allows it's customers to download products for as little as 99 cents. Business student Mitchel Hunt likes the customer-friendly system: "I can download the videos I want very cheaply." However, selling digital singles has reportedly badly hurt recording companies profits. Many artists also claim they're losing money from this model. In 2013, in the article   A Decade of iTunes Killed the music Industry,   Adrian Covert reported that the record industry earned nearly 40 percent less in revenue than in 2003, despite a huge increase in online sales.

The Writer's Room

Write about one of the following topics. Ensure that your punctuation is correct.

1. What is success? Define success and, as a supporting example, describe a successful person whom you know.
2. What are the effects of the Internet on small businesses?

36 Capitalization and Other Punctuation Marks

SECTION THEME: The Workplace

In this chapter, you read about topics related to new innovations.

LEARNING OBJECTIVES

36.1 Use capital letters correctly.

36.2 Use other punctuation marks correctly.

The Writer's Journal

Do you buy products online? Why or why not? Express your opinion about online shopping.

Capitalization

36.1 Use capital letters correctly.

There are many instances in which you must use capital letters. Always capitalize the following words:

- **The pronoun *I* and the first word of every sentence**

    My coworkers and **I** share an office.

- **Days of the week, months, and holidays**

    Thursday   June 23   Thanksgiving

Do not capitalize the seasons: summer, fall, winter, spring.

- **Titles of specific institutions, departments, companies, and schools**

    Apple Computer   Department of Finance   Daleview High School

  Do not capitalize general references.

    the company   the department   the school

- **The names of specific places such as buildings, streets, parks, cities, states, countries, continents, and bodies of water**

    Market Street   Times Square   Los Angeles, California
    Brazil   Asia   Lake Erie

  Do not capitalize general references.

    the street   the state   the lake

- **The names of specific planets, but not the sun or moon**

    Earth   Mars   Venus   sun

- **The names of specific languages, nationalities, tribes, races, and religions**

    Spanish   Mohawk   Buddhist   an Italian restaurant

- **Titles of specific individuals**

    General Dewitt   President Lincoln   Dr. Blain

    Professor Cruz   Prime Minister Cameron   Mrs. Ellen Ross

  Do not capitalize titles if you are referring to the profession in general, or if the title follows the name.

    my doctor   the professors   Dianne Feinstein, a senator

- **Specific course and program titles**

    Economics 201   Topics in Electrical Engineering   Nursing 402

  Do not capitalize if you refer to a course but do not mention the course title.

    an economics course   an engineering program   a nursing class

- **Major words in titles of literary or artistic works**

    Washington Post   *Silver Linings Playbook*   *Lord of the Flies*

- **Historical events, eras, and movements**

    World War II   Cubism   the Middle Ages

HINT: Capitalizing Computer Terms and Brand Names

Brand names for hardware, software, and devices often use informal capitalization rules (iPhone, MS Word, and so on). When in doubt, check the manufacturer's website for the exact spelling. Here are some examples:

    iPad   YouTube   QuickBooks

Practice 1

Add fifteen missing capital letters.

EXAMPLE: Many countries such as India want to manufacture green vehicles.

1.　In recent times, some people have produced interesting inventions, including google's self-driving car. In the mid-2000s, the magazine *Popular mechanics* reported on another type of automobile. In france, Motor development International has developed a car that runs on compressed air. It was invented by Guy Negre. He used to be an engineer on the Formula one circuit. The american distribution center is on canaan street in New paltz, New York. In a promotional video, the inventor proudly stated, "i share the same birthday as science fiction writer Jules Verne." Verne predicted that automobiles would run on air.

2.　In november 2015, a compressed air car was ready to launch. When tata motors of India developed the tiny vehicle, it called the car AIRpod. A partner company, Zero pollution Motors, builds the AIRpod at its factory in hawaii.

Other Punctuation Marks

36.2　**Use other punctuation marks correctly.**

Colon (:)

Use a colon

- to introduce a quotation with a complete sentence.

  The writer Oscar Wilde stated his opinion: "All art is quite useless."

- to introduce a series or a list after a complete sentence.

  In recent years, these novelists won Pulitzer Prizes for writing fiction: Anthony Doerr, Donna Tartt, Adam Johnson, Jennifer Egan, and Junot Diaz.

- after the expression *the following*.

  Please do the following: read, review, and respond.

- to introduce an explanation or example.

  In 1929, investors witnessed a tragedy: the Stock Market Crash.

- to separate the hour and minutes in expressions of time.

  The meeting will begin at 11:45.

Hyphen (-)

Use a hyphen

- when you write the complete words for numbers between twenty-one and ninety-nine.

    twenty-six   ninety-nine   seventy-two

- when you use a compound adjective before a noun. The compound adjective must express a single thought.

No hyphen	The new employee must work under high pressure.
Hyphen	The new employee has a <u>high-pressure</u> **job**.
	(You cannot say a "high job" or a "pressure job." *High* and *pressure* must go together.)
No hyphen	Our boss is thirty years old.
Hyphen	We have a <u>thirty-year-old</u> **boss**.
	(The words *thirty*, *year*, and *old* express a single thought. You cannot remove one of those words.)

If the adjectives before a noun function independently, do *not* add hyphens.

No hyphen	They renovated an old red barn.
	(The two adjectives function separately.)

HINT: Nonhyphenated Compound Adjectives

Some compound adjectives never take a hyphen, even when they appear before a noun.

World Wide Web   high school senior   real estate agent

Practice 2

Add eight missing colons and hyphens.

EXAMPLE: My ~~brother in law~~ <u>brother-in-law</u> is an inventor.

1. Some of the most high tech innovations of the twenty first century auto industry have come from Tesla Motors CEO Elon Musk. Tesla Motors has a long range project: The company aims to sell fully automated, driverless cars by 2029. This plan has two steps building the cars and creating the program to drive the cars.

2. Elon Musk has had many other successful business SpaceX, Zip2, PayPal, and more. He also has a futuristic idea for replacing high speed rail. His plan, known as the HyperLoop, involves a pressurized tube between Los Angeles and San Francisco. Passengers could theoretically make this trip faster with the HyperLoop than on an airplane.

3. Electric cars are likely to be the wave of the future. Tesla Motors is currently working on their long anticipated Model 3. The car has the following features fast acceleration, 200-mile battery range, and innovative online features. Tesla says they are also trying to make the car affordable for the average consumer.

Ellipsis Marks (. . .)

You may want to quote key ideas from an author, but you do not always want to quote an entire paragraph. Use ellipsis marks to show that you have omitted information from a quotation. The new sentence with an ellipses must be grammatically correct.

When you type an ellipsis mark, leave a space before and after each period. If the omitted section includes complete sentences, then add a period before the ellipses. In the next examples, notice how the quotation changes when ellipses are used.

Original Selection

Many people think that the Inuit language has ten different ways to say the word *snow*. Certainly, snow plays an important role in the daily life of the Inuit. However, this belief is a fallacy.

—Ling Park, student

Quotation with Omissions

Many people think that the Inuit language has ten different ways to say the word *snow*. . . . However, this belief is a fallacy.

—Ling Park, student

GRAMMAR LINK
For more information about quotations, see Chapter 35.

Practice 3

Write quotations incorporating material from each of the next passages. Use ellipses to show where you omit words, and remember to keep important information.

1. Normal thoughts of my future (not pertaining to football), friends, family, reputation, moral status, etc., were entirely beyond me.

—From H.D.'s "Dying to Be Bigger"

According to H.D., _____

_____

_____

2. To top it off, our kids are imbued with victimology, which today has become the American way of blame. It is too routine for adults and their kids to explain all their problems as victimization. When a boy in trouble sees himself as a victim, this festers into seething anger. With easy availability of guns, it can explode as murder.

—From Martin Seligman's "The American Way of Blame"

Martin Seligman says, _____

_____

_____

_____

Reflect On It

Think about what you have learned in this unit. If you do not know an answer, review that concept.

1. List five types of words that require capitalization. For instance, the days of the week begin with capital letters.

   _____

   _____

2. Add hyphens, where necessary, to the following sentences.

   He is a twenty five year old man who carries a small red book in his back pocket.

   He has a high pressure job, but he remains relaxed at work.

3. Correct the four errors in punctuation and capitalization.

   Alberto Vinicio Baez was a prominent mexican-american physicist. Born in Mexico, Baez moved to brooklyn, New York, when he was a boy. After earning several university degrees, he developed the first x-ray microscope and telescope. Two of his daughters became famous folk singers Joan Baez and Mimi Fariña.

Final Review

Correct fifteen capitalization and punctuation (colon and hyphen) errors in the next selection.

EXAMPLE: Facebook developer Mark Zuckerberg is a self-made millionaire.

1.   Facebook has become extremely popular over the years. Millions of people use similar social media sites to reconnect with their long lost friends. Facebook's developer was a twenty-year old Harvard university student. Mark Zuckerberg launched the site in february 2004. The user friendly site fascinated the public. Researchers give three positive outcomes for people using such sites mastering new computer skills, sharing professional information, and increasing social contacts.

2.   However, critics complain about privacy issues on sharing and social media sites. In 2005, two Massachusetts Institute of technology students easily downloaded the personal information of around 70,000 Facebook users. In 2008, the BBC program *click* also acquired personal information of Facebook clients.

3.   People should be careful when using sites like Facebook, instagram, and Snapchat. Avoid sharing the following your birthday, phone number, school, job, and embarrassing photos. Malicious people often search for such information to steal identities. In addition, around 25 percent of employers say that they check the pages of job applicants. For example, Luther Hudson of Wayne and smith, a marketing firm, accessed the personal information of an interviewee on friday, august 6, at 2 20 P.M., about one hour after he had read the applicant's résumé. Hudson saw an embarrassing photo of the candidate mooning her friends. He thought the Applicant lacked good judgment and would not fit into the culture of the company.

The Writer's Room

Write about one of the following topics. Ensure that your capitalization and punctuation are correct.

1. Describe your work environment.
2. What types of jobs does society place a high value on? Describe at least three different categories or types of workers who get a lot of respect.

READING LINK
Readings on workplace issues:
"The Wonders of Power Point" (p. 193)
"Why Small Businesses Fail" (p. 210)
"Aunt Tee" (p. 514)
"Advertising Appeals" (p. 517)
"The Beeps" (p. 519)
"Of Rags and Riches and Social Responsibility" (p. 522)

The Writers' Circle: Collaborative Activity

Work with a partner and think about a job that would interest you. Find a job advertisement from a newspaper, a magazine, or an online site. You could refer to one of the following or look on a local jobs site.

    Monster.com   *Jobs.net*   *usajobs.gov*   *Jobs.org*

    Compose a letter of application. In the first paragraph, explain what job you want, and tell where you heard about the job. In the second paragraph, briefly detail your qualities and experience. Then, in a third paragraph, explain your availability and how you can be contacted. Ask your partner to help you compose each part of the letter.

    Remember to be as direct as possible. After you finish writing, proofread your letter and ensure that you have used correct punctuation and capitalization. Exchange letters with your partner, and proofread your partner's letter.

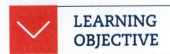

**LEARNING
OBJECTIVE**

37.1 Practice editing
different types of
writing.

In this chapter, you have opportunities to edit different types of writing, including a memo and a letter.

Practice Editing

37.1   Practice editing different types of writing.

After writing the first draft of a paragraph or essay, it is important to edit your work. When you edit, carefully review your writing to verify that your grammar, punctuation, sentence structure, and capitalization are correct. In this chapter, you can practice editing written pieces that you see every day, including e-mail messages, paragraphs, essays, and business correspondence.

Practice 1

Correct twenty errors in the next selection. An editing symbol appears above each underlined error. To understand the meaning of the symbol, refer to the chart at the back of this book.

1.   ^{wc}
     Much news articles focus on natural disasters such as deforestation,

water pollution, and focus on climate change. Such gloomy information

make people very pessimistic about the future of the planet. However the

environmental movement has had some success stories.

2.   In the 1980's, scientists brought a serious problem to the attention of the public who were studying the environment. They noticed that the ozone layer in Earths atmosphere was disappearing. A hole in the ozone was getting more bigger. This phenomena was serious because the ozone protects our planet from the sun's radiation. Chlorofluorocarbons (CFCs) from refrigerators and aerosol sprays were damaging the ozone. Eventually, 197 countrys signed an agreement to limit CFCs in industrial products, and the ozone hole has started to shrink.

3.   By the 1970s, scientists realized that forests and lakes were dying due to acid rain. When fossil fuels burn, they emit chemicals into the air. Causing them to turn into acid. Acid rain damages flora and fauna. In 1990, President George H.W. Bush signs the Clean Air Act Amendments, this act limits the amount of air pollution companies can generate. Since then, air pollution has been reduced.

4.   In 1969, the Cuyahoga River in ohio caught fire because it was one of the most polluted river in the world. As a result, in 1972, Congress past an important piece of legislation: the Clean Water Act. The act focuses on stopping factories from dumping toxic chemicals into rivers. Before the act was approved, most rivers were polluted. Since then, more then two-thirds of all waterways have improved there water quality. Also wetlands are better protected and soil erosion have lessened.

5.   Certainly, the United States faces many challenges to improve the ecosystem. However, Americans will be able to find solutions for environmental problems with creative thinking.

Practice 2

Correct fifteen errors in the next selection. An editing symbol appears above each underlined error. To understand the meaning of the symbol, refer to the chart at the back of this book.

1. Many people think that young <u>americans</u> [cap] are uninterested in politics. However, young people <u>is</u> [agr] at the forefront of some modern political movements. For example, the group Occupy Wall Street was largely composed of young <u>adult</u> [pl]. The group was formed to <u>protested</u> [vt] economic inequality and government bailouts of large banks after the 2008 financial crisis. The protesters fought for the <u>principal</u> [wc] that everyone should be treated <u>equaly</u> [sp] regardless of <u>their</u> [shift] financial wealth. Eventually, the movement lost its force, but the message was <u>real</u> [ad] successful in changing the public perception of income inequality.

2. Police in many countries <u>been criticized</u> [vt] for using excessive force when making arrests. In particular, the treatment of young African American men by police was called into question by members of a political movement that became known as Black Lives Matter. Teenager Michael <u>Browns</u> [P] death at the hands of the police inspired protests in <u>ferguson</u> [cap], Missouri. His death also sparked demonstrations around the country. While some protesters were violent, many were <u>conscious</u> [wc] young people peacefully protesting for social justice. The <u>arguement</u> [sp] about racial bias in <u>goverment</u> [sp] institutions is important. Young people <u>are</u> [vt] a part of the fight for civil rights in the 1960s, and they still play an important role today.

Practice 3

EDIT A PARAGRAPH

There are no editing symbols in the next paragraph. Proofread it as you would your own writing, and correct fifteen errors.

Identity theft is the ilegal use of someones personal information. It is a serious crime, in fact, last year there was over 10 million cases of identity theft in the United States. To find identities, thieves go threw recycling bins, empty garbage cans, and stealing mail to obtain somebodys personal information. Computer hackers can even steal identities by tapping into personal information that persons keep on their computers. When a criminal has stolen a name, birthplace, address, and Social Security number, they can take out credit cards in the victim's name. For example, my coworker, Nick Matsushita. He came home one day and found a large bill from a credit card company. Somebody had use his personal information to apply for credit. Nick and me are good friends, and I know that the identity theft has caused him alot of pain. He says that if he would have known about the way identity thieves work, he would have been more careful with his personal papers. Certainly, victims of identity theft loose time and money trying to fix the problem. To avoid being a victim, be prudent when sharing personal information.

Practice 4

EDIT A WORKPLACE MEMO

Correct nine errors in the next excerpt from a memo.

Re: Parking

To: All Employees

It has been bought to my attention that employees are having problems parking. Because of construction of the new building. To solve a problem, the company have acquired extra parking spaces in the lot across the street. If employees wanna have a parking space, you need an entrance card. The cards are available at the front desk with names of employees. The parking inconvenience is temporary all staff members will be able to park in the regular parking lot in a few weaks.

Chad Renforth

Human Resources Department

Practice 8

EDIT AN ESSAY

Correct twenty errors in the next student essay.

1.   Sports surround us every day in the papers, on television, and on the radio. College sports are particularly popular in the United States. Some critics say that colleges' should pay their student athletes. While the National Collegiate athletic association (NCAA) touts the achievments of athletes in the classroom, the fact is that college sports are a billion-dollar industry. The athletes who provide the entertainment deserve to get remunerated.

2.   First, colleges with good sports teams gets a lot of publicity. A popular football or basketball team could boost enrollment to the school, and three major television networks pays a huge amount of money to broadcast college football games CBS, NBC, and ABC. For the rights to broadcast the college basketball playoffs, March Madness CBS and Time Warner agreed to pay over 10 billions dollars. While NCAA athletes get college scholarships, the organization is not giving any of the huge profits from its television deals to the athletes. The publicity that colleges receive from sports also attract more students to the academic programs, which brings in even more revenue for schools.

3.   In addition several recent studies from prominent economists show that schools are definitely capable of paying their student-athletes. While the NCAA claims that many schools are losing money, some economists think this is a real dubious claim. Most schools don't lose money. They just spend all of the money that come in. These profits are spent in a variety of ways, including on lavish new training facilities for the sports teams and on huge salaries for some coaches.

4.   Moreover, economists have even determined the exact fair market value for high-level college athletes. A 2013 study determined that college football players was worth about $140,000 per year, on average. If college sports teams distributed revenue the same way professionel teams do, they would give over $250,000 per year. To the average men's basketball player.

5.   College administrators and coaches are mostly opposed to paying there student-athletes. So far, they have suceeded in their goal. However, because of public pressure and challenges in the courts the NCAA may be forced to rethink its stance on this issue.

Part V
Reading Strategies and Selections

In Chapter 38, you will learn strategies that can help you improve your reading skills. You will review the reading process, practice previewing, and apply active reading techniques to determine main and supporting ideas. You will also determine word meanings by using context clues, looking at word parts, and using dictionaries effectively. Finally, you will use critical thinking strategies such as inferencing.

In Chapter 39, you will see a number of thought-provoking essays that present a wide range of viewpoints about topics related to popular culture and college life; psychology and health care; our environment and the workplace; and spies, hackers, and the legal world. The writers of these essays achieve their purpose using one or more of these writing patterns: Illustration, Narration, Description, Process, Definition, Classification, Comparison and Contrast, Cause and Effect, and Argument.

38   Reading Strategies

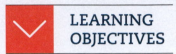

LEARNING OBJECTIVES

38.1 Review steps to become a proficient reader.

38.2 Preview title, headings, and visual cues to determine subject and activate prior knowledge.

38.3 Apply active reading techniques to determine main idea and support.

38.4 Apply vocabulary development skills to figure out word meanings.

38.5 Use clues in the text to infer meaning.

Music students study techniques when they learn to play their instruments. In the same way, you can improve your reading skills by learning different reading strategies.

An Overview of the Reading Process

38.1 Review steps to become a proficient reader.

In college, you will read different types of texts and view many images and videos that may be part of print or online textbooks. You will also write responses or essays to clarify what you have read or offer your own opinions. As a reader and a writer, you engage in similar activities to understand written passages and produce your own texts. For example, when reading an article, you intuitively try to figure out what the writer aims to say and the details used to support that main idea. As a writer, you try to express a clear point of view and give relevant facts, examples, and anecdotes to support your main idea.

Becoming a Proficient Reader

To improve your reading skills, actively engage with what you read. The reading process involves the following steps:

- **Exploring:** Preview the text to get a basic idea of what subject it is about.
- **Understanding vocabulary:** Use strategies to comprehend and remember new vocabulary words.
- **Analyzing the text:** Demonstrate your understanding of the main and supporting ideas by mapping (similar to clustering explained in Chapter 1) as well as summarizing and paraphrasing (see Chapter 15). Also, think critically about the text and formulate opinions about it.

Previewing

38.2 **Preview title, headings, and visual cues to determine subject and activate prior knowledge.**

Previewing is like browsing an online store; it gives you a chance to see what the writer is offering. One way to preview is to **skim** a text. Read it quickly and get the gist or general overview. You can also **scan**, or look, for particular information, such as **key words** and visual clues, so that you can determine the selection's key points. Preview the following:

- Titles or subheadings (if any)
- Table of contents
- The first and last sentences of the introduction
- The first sentence of each paragraph
- The concluding sentences of the selection
- Key words (which may be in bold)
- Any photos, graphs, or charts
- The index, which is at the back of the book

Consider the Topic, Audience, and Purpose

Another previewing strategy is to determine the main point of view of an article. You can examine the **subject** of the text, **purpose** of the author, and the **audience** the author is writing for.

TOPIC

In reading material, the subject or **topic** is what the text is about. Often, the title hints at the subject of a text. For example, a newspaper article titled "Excess Drinking on College Campuses" is likely about student alcohol abuse.

AUDIENCE

Writers write for an intended **audience**. For example, you are the intended audience for your course textbooks. Other types of texts (novels, blogs, journal articles) target different audiences. In those situations, ask yourself who the intended audience might be. For instance, an article in a local newspaper about recycling is probably intended for the town's citizens, while a complex article about neuroscience may be aimed at medical students who have specific knowledge of the subject. If you are asked to read a challenging article, don't panic. Follow the reading process, and you'll be surprised how much information you can grasp.

PURPOSE

An author writes a text for a specific reason. The **purpose** of most texts is to inform, to persuade, or to entertain. Sometimes a writer may have more than one purpose. For example, in an opinion article about the benefits of organic foods, the purposes could be to inform and persuade.

Practice 1

Preview this textbook and answer the following questions.

1. What is the main title of this textbook? _____

2. On what pages is the Table of Contents? _____

3. How many parts does this textbook have? _____

4. What is the title of Chapter 1? _____

5. How many subtitles does Chapter 2 have? _____

6. Refer to the index of this textbook. On what page is "The Sanctuary of School" by Lynda Barry? _____

7. Who is the audience for this textbook? _____

8. What is the purpose of this textbook? _____
   _____

Practice 2

Skim and scan the following text and answer the questions.

CHANGING COMPLEXION OF FARMING

The nature of farming and ranching operations in the U.S. farm sector has changed dramatically during the post–World War II period. The focus of this section is on the collective structure and performance of farmland ranches and on the changing complexion of farming activities in the United States. We can assess these attributes by examining recent trends in the physical structure, productivity, profitability, and financial structure of farms in general.

Physical Structure

An examination of the changing physical structure of the farm sector must necessarily focus on things such as the number and size of farms and ranches, their ownership and control, and the ease of entry into the farm sector.

Number and Size of Farms

A trend toward fewer but larger farms has been occurring. The number of farms has declined from 6.8 million in 1935 (the peak) to about 2.2 million currently (U.S. Department of Agriculture). The number of farms dropped by two-thirds between 1935 and 1974, from 6.8 million to 2.5 million. Since 1974, farm numbers have been more stable, especially since the 1990s.

From John B. Penson Jr., et al. *Introduction to Agriculture Economics*, 6th ed., Pearson, page 19.

1. What is the title of this text? _____

2. By looking only at the title, what is this text about?
   _____

3. Does this text have any subtitles? _____
   If yes, list them. _____

4. What is the third paragraph about? _____
   _____
   _____

Activate Your Prior Knowledge

After you have determined the topic, audience, and purpose of the text, you can activate prior knowledge. What do you already know about the subject? Make a connection between the text and your own experiences and the world at large. For example, you've been asked to read an article titled "Parents Mistrust Vaccinations." You may not know a lot about vaccinations, but you probably know a little. Maybe you've had to decide whether to be vaccinated or have your children vaccinated. Or you might have seen some online headlines about the topic. Here are tips to tap into your prior knowledge about a subject.

- **Brainstorming:** Make a list of the information you already know about the subject. You may also write down what your opinions are on the subject. In this way, you can have a point of reference for further research.

- **Mapping:** Write down the most important word or concept about the topic. Then, think of other ideas that relate to that word and connect them. Keep adding words or even images that link to each other.

Reading Actively

38.3 **Apply active reading techniques to determine main idea and support.**

Find the Main Idea

After you finish previewing, engage in active reading. Search for the **main idea**, which is the central point that the writer is trying to make. In an essay, a college writer usually places the main idea somewhere in the first few paragraphs in the form of a **thesis statement**. However, some professional writers build up to the main idea and state it only in the middle or at the end of the essay. Additionally, some professional writers do not state the main idea directly.

HINT: Missing Statement of Main Idea

If a reading does not contain a clear thesis statement, you can determine the main idea by asking yourself *who*, *what*, *when*, *where*, *why*, and *how* questions. Then, using the answers to those questions, write a statement that sums up the main point of the reading.

Find the Supporting Ideas

Different writers use different types of supporting ideas. They may give steps for a process, use examples to illustrate a point, give reasons for an argument, and so on. Try to identify the author's supporting ideas.

Highlight and Make Annotations

After you read a long text, you may forget some of the author's ideas. To help you remember and quickly find the important points, you can highlight key ideas and make annotations. An **annotation** is a comment, question, or reaction that you write in the margin of a page. Each time you read a passage, follow the next steps.

- Look in the introductory and concluding paragraphs. Underline sentences that sum up the main idea. Using your own words, rewrite the main idea in the margin.

- Underline or highlight supporting ideas. You might even number the arguments or ideas. This will allow you to understand the essay's development.

- Circle words that you do not understand.

- Write questions in the margin if you do not understand the author's meaning.

- Write notes beside passages that are interesting or that relate to your own experiences.

- Jot down any ideas that might make interesting writing topics.

Here is an annotated passage from an essay titled "Don't Worry, Act Happy" by Albert Nerenberg.

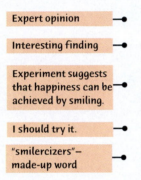

Expert opinion

Interesting finding

Experiment suggests that happiness can be achieved by smiling.

I should try it.

"smilercizers"— made-up word

Robert Kall is a Philadelphia-based Positive Psychology conference organizer. While working as a therapist, he tried simple smiling as a way to treat depression. "I would put surface electrodes on the smile muscles in people's faces and, using electromyography, would measure the strength of their smiles," he said. "People who were not depressed had smile muscles that were on average four times stronger than people who were depressed," he said. This amazed him. So he began developing what could only be described as a smiling exercise program. "I would have depressed people pump 'smile' iron," he said. "I would have them do repetitions: three sets of 12 every day." By naturally triggering smiles, the 'smilercizers' would seem to drive themselves to happier states.

Use the SQ3R Method

Another reading strategy you can use to understand a text is SQ3R, which stands for survey, question, read, recite, and review.

- **Survey** the organization of the text. Look for titles, key words, subtitles, and so on.

- **Question** while you survey. Brainstorm a list of questions about the text. For instance, you can turn titles and headings into questions. You can also ask yourself what you know about the topic.

- **Read** the text and look for answers to your questions.

- **Recite** what you have read. Look away from the text and orally answer the questions. Only look at the text if you can't find an answer.

- **Review** what you have read. Check the main headings and subheadings again and recall your questions.

Understanding Difficult Words

38.4 **Apply vocabulary development skills to figure out word meanings.**

When you read a document and come across a new word, what do you generally do? If you skip over difficult words, you might end up with a very fuzzy idea about what you read. Constantly using a dictionary or glossary slows down your reading and may make you feel frustrated.

An effective way to determine a word's meaning is to look for hints in the surrounding words and sentences. **Context clues** are hints in the text that help define a word.

> For example, can you define *fabricated*? Yes ___ No ___
>
> Can you define *cognizant*? Yes ___ No ___

Now read the words in context, and you should be able to guess what they mean.

> Maude's classmates had stopped believing her stories. They knew that Maude had fabricated most of them. She slowly became cognizant of their attitude.

Now write your own definitions of the words.

1. fabricated: _____

2. cognizant: _____

HINT: Cognates

Cognates are English words that may look and sound like words in another language. For example, the English word *adoption* is similar to the Spanish word *adopcion*, but it is spelled differently.

If English is not your first language, and you see an English word that looks similar to a word in your language, check how the word is being used in context. It may or may not mean the same in English that it means in your language. For example, in English, *actual* means "real." In Spanish, *actual* means "current." Both English and German have the word *fast*, but in German it means "almost." If you are not sure of a word's meaning, you can always consult a dictionary.

Use Context Clues

An effective way to determine a word's meaning is to look for **context clues**—hints in the surrounding words and sentences. Look for the following types of context clues.

DEFINITION OR RESTATEMENT

Writers, and especially textbook authors, often provide complete definitions of difficult words to ensure that readers will understand.

> A **correlation** shows the relationship between two variables.

SYNONYM

Sometimes, instead of defining a word, writers simply put a **synonym**—a word or phrase that is close in meaning—to help readers understand the term.

> Anya coveted—or desired—the silver bracelet.
>
> (*Desired* is a synonym for *coveted*.)

ANTONYM

An **antonym** is a word that has the opposite meaning of another word. By understanding the contrasting word, you can guess the difficult word's meaning.

> Sean Drake was optimistic after his job interview but became pessimistic when he didn't hear from the human resources recruiter for a week.
>
> (*Optimistic* is the opposite of *pessimistic*, which means "gloomy.")

EXAMPLE

Writers sometimes include examples that make a word's meaning clear.

> The water in the pond was foul. Oily scum, banana peels, and cigarette butts were floating on top.
>
> (The examples help you understand that *foul* means "filthy.")

LOGICAL DEDUCTION

Often, you can **infer**—or guess—a word's meaning simply by using your reasoning skills. Maybe the tone or atmosphere helps you guess. The surrounding sentences can also help you determine the word's meaning. In the following sentence, you can guess the meaning of *disconcerted*.

> Samira was disconcerted when she heard that she was being transferred to a new city. She had just started to make friends here and did not want to move again.
>
> (You can deduce that *disconcerted* means "upset.")

Practice 3

Guess the meanings of the words in bold. First, look for and underline the context clues in the sentence. Then use your own words to define each word.

EXAMPLE:

During the 1950s, the sitcom *I Love Lucy* was popular and influential, but the writers could not **breach** the censorship rules.

      breach: _break_

1. In 1952, Lucille Ball could not **utter** the word "pregnant" on air when she was expecting her baby. At the time, "pregnant" was considered a vulgar and distasteful term.

      utter: _____

2. Censorship rules were very **stringent** at that time. There were severe penalties if television networks broadcast certain profane words.

      stringent: _____

3. To avoid using the word "pregnant," Lucille Ball used **euphemisms** such as "expecting" or "in the family way."

      euphemisms: _____

4. The actress could only use words that were **deemed** appropriate by the censorship board. Banned words, such as "sex" and "virgin," were considered scandalous.

      deemed: _____

5. CBS executives even **balked** at the idea that Lucy could share a bed with her on-screen—and real-life—husband Desi Arnaz Jr. Instead, the couple's TV bedroom had two single beds.

      balked: _____

6. In many ways, *I Love Lucy* was a groundbreaking series, and Lucille Ball was a powerful **trailblazer**. For instance, she insisted on casting her Cuban husband in the series, even though the network strongly objected.

      trailblazer: _____

Practice 4

Guess the meanings of difficult words by using context clues. Choose the word that best defines the word in bold.

1. According to Desmond Morris, some gestures originate in infancy. A baby's earliest activity is to suck at its mother's breast. This involves **pursing** the lips, and the expression survives into adulthood as a kiss.

    a. opening   c. putting into a handbag

    b. raising the corners in a smile   d. pushing together

2. The refugees on the border are in **dire** need of food and water. They have not eaten for two days.

    a. desperate   c. said

    b. unnecessary   d. reduced

3. The officer's **demeanor** was respectful and polite. She listened and responded thoughtfully.

    a. appearance   c. behavior

    b. agreement   d. information

4. After looking at the architect's plans and recommendations, the committee determined that the project was **viable**. They would find contractors and begin the job in the spring.

    a. workable   c. harmful

    b. impossible   d. expensive

Understand Word Parts

Another effective way to understand difficult words is to look at the word's structure. Often, there are clues within a word that can help you determine the meaning. All words have a root, but some longer and more complex words may have a **prefix** before the root word or a **suffix** after it.

Words have the following parts. Become familiar with the following terms.

ROOT WORDS AND BASE WORDS

The **root** is the basic part of a word that contains the core meaning. For example, *compilation* contains the root word *compile*. Most root words are also **base words**: That is, they can stand alone. *Interest*, *help*, and *play* are root—and base—words.

Some words have more than one root. A **compound word** has two.

    root   root

note + book = notebook

Some Common Root Words

Some root words are the starting points for larger words. For instance, *bio* means "life," but it can't stand alone. It needs to be combined with a suffix such as *-logy* to create the word *biology*. Review some common root words that generally do not stand alone.

Root	Meaning	Example	Definition
aud / audit	sound	audible	able to be heard
bio	life	biography	story of a life
corp	body	corpse	dead body
cred	believe	credible	believable
man	hand	manual	done by hand
mater	mother	maternal	motherly
pater	father	patricide	killing of a father
psych	mind	psychology	study of the mind
socio	society	sociology	study of society
spect	see	spectator	viewers

PREFIXES

A prefix appears at the beginning of a word, and it modifies the word's meaning. For example, *un-* means "not," *anti-* means "against," and *pre-* means "before."

prefix root
anti + biotic = antibiotic

Some Common Prefixes

Prefix	Meaning	Example	Definition
ante- / pre-	before	prejudge	judge before
bi-	two	bicycle	two wheels
semi-	half	semicircle	half a circle
multi- / poly-	many	multipurpose	many purposes
micro- / mini-	small	minibus	small bus
mega-	large	megaproject	large project
post-	after	postpartum	after birth
quad-	four	quadruped	four footed
re-	again	review	view again
tri-	three	triangle	three angles
uni- / mono-	one	monochrome	one color

SUFFIXES

A suffix is added to the ending of a word, and it can change a word's meaning and part of speech. For example, when you add the suffix *-ful* to the verb *hope,* you end up with the adjective *hopeful.* Words can have more than one suffix. For instance, *helpfully* is made of the root word *help* and two suffixes: *ful + ly.*

root verb suffix noun
suggest + ion = suggestion

Some Common Suffixes

Suffix	Meaning	Example	Definition
-al	process of	refusal	process of refusing
-able	able to be	preventable	able to be prevented
-aholic / -oholic	with an obsession	workaholic	obsessed with work
-arian	a person who	vegetarian	a person who eats vegetables
-arium / -orium	a place for	auditorium	a place for listening
-dom	quality / realm	kingdom	realm or place of the king
-er / -or	one who	teacher	one who teaches
-ful	full of	peaceful	full of peace
-less	without	hopeless	without hope
-ness / -ship	state of being	sadness	state of being sad
-phile	love of	anglophile	one who admires English culture

Practice 5

Underline the root word in each item.

EXAMPLE: <u>employ</u>ment

1. movement
2. magician
3. uninteresting
4. nonconformist
5. disorderly
6. unlockable
7. hyperactivity
8. undependable
9. disrespectable

Practice 6

Use your own words to define the words in bold. Look at the parts of the word to help you guess the meaning.

1. The journalist made mistakes partially because she was rushing to meet the **inescapable** deadlines of the daily newspaper.

_____

2. Micropreneurs start their own businesses but are satisfied with keeping their businesses small in an effort to achieve a balanced lifestyle.

_____

3. The emotions that most often **underlie** riots are anger and hostility.

_____

4. The lawyer's actions were **indefensible**, and the bar association forced her to leave the profession.

_____

5. The patients' **socioeconomic** status was considered before the doctor decided on the course of treatment.

_____

6. The Wrights are **francophiles**; they visit Quebec each summer to revel in the unique cuisine and culture.

_____

7. Our neighbour's son Casey is **multlingual**; he speaks Vietnamese, French, and some Russian.

_____

8. The new high school principal is a harsh **disciplinarian**.

_____

HINT: Economic or Economical?

Economic refers to the economy. *Economical* means "cheap or inexpensive."

> The government will unveil its new **economic** policy.
> An **economical** way to visit New York is by train.

Use a Dictionary and Thesaurus

DICTIONARY

If you do not understand the meaning of an unfamiliar word after using context clues, look up the word in a dictionary. You might check an online dictionary, a smartphone app, or a word processor's built-in dictionary. Review the following tips.

- **Look at the dictionary's front matter if using a print dictionary.** The preface contains explanations about the various symbols and abbreviations.
- **Read all of the definitions listed for the word.** Look for the meaning that best fits the context of the sentence you are reading.
- **Look up root words, if necessary.** If the difficult word has a prefix such as *un-* or *anti-*, you may have to look up the root word.

THESAURUS

A thesaurus provides **synonyms** (words with a similar meaning) and **antonyms** (words with an opposite meaning). To avoid repeating the same word over and over in a text, writers use synonyms. When reading a text, make sure that you understand the meaning of the word that the writer intended. Sometimes synonyms are similar but not exactly the same in meaning. For example, look at the various synonyms for the word *lazy*. Some of the words have particular nuances, or shades of meaning.

> **lazy**, adj: easygoing, idle, lax, lackadaisical, laidback, lethargic, negligent, slothful, slack

ONLINE AND ELECTRONIC RESOURCES

Here are some digital options for looking up words:

- Online sites—including *Merriam-Webster, Oxford, Dictionary.reference.com*, and the *Longman Dictionary of Contemporary English*—offer word origins, spellings, meanings, pronunciations, and more.
- Smartphone apps offer word meanings, synonyms, antonyms, and even language translations.
- Word processing programs have built-in dictionary and thesaurus functionality. For example, in MS Word, you can right-click on words, and a menu appears that includes a definition, synonym, and translation.

Review some features of an online dictionary.

Part of Speech
You can see that *deception* is a noun.

Word Division
Black dots indicate places for dividing words.

Pronunciation
Click on loudspeakers to hear the word's pronunciation.

deception *noun*

◀)) | Menu

de·cep·tion [uncountable and countable]
the act of deliberately making someone believe something that is not true [↪ deceive]:
◀) *She didn't have the courage to admit to her deception.*
◀) *He was convicted of **obtaining money by deception**.*

Definition from the Longman Dictionary of Contemporary English
Advanced Learner's Dictionary.

Making Inferences

38.5 Use clues in the text to infer meaning.

Sometimes, writers do not state points of view obviously. That is, in a paragraph, you may not find the topic sentence because the author has not stated it concretely. He or she may have suggested the point of view. You, the reader, must use critical thinking skills, or inferring, to figure it out. When you **infer**, you "read between lines" and use clues in the text to understand its meaning. To infer, follow the next steps:

- Read the paragraph carefully and search for details.
- Verify any meanings of words you don't know.
- Ask *who*, *what*, *where*, *when*, *why*, and *how* questions.
- Jot down the facts and other important ideas. Make a list of any details, opinions, or information given by the author.
- Think about causes and effects.
- Activate your background knowledge of the topic. What information or opinion do you already have?

EXAMPLE

Henry sat down in the chair and laid two pens and a pencil on his desk. His teacher reminded students to put their names on the upper right-hand corner of the paper. Henry slowly picked up the document in front of him and began to read. He frowned as he started looking at the first question. But as he continued reading, he wriggled in his chair to become more comfortable. His shoulders relaxed. He placed the sheet of paper carefully down on his desk and picked up his pen. He was smiling as he started to write the answer to the question.

1. Who is Henry? _He is a student._
2. Where is Henry? _He is in class or in an exam room._
3. What is Henry doing? _He is taking a test._

You can infer that Henry knew the answers to the test because _he became comfortable, his shoulders relaxed, and he smiled as he started to answer the questions_.

Practice 7

Read the next paragraphs and answer the questions. Read between the lines and make inferences, or guesses, based on the information in the text.

A.   Brandon strolled down the country lane. Tiffin ran in circles around Brandon barking and yelping. It was their first outing together since Brandon had adopted Tiffin, who was very excited and wagged his tail continuously. Brandon spotted a stick, bent down, picked it up, and raised his arm to throw it. Tiffin's demeanor suddenly changed; he whimpered and cowered.

1. Who is Tiffin? _____

2. How did Brandon get Tiffin? _____

3. What did Tiffin do when Brandon raised his arm? _____

_____

4. What can you infer about Tiffin's behavior when Brandon wanted to throw a stick?

_____

_____

B.   Lindsay stood on the rock staring at the whirling water all around her. Then she saw the puffed-up blue denim shirt and the thin white arm sticking out of it. She came to her senses and lay down on her stomach on the rugged rock and inched her way forward until she was half hovering over the flowing water. With her left hand, she grabbed the arm and with her right hand, she grabbed the pant legs by the belt. She pulled with all her might and dragged Lucius onto the rock. His frightened eyes stared at her as he started coughing.

1. Where was Lindsay? _____

2. What did Lindsay see in the water? _____

_____

3. What did Lindsay do? _____

_____

4. What can you infer happened to Lucius? _____

_____

In the next chapter, you practice the reading strategies you've learned in this chapter (and throughout *The Writer's World*) by reading professional essays, articles, and other texts. The questions about each selection help reinforce previewing, focusing on vocabulary, and looking for bias and hidden meaning.

LEARNING OBJECTIVES

39.1 Analyze reading selections.

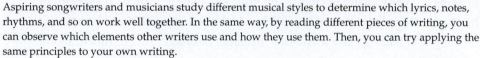

Aspiring songwriters and musicians study different musical styles to determine which lyrics, notes, rhythms, and so on work well together. In the same way, by reading different pieces of writing, you can observe which elements other writers use and how they use them. Then, you can try applying the same principles to your own writing.

The Link Between Reading and Writing

The ability to understand another writer's ideas and express your own ideas in written form is very useful in your personal, academic, and professional life.

After you finish reading a selection, you could try these writing strategies to make sure that you have understood it.

Summarize the reading. When you summarize, you use your own words to write a condensed version of the reading. You leave out all information except for the main points. You can find a detailed explanation about summaries in Chapter 15.

Outline the reading. An outline is a visual plan of the reading that looks like an essay plan. First, you write the main idea of the essay, and then write down the most important idea from each paragraph. You could make further indentations, and under each idea, include a detail or example.

Analyze the reading. When you read, look critically at the writer's arguments and evaluate them, point by point. Also analyze how the writer builds the argument and ask yourself questions such as *Do I agree? Are the author's arguments convincing?* Then, when you write your analysis, you can break down the author's explanations and either refute or agree with them, using your own experiences and examples to support your view.

Write a response. Your instructor may ask you to write about your reaction to a reading. These are some questions you might ask yourself before you respond in writing.

- What is the writer's main point?
- What is the writer's purpose? Is the writer trying to entertain, persuade, or inform?
- Who is the audience? Is the writer directing his or her message at someone like me?
- Do I agree or disagree with the writer's main point?
- Are there any aspects of the topic to which I can relate? What are they?

Reading Selections

Popular Culture and College Life

Psychology and Health Care

Our Environment and The Workplace

Spies and Hackers and The Legal World

Reading Selections

39.1 Analyze reading selections.

Themes: Popular Culture and College Life

Reading 1
Being a Hyphenated American

Zaina Arafat

Zaina Arafat is a young Arab American. In the next essay, she reflects on identity and culture. As you read this definition essay, also look for elements of narration and comparison and contrast.

1   During the 1991 Persian Gulf War, I came home from school one day in tears. My classmates had been ridiculing me, and when I told my mother, she went straight to the administration. She said that during this particularly emotional time, they should make extra efforts to prevent discrimination against Arab-American students. They agreed, and assured her that they would. Months later, I came home complaining of the same torment: "They're still calling me fat! Zaina AraFAT!" Right then, my mother realized the teasing had nothing to do with my ethnic background. It was simply kids being kids. As a first-generation Arab-American, my ethnic duality has exposed me to a series of assumptions that stem from both ignorance and fear of the unknown. But these assumptions exist on both sides.

2   My parents moved to the United States from the West Bank a year before I was born. Growing up in the suburbs of Washington, D.C., my family seemed just like everyone else's, with a few variations that most wouldn't have noticed. For example, while my friends' fathers cracked open a bag of chips after work, my dad went straight for pumpkin seeds. My friends' moms drove minivans; mine, a two-seater. Their parents were big on curfews, grammar, "time outs," and seat belts. Soda was strictly forbidden in their houses, as were Cocoa Puffs for breakfast, and television was allowed only on weekends.

3   I really didn't understand these rules. Since the American tendency toward overparenting contradicted my parents' Mediterranean, **laissez-faire** approach, the structure and what I saw as rigidity that existed in my friends' houses were absent in ours. Rather, our family was informal and spontaneous.

laissez-faire: permissive

4   My friends found much in my life to be confused by, too, such as why my mom and dad called me mom and dad, as is tradition in Arab culture. They wondered why my parents and their friends seemed to be yelling at each other whenever they conversed, why every social gathering inevitably ended with dancing, and why our nicknames were longer than our actual ones: Zanzoon for Zaina; Abu Zooz for my brother, Zaid.

5   As a kid, I was insecure about the nuances that set us apart, especially when friends asked for a bologna sandwich as soon as they saw whatever we were serving. But as I grew older, I began to appreciate my parents' attempt

hummus: a spread made with chickpeas, lemon, garlic, and salt, very common in Middle Eastern cooking

to assimilate while retaining our own traditions. We always had a turkey on Thanksgiving—that it was stuffed with rice and served with **hummus** seemed a fair compromise.

6   I found that while being an Arab-American in the US got better with age, the reverse applied when I visited the Middle East. As a kid, I couldn't wait for these summer excursions. The moment I arrived in Jordan, where my extended family lives, I felt like a celebrity. I was coming from America, and that alone brought me relative fame and adoration. But eventually, things began to change. No longer able to get a free ride because of my American identity, I found there were many unspoken rules that were unfamiliar to me, such as when to put out my hand versus going for the cheek, and if the latter, two kisses or three? Also, no one wears shorts past the age of twelve. (Once on a visit to Bethlehem, my uncle had to trade me his trousers for my cutoffs.)

7   Despite the humbling, awkward moments that accompanied these lessons, I've begun to accept the potential for mistakes as an inevitable cross-cultural byproduct. And in doing so, I've realized that being Arab-American has different meanings, depending on where I am. In the Middle East, it often means having to stress that Americans shouldn't be equated with their country's foreign policy. In the US, it involves explaining that the Islamists shown on television represent a sliver of the Muslim population. It also entails reminding Americans that while **Al Jazeera** may seem oversensationalized, American media seems sanitized to Arabs.

Al Jazeera: a news network based out of Qatar

8   In many ways, "having a foot in both worlds" means having a full presence in neither. Although the phrase isn't meant to be interpreted literally, after twenty-seven years of balancing between two cultures and continents, I can say with certainty that it's far from figurative. But it's from such a vantage point that stereotypes are abolished. And as I get further away from a cultural identity crisis—and as a Kenyan-American was able to become US president—I realize that having dual ethnicity may be a great thing after all.

Vocabulary and Comprehension

1. In paragraph 5, what does the word *nuances* mean?
   a. colors   b. problems   c. subtle differences

2. Find a word in paragraph 6 that means the "second of two choices."

   _____

3a. Where are the writer's parents originally from?

   _____

3b. Where do they live presently?

   _____

4. What were some cultural differences the author mentions between her "American" friends and her own family? List at least three differences.

   _____

   _____

   _____

   _____

Critical Thinking

5. What is the significance of the title?

_____

_____

6. What example does the author use to show that her family tried to integrate into American society?

_____

_____

7. How does the author show that cultural misunderstandings are not just one-sided?

_____

_____

_____

_____

_____

8. How does the author's attitude toward her dual heritage change?

_____

_____

Writing Topics

Write about one of the following topics. Remember to explore, develop, and revise and edit your work.

1. In paragraph 8, the author writes, "'having a foot in both worlds' means having a full presence in neither." Do you agree or disagree with this statement? Give examples to support your ideas.

2. How do you define yourself: as an American or a hyphenated American? Explain your answer.

3. America promotes itself as a melting pot rather than a mosaic. In your opinion, which idea is better?

Reading 2
Domains of Sacred Consumption

Michael R. Solomon

Michael R. Solomon teaches marketing and consumer behavior at St. Joseph's University. His articles have appeared in *Psychology Today*, *Newsweek*, and *The New York Times*. As you read this classification essay, look for elements of illustration, definition, and cause and effect.

1   Many types of consumer activities involve the demarcation of categories, such as good versus bad, male versus female—or even regular cola versus diet. One of the most important categories is sacred consumption. Sacred consumption occurs when we "set apart objects and events from normal activities and treat them with respect or awe." Note that in this context the term sacred does not necessarily carry a religious meaning. We find ways to set apart

all sorts of places, people, and events. Sacred consumption permeates many aspects of our lives.

Sacred Places

2   A society sets apart sacred places because they have religious or mystical significance (e.g., Bethlehem, Mecca, Stonehenge) or because they commemorate some aspect of a country's heritage (e.g., the Kremlin, the Emperor's Palace in Tokyo, the Statue of Liberty, or, more recently, Ground Zero in Manhattan). Contamination makes these places sacred: Something sacred happened on that spot, so the place itself takes on sacred qualities. Hard-core fans buy Yankees Sod, the first officially licensed grass. Although it costs a few thousand dollars to fill out a good-sized lawn, proud fans can boast of turf that grows from the same seeds the groundskeepers use at the stadium, and the sod comes with a certificate of authenticity from Major League Baseball and a counterfeit-proof hologram that declares it the official grass of the New York Yankees.

3   Still other places start out as profane, but we endow them with sacred qualities. Grauman's Chinese Theater in Hollywood, where movie stars leave their footprints in concrete for posterity, is one such place. Theme parks are a form of mass-produced fantasy that take on aspects of sacredness. In particular, Disney World and Disneyland—and their outposts in Europe, Japan, and China—are destinations for "pilgrimages" by consumers around the globe. Disney World displays many characteristics of more traditional sacred places. Some even believe it has healing powers, which helps to explain why a trip to the park is the most common "last wish" for terminally ill children.

4   As the saying goes, "Home is where the heart is." In many cultures, the home is a particularly sacred place. It's a barrier between the harsh, external world and consumers' "inner space." Americans spend more than $50 billion a year on interior decorators and home furnishings, and their home is a central part of their identity. People all over the world go to great lengths to create a feeling of "homeyness." They personalize their dwellings with door wreaths, mantel arrangements, and a "memory wall" for family photos. Even public places such as Starbucks cafés strive for a homelike atmosphere to shelter customers from the harshness of the outside world.

Sacred People

5   At her Web site *livingoprah.com*, superfan Robyn Okrant blogs about her devotion to Oprah Winfrey—and the year she spent living her life completely guided by Oprah's advice about what to eat, wear, and read. In her mission statement, she speculates, "I wonder, will I find bliss if I commit wholeheartedly to her lifestyle suggestions?"

6   We idolize sacred people as we set them apart from the masses, and sometimes people come to believe that these individuals have "superhuman" abilities. Souvenirs, memorabilia, and even mundane items these celebrities have touched acquire special meanings (the celebrities "contaminate" the items). Newspapers pay paparazzi hundreds of thousands of dollars for candid shots of stars or royalty. Indeed, many businesses thrive on consumers' desire for products they associate with the famous. There is a flourishing market for autographs of celebrities, and objects owned by celebrities, such as Princess Diana's gowns or John Lennon's guitars.

Sacred Events

7   Sometimes public events resemble sacred, religious ceremonies. Think about fans who hold their hands over their hearts and solemnly recite the "Pledge of Allegiance" before a ballgame, or how others reverently light matches (or hold up illuminated cell phones) during a rock concert.

8   The world of sports is sacred to many of people—recent doping and gambling scandals aside. We find the roots of modern sports events in ancient religious rites, such as fertility festivals (e.g., the original Olympics). And it's not uncommon for teams to join in prayer prior to a game. The sports pages are like the scriptures (and we all know ardent fans who read them "religiously"), the stadium is a house of worship, and the fans are members of the congregation. Devotees engage in group activities, such as tailgate parties and the "Wave," where sections of the stadium take turns standing up. The athletes and coaches that fans come to see are godlike; devotees believe they have almost super-human powers. One study documented more than 600 children whose parents named them after the legendary University of Alabama coach Paul "Bear" Bryant!

9   Athletes are central figures in a common cultural myth known as the *hero tale*. In these stories, the player must prove himself under strenuous circumstances, and he achieves victory only through sheer force of will. On a more mundane level, devotees consume certain ritual artifacts during these ceremonies (such as hot dogs at the ballpark). Sales of snack foods and beverages spike around the time of the Super Bowl; people spend $10 million more on tortilla chips than during a normal two-week period and more than $15 million extra on beer in the weeks surrounding the big game.

10   Tourism is another category of sacred experience. People occupy sacred time and space when they travel on vacation—though they may not think so if they get stuck sleeping on an airport floor because of a flight delay. The tourist searches for "authentic" experiences that differ from his normal world (think of Club Med's motto, "The antidote to civilization"). This traveling experience involves binary oppositions between work and leisure and being "at home" versus "away." Often, people relax everyday (profane) norms regarding appropriate behavior as tourists, and participate in illicit or adventurous experiences they would never engage in at home. ("What happens in Vegas, stays in Vegas.")

11   The desire of travelers to capture these sacred experiences in objects forms the bedrock of the souvenir industry, which really sells sacred memories. Whether it's a personalized matchbook from a wedding or New York City salt-and-pepper shakers, a souvenir represents a tangible piece of the consumer's sacred experience. In addition to personal mementos, such as ticket stubs someone saves from a favorite concert, these are some other sacred souvenir icons: local products (wine from California); pictorial images (postcards); "piece of the rock" (seashells, pine cones); symbolic shorthand in the form of literal representations of the site (a miniature Statue of Liberty); and markers (Hard Rock Café t-shirts).

Vocabulary and Comprehension

1. Find a word in paragraph 10 that means *illegal*. _____

2. Highlight the thesis statement.

3. What are the three main categories explained in this essay?

   _____

   _____

4. What is this essay's classifying principle?

   _____

   _____

5. In your own words, define each category.

   _____

   _____

   _____

   _____

6. Give some examples in each category.

   _____

   _____

   _____

   _____

   _____

Critical Thinking

7. List other examples of sacred places, people, or events. You will have to use your prior knowledge (see Chapter 38, "Reading Strategies," page 475).

   _____

   _____

8. Why do people make certain places, people, or events "sacred"? You will have to infer or make a guess.

   _____

   _____

9. This essay lacks a conclusion. On a separate piece of paper, write a possible conclusion.

Writing Topics

1. Classify your hobbies or interests. Give examples to support each category.

2. What family traditions do you follow? Classify your family traditions into three categories.

_____

Reading 3
Emojis

Celine Cooper

Celine Cooper is a columnist for the *Montreal Gazette*. Her articles have appeared in *BBC World News*, *Inside Policy*, and others. As you read this definition essay, look for elements of illustration and argument.

1   Last week, the Oxford Dictionaries chose its Word of the Year for 2015: "Face with Tears of Joy" emoji. Citing a swell in emoji culture over the last year, Oxford Dictionaries and the London-based Swiftkey, a company that develops keyboard

apps for smartphones, undertook research to see which images were being most frequently used. They found that "Face with Tears of Joy"—a yellow, saucer-shaped face with an open smile and tears of laughter spurting out of its eyes—totalled 20 percent of all emoji use in the United Kingdom and 17 percent in the United States. Emoji, for the uninitiated, are small digital images used in electronic communication that are designed to express a feeling, idea, or emotion. Emojis are emerging as a language of the global elite.

2   A man named Shigetaka Kurita who worked for a telecom company called NTT DoCoMo originally developed them in Japan during the late 1990s. The word "emoji" is derived from a combination of the Japanese terms *e* meaning "picture," and *moji* meaning "word." Today, these small images take on hundreds of shapes. You can find pictures of sushi rolls and burritos, hands clapping and clasped in prayer, sad and happy faces, hearts, cigarettes, wine glasses and high-heeled shoes. They can be beamed all over the world by all kinds of people who may not speak the same language but can express complex ideas with a shared use of a simple image.

3   It has been noted that the 2015 Word of the Year selection follows a recent trend from Oxford Dictionaries in highlighting "words" that are associated with tech culture. For example, the US Word of the Year in 2012 was "GIF" and 2013's Word of the Year was "selfie."

4   The "Face with Tears of Joy" emoji beat out a bunch of other contenders on the shortlist this year. Some of those include Ad blocker ("a piece of software designed to prevent advertisements from appearing on a web page") and On Fleek ("extremely good, attractive, or stylish"—a term popularized in 2014 by a woman named Kayla Newman as she referred to her eyebrows in a short online Vine video). Other contenders are the following: Brexit ("A term for the potential or hypothetical departure of the United Kingdom from the European Union"); sharing economy ("An economic system in which assets or services are shared between private individuals either for free or for a fee, typically by means of the Internet"—think Airbnb or Uber); and lumbersexual ("a young urban man who cultivates an appearance and style of dress typified by a beard and check shirt suggestive of a rugged outdoor lifestyle").

5   Languages are always evolving and adapting to the needs of their users. The President of Oxford Dictionaries, Casper Grathwohl, issued a statement saying, "You can see how traditional alphabet scripts have been struggling to meet the rapid-fire, visually focused demands of 21st century communication. . . . It's not surprising that a pictographic script like emoji has stepped in to fill those gaps—it's flexible, immediate, and infuses tone beautifully. As a result, emoji are becoming an increasingly rich form of communication, one that transcends linguistic borders." In other words (or pictures, as the case may be), emojis are a trend pointing us toward a changing language in a changing society.

6   At the same time, it is important to point out that most people in the world still have no access to the new communication technologies—smartphones, tablets, computers—that offer these new linguistic shortcuts. This is why, in a strange way, these little electronic images may already be emerging as a language of the global elite. I wonder if there is an emoji for that.

Vocabulary and Comprehension

1. In your own words, define an "emoji." _____

_____

2. Find a word in paragraph 2 that means "sent." _____

3. How was the first "emoji" developed? _____

_____

4. Which category of words has increased in dictionaries such as Oxford?

_____

Critical Thinking

5. How have emojis helped people overcome language barriers? _____

_____

6. What are some advantages of using emojis to communicate? You will have to infer or guess.

_____

_____

7. What are some disadvantages of using emojis as a method of communication? You will have to infer or guess.

_____

_____

_____

_____

8. What is the author's attitude toward the subject?

_____

_____

Writing Topics

1. What is *popular culture*? Write about popular culture and use examples to illustrate your point.

2. What steps should people take to learn another language?

_____

Reading 4
This Boat Is My Boat

Drew Hayden Taylor

Drew Hayden Taylor is a playwright and author. His writings include essays and short stories about First Nations cultures and concerns. As you read this comparison and contrast essay, also look for elements of argument and cause and effect.

1 F. Scott Fitzgerald once wrote, "The rich are different from you and me," to which everybody usually responds, "Yeah, they've got more money." On a similar theme, it's been my Ojibwa-tainted observation over the years that "middle-class white people are different from you and me." They're insane. Much has been written over the years about the differences between native

people and nonnative people, and the way they view life. There's no better example of this admittedly broad opinion than in the peculiar world of outdoor recreational water sports and the death wish that inspires them.

2   As a member of North America's indigenous population, I've cast a suspicious glance at all these waterlogged enthusiasts for several reasons. The principal one is the now familiar concept of cultural appropriation—this time of our methods of water transportation. On any given weekend, our rivers are jam-packed with plastic and fiberglass kayaks and canoes, hardly any of them filled with authentic Inuit or First Nations people, all looking to taunt death using an aboriginal calling card.

3   Historically, kayaks and canoes were the life's blood of Inuit and native communities. They were vital means of transportation and survival, not toys to amuse bored weekend warriors. For instance, there is a brand of gloves used by kayakers to protect their hands from developing calluses, called Nootkas. To the best of my knowledge, the real Nootka, a West Coast First Nation, neither kayaked nor wore gloves.

White-water kayaking

4   Let's examine the different ways these two cultural groups react to a single visual stimulus. A group of native people and white people sit in two separate canoes before a long stretch of roaring rapids—with large pointy rocks and lots and lots of turbulent white water. Watch the different reactions. Granted, I'm generalizing, but I think I can safely say the vast majority of native people, based on thousands of years of traveling the rivers of this great country of ours, would probably go home and order a pizza, or possibly put the canoe in their Ford pickup and drive downstream to a more suitable and safe location. Usually, the only white water native people enjoy is in their showers. Hurtling toward potential death and certain injury tends to go against many traditional native beliefs. Contrary to popular assumption, "portage" is not a French word—it is Ojibwa for "Are you crazy? I'm not going through that! Do you know how much I paid for this canoe?" When sunburned Caucasian canoeists are in the same position, their natural inclination is to aim directly for the rapids, paddling as fast as they can toward the white water.

5   Recently, for purely anthropological reasons, I risked my life to explore the unique subcultures of white-water canoeing and sea kayaking. There is also a sport known as white-water kayaking, but I have yet to put that particular bullet in my gun. So for three days, I found myself in the middle of Georgian Bay, during a storm, testing my abilities at sea kayaking. With me were a former Olympic rower, a Quebecois lawyer, a leading diabetes specialist, and a six-foot-seven ex-Mormon. We bonded over four-foot swells and lightning. The higher the waves, the more exciting they found the experience.

6   Various indigenous populations developed other sports that have been corrupted and marketed as something fun to do when not sitting behind a desk in a high-rise office building. The Scandinavian **Sami** were instrumental in the development of skiing, though I doubt their motivation was to hurl themselves down as fast as gravity and snow would allow. The same could be said of bungee jumping. Originally a coming-of-age ritual in the South Pacific, young boys would build platforms, tie vines to their legs, and leap off to show their bravery and passage into adulthood. The same motivation doesn't drive today's bungee jumpers.

Sami: indigenous people inhabiting the Arctic area of Sápmi

7   I have brought up the issue of recreational cultural appropriation many times with a friend who organizes these outdoor adventures. The irony is she works at a hospital, and she chews me out for not wearing a helmet while biking. She says there is no appropriation. If anything, her enthusiasm for the sports is a sign of respect and gratefulness.

8   People should pay a royalty of sorts every time they try to kill themselves using one of our aboriginal cultural legacies. Of course, no aboriginal group has ever sought a patent or copyright protection for kayaks or canoes—that was not part of the treaty negotiations. But somebody should definitely investigate the possibility. Or better yet, every time nonnatives go white-water canoeing or kayaking, they should first take an aboriginal person to lunch. That is a better way of showing respect and gratefulness, and it involves much less paperwork.

Vocabulary and Comprehension

1. What is the ethnic background of the author of this text?

_____

2. In your own words, describe the author's thesis. Write a thesis statement.

_____

_____

_____

3. What examples does the author use to support his thesis?

_____

_____

_____

_____

_____

_____

4. In paragraph 2, what is *cultural appropriation*?

_____

_____

Critical Thinking

5. What does the author think about white middle-class people who borrow native traditions?

_____

_____

6. In which paragraph does the author acknowledge the opposition when he discusses *cultural appropriation*? What point does he make?

_____

_____

7. What is the general tone of the author toward his subject?
  a. angry   b. sad   c. amused   d. serious

8. What does the author want the nonnatives to understand?

_____

_____

Writing Topics

Write about one of the following topics. Remember to explore, develop, and revise and edit your work.

1. Compare and contrast one of the following: two risky sports, two different holidays, two different brands of the same product, two different cultural traditions, or two different vacations.

2. Do you have a favorite activity or pastime? Describe it. It could be a sports activity or a leisure activity.

3. Drew Hayden Taylor uses humor to make fun of an ethnic group: Caucasians. What are some positive and/or negative effects of ethnic humor?

Reading 5
It's Class, Stupid!

Richard Rodriguez

Richard Rodriguez is a writer and an essayist who published the novel *Days of Obligation*. He also writes for the *Los Angeles Times* and *Harper's*. The next selection is an argument essay about affirmative action that originally appeared in the online magazine *Salon.com*. As you read, also look for elements of the comparison and contrast writing pattern.

1   Some weeks ago, a law professor at the University of Texas got in trouble for saying that African Americans and Mexicans are at a disadvantage in higher education because they come from cultures that tolerate failure. Jesse Jackson flew to Austin to deliver a fiery speech; students demanded the professor's **ouster**.

ouster: dismissal

2   It was all typical of the way we have debated affirmative action for years. Both sides ended up arguing about race and ethnicity; both sides ignored the deeper issue of social inequality. Even now, as affirmative action is finished in California and is being challenged in many other states, nobody is really saying what is wrong with affirmative action: It is unfair to poor whites.

3   Americans find it hard to talk about what Europeans more easily call the lower class. We find it easier to sneer at the white poor—the "rednecks," the trailer-park trash. The rural white male is Hollywood's politically correct villain **du jour**.

du jour: French term meaning "of the day" or "at the present time"

4   We seem much more comfortable worrying about race; it's our most important metaphor for social distinction. We talk about the difference between black and white, not the difference between rich and poor. American writers—Richard Wright, James Baldwin, Toni Morrison—are brilliant at describing what it is like to be a racial minority. But America has few writers who describe as well what it is like to be poor. We don't have a writer of the stature of D.H. Lawrence—the son of an English coal miner—who grew up embarrassed by his soft hands. At the University of Texas, it was easier for the Sicilian-born professor Lino Graglia to notice that the students who dropped out of school were Mexican American or black than to wonder if they might be poor.

5   At the same time, the angry students who accused the law professor of racism never bothered to acknowledge the obvious: Poor students *do* often come from neighborhoods and from families that tolerate failure or at least have learned the wisdom of slight expectations. Education is fine, if it works. I meet young people all the time who want to go to college, but Mama needs her oldest son to start working. It is better to have a dollar-and-cents job working at Safeway or McDonald's than a college diploma that might not guarantee a job.

6   Anyone who has taught poor children knows how hard it is to persuade students not to be afraid of success. There is the boy who is mocked by male classmates for speaking good English. There is the girl who comes from a family where women are assumed not to need, or want, education.

7   We also don't like to admit, though we have argued its merits for twenty years, that the chief beneficiaries of affirmative action—black, brown, female—are primarily middle class. It still doesn't occur to many progressives that affirmative action might be unfair to poor whites. That is because poor whites do not constitute an officially recognized minority group. We don't even notice the presence or, more likely, the absence of the poor white on college campuses. Our only acknowledgment of working-class existence is to wear fashionable working-class denim.

8   A man I know, when he went to Harvard, had only a pair of running shoes to wear and had never owned a tie. He dropped out of Harvard after two years. I suppose some of his teachers imagined it was because he was Hispanic, not that he was dirt poor. The advantage I had, besides my parents, were my Irish nuns—who themselves had grown up working class. They were free of that middle-class fear (typical today in middle-class teachers) of changing students too much. The nuns understood that education is not an exercise in self-esteem. They understood how much education costs, the price the heart pays.

9   Every once in a while, I meet middle-class Americans who were once lower class. They come from inner cities and from West Texas trailer parks. They are successful now beyond their dreams, but bewildered by loss, becoming so different from their parents. If only America would hear their stories, we might, at last, acknowledge social class. And we might know how to proceed, now that affirmative action is dead and so many poor kids remain to be educated.

Vocabulary and Comprehension

1. Find a word in paragraph 6 that means "made fun of."

   _____

2. What does the word *constitute* in paragraph 7 mean? Circle the best answer.
   a. govern   b. appoint   c. represent

3. Look in the first two paragraphs and underline the thesis statement.

4. According to the author, what prevents many poor people from attending college? Give at least three reasons.

_____

_____

_____

5. Who benefits the most from affirmative action, according to the author?

_____

_____

Critical Thinking

6. Explain why Rodriguez disagrees with affirmative action.

_____

_____

_____

7. The author compares English writer D.H. Lawrence with American writers such as Toni Morrison. How is this comparison relevant for this essay?

_____

_____

_____

8. In paragraph 1, Rodriguez includes an anecdote about a University of Texas law professor. Explain why the author agrees or disagrees with the professor.

_____

_____

_____

_____

9. The author writes that his teachers, Irish nuns with working-class backgrounds, "understood how much education costs, the price the heart pays." What does he mean? (Look in paragraphs 8 and 9 for clues.)

_____

_____

_____

_____

Writing Topics

Write about one of the following topics. Remember to explore, develop, and revise and edit your work.

1. In your employment or education, have you had any positive or negative experiences because of your economic, gender, ethnic, or racial background?

2. Do you agree or disagree with the author's argument? Support your point of view with specific examples.

3. Writer James Baldwin once said that being poor has high costs. What are the costs? Give examples or anecdotes to support your ideas.

Reading 6
Why Diversity on Campus Matters

Matthew Lynch

Matthew Lynch is a writer, blogger, and educator. He has written *The Call to Teach* and is the editor of *The Edvocate*. As you read this argument essay, also look for elements of illustration and cause and effect.

1   It's easy to think of college campuses as islands—academic havens that have little interaction with the greater world beyond. In reality, the work done on the grounds of colleges and universities has a big impact on society, from medical breakthroughs to mass adoption of social change. It's important then that US institutions of higher learning are representative of society as a whole in their student bodies and staff. That's easier said than done, of course, but multicultural representation on college campuses should be a top priority. Beyond the boost a multicultural campus brings to the immediate student and faculty body, it also contributes to the "real" after-college world.

2   First, feeding diversity from colleges into the professional workforce goes a long way toward pay equality and ups the standard of living for minorities and women. The latest numbers from the Bureau of Labor Statistics finds that women make 78 cents for every dollar earned by a man in the United States. The racial pay gap varies, but in industries such as technology, minority workers make $3,000 to $8,000 less than their white counterparts. By having more diversity in the amount of highly educated workers, Americans have a better shot at getting rid of the nasty wage gap for good. Not only will these educated workers be more apt to ask for what they are worth, but more diversity will emerge in positions of leadership, those that make salary decisions.

3   Racial tensions have spiked in recent years, accented by the deaths of Michael Brown in Ferguson, Missouri, and Eric Garner in New York City. Diversity on campus could help ease such tensions in society as a whole. It is easier to judge and alienate hypothetical people whom we have never actually met. And in our nation's public schools, diversity is difficult to achieve in districted areas. Children go to school alongside their neighbors—people who often look like them, have a similar socioeconomic background, and have the same basic life experience. Colleges and universities are able to break out of this mold, and they can be the first pass at diversity that students experience. It's important to maximize that opportunity by making sure not just campuses, but individual programs, are well represented with students from a variety of racial and socioeconomic backgrounds.

4   Moreover, diversity in colleges will help the United States compete better on the world stage. The more ideas brought to a discussion, the better the chance of a good one. When a variety of perspectives are pooled, innovation and creativity emerge. Nations such as Japan have always had an academic edge, but Americans often win out because of the one thing that just can't be taught: visionary thinking. When everyone brings the same experience to a problem, there will be fewer ways to solve it. A diverse college body means a more diverse workforce after graduation. This heterogeneity helps everyone. When the United States succeeds on the world stage, all Americans benefit.

5   Diversity matters on college campuses and not just for the benefit of those institutions. Could the next generation of college grads be the one to help the United States surge ahead of world competitors through collective creativity? Could the next generation of college grads be the one to eliminate the wage gap and to put an end to discrimination? All of these accomplishments are on the horizon in the United States, and colleges and universities can give them all a boost by fostering multiculturalism and diversity on campuses.

Vocabulary and Comprehension

1. In paragraph 3, what does *alienate* mean?
   a. turn off   b. be strange   c. create a distance

2. In paragraph 4, find a word that means "combined"? _____

3. Highlight the thesis statement.

4. Underline the topic sentences of each body paragraph.

5. In your own words, sum up the three points the author makes to support the thesis. _____

_____

Critical Thinking

6. What types of details does the author use to support his main idea? You can circle more than one answer.

   a. statistics   d. logical consequences
   b. informed opinions   e. answering the opposition
   c. facts

7. How will diversifying a college student body help women and minorities in the workforce?

_____

_____

8. How can student diversity help ease racial tensions?

_____

_____

9. How does the United States have an economic advantage over Japan?

_____

_____

_____

10. What are some factors that may prevent colleges from attracting students from different backgrounds? Make inferences or guesses based on information in the text.

_____

_____

_____

Writing Topics

1. What is your view about equality? Should laws protect some members to ensure equal access to work, education, and housing? Why or why not?

2. List examples of ways in which people are stereotyped. You can discuss age, gender, race, and so on.

Themes: Psychology and Health Care

Reading 7
The Catcher of Ghosts

Amy Tan

Amy Tan is an American writer. One of her most well-known novels is *The Joy Luck Club*. She has explored themes such as mother–daughter relationships and cultural issues. As you read this descriptive story, which appeared in her book *The Bonesetter's Daughter*, also look for elements of narration and cause and effect.

1   When we returned home, Mother and Father, as well as our aunts and uncles, were bunched in the courtyard talking in excited voices. Father was relating how he had met an old Taoist priest at the market, a remarkable and strange man. As he passed by, the priest had called out to him: "Sir, you look as if a ghost is plaguing your house."

2   "Why do you say that?" Father asked.

3   "It's true, isn't it?" the old man insisted. "I feel you've had a lot of bad luck and there's no other reason for it. Am I right?"

4   "We had a suicide," Father admitted, "a nursemaid whose daughter was about to be married."

5   "And bad luck followed."

6   "A few calamities," Father answered.

7   The young man standing next to the priest then asked Father if he had heard of the famous Catcher of Ghosts. "No? Well, this is he, the wandering priest right before you. He's newly arrived in your town, so he's not yet as well known as he is in places far to the north and south. Do you have relatives in **Harbin**? No? Well, then! If you had, you'd know who he is." The young man, who claimed to be the priest's acolyte, added, "In that city alone, he is celebrated for having already caught one hundred ghosts in disturbed households. When he was done, the gods told him to start wandering again."

8   When Father finished telling us how he had met these two men, he added, "This afternoon, the famous Catcher of Ghosts is coming to our house."

9   A few hours later, the Catcher of Ghosts and his assistant stood in our courtyard. The priest had a white beard, and his long hair was piled like a messy bird's nest. In one hand he carried a walking stick with a carved end that looked like a flayed dog stretched over a gateway. In the other, he held a short beating stick. Slung over his shoulders was a rope shawl from which hung a large wooden bell. His robe was not the sand-colored cotton of most wandering monks I had seen. His was a rich-looking blue silk, but the sleeves were grease-stained, as if he had often reached across the table for more to eat.

10   I watched hungrily as Mother offered him special cold dishes. It was late afternoon, and we were sitting on low stools in the courtyard. The monk

Harbin: a large town in northeastern China

helped himself to everything—glass noodles with spinach, bamboo shoots with pickled mustard, tofu seasoned with sesame seed oil and coriander. Mother kept apologizing about the quality of the food, saying she was both ashamed and honored to have him in our shabby home. Father was drinking tea. "Tell us how it's done," he said to the priest, "this catching of ghosts. Do you seize them in your fists? Is the struggle fierce or dangerous?"

11   The priest said he would soon show us. "But first I need proof of your sincerity." Father gave his word that we were indeed sincere. "Words are not proof," the priest said.

12   "How do you prove sincerity?" Father asked.

13   "In some cases, a family might walk from here to the top of Mount Tai and back, barefoot and carrying a load of rocks." Everyone, especially my aunts, looked doubtful that any of us could do that.

14   "In other cases," the monk continued, "a small offering of pure silver can be enough and will cover the sincerity of all members of the immediate family."

15   "How much might be enough?" Father asked.

16   The priest frowned. "Only you know if your sincerity is little or great, fake or genuine."

17   The monk continued eating. Father and Mother went to another room to discuss the amount of their sincerity. When they returned, Father opened a pouch and pulled out a silver **ingot** and placed this in front of the famous Catcher of Ghosts.

> **ingot:** pieces of metal historically used as currency

18   "This is good," the priest said. "A little sincerity is better than none at all."

19   Mother then drew an ingot from the sleeve of her jacket. She slid this next to the first so that the two made a clinking sound. The monk nodded and put down his bowl. He clapped his hands, and the assistant took from his bundle an empty vinegar jar and wad of string.

20   "Where's the girl that the ghost loved best?" asked the priest.

21   "There," Mother said, and pointed to me. "The ghost was her nursemaid."

22   The priest said to me, "Fetch me the comb she used for your hair."

23   My feet were locked to the ground until Mother gave me a little knock on the head to hurry. So I went to the room Precious Auntie and I had shared not so long before. I picked up the comb she used to run through my hair. It was the ivory comb she never wore, its ends carved with roosters, its teeth long and straight. I remembered how Precious Auntie used to scold me for my tangles, worrying over every hair on my head.

24   When I returned, I saw the assistant had placed the vinegar jar in the middle of the courtyard. "Run the comb through your hair nine times," he said. So I did.

25   "Place it in the jar." I dropped the comb inside, smelling the escape of cheap vinegar fumes. "Now stand there perfectly still." The Catcher of Ghosts beat his stick on the wooden bell. It made a deep kwak, kwak sound. He and the acolyte walked in rhythm, circling me, chanting, and drawing closer. Without warning, the Catcher of Ghosts gave a shout and leapt toward me. I thought he was going to squeeze me into the jar, so I closed my eyes and screamed, as did **GaoLing**.

> **GaoLing:** the girl's younger sister

26   When I opened my eyes, I saw the acolyte was pounding a tight-fitting wooden lid onto the jar. He wove rope from top to bottom, bottom to top, then all around the jar, until it resembled a hornet's nest. When this was done, the Catcher of Ghosts tapped the jar with his beating stick and said, "It's over. She's caught. Go ahead. Try to open it, you try. Can't be done."

27   Everyone looked, but no one would touch. Father asked, "Can she escape?"

28   "Not possible," said the Catcher of Ghosts. "This jar is guaranteed to last more than several lifetimes."

Vocabulary and Comprehension

1. Find a word in paragraph 7 that means "helper."

_____

2. Why do Mother and Father need the services of the Catcher of Ghosts?

_____

_____

3. Who is the ghost and what relationship did it have with the family?

_____

4. A simile is a comparison using *like* or *as*. Underline an example of a simile that the author uses to describe the priest.

5. The author uses imagery in this essay. Give an example of the following.

sight: _____

_____

sound: _____

_____

smell: _____

_____

touch: _____

_____

Critical Thinking

6. Who is Precious Auntie?

_____

_____

7. What can you infer, or guess, about the Catcher of Ghosts when he asks for "proof of sincerity?"

_____

_____

8. What can you infer about the characters of Mother and Father from their actions?

_____

_____

_____

Writing Topics

Write about one of the following topics. Remember to explore, develop, and revise and edit your work.

1. Describe an incident from your childhood or the childhood of your parents or grandparents. Try to use descriptive imagery.

2. Describe a family tradition. Give as many details as possible using the five senses.

3. What are some examples of superstitions that people have?

Reading 8
The Sanctuary of School

Lynda Barry

Lynda Barry is a cartoonist, writer, and playwright. Her work includes graphic novels and the syndicated comic strip *Ernie Pook's Comeek*. As you read this narrative essay, also look for elements of description.

1   I was seven years old the first time I snuck out of the house in the dark. It was winter, and my parents had been fighting all night. They were short on money and long on relatives who kept "temporarily" moving into our house because they had nowhere else to go.

2   My brother and I were used to giving up our bedroom. We slept on the couch, something we actually liked because it put us that much closer to the light of our lives, our television. At night when everyone was asleep, we lay on our pillows watching it with the sound off. We watched Steve Allen's mouth moving. We watched Johnny Carson's mouth moving. We watched movies filled with gangsters shooting machine guns into packed rooms, dying soldiers hurling a last grenade, and beautiful women crying at windows. Then the sign-off finally came, and we tried to sleep.

3   The morning I snuck out, I woke up filled with a panic about needing to get to school. The sun wasn't quite up yet, but my anxiety was so fierce that I just got dressed, walked quietly across the kitchen, and let myself out the back door.

4   It was quiet outside. Stars were still out. Nothing moved, and no one was in the street. It was as if someone had turned the sound off on the world.

5   I walked the alley, breaking thin ice over the puddles with my shoes. I didn't know why I was walking to school in the dark. I didn't think about it. All I knew was a feeling of panic, like the panic that strikes kids when they realize they are lost.

6   That feeling eased the moment I turned the corner and saw the dark outline of my school at the top of the hill. My school was made up of about fifteen nondescript portable classrooms set down on a fenced concrete lot in a rundown Seattle neighborhood, but it had the most beautiful view of the Cascade Mountains. You could see them from anywhere on the playfield, and you could see them from the windows of my classroom—Room 2.

7   I walked over to the monkey bars and hooked my arms around the cold metal. I stood for a long time just looking across Rainier Valley. The sky was beginning to whiten, and I could hear a few birds.

8   In a perfect world, my absence at home would not have gone unnoticed. I would have had two parents in a panic to locate me, instead of two parents in a panic to locate an answer to the hard question of survival during a deep financial and emotional crisis.

9   But in an overcrowded and unhappy home, it's incredibly easy for any child to slip away. The high levels of frustration, depression, and anger in my house made my brother and me invisible. We were children with the sound turned off. And for us, as for the steadily increasing number of neglected children in this country, the only place where we could count on being noticed was at school.

10   "Hey there, young lady. Did you forget to go home last night?" It was Mr. Gunderson, our janitor, whom we all loved. He was nice and he was funny and he was old with white hair, thick glasses, and an unbelievable number of keys. I could hear them jingling as he walked across the playfield. I felt incredibly happy to see him.

11   He let me push his wheeled garbage can between the different portables as he unlocked each room. He let me turn on the lights and raise the window shades, and I saw my school slowly come to life. I saw Mrs. Holman, our school secretary, walk into the office without her orange lipstick on yet. She waved. I saw the fifth-grade teacher, Mr. Cunningham, walking under the breezeway eating a hard roll. He waved.

12   And I saw my teacher, Mrs. Claire LeSane, walking toward us in a red coat and calling my name in a very happy and surprised way, and suddenly my throat got tight and my eyes stung and I ran toward her crying. It was something that surprised us both.

13   It's only thinking about it now, twenty-eight years later, that I realize I was crying from relief. I was with my teacher, and in a while I was going to sit at my desk, with my crayons and pencils and books and classmates all around me, and for the next six hours I was going to enjoy a thoroughly secure, warm, and stable world. It was a world I absolutely relied on. Without it, I don't know where I would have gone that morning.

14   Mrs. LeSane asked me what was wrong, and when I said, "Nothing," she seemingly left it at that. But she asked me if I would carry her purse for her, an honor above all honors, and she asked if I wanted to come into Room 2 early and paint.

15   She believed in the natural healing power of painting and drawing for troubled children. In the back of her room, there was always a drawing table and an easel with plenty of supplies, and sometimes during the day she would come up to you for what seemed like no good reason and quietly ask if you wanted to go to the back table and "make some pictures for Mrs. LeSane." We all had a chance at it—to sit apart from the class for a while to paint, draw, and silently work out impossible problems on 11 × 17 sheets of newsprint.

16   Drawing came to mean everything to me. At the back table in Room 2, I learned to build myself a life preserver that I could carry into my home.

17   We all know that a good education system saves lives, but the people of this country are still told that cutting the budget for public schools is necessary, that poor salaries for teachers are all we can manage, and that art, music, and all creative activities must be the first to go when times are lean.

18   Before- and after-school programs are cut, and we are told that public schools are not made for baby-sitting children. If parents are neglectful temporarily or permanently, for whatever reason, it's certainly sad, but their unlucky children must fend for themselves. Or slip through the cracks. Or wander in a dark night alone.

19   We are told in a thousand ways that not only are public schools not important, but that the children who attend them, the children who need them most, are not important either. We leave them to learn from the blind eye of a television or to the mercy of "**a thousand points of light**" that can be as far away as stars.

a thousand points of light: a spirit of volunteerism encouraged by former president Bush

20   I was lucky. I had Mrs. LeSane. I had Mr. Gunderson. I had an abundance of art supplies. And I had a particular brand of neglect in my home that allowed me to slip away and get to them. But what about the rest of the kids who weren't as lucky? What happened to them?

21   By the time the bell rang that morning, I had finished my drawing, and Mrs. LeSane pinned it up on the special bulletin board she reserved for drawings from the back table. It was the same picture I always drew—a sun in the corner of a blue sky over a nice house with flowers all around it.

22   Mrs. LeSane asked us to please stand, face the flag, place our right hands over our hearts, and say the Pledge of Allegiance. Children across the country do it faithfully. I wonder now when the country will face its children and say a pledge right back.

Vocabulary and Comprehension

1. Find a word in paragraph 6 that means "uninteresting."

_____

2. What type of narrator is telling this story?
   a. first person   b. third person

3. When and where does the story take place?

_____

_____

4. Why did the author sneak out of her house and go to the school?

_____

_____

Critical Thinking

5. Describe the author's family life. You will have to infer or guess.

_____

_____

_____

6. In paragraph 6, the author writes that she stopped feeling anxious when she saw the school. What are some reasons that she felt secure at the school?

   _____

   _____

   _____

7. In paragraph 9, the author writes, "We were children with the sound turned off." What does she mean?

   _____

   _____

8. What role did Mrs. LeSane play in the author's childhood?

   _____

   _____

   _____

9. According to the author, how does the public school system of her childhood compare to the public school system of today?

   _____

   _____

   _____

10. The author uses imagery—description using the senses—to depict her environment. Give an example of each of the following types of imagery.

    Sight: _____

    _____

    Sound: _____

    _____

    Touch: _____

    _____

Writing Topics

1. Narrate an event that happened in your childhood at school. How did you feel?
2. Who was your childhood role model? Was it a parent, a teacher, or another adult? Explain why you respected this person.
3. Describe what the ideal classroom would look like. Mention the space, the type of teachers, and the activities in an ideal classroom.

Reading 9
Planting False Memories

Sarah Barmak

Sarah Barmak is a freelance journalist and author. Her work has appeared in *Macleans'*, The *Globe and Mail*, and *The Toronto Star*, among other publications. In this illustration essay, she examines how fragile memory can be. As you read, also look for elements of cause and effect and argument.

1   **Subject:** "I remember the two cops. There were two. I know that for sure. . . I have a feeling, like, one was white, and one maybe Hispanic. . . I remember getting in trouble. And I had to like, tell them what I did. And why I did it, and where it happened. . ."

2   **Interviewer:** "You remember yelling?"

3   **Subject:** "I feel like she called me a slut. And I got ticked off and threw a rock at her. And the reason why I threw a rock at her was because I couldn't get close to her. . ."

4   The person being interviewed is confessing on videotape to a serious crime—throwing a rock so hard at a girl's head that it left her bleeding and unconscious. But the assault in this story never happened. The interviewee was the unknowing subject of an experiment showing that innocent people can be led to falsely remember having committed crimes as severe as assault with a weapon. The new study proves for the first time what psychologists have long suspected: Manipulative questioning tactics used by police can induce false memories and produce false confessions.

5   Published in *Psychological Science* by Julia Shaw and Stephen Porter, the study holds striking implications for the justice system. "The human mind is very vulnerable to certain tactics in interviews," Porter said. Shaw and Porter recruited seventy University of British Columbia (UBC) students who had never committed a crime and told them they would be taking part in a study about how well people could remember their childhoods. They asked students' past caregivers for details about a vivid event that had taken place in the students' lives between ages eleven and fourteen, such as an accident or an emotional first day at school. Caregivers and students agreed not to communicate about the experiment while it was ongoing.

6   Researchers questioned the students for three sessions of about forty minutes each. The researchers told participants that their caregivers had discussed two past events. One event was true and one was fabricated by the psychologists. The false event was described in general terms—simply "an assault" or an incident where the student was in contact with the police. If subjects said they couldn't remember the false event, questioners reassured students that they would be able to retrieve their "lost memories" if they tried hard enough. If they began to "remember," experimenters asked for more detail: "Do you recall any images? How did you feel? Visualize what it might have been like, and the memory will come back to you."

7   By the end of the third interview, more than 70 percent of subjects came to believe that they had committed a crime just five or so years in the past. They didn't merely agree that they had done what the experimenters suggested; they generated all the details of the crime. They recalled vivid sensory memories and often became emotional and guilt-ridden. Some students persisted in believing they were guilty even after they were told the "crime" had been invented. "A few people argued with the experimenter and said, 'Well, no, I know this happened,'" says Porter.

8   Do you think that's scary? The psychologists did. "We ended the study prematurely," says Porter. Once he and Shaw had interviewed sixty of the students and realized the proportion of them generating false memories was high enough to support their hypothesis, they decided to spare the remaining subjects the unnecessary upheaval. It's the stuff of disturbing sci-fi fantasies such as *Inception* and *Blade Runner*: planting an idea or memory in another's

mind that's so convincing, the person believes it's his own. Except it isn't science fiction; it's science fact. And instead of fanciful technology, all the psychologists needed to implant a false idea was a room, three hours, and some innocent-sounding questions.

9   A few details make this study different from a police interrogation. Subjects may have been less afraid to admit a crime to psychologists than to police. Also, subjects were being questioned about an act committed five years in the past, but police investigations often involve questioning about events that are decades old. Police regularly interrogate suspects for far longer, are more confrontational, and wear suspects down emotionally.

10   The UBC study is only the latest to show that false memories can be induced, adding to a growing consensus that memory is inherently fragile. Harvard psychologist Daniel Schacter has shown that memory is always in part a construction—a delicate process of rebuilding. Even vivid recollections can get distorted because of the way we recount them to others, our mood, or whether we've had enough sleep. While this changeable, plastic model of memory has become standard in psychology and neuroscience, in the justice system, an older, outdated model persists. "(It's) the old view that memory works as a videotape," says Porter. "The ancient Greeks used to talk about the storehouse of memory or the wax tablet of memory."

11   The Reid police questioning model is an often aggressive technique meant to confirm suspects' guilt rather than uncover the facts. The American technique, which allows interviewers to lie to suspects, has become standard around the world. False memories are responsible for countless false convictions and wrongful imprisonments, Porter believes. A well-known US exoneration involved a man convicted on the basis of the Reid interrogation technique. Texan Chris Ochoa spent twelve years in prison for a murder he confessed to after two lengthy interrogations. He was freed when DNA evidence proved his innocence. In fact, the Innocence Project has found that at least 30 percent of cases in which convicts have been exonerated by DNA testing involved false confessions. Some of those may have involved falsely-induced memories.

12   Porter believes both police and the law need an overhaul in the way they treat testimony and confessions. He argues eyewitness testimony is valuable and can be largely accurate if suspects are questioned in ways that help preserve their recall. "The message I try to get across to the officers is that memory is like a crime scene," says Brent Snook, a professor of psychology. "One of the first things you don't want to be doing at a crime scene is contaminating it. You make sure no one gets in there and starts moving evidence around." Advocates hope that changes to interrogation methods will come soon.

Vocabulary and Comprehension

1. Find a word in paragraph 6 that means "invented." _____
2. What introductory style does the author use?
    a. general background   b. anecdote   c. historical
3. Highlight the thesis statement.

4. This essay uses an extended example to support the main idea. Briefly describe the extended example. Answer these questions about the study.

   a. Who conducted the study? _____

   b. How many students participated in the study? _____

   c. What did the students think the study was about?

   _____

Critical Thinking

5. In the study, what techniques did the researchers use to manipulate the participants?

   _____

   _____

6. Why did the students believe the lie even after they were told that the crime had been invented? Make an inference or guess.

   _____

   _____

   _____

7. Why did the psychologists end the study early? Read paragraphs 7 and 8 and make an inference or guess.

   _____

   _____

   _____

8. The writer compares and contrasts the UBC study and police interrogation techniques. What are some similarities and differences?

   Similarities: _____

   _____

   _____

   _____

   _____

   Differences: _____

   _____

   _____

   _____

9. In this illustration essay, the writer also makes an argument. What does she hope to achieve with this essay?

   _____

   _____

   _____

Writing Topics

1. Write an illustration essay about some of your best memories. List at least three memories.

2. Write about a time when you lied to someone. What happened? What were the repercussions?

Themes: Our Environment and The Workplace

Reading 10
Mother Nature's Melting Pot

Hugh Raffles

Hugh Raffles is an anthropologist and author who writes about the relationship between humans and animals. His most recent book is *Insectopedia*. As you read this cause and effect essay, also look for patterns in illustration and comparison and contrast.

1 The anti-immigrant sentiment sweeping the country, from draconian laws in Arizona to armed militias along the Mexican border, has taken many Americans by surprise. It shouldn't—nativism runs deeply in the United States. Just ask our nonnative animals and plants: They too are commonly labeled as aliens, even though they also provide significant benefits to their new home. But just as America is a nation built by waves of immigrants, our natural landscape is a shifting mosaic of plant and animal life. Like humans, plants and animals arrive unannounced, encounter unfamiliar conditions, and proceed to remake each other and their surroundings.

2 Designating some species as native and others as alien denies this ecological and genetic dynamism. It draws an arbitrary historical line based as much on aesthetics, morality, and politics as on science, a line that creates a mythic time of purity before places were polluted by interlopers. What's more, many of the species we now think of as natives may not be especially well suited to being here. They might be, in an ecological sense, temporary residents, no matter how permanent they seem to us. These "native" species can have serious effects on their environment. Take the mountain pine beetle: Thanks to climate change, its population is exploding in the West, devastating hundreds of thousands of square miles of forest.

3 It's true that some nonnative species have brought with them expensive and well-publicized problems; zebra mussels, nutria, and kudzu are prime examples. But even these notorious villains have ecological or economic benefits. Zebra mussels, for example, significantly improve water quality, which increases populations of small fish, invertebrates, and seaweeds—and that, in turn, has helped expand the number of larger fish and birds. Indeed, nonnative plants and animals have transformed the American landscape in unmistakably positive ways. Honeybees were introduced from Europe in the 1600s, and new stocks from elsewhere in the world have landed at least eight times since. They have succeeded in making themselves indispensable, economically and symbolically. In the process, they have made us grateful that they arrived, stayed, and found their place.

4 But the honeybee is a lucky exception. Today, a species' immigration status often makes it a target for eradication, no matter its effect on the environment. Eucalyptus trees, charged with everything from suffocating birds with their resin to elevating fire risk with their peeling bark, are the targets of large-scale

Eucalyptus trees

felling. Yet eucalyptuses are not only majestic trees popular with picnickers, but are also one of the few sources of nectar available to northern Californian bees in winter and a vital destination for migrating monarch butterflies.

5   There are plenty of less controversial examples. Nonnative shad, crayfish, and mud snails provide food for salmon and other fish. Nonnative oysters on the Pacific Coast build reefs that create habitat for crab, mussels, and small fish, appearing to increase these animals' populations. The ice plant, a much-vilified Old World succulent, spreads its thick, candy-colored carpet along the California coast. Concerned that it is crowding out native wildflowers, legions of environmental volunteers rip it from the sandy soil and pile it in slowly moldering heaps along the cliffs. Yet the ice plant, introduced to the West Coast at the beginning of the twentieth century to stabilize railroad tracks, is an attractive plant that can also deter erosion of the sandstone bluffs on which it grows.

6   Efforts to restore ecosystems to an imagined pristine state almost always fail. Once a species begins to thrive in a new environment, there's little we can do to stop it. Indeed, these efforts are often expensive and can increase rather than relieve environmental harm. An alternative is to embrace the impurity of our cosmopolitan natural world and, as some biologists are now arguing, to consider the many ways that nonnative plants and animals—not just the natives—benefit their environments and our lives.

7   Last month, along with 161 other immigrants from more than 50 countries, I attended an oath-swearing ceremony in Lower Manhattan and became a citizen of the United States. In a brief speech welcoming us into a world of new rights and responsibilities, the presiding judge emphasized our diversity. It is, he said, the ever-shifting diversity that immigrants like us bring to this country that keeps it dynamic and strong. These familiar words apply just as meaningfully to our nation's nonnative plants and animals. Like the humans with whose lives they are so entangled, they too are in need of a thoughtful and inclusive response.

Vocabulary and Comprehension

1. Find a word in paragraph 1 that means "harsh." _____

2. Underline the thesis statement of this essay.

3. What are some positive effects that at least two nonnative species might have on the environment?

_____

_____

_____

4. What measures do well-meaning eco-volunteers take to protect the landscape from nonnative species?

_____

5. Why do such measures usually fail?

_____

_____

_____

Critical Thinking

6. Why does the author compare anti-immigrant sentiment to plants and animals?

_____

_____

7. Why does the author think it is wrong to categorize some species as nonnative and others as native?

_____

_____

_____

_____

8. What lessons about human immigration can we learn from animal and plant migration?

_____

_____

Writing Topics

Write about one of the following topics. Remember to explore, develop, and revise and edit your work.

1. What are some causes and effects of natural disasters?

2. What are some reasons that people move to other countries?

3. Most Americans are descendants of immigrants. Luis Gutierrez, a politician, once said that the older immigrants fear the newcomers. Write a response. For instance, you can define a "real American" or discuss fear of outsiders, or you could explain how you are a descendant of immigrants.

Reading 11
Aunt Tee

Maya Angelou

Maya Angelou is a poet, historian, civil rights activist, and writer. In this next essay from her collection *I Wouldn't Take Nothing for My Journey Now*, Angelou writes about an important person in her life. As you read this description essay, also look for elements of narration and comparison and contrast.

1   Aunt Tee was a Los Angeles member of our extended family. She was seventy-nine when I met her, sinewy, strong, and the color of old lemons. She wore her coarse, straight hair, which was slightly streaked with gray, in a long braided rope across the top of her head. With her high cheekbones, old gold skin, and almond eyes, she looked more like an Indian chief than an old black woman. (Aunt Tee described herself and any favored member of her race as Negroes. *Black* was saved for those who had incurred her disapproval.)

2   She had retired and lived alone in a dead, neat ground-floor apartment. Wax flowers and china figurines sat on elaborately embroidered and heavily starched doilies. Sofas and chairs were tautly upholstered. The only thing at ease in Aunt Tee's apartment was Aunt Tee.

3   I used to visit her often and perch on her uncomfortable sofa just to hear her stories. She was proud that after working thirty years as a maid, she spent the next thirty years as a live-in housekeeper, carrying the keys to rich houses and keeping meticulous accounts. "Living in lets the white folks know Negroes are as neat and clean as they are, sometimes more so. And it gives the Negro maid a chance to see white folks ain't no smarter than Negroes. Just luckier. Sometimes."

4   Aunt Tee told me that once she was housekeeper for a couple in Bel Air, California, and lived with them in a fourteen-room ranch house. There was a day maid who cleaned, and a gardener who daily tended the lush gardens. Aunt Tee oversaw the workers. When she began the job, she cooked and served a light breakfast, a good lunch, and a full three- or four-course dinner to her employers and their guests. Aunt Tee said she watched them grow older and leaner. After a few years, they stopped entertaining and ate dinner, hardly seeing each other at the table. Finally, they sat in a dry silence as they ate evening meals of soft scrambled eggs, melba toast, and weak tea. Aunt Tee said she saw them growing old but didn't see herself aging at all.

5   She became the social maven. She started "keeping company" (her phrase) with a chauffeur down the street. Her best friend and her friend's husband worked in service only a few blocks away.

6   On Saturdays, Aunt Tee would cook a pot of pigs' feet, a pot of greens, fry chicken, make potato salad, and bake a banana pudding. Then, that evening, her friends— the chauffeur, the other housekeeper, and her husband—would come to Aunt Tee's **commodious** live-in quarters. There the four would eat and drink, play records and dance. As the evening wore on, they would settle down to a serious game of bid whist. Naturally, during this revelry, jokes were told, fingers were snapped, feet were patted, and there was a great deal of laughter.

commodious: large; spacious

7   Aunt Tee said that what occurred during every Saturday party startled her and her friends the first time it happened. They had been playing cards, and Aunt Tee, who had just won the bid, held a handful of trumps. She felt a cool breeze on her back and sat upright and turned around. Her employers had cracked her door open and beckoned to her. Aunt Tee, a little peeved, laid down her cards and went to the door. The couple backed away and asked her to come into the hall, and there they both spoke and won Aunt Tee's sympathy forever.

8   "Theresa, we don't mean to disturb you," the man whispered, "but you all seem to be having such a good time."

9   The woman added, "We hear you and your friends laughing every Saturday night, and we'd just like to watch you. We don't want to bother you. We'll be quiet and just watch."

10   The man said, "If you'll just leave your door ajar, your friends don't need to know. We'll never make a sound." Aunt Tee said she saw no harm in agreeing, and she talked it over with her company. They said it was OK with them, but it was sad that the employers owned the gracious house, the swimming pool, three cars, and numberless palm trees, but had no joy. Aunt Tee told me that laughter and relaxation had left the house; she agreed it was sad.

11   That story has stayed with me for nearly thirty years, and when a tale remains fresh in my mind, it almost always contains a lesson which will benefit me. I draw the picture of the wealthy couple standing in a darkened hallway, peering into a lighted room where black servants were lifting their voices in merriment and comradery, and I realize that living well is an art which can be developed. Of course, you need the basic talents to build upon: They are a love of life and the ability to take great pleasure from small offerings, an assurance that the world owes you nothing, and awareness that every gift is exactly that, a gift. Because of the routines we follow, we often forget that life is an ongoing adventure.

Vocabulary and Comprehension

1. What is a *social maven* in paragraph 5?

_____

2. What is the meaning of *revelry* in paragraph 6?

_____

3. Angelou uses descriptive imagery. Descriptive imagery includes active verbs, adjectives, and other words that appeal to the senses (sight, smell, touch, sound, taste). Underline at least six examples of descriptive imagery.

4. Why was it so important for Aunt Tee to be neat and tidy?

_____

_____

Critical Thinking

5. Why does Angelou call her aunt's apartment *dead* in paragraph 2?

_____

_____

6. In paragraph 3, Angelou quotes Aunt Tee. Why does the author use the slang word *ain't*?

_____

_____

7. What can you infer about the lives of Aunt Tee's wealthy employers? What types of people are they?

_____

_____

_____

8. In paragraph 4, Aunt Tee says that she does not see herself aging. Why does she say this?

_____

_____

Writing Topics

Write about one of the following topics. Remember to explore, develop, and revise and edit your work.

1. Write about a time when you saw an event that changed your perception of someone.

2. Angelou tells a story to make a point about living life to the fullest. Write about a moment in time when you felt that you were living life to its fullest. Use descriptive imagery in your writing.

3. Do you live in a clean, organized environment or a messy one? Describe a clean or messy room in your home. (You might reread Angelou's depiction of Aunt Tee's home to get some ideas.)

Reading 12
Advertising Appeals

Michael R. Solomon, Greg W. Marshall, and Elnora W. Stuart

The next essay, which appeared in *Marketing: Real People, Real Choices*, focuses on advertising. As you read this classification essay, also look for the illustration and argument writing patterns.

1   An advertising appeal is the central idea of the ad. Some advertisers use an emotional appeal, complete with dramatic color or powerful images, while others bombard the audience with facts. Some feature sexy people or stern-looking experts—even professors from time to time. Different appeals can work for the same product, from a bland "talking head" to a montage of animated special effects. Although an attention-getting way to say something profound about cat food or laundry detergent is more art than science, there are some common appeals that are highly effective.

2   Testimonials are a useful type of endorsement. A celebrity, an expert, or a "man in the street" states the product's effectiveness. The use of celebrity endorsers is a common but expensive strategy. It is particularly effective for mature products that need to differentiate themselves from competitors, such as Coke and Pepsi, which enlist celebrities to tout one cola over another. For example, Michael Jackson and Shakira have been in Pepsi ads, and Bill Cosby and Bill Gates have endorsed Coke. Makeup and perfume companies also hire well-known faces to promote their brands. For instance, Penelope Cruz advertises L'Oreal mascara, and Nicole Kidman promotes Chanel.

3   A slice-of-life format presents a dramatized scene from everyday life. Slice-of-life advertising can be effective for everyday products such as peanut butter and headache remedies that consumers may feel good about if they see "real" people buying and using them. Tide, for instance, regularly depicts ordinary kids playing a rough and tumble game and arriving home covered in dirt and grass stains. Old El Paso shows a family of four sitting around the kitchen table enjoying their tacos.

4   Fear appeal ads highlight the negative consequences of not using a product. Some fear appeal ads focus on physical harm, while others try to create concern

for social harm or disapproval. Mouthwash, deodorant, and dandruff shampoo products play on viewers' concerns about social rejection. Also, life insurance companies successfully use fear appeals, as do ads aimed at changing behaviors, such as messages discouraging drug use or encouraging safe sex. Axe, for instance, has a humorous ad depicting a young man with very dirty, messy hair. The young fellow gets ambushed by a group of girls who wash his hair with Axe shampoo. Election campaigns make particular use of fear advertising. For example, during the country's health care debate, many political ads warned about seniors dying and about socialized medicine. Senators regularly warn voters about their opponents' tax plans.

5   Advertising creative types, including art directors, copywriters, photographers, and others, work hard on a "big idea"—a concept that expresses the aspects of the product, service, or organization in a tangible way. The best ads are attention-getting, memorable, and appealing to consumers.

Vocabulary and Comprehension

1. Find three words in paragraph 2 that mean the same thing as "promote."

   _____   _____   _____

2. Highlight the thesis statement in the essay.
3. What introduction style does the author use? Circle the best answer.
   a. general background   b. anecdote   c. definition
4. Underline the topic sentence in paragraphs 2 to 4.
5. What is the author's purpose?
   a. to persuade   b. to inform   c. to entertain

Critical Thinking

6. Add an appropriate transitional word or phrase to the beginnings of paragraphs 2 to 4. Write your ideas here.

   Para. 2 _____

   Para. 3 _____

   Para. 4 _____

7. Include an additional example of each type of ad. Think about some ads that you have seen.

   testimonial _____

   _____

   _____

   slice-of-life _____

   _____

   _____

   fear appeal _____

   _____

   _____

8. What are ethical problems with fear-appeal ads? Think of examples to support your point.

_____

_____

_____

_____

9. Which type of advertising is most effective, in your opinion? Which type of ad is least effective? Explain your answers.

Most effective: _____

_____

_____

Least effective: _____

_____

_____

Writing Topics

Write about one of the following topics. Remember to explore, develop, and revise and edit your work.

1. Develop another way to classify advertising into at least three categories. List characteristics and examples of each category.

2. Describe a very effective advertising campaign. Include details to support your point.

3. What products have been elevated into necessities when they are actually quite useless? Have you ever been influenced to buy a useless item because of a really good advertisement? Write about the power of advertising to influence people.

Reading 13
The Beeps

Josh Freed

Josh Freed is an award-winning journalist and documentary film writer. In the following example of an illustration essay, also look for elements of comparison and contrast and cause and effect.

1   Uh-oh. Something in the house is beeping—but what? Is it the stove announcing that dinner is cooked? Or is the dryer proclaiming my clothes are ready? Is the fridge defrosting, the thermostat adjusting, the smoke alarm dying, or is my cell phone dead? I'm living in an electronic jungle, trained to leap at every beep—if I could just figure out which beep it is.

2   I grew up in a time of easier-to-identify sounds, when telephones ding-a-linged, cash registers ka-chinged, and typewriters clacked; when school bells clanged, fire alarms rang, and ambulance sirens wailed—instead of today's digital whooping. Now they are all being replaced by the beep-beeps and bing-bings that are the frantic soundtrack of the twenty-first century.

3   Many of these high-pitched beeps are strangely hard to locate, even when they are right beside me. I usually fumble around for my cell phone when it rings

because I can't figure out which pants pocket it's in—or which pants. Maybe it's lost under the armchair again? Several times a week, a mystery beeping goes off somewhere in our house, and I run around like a lunatic trying to find whatever it is. I listen to our bookshelves, to our laundry piles, and even to the inside of the fridge. But the beeping always stops long before I crack the mystery.

4   Meanwhile, I am bombarded on every side by other urgent electronic sounds. My car beeps constantly, nagging me to put on my seat belt, or turn off the lights, or lock the trunk, or whatever else it's trying to tell me—probably: "Wipe your shoes before you mess up my floor, mister!" My printer beeps identically when it's out of paper, or out of toner, or when something is jammed—but which is it? My microwave beeps all the time, just for fun.

5   Out in the world, elevators and ATM machines beep constantly. TV shows beep when they bleep out swear words. Store machines beep when they swipe your groceries, or you try to swipe theirs without paying. Then there are security beeps: the loud BEEEEP . . . BEEEEP . . . BEEEEP that says you're about to be run down by a city street cleaner that's backing up; the shrill beep-beep-beep-beep that says you have 15 seconds to punch in the house alarm code or an old-fashioned siren will go off alerting a security firm that you are an intruder in your own home. The simple but dreaded beep of an airline security wand means it's time to start your striptease act.

6   Even life itself is measured in beeps. Hospitals are full of machines whose soft beeps indicate you are still alive. "I beep, therefore I am." We are born into the world in a noisy jungle of beeping medical monitors and wires. We will probably leave it the same way—for most of us, the world will end with a beep, not a bang.

7   Who would have guessed the sound of the twenty-first century would be the cry of the cartoon Road Runner, the fast-stepping bird that was always pursued by Wile E. Coyote, crying beep-beep as it ran? Today we are all Road Runners, frantically beeping as we run for our lives, chased by our own high-speed machines and hectic lifestyles.

8   Beep-beep! Fasten your seat belt. Beep-beep! You have another new e-mail . . . NOW. "BEEP! BEEP! Hello, we value your call, but we can't be bothered to take it now, so please don't speak until the beep." Electronic sounds have become so widespread, ornithologists report many birds are now mimicking our beeps, buzzes, and chirps as part of their mating songs. There are parrots that sound like cell phones, mockingbirds that mimic microwaves, and white-bellied caiques that do perfect car alarms.

9   Will the entire animal kingdom eventually chirp, roar, and growl electronically? Or will a new generation of humans choose more soothing sounds, like a phone ring that sounds exactly like birdsong, instead of vice-versa? Or an alarm clock that sounds like a rooster? Or a cash register that once again makes a genuine ka-ching? Perhaps we will all have truly personalized ring tones made by gentle New Age mechanical voices that show some respect for our space: "Jossshhh . . . This is your sto-o-ove speaking. Dinner is ready whenever you are, but don't rush—I'll keep it warm. Sorry if I disturbed you." "Suu-ssan . . . This

is your phone ringing. Suu-ssan. I'm in your brown purse, under your make-up and your dirty gym socks. Will you take the call . . . or should I?" To beep or not to beep? That is the question future generations must face. But for now, I've got to run. That beeping just started again, and I've just figured out what it is: my computer.

Vocabulary and Comprehension

1. Find a word in paragraph 8 that means "imitating." _____

2. Freed states that he is "living in an electronic jungle." What does he mean?

_____

_____

_____

3. The author discusses three main locations where he is bombarded with electronic beeps. List at least three locations and give examples of some noise-making machines in each category.

_____

_____

_____

_____

_____

4. How has new office technology affected nature?

_____

_____

Critical Thinking

5. Why is the author frustrated with the new technology? Give at least two reasons.

_____

_____

_____

6. What is the tone of the essay? Circle the best answer.

a. serious   c. humorous

b. angry   d. neutral

7. The author is indirectly comparing two worlds. What are they?

_____

_____

Writing Topics

Write about one of the following topics. Remember to explore, develop, and revise and edit your work.

1. In your daily life, what actions or objects frustrate you? List some examples to support your point.

2. What is your most valuable possession? Give examples of why it is valuable.

3. Does modern technology make life easier or was life better when technology was simpler? Use examples to support your point of view.

Reading 14
Of Rags and Riches—and Social Responsibility

Dorothy Nixon

Dorothy Nixon, a freelance writer, has written ads for radio and television and articles for many well-known publications. She is also the author of *Furies Cross the Mersey* and several other historical novels set in the 1910 era. Her novels are available on Amazon's Kindle. In the following text, she examines the fast fashion industry. As you read this comparison and contrast essay, also look for elements of process and argument.

1   The somewhat comical work-of-art called *Venus of the Rags*, by Michaelangelo Pisoletto, is part of the permanent collection of the Tate Modern, in London, England. It consists of classical statue of a nude woman pushed up against an immense, ugly, pile of cloth. When I look at it, I see a young woman deciding what to wear, and I can relate. We live in an era where clothing has become so cheap, so throw-away, that we can toss it away without feeling guilty.

2   Because fine art always inspires reflection, I've asked myself some uncomfortable questions: How many people work their fingers to the bone to produce all this modern, throw-away clothing? How many have died? Why, when I buy a skirt or a blouse, do I only consider the price, the cut, and the color, and not the person who actually made the piece of clothing? Unfortunately, conditions for most garment factory workers are no better today than they were one hundred years ago.

3   Around 1910, ready-to-wear women's apparel became widely available in the United States. After all, young women were going out to work in droves, and they needed something to wear. The centerpiece of their working wardrobe was the shirtwaist, a plain, tailored blouse often worn with a tie. But, if those young working women didn't want to make their own clothing, someone had to do it. That task fell to immigrant women, often Jewish or Italian, who usually worked in large factories, often under oppressive conditions. One such business was the Triangle Shirtwaist Factory in New York City, a sweatshop where employees, mostly non-English speaking immigrants, labored twelve-hour days, every day, for 15 dollars a week.

4   On March 25, 1911, the ten-storey Triangle Shirtwaist building went up in flames, killing 146 workers, mostly women. All of the factory doors had been locked by the owners to prevent theft. The women, some as young as fourteen, died from suffocation or by jumping out of the windows onto the pavement below. That workplace tragedy was widely publicized in the press, and the political fallout led to the Sullivan-Hoey Fire Prevention Law. It included progressive measures to improve conditions for workers, such as the installation of sprinklers in all New York factories. The ranks of the International Ladies Garment Workers Union swelled because of the tragedy, and that union went on to become a powerful force in the 1920s and 1930s.

5   Late in the twentieth century, profit-hungry retailers began to outsource production to countries like Pakistan and Bangladesh, places with enormous populations and very frail economies. In recent years, there has unfolded a series of fires and tragic accidents reminiscent of the Triangle Shirtwaist Factory fire one hundred years before. In September 2012, a fire in a garment factory in Karachi, Pakistan killed about 300 people and seriously injured twice that number. Frantic workers encountered locked doors and stairwells that were blocked by piles of clothing. There were no fire exits. Two months later, in November 2012, a Dhaka, Bangladesh factory—Tazreen Fashion—also caught fire, killing 112. It was later reported to be an act of sabotage. Then there was the April 2013 disaster at the Rana Plaza, also in Dhaka, where an eight-story building came down on workers inside, killing over a thousand people and injuring even more than that.

6   The Rana Plaza event is the deadliest garment industry accident in history. As it happens, I had recently purchased a cute little green striped t-shirt, for a mere five dollars, from a popular local discount retailer. That store's goods were found in the rubble of the Rana Plaza. I had tucked away the top in a drawer and had never worn it. After reading the harrowing account of the Rana Plaza collapse, I took the pretty thing out and put it on. I was feeling a little guilty, I guess. But, should I feel guilty? Are we in the West to blame for not caring about the origins of the clothing we purchase? According to Human Rights Watch, garment factory tragedies like the ones in Asia are unlikely to spur a vigorous union movement such as the one that occurred after the Triangle Shirtwaist Factory fire. There are too many political obstacles to that happening, and, some say, western retailers are in collusion.

7   I wonder if boycotting the western companies would help the situation. Some of those frail Asian economies have become dependent on the textile industry. So the question posed to me by that comical classical goddess in the Tate Gallery remains unanswered, for now. But I wonder how many more textile workers have to needlessly die—for my casual dressing pleasure and to pad my overflowing wardrobe—before I eventually take a stand. Perhaps there comes a time in a person's life when she should remove the blinkers and assume some social responsibility as a consumer, even when it seems innocuous, such as how she chooses to dress.

Vocabulary and Comprehension

1. Find a word in paragraph 7 that means "harmless." _____

2. Highlight the thesis statement. Remember that the thesis might not be in the first paragraph.

3. What type of introduction is used?
   a. anecdote   b. historical background   c. opposing position

4. What is the author comparing and contrasting?

   _____

5. What are some similarities and differences between garment factory conditions in the past and present?

Similarities: _____

_____

Differences: _____

_____

Critical Thinking

6. Why does the writer begin by discussing an artwork?

_____

_____

7. Why is clothing so inexpensive today? Make an inference or guess based on information in the reading.

_____

_____

8. This comparison and contrast essay also presents an argument. What is the argument?

_____

_____

_____

Writing Topics

1. Compare and contrast two pieces of clothing. You could choose an item that you love and one that you hate.

2. Compare and contrast the way that you dressed in the past and the way that you dress today.

Themes: Spies and Hackers and The Legal World

Reading 15
My Father Taught Me to Love Guns

Tricia Braun

Tricia Braun, a native Texan, is a former prosecutor and mother of three. She is also a writer, and she is working on a memoir. As you read this narrative essay, also look for elements of comparison and contrast, description, and argument.

1   My father taught me to always carry a handgun when I was driving long distances alone. My father had grown up in rural South Texas, just north of the Mexican border. Guns and hunting were a part of the landscape. He was a former boxer who had spent his entire adult life as a criminal defense lawyer. He represented accused murderers, rapists, and drug dealers, listening to their stories day after day. He knew the kind of violence that most people only saw on episodes of *Law and Order*. My father trained me to be ready, to be on the lookout, and to fight back. He taught me to shoot.

2   When I graduated at twenty-one, I left my home state of Texas to work and ski in Colorado. That first spring, I set off on the two-day drive back home to South Texas. One night, I called my father from a motel, and he gave me an earful of gun advice. "Keep it under your pillow," he said. His voice was forceful, almost urgent. He had been giving me this same advice since I was twelve. "The element of surprise is very important," he emphasized, "especially in a motel room."

3   The next day, the clutch broke. I slowly glided onto the dirt beside the highway. The road stretched flat in either direction—no houses, no gas stations, and no phones. I would have to hitchhike. At 5-foot-3 and 115 pounds, I was no physical match for any man who might pick me up. I tried not to think of the dangers as I stuffed my two most valuable possessions in my backpack: my typewriter and my gun.

4   Within 15 minutes, an 18-wheeler pulled over. I climbed into the rig and sat on the passenger seat. The driver had leathery skin and looked to be in his late fifties. I surveyed the cab of the truck, watching and evaluating his every move. I tried to anticipate every possible attack scenario as I fastened my seatbelt. He looked into his side mirror and pulled back onto the highway. I put my backpack on the floor next to the passenger door so he couldn't grab it while driving, hoping I wasn't obvious. As we rode to San Antonio, I periodically brushed the back of my hand against the front pocket of my pack, feeling the hard surface of the revolver's cylinder.

5   Afterwards, I called my dad on a pay phone, telling him what had happened. He listened without interruption, finally asking, "Did you have your gun?"

6   "Yeah," I said.

7   "Did you show it to him?"

8   "Dad! That's not hitchhiking—that's carjacking."

9   "Yeah, I guess you're right," he said, with a chuckle. "All right, well, I'll come down there and get you."

10   As an adult, I sometimes hear liberal friends and acquaintances deride gun enthusiasts as "gun nuts" or "gun fanatics." I know they don't mean to insult my family or me. I know they can't comprehend how a parent would give his twenty-two-year-old daughter a gun. But where I come from, that isn't so unusual. When I moved into my first apartment in college, both of my roommates' fathers had given them guns, too. From my dad's perspective, he was protecting me, empowering me to defend myself against an unpredictable and dangerous world. I, being young and female, welcomed that power and security.

11   But I had never had to use a gun in a high-stress situation. I didn't have military or police training. If danger was a paper target, an empty beer can, even a flying bird, I was prepared. But what if it was a person, someone unpredictable and on the attack? My only preparation was my father's advice, movies I had seen, and my own imagined scenarios. And yet, the idea that a gun was essential for my protection was imbedded in me from childhood. I checked it regularly, under my mattress or car floor mat. It was my touchstone of safety. My gun gave me the confidence to drive 1,000 miles alone.

12   When I left Texas for the return drive to Colorado, a brand-new clutch under the hood, my dad gave me a 9 mm Glock. For many years after that I always traveled armed. I lived in Texas, Colorado, Utah, and Connecticut and drove thousands of miles by myself with no cellphone and no companion other than my own personal bodyguard: the Glock under the driver-side floor mat.

13   In 1993, I graduated from law school in Connecticut and moved back to Texas to clerk for a federal judge. The tenor of Texas gun culture had intensified. Two years before my return, a man named George Hennard had shot forty-four people. It was the worst mass murder in U.S. history at the time. Texas lawmakers responded with the now-familiar refrain that a good guy with a gun could have stopped a bad guy with a gun. Legislators passed a law permitting gun owners to apply for licenses to carry concealed weapons.

14   The following summer, I finished my clerkship and prepared to move to Boulder, Colorado, to work for a law firm. In between jobs, I took a road trip with a good friend from law school. She had grown up on the Upper East Side of New York. As we set out for our first leg of our trip, she told me her dad's theory: "My dad says, 'There's always one thing you need to take with you on a road trip: your AAA card.'"

15   "*My* dad says the only thing you need is your gun," I said.

16   We laughed, and she shook her head. "Do you have yours now?" she asked.

17   "Of course," I said.

18   There was a long, awkward pause. "Ah," she said. "I'm not sure how I feel about that."

19   "Really?" For the first time in my life it occurred to me that my having a gun might not be reassuring to someone. I had never thought to ask how she felt beforehand. I had never been close friends with someone who would object. But what could I do? I couldn't just throw it away. We drove from New Mexico all the way up to Montana and back with both the AAA card and the gun, but we never needed either.

20   After that trip, I moved back to Colorado, a middle-ground state as far as guns were concerned. I practiced criminal defense and civil law, and then joined the DA's Office. I continued to drive with the Glock in my car for long-distance and night drives, but the fog of gun obsession lifted. The only people I knew who had guns in Colorado were law enforcement and hunters. I worked closely with police who recertified their weapons' proficiency quarterly. The more I saw of their training, the more I saw the inadequacy of my own.

21   While I grappled with this, a man in Boulder named Forrest Leigh, an ex-Marine and **NRA** member, was cleaning his guns and accidentally shot one. The bullet ripped through the wall of his apartment and into the next, piercing the forehead of his 27-year-old neighbor, Tara Coakley, killing her. She had been sitting down to eat pizza with her brother and his fiancé. Hearing this story froze something inside me. My unease about carrying guns grew. The consequences of an accident—a literal slip when clearing a chamber or cleaning a barrel—cast a long, dark shadow over my confidence in having guns.

NRA: National Rifle Association

22   Ten years after, newly married, I moved from Boulder, Colorado, to Brooklyn, New York. The night before the movers arrived, I gave my sister my guns. It was the red tape, really. I knew the gun laws in New York were strict. It was easier to get rid of the guns than to research all of the laws and regulations about owning them in the city. Also, I had more guns than I had realized. I pulled them from under the floor mat of my car, out of my closet, and from under my mattress. There was the Glock, the .38, a .22 revolver, a .22 rifle, and one more I can no longer remember. I was surprised and somewhat embarrassed by the little armory I had built up over the years.

23   As I handed the last gun over to my sister, it hit me that I had never lived without guns. What if our car broke down on our way to New York? It's not that I expected danger, but if danger came my way, I expected it to be armed. How did people without guns protect themselves? "They're still mine," I said to my sister. "I'll want them when we move back."

24   It's been sixteen years and I never did move back. I lived through 9/11 in New York City and the East Coast blackout the following year. During the blackout, I heard people walking on the roof of our brownstone apartment in the night, and I thought about my guns in Colorado. I lay in the stifling dark, longing for a gun under the mattress. I thought about protecting my sleeping toddler in the next room. But I also thought about how his curiosity and physical abilities so far outpaced his reason. How would I ever be able to keep a gun accessible to me but not to him? I pushed away images of him finding the gun, his chubby little hands wrapping around the stock and the trigger.

25   I had long agonized about whether I could safely raise a child in a home with guns. I knew that to do so, I would have to spend lots of time and effort teaching firearm safety and skills. Even then, accidents happen. The statistics about accidental child shootings, I knew, were stunning. But I also had personal experience. When I was twelve, I accidentally shot a hole in the ceiling of my parents' bedroom with a .357 magnum, barely missing my own face. As a child that was an embarrassment. As a parent looking back, I couldn't even breathe.

26   That night in Brooklyn, I thought about the sheer density of the city. It meant there were always people around if I called for help. That same density also meant that bullets could easily pierce through walls, endangering neighbors. I was grateful for the lack of guns. I knew no matter how drunk and out of control my alcoholic neighbor got, I never worried about him killing himself or anyone else in a blind rage because a gun was so easy to grab. I was astonished to realize that my faith had outpaced my fears.

27   Scary and terrible things happen. How do you defend yourself against true evil? I think of the Petit family in Connecticut, where two sociopaths broke into a randomly selected home and raped and killed the daughters and wife. The father was beaten on the head with a baseball bat from his own garage and tied up, unable to save his family. What if he had had a gun? Would he have been able to get to it and save them? My father absolutely believes he would have. But the facts of the case suggest otherwise. For my father, having a gun is a kind of insurance against tragedy. With his gun, he was not afraid. I used to feel the same.

28   Then, on Dec. 14, 2012, I had just returned home from dropping my first-grader off at a reunion with her kindergarten teacher when I read the breaking news of the Sandy Hook school shooting on my phone. My sister called me immediately. "What is wrong with this country?" she cried. I hurried upstairs and closed myself in my bedroom so that my other children couldn't hear me crying.

29   My sister and I both had first-graders, like twenty of the child victims that day. We knew the dimples on the back of their hands and the feel of their breath on our necks when we kissed them goodnight. We knew how much they loved their teachers, and that four of the victims at Sandy Hook were teachers. All of those bodies were ripped apart by a semi-automatic machine gun in the hands of a damaged boy.

30   "Those guns I left," I said, wiping tears and snot off my face. "I don't want them back. Ever. I don't care what you do with them. I can't be a part of this anymore. Sell them; turn them into a buy-back program. I never want them back."

31   I have grown beyond my father's world. I left his home. I left his state. I left his guns behind. People sometimes ask how my dad feels about my evolution on guns. I tell them that we are family. We love and respect each other. I tell them it's a continuing conversation, and we find much on which we can agree: rules and regulations we could both accept. Whatever my personal choices, my children will never live in a gun-free world.

32   When I drove east out of Colorado gun-free, I left behind much more than my guns. Over time, I came to realize that I left behind the feeling that I was always under siege, the feeling that every moment I must be vigilant. I left behind the burden of responsibility and the fear of the wrong person using my gun. Most of all, I left behind the fear of being that parent on the 911 call—the one with the animal scream because her child accidentally shot herself or her sibling.

33   I left gun country, and then gun country left me.

Braun, Tricia, "My Father Taught Me to Love Guns," December 13, 2015. This article first appeared in Salon.com, at http://www.Salon.com. An online version remains in the Salon archives. Reprinted with permission.

Vocabulary and Comprehension

1. In paragraph 10, what does *deride* mean?
   a. use carefully   b. laugh   c. express contempt

2. What type of narration is used?
   a. first person   b. third person

3. Where did the writer live during her childhood? _____

4. This narrative essay uses elements of imagery, which appeals to the senses. Find an example of the following types of imagery.

   Sight: _____

   _____

   Touch: _____

   _____

   Sound: _____

   _____

5. Which statement from the essay best expresses the thesis or main idea of the essay?

   a. My father taught me to love guns.

   b. I had long agonized about whether I could safely raise a child in a home with guns.

   c. How do you defend yourself against true evil?

   d. I left gun country, and then gun country left me.

Critical Thinking

6. Why did the writer change her views about gun ownership? List at least four reasons.

   _____

   _____

   _____

   _____

   _____

   _____

7. Both the father and daughter work for the criminal justice system. Why are their viewpoints about guns so different?

   _____

   _____

8. The writer lives and works in different states. How does her location influence her thinking?

   _____

   _____

   _____

9. Near the end of the essay, the writer discusses a major change in her emotions and the way she faces life. How is she different today?

   _____

   _____

   _____

Writing Topics

1. How have your emotions evolved over the years? These days, are you happier, sadder, or angrier than you were in the past? Write about an emotional change that you have undergone in your life. Explain what happened to make you feel differently today.

2. What is your opinion about open-carry laws? Argue that people should or should not be allowed to carry guns in public.

Reading 16
The Criminal Justice Process

John Randolph Fuller

John Randolph Fuller teaches criminology at the University of West Georgia. He has also been a parole officer and criminal justice planner. This excerpt is taken from his book *Criminal Justice Mainstream and Crosscurrents*. As you read this process essay, also look for elements of illustration and cause and effect.

1   In April 1983, the pelvic portion of a female torso was found on the banks of the Mississippi River near Davenport, Iowa. In an autopsy, the pathologist estimated that the victim was between eighteen and forty years old, had probably given birth, and had likely been dismembered with a chainsaw. With the help of techniques considered cutting-edge at the time, including DNA evidence, investigators matched the woman's characteristics to those of Joyce Klindt, a Davenport woman who had gone missing the month before. Eventually, her husband admitted murdering her, cutting her up with a chainsaw, and dumping her remains in the river.

2   The criminal justice system is extremely complex. It is clear to most observers of the system that only a very small percentage of the crimes committed result in someone going to prison. The criminal justice system is frustrating not only for the general public, but also for those who work in the system, as well as for victims, offenders, and their respective families because it is close to being overloaded. It is useful to envision the criminal justice system as a large funnel in which cases move downward toward their final disposition. The problem with the funnel is that it is too small to hold all the cases, and so a considerable amount of leakage occurs. Police officers, prosecutors, and judges use discretion to decide which cases are pushed further into the funnel of the criminal justice system and which ones are kicked out.

3   Processing criminal cases begins with reported crimes. At the wide mouth of the funnel are all the crimes committed in society, such as murder, rape, burglary, insurance fraud, shoplifting, and car theft. It includes all the acts that can be defined as crime whether they have been reported or not. Many, maybe even most, crimes are never reported, or if they are, they get handled informally and never make it into the official crime reporting systems. Criminologists call these unreported acts the dark figures of crime. A bit lower and at a point narrower in the funnel are crimes known to the police. These are the behaviors that the police include in their reports and are officially measured. However, individual police officers or police administrators can exercise considerable discretions in determining just how a behavior will be categorized for reporting purposes.

4   After a crime has been reported, police investigate and try to solve the crime. The investigation into the death of Joyce Klindt has been cited as a classic example of good investigation, and it set precedents for the use of scientific evidence in courts. But such success stories are not the norm. In probing the 1996 murder of JonBenet Ramsey, a local police detective was accused of making crucial mistakes in the investigation. The investigation into the little girl's death is ongoing with no clear results to date. In other less sensational cases, police investigate to the best of their abilities but must deal with limited resources, poor physical evidence, a cold trail, or just bad luck. Typically, police gather tissue samples and fingerprints, talk with witnesses and victims, and examine police records of potential suspects. Sometimes, the evidence is gathered quickly, and a suspect is apprehended at once. Other times, cases languish and are solved years later or never solved at all.

5   Once the police have enough evidence of a crime, they make an arrest. It should come as no surprise that the police do not make an arrest for every crime they detect. In fact, clearance rates can vary widely, depending on the type of crime and the priorities of the police department. For instance, most Driving Under the Influence (DUI) offenses go undetected, but proactive police practices such as sobriety checkpoints can greatly increase the arrest statistics for a police agency. Arrests are an important measure in our crime funnel because they provide a good indication of what will happen in the rest of the criminal justice system. Arrests provide the system with the cases it must handle.

6   After a suspect is arrested, the police must make an official report of the charges. Booking occurs at the police station, where a suspect's name, age, and address are recorded, as well as information on the time, place, and reason for arrest. Usually, a photograph and fingerprints are taken, and the suspect's clothing and personal effects are stored. The suspect is usually placed in a holding cell until he or she can be questioned further. The suspect is advised of her rights and signs the report that she understands her rights.

7   Of all the arrests made by the police, only a percentage result in a person being charged with a crime by the prosecutor and funneled deeper into the criminal justice system. The discretion used by the prosecutor to decide which cases to eliminate is determined by a number of factors. The first factor is resources. The decision to prosecute is dependent on personnel, budget, space, and agency priorities. The prosecutor may have too many other cases deemed more important, or may decide there is insufficient evidence to charge a suspect. The prosecutor may think that the police made too many procedural errors. Finally, the prosecutor may have personal or agency priorities concerning what types of cases will be pressed. Political corruption cases may be encouraged or discouraged depending on the part affiliation of the state attorney versus the defendant.

8   Suspects must be brought before a judge within a reasonable time of their arrest for an initial appearance. At this stage, the defendant is formally charged with a crime and will respond by pleading guilty, not guilty, or **no contest** at a first court hearing or arraignment. The defendants then have a preliminary hearing where the prosecutor presents evidence to show that the defendant has committed the crime, also known as probable cause. The judge decides if the defendant will be granted bail. Bail is money paid to the court to ensure that a suspect who is released from jail will appear in court.

no contest: the defendant does not admit guilt or proclaim innocence

9   Few cases actually make it to the trial phase of the criminal justice process. Many cases get resolved by plea-bargaining, a negotiation between defense attorneys and prosecutors that results in some type of punishment. Of the cases that go to trial, only a small percentage end up in guilty verdicts that require further processing of the case. Some defendants are acquitted or found not guilty. Sometimes a case is dismissed because the prosecution is unable to present a viable case against the defendant. Most of the legal decisions are made behind the scenes, and the excitement and drama in the courtroom are actually quite rare.

10   The criminal justice system is very complex from the initial police investigation to the final verdict in a trial. The funnel analogy serves to point out how the numbers of cases dwindle drastically as they go through the criminal justice system.

Vocabulary and Comprehension

1. What are *the dark figures of crime*? See paragraph 3.

   _____

2. Highlight the thesis statement.

3. What are some obstacles police face when they investigate a crime?

   _____

   _____

4. What are some factors that prosecutors must consider before deciding to prosecute a case?

   _____

   _____

   _____

   _____

5. What type of introductory style does the author use?

   a. opposing position   b. anecdote   c. definition

Critical Thinking

6. Using your own words, explain how criminal cases are processed in the criminal justice system.

   _____

   _____

   _____

   _____

   _____

   _____

   _____

7. Why does the author refer to a funnel when explaining the criminal justice system?

   _____

   _____

8. In paragraph 2, the author mentions that many crimes are never reported. Using your own ideas, give some reasons why a victim may not want to report a crime.

   _____

   _____

   _____

9. In paragraph 9, the author states that many cases may get resolved through plea bargaining. Think of some reasons why a defense attorney and a prosecutor might want to avoid a court trial, and therefore, want to plea-bargain.

   _____

   _____

   _____

   _____

Writing Topics

1. Have you or someone you know ever been a victim of a crime or conducted a criminal act? What did you do? Describe the process you went through.

2. Describe some steps people should take to be safer on their college campus or in their neighborhood.

3. Argue that certain types of criminals are treated too leniently or too harshly.

Reading 17
How Spies Are Caught

This process essay recounts how spies are caught. As you read the text, also look for definition and cause and effect writing patterns.

1   Espionage is a high-risk criminal offense. The traitor must fear arrest for the rest of his or her life, as the statute of limitations does not apply to espionage. Former National Security Agency employee Robert Lipka was arrested in 1996—thirty years after he left NSA and twenty-two years after his last contact with Soviet intelligence. There are four principal ways by which spies are detected: Reporting by U.S. sources within the foreign intelligence service, routine counterintelligence monitoring, a tip from a friend or spouse, or the traitor's own mistakes.

2   Of the Americans who held a security clearance who have been arrested for espionage, about half were caught as a result of information provided by a defector from the foreign intelligence service or an agent or friend within the foreign service that the spy was working for. People who betray their country often have little fear of being caught because they think they are smarter than everyone else. They think they can easily get away with it. However, no matter how smart or clever a spy may be, he or she has no protection against U.S. Government sources within the other intelligence service.

3   If the spy is not reported by sources within the other intelligence service, there is a strong likelihood of detection through routine counterintelligence operations. Of the cleared Americans arrested for espionage or attempted espionage during the past twenty years, 26 percent were arrested before they could do any damage, and 47 percent were caught during their first year of betrayal. This is not surprising, as counterintelligence agents know many of the foreign intelligence officers active in the United States and know where they work, where they live, where they hang out, and how they ply their trade. Any would-be spy who doesn't know how the counterintelligence system works is likely to be caught in the counterintelligence web.

4   Espionage usually requires keeping or preparing materials at home, traveling to signal sites or secret meetings at unusual times and places, a change in one's financial status with no corresponding change in job income, and periods of high stress that affect behavior. All of these changes in the normal pattern of behavior often come to the attention of other people and must be explained. Other people become suspicious and pass their suspicions on. This sometimes comes out during the periodic security clearance reinvestigation.

5   Spying is a lonely business. To explain these changes in behavior, or because of a need to confide in someone else, spies often confide in a spouse or try to enlist the help of a friend. The friend or spouse in whom the spy confides often does not remain a friend or loyal spouse after he or she realizes what is going on.

6   Most people who betray their country are not thinking rationally, or they would not be involved in such a self-destructive activity. They are driven, in large part, by irrational emotional needs to feel important, successful, powerful, or to get even or to take risks. These emotional needs are out of control, so the same emotional needs that lead them to betray also cause them to flaunt their sudden affluence or to brag about their involvement in some mysterious activity. Because they are so mixed up psychologically, they make mistakes that get them caught.

Vocabulary and Comprehension

1. Find a word in paragraph 6 that means "to show off." _____

2. What are the four ways in which spies are usually caught?

   _____

   _____

   _____

   _____

3. Give an example of the following types of support.

   Statistic: _____

   _____

   Anecdote: _____

   _____

4. How might a friend or coworker suspect that someone is a spy?

   _____

   _____

Critical Thinking

5. Give at least three reasons that people betray government secrets.

   _____

   _____

   _____

6. By making inferences, determine some consequences of espionage on the individual spy.

   _____

   _____

   _____

7. In your opinion, how does treachery affect a country?

   _____

   _____

   _____

Writing Topics

Write about one of the following topics. Remember to explore, develop, and revise and edit your work.

1. Many people feel insecure in this post-9/11 society. What steps can people take to feel safe in their own homes? Explain.

2. Most people value their privacy. Should government agencies in the United States have the right to spy on citizens by any means?

3. These days, citizens can use social media tools to spy on each other. For example, teachers and police officers have been caught on cell phone videos doing misdeeds. Ordinary people have also been humiliated if they have done something embarrassing and it was caught on video and posted online. What are some benefits or disadvantages of citizen spying?

Reading 18
The Real Reason Crime Is Falling

Zoe McKnight

Zoe McKnight is a journalist and writer. In this cause and effect essay, she examines the connection between technology and crime. As you read this cause and effect essay, also look for elements of comparison and contrast and argument.

1   Technology is blamed for obesity, dwindling attention spans, and sedentary lifestyles. Texting and walking is hazardous, while texting and driving can be fatal. Anxieties about video games became entrenched after of the 1999 Columbine High School massacre. And in Brampton, Ontario, Jeremy Cook was just eighteen when he was murdered for his iPhone. The crime, which became known as the "cellphone slaying," left the nation stunned. For those who believe that crime is out of control and who are upset by society's dangerous addiction to technology, Cook's tragic death confirmed their worst fears.

2   But there's another side to the story of youth crime and technology. In North America, Europe, and Australia, many common street crimes have fallen by half since the early 1990s. Last year, the overall crime rate hit a low not seen since 1969. When the statistics are broken down by age group, the most powerful and dramatic trend becomes apparent: Huge numbers of those aged eighteen to twenty-four—the slice of the population historically responsible for the largest share of crimes—are staying on the right side of the law.

3   What's behind the phenomenon? Theories abound, including better security—improved locks, CCTVs, and home alarm systems—as well as the sheer number of police on the street and bodies in prison. But a growing number of criminologists are also considering another factor—namely, our obsession with technology. Leading British criminologist Ken Pease argues that the staggering reach of the online world—video games, social media, access to instant and unlimited video and texting—is reshaping the modern world to such an extent that it may even be affecting crime rates. "Frankly, there are more interesting things to do indoors now than going out and **nicking** things," says Pease. Other researchers, as well as those working in law enforcement,

nicking: stealing

are observing fundamental changes taking place among the most digitally connected generation. Our chronic technology habit is actually keeping us safe.

4   Criminologist Mike Sutton and psychologist Mark Griffiths, who both teach at Nottingham Trent University, proposed the crime substitution hypothesis: If substantial numbers of young people are inside and not on the streets, they are less likely to become offenders. Though Griffiths admits their theory is "speculative and correlational," it rings true. In the past, when youths got bored and hung around with friends outdoors, they might have engaged in crimes such as shoplifting or vandalism. Those petty crimes often served as gateways to more serious crimes later in life. But nowadays, people have an almost pathological need to look at their phones when the devices buzz with an incoming text or message.

5   Harvard economist Lawrence Katz suggests that "video games and websites" may have provided such an effective distraction during the 2008 financial collapse that the predicted crime wave did not materialize. Meanwhile, a 2013 study published by the American Psychological Association found that violent crime actually went down, even as video game sales went up. The authors chalk it up to either catharsis through simulated violence, or the simple fact that if violent people are drawn to violent video games, they keep the streets safer by staying—and playing—at home.

6   Sixteen-year-old Corick Henlin grew up in a tough part of town. He and his friends can spot gangs by their crews or their cars, but they have no interest in that lifestyle. They spend most of their time playing video games, chatting to their thousands of Facebook friends, and texting girls. Henlin, a digital native, or "screenager" (someone who can't recall a time before the Internet), admits that all that screen time can breed laziness, but he sees it as a useful diversion. "Before electronics, people were forced to go outside to have fun, but that's why there were more problems on the streets," he says. "Nowadays, with electronics, you can play, like, a fighting game on PS3. When you play games, you can cause trouble and not actually get in trouble."

7   Of course, technology has also created brand-new problems for police, such as cyberbullying and smartphone thefts. But technology is also helping to turn that around. The introduction of so-called "kill switches" on smartphones, which allow owners to remotely disable their devices, contributed to a 30 per cent drop in the number of phone thefts last year, according to a recent *Consumer Reports* study. Devices such as camera phones may also serve to deter crime because the risk of getting caught is higher. A victim or bystander can easily phone 911 or record a video of an attack.

8   Not everyone is convinced that chronic use of technology is helping to bring down crime. Simon Fraser University criminology professor Graham Farrell is skeptical that new technology has contributed to the crime drop. Crime rates began their slide in 1991, before Google and texting. He's quick to point out that correlation is not causation.

9   Even if the proof isn't absolute, investment in technology has worked its way into social programs, which provide at-risk youths with access to mobile phones. The Youth Restorative Action Project in Edmonton has distributed

phones to thirty teens aged seventeen and under. Program coordinator Taylor-Rae Foster acknowledges that the devices could facilitate drug deals or gang activity. Instead, she says they've been used by youth to find safe places to sleep and to keep in touch with friends.

10   While it's easy to worry about kids these days being attached to their devices, it's clear the digital revolution has brought enormous positive changes, often in unexpected ways. Society will continue to grapple with social ills such as crime and addiction. But it's possible our very dependence on technology has actually made the world a little safer.

Vocabulary and Comprehension

1. Find a word in paragraph 1 that means "shrinking." _____

2. Highlight the thesis statement. Hint: It is not in the first paragraph.

3. What are the possible causes of the falling crime rate? List four ideas.

   _____

   _____

4. The writer suggests that technology is helping keep crime down. How does she support her main point? Circle one or more answers.

   a. statistics   b. expert opinions   c. anecdotal evidence

5. Underline the names of three experts who support the idea that technology is affecting crime rates.

6. This cause and effect essay also presents an argument. Which person presents an opposing position to the main argument?

   a. Lawrence Katz   b. Graham Farrell   c. Taylor-Rae Foster

Critical Thinking

7. List four ways that technology is helping reduce crime.

   _____

   _____

   _____

   _____

   _____

8. In paragraph 2, the writer calls those aged eighteen to twenty-four "the slice of the population historically responsible for the largest share of crimes." What are some reasons that age group gets into more trouble than other age groups?

   _____

Writing Topics

1. How has technology affected you and your friends? Write about the effects of technology on your generation.

2. Have you ever been the victim of a crime? Narrate what happened.

Appendix 1 Grammar Glossary

The Basic Parts of a Sentence

Parts of Speech	Definition	Some Examples
Adjective	Adds information about the noun	cautious, cold, easy, happy, slow, strange
Adverb	Adds information about the verb, adjective, or other adverb; expresses time, place, and frequency	cautiously, coldly, easily, happily, slowly, strangely, sometimes, usually, never
Conjunctive adverb	Shows a relationship between two ideas	also, consequently, finally, however, furthermore, moreover, therefore, thus
Coordinating conjunction	Connects two ideas of equal importance	for, and, nor, but, or, yet, so
Determiner	Identifies or determines if a noun is specific or general	a, an, the, this, that, these, those, any, all, each, every, many, some
Interjection	A word expressing an emotion	Ouch! Yikes! Wow . . . . Yeah. Oh.
Noun	A person, place, or thing	singular: woman, office, mouse plural: women, offices, mice
Preposition	Shows a relationship between words (source, direction, location, etc.)	at, to, for, from, behind, above
Pronoun	Replaces one or more nouns	he, she, it, us, ours, themselves
Subordinating conjunction	Connects two ideas when one idea is subordinate (or inferior) to the other idea	after, although, because, unless, until
Verb	Expresses an action or state of being	action verb: run, eat, walk, think state of being or linking verb: is, become, seem

Practice 1

Label each word with one of the following terms.

adjective	noun	verb	adverb
conjunction	preposition	pronoun	interjection

EXAMPLE: easy <u>adjective</u>

1. pants _____

2. into _____

3. below _____

4. herself _____

5. wow _____

6. was _____

7. whispered _____

8. quickly _____

9. because _____

10. children _____

11. they _____

12. ouch _____

Types of Clauses and Sentences

Other Key Terms	Definition	Example
clause	An **independent clause** has a subject and a verb and expresses a complete idea. A **dependent clause** has a subject and a verb but cannot stand alone. It "depends" on another clause in order to be complete.	The movie is funny. although it is violent
phrase	A group of words that is missing a subject, a verb, or both, and is not a complete sentence	in the morning after the storm
simple sentence	One independent clause that expresses a complete idea	The movie is funny.
complex sentence	At least one dependent clause joined with one independent clause	Although the movie is violent, it conveys an important message.
compound sentence	Two or more independent clauses that are joined together	Some movies are funny, and others are deeply moving.
compound-complex sentence	At least two independent clauses joined with at least one dependent clause	Although the movie is violent, it is very entertaining, and it conveys an important message.

Practice 2

Identify the types of sentences. Beside each sentence, write one of the following:

S   simple sentence

C   compound sentence

CX   complex sentence

CCX   compound-complex sentence

1. I took a university course that was very interesting. _____

2. In the course, I read a book about a famous women's rights crusader, and I finished the book in an hour. _____

3. Elizabeth Cady Stanton was born in 1915, and her father was a lawyer, judge, and congressman. _____

4. When Elizabeth was a young girl, she heard about an unfair law. _____

5. The law restricted a woman's right to own property. _____

6. One day, she took a pair of scissors, and she cut out the law from her father's law book. _____

7. She thought that the law would be cancelled. _____

8. Her plan didn't work, of course, but her father had an unusual reaction to her act. _____

9. He put down his pen and looked at Elizabeth. _____

10. With a serious expression on his face, he told Elizabeth that she could change things, and he asked her to think about his words. _____

A Quick Guide to Verb Tenses

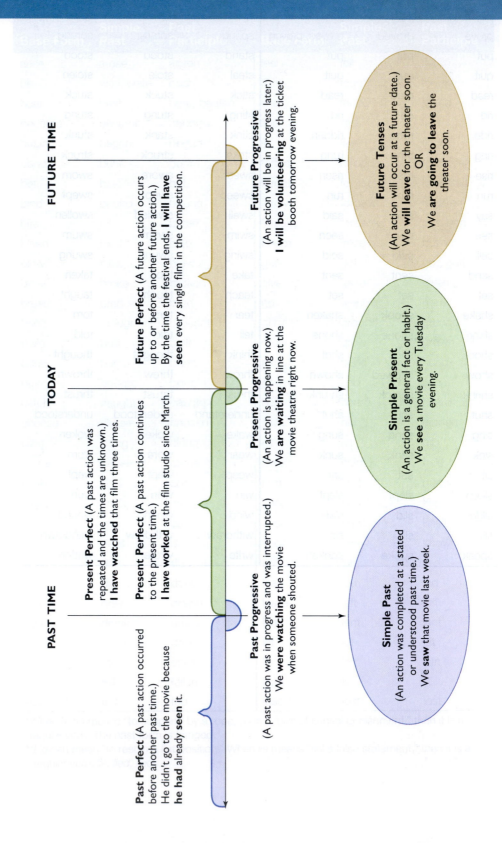

Past Perfect (A past action occurred before another past time.)
He didn't go to the movie because **he had** already **seen** it.

Present Perfect (A past action was repeated and the times are unknown.)
I have watched that film three times.

Present Perfect (A past action continues to the present time.)
I have worked at the film studio since March.

Future Perfect (A future action occurs up to or before another future action.)
By the time the festival ends, **I will have seen** every single film in the competition.

PAST TIME

TODAY

FUTURE TIME

Past Progressive
(A past action was in progress and was interrupted.)
We **were watching** the movie when someone shouted.

Present Progressive
(An action is happening now.)
We **are waiting** in line at the movie theatre right now.

Future Progressive
(An action will be in progress later.)
I will be volunteering at the ticket booth tomorrow evening.

Simple Past
(An action was completed at a stated or understood past time.)
We **saw** that movie last week.

Simple Present
(An action is a general fact or habit.)
We **see** a movie every Tuesday evening.

Future Tenses
(An action will occur at a future date.)
We **will leave** for the theater soon.
OR
We **are going to leave** the theater soon.

Combining Ideas in Sentences

Making Compound Sentences

A.

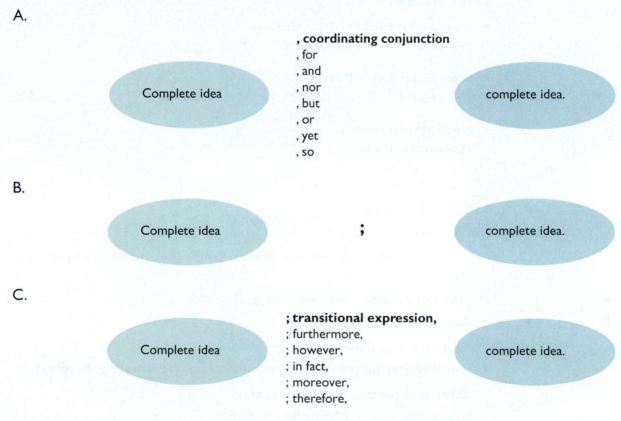

, **coordinating conjunction**
, for
, and
, nor
, but
, or
, yet
, so

B.

Complete idea ; complete idea.

C.

; **transitional expression,**
; furthermore,
; however,
; in fact,
; moreover,
; therefore,

Making Complex Sentences

D.

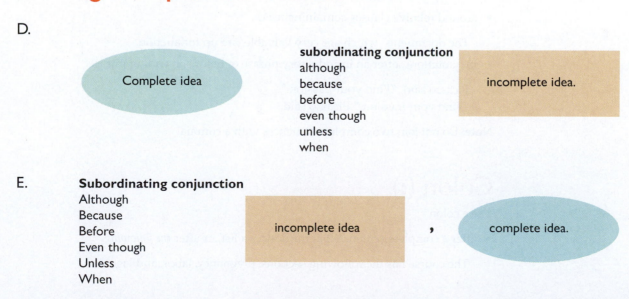

subordinating conjunction
although
because
before
even though
unless
when

E. **Subordinating conjunction**
Although
Because
Before
Even though
Unless
When

incomplete idea , complete idea.

Punctuation and Mechanics

Apostrophe (')

Use an apostrophe

- to join a subject and a verb together.

    We're late.

- to join an auxiliary with *not*.

    I **can't** come.

- to indicate possession.

    Ross's computer is new.

Comma (,)

Use a comma

- to separate words in a series (more than two things). Place a comma before the final *and*.

    The doctor is kind, considerate, and gentle.
- after an introductory word or phrase.

    In the evenings, Carson volunteered at a hospital.
- around interrupting phrases that give additional information about the subject.

    Alan, an electrician, earns a good salary.
- in compound sentences before the coordinator.

    We worked for hours, and then we rested.
- around relative clauses containing *which*.

    The documents, which are very valuable, are up for auction.
- in quotations, after an introductory phrase or before an ending phrase.

    Picasso said, "Find your passion."
    "Find your passion," Picasso said.

Note: Do not join two complete sentences with a comma!

Colon (:)

Use a colon

- after a complete sentence that introduces a list, or after *the following*.

    The course has the following sections: pregnancy, labor, and lactation.

- after a complete sentence that introduces a quotation.

    Picasso's advice was clear: "Find your passion."

- before an explanation or example.

    Carlos explained what he really needed: a raise.

- to separate the hours and minutes in expressions of time.

    The mall opens at 9:30 A.M.

Semicolon (;)

Use a semicolon to join two independent but related clauses.

    Mahatma Gandhi was a pacifist; he believed in nonviolence.

Quotation Marks (" ")

Use quotation marks around direct speech. When a quotation is a complete sentence, capitalize the first word in the quotation. Place the end punctuation inside the closing quotation marks.

    My boss wrote, "We need to cut back on expenses."

If the end of the quotation is not the end of your sentence, end the quotation with a comma. If your quotation ends with other punctuation, put it inside the closing quotation marks.

    "We need to cut back on expenses," my boss wrote.

    "You can't be serious!" she shouted.

    "What did you call me?" he replied.

Integrated Quotations

If you integrate a quotation in a sentence, add quotation marks around the words the speaker quoted.

    Dorothy Nixon calls herself a "terrible mother."

"Inside" Quotations

If one quotation is inside another quotation, add single quotation marks (' ') around the inside quotation.

    Sondra explained, "My mother said, 'Your teacher wants to meet me.' "

Citing Page Numbers

If you are using MLA style, write the page number in parentheses and place it after the quotation. Place the final period *after* the parentheses if the quotation ends the sentence.

    In her essay, the writer Stella McStreet states, "We need to focus on our career paths" (8).

Capitalization

Always capitalize

- the pronoun *I* and the first word of every sentence.
- the days of the week, months, and holidays.

Tuesday	**May 22**	**Labor Day**

- the names of specific places, such as buildings, streets, parks, public squares, lakes, rivers, cities, states, and countries.

Kelvin Street	**Lake Erie**	**White Plains, New York**

- the names of languages, nationalities, tribes, races, and religions.

Spanish	**Mohawk**	**Buddhist**

- the names of specific planets (but not the sun or moon).

Venus	**Saturn**	**Earth**	moon

- specific course or program titles (but not when the course is mentioned without the title).

Economics 201	**Nursing 411**	an economics course

- the titles of specific individuals.

General Dewitt	**Dr. Franklin**	**Mr. Blain**

- the major words in titles of literary or artistic works.

The Great Gatsby	*The Diviners*	*Crime and Punishment*

- the names of historical eras and movements.

World War I	**Cubism**	the **Middle Ages**

Punctuating Titles

Place the title of short works in quotation marks. Capitalize the major words. Short works include songs, short stories, newspaper and magazine articles, essays, and poems.

The Beatles' worst song was "Help."

Italicize the title of a longer document. If the title is in handwritten text, underline it. Long works include television series, films, works of art, magazines, books, plays, and newspapers.

Handwritten	We watched the classic movie <u>West Side Story</u>.
Typed	We watched the classic movie *West Side Story*.

Appendix 6 — Writing Paragraphs and Essays in Exams

In many of your courses, you will have to answer exam questions with a paragraph or an essay. Although taking any exam can be stressful, you can reduce test anxiety and increase your chances of doing well by following some preparation and exam-writing strategies.

Preparing for Exams

Here are some steps you can take to help prepare for exams.

- Before you take an exam, make sure that you know exactly what material you should study. Do not be afraid to ask the instructor for clarification. Also ask what materials you should bring to the exam.
- Review the assigned information, class notes, and the textbook, if any.
- Read and repeat information out loud.
- Take notes about important points.
- Study with a friend.

HINT: Predict Exam Questions

An effective study strategy is to predict possible exam questions. Here are some tips:

- Look for important themes in your course outline.
- Study your notes and try to analyze what information is of particular importance.
- Look at your previous exams for the course. Determine whether any questions or subjects are repeated in more than one exam.

After you have looked through the course outline, your notes, and previous exams, write out possible exam questions based on the information that you have collected. Then practice writing the answers to your questions.

Writing Exams

Knowing your material inside and out is a large part of exam writing; however, budgeting your time and knowing how to read exam questions are important, too. When you receive the exam paper, look it over carefully and try these test-taking strategies.

Schedule Your Time

DETERMINE POINT VALUES

One of the most stressful things about taking an exam is running out of time. Before you write, find out exactly how much time you have. Then, plan how much time you will need to answer the questions.

As soon as you get an exam, scan the questions and determine which questions have a larger point value. For example, you might respond to the questions with the largest point value first, or you might begin with those that you understand well. Then go to the more difficult questions. If you find yourself blocked on a certain answer, do not waste a lot of time on it. Go to another question, and then go back to the first question later.

Carefully Read the Exam Questions

It is important to read exam instructions thoroughly. Follow the next steps.

IDENTIFY KEY WORDS AND PHRASES

When you read an exam question, underline or circle key words and phrases in order to understand exactly what you are supposed to do. In the next example, the underlined words highlight three different tasks.

1. Discuss how each time period differs from the other.

2. Organize the essay according to each period's date.

3. Discuss what people did for shelter, food, and leisure activities.

Distinguish between Paleolithic, Mesolithic, and Neolithic. Place these periods in chronological order and describe how the people lived during those times.

EXAMINE COMMON QUESTION WORDS

Exam questions direct you using verbs (action words). This chart gives the most common words that are used in both paragraph- and essay-style questions.

Verb	Meaning
describe discuss review	Examine a subject as thoroughly as possible. Focus on the main points.
narrate trace	Describe the development or progress of something using time order.
evaluate explain your point of view interpret justify take a stand	State your opinion and give reasons to support your opinion. In other words, write an argument paragraph or essay.
analyze criticize classify	Explain something carefully by breaking it down into smaller parts.
enumerate list outline	Go through important facts one by one.
compare contrast distinguish	Discuss important similarities and/or differences.
define explain what is meant by	Give a complete and accurate definition that demonstrates your understanding of the concept.
explain causes	Analyze the reasons for an event.
explain effects	Analyze the consequences or results of an event.
explain a process	Explain the steps needed to perform a task.
summarize	Write down the main points from a larger work.
illustrate	Demonstrate your understanding by giving examples.

Practice 1

Determine the main type of response that you would use to answer each essay question. Choose one of the following essay patterns.

narrate	explain a process	explain causes/effects	define
argue	classify	compare and contrast	

EXAMPLE: Discuss the term *affirmative action*.

define

1. Differentiate between capitalism and communism.

   _____

2. Describe what happened during the Liberation of Kuwait.

   _____

3. List and describe three types of clean energy sources

   _____

4. What steps are required to improve your city's transportation system?

   _____

5. What effect did the Women's Movement have on employment in the 1960s?

   _____

6. Give a short but thorough description of the term "statute of limitations."

   _____

7. Discuss whether religious symbols should be banned from schools.

8. _____

Follow the Writing Process

When you answer paragraph or essay exam questions, remember to follow the writing process.

Explore
- Jot down any ideas that you think can help you answer the question.

Develop
- Use the exam question to guide your topic sentence or thesis statement.
- List supporting ideas. Then organize your ideas and create a paragraph or essay plan.
- Write the paragraph or essay. Use transitions to link your ideas.

Revise and edit
- Read over your writing to make sure it makes sense and that your spelling, punctuation, and mechanics are correct.

Practice 2

Choose three topics from Practice 1 and write topic sentences or thesis statements.

EXAMPLE: Discuss the term *affirmative action*.

Topic sentence or thesis statement: <u>Affirmative action policies give</u>
<u>certain groups in society preferential treatment to correct a</u>
<u>history of discrimination</u>.

1. _____

_____

_____

2. _____

_____

_____

3. _____

_____

_____

Practice 3

Read the following test material and answer the questions that follow.

Essay Exam

You will have ninety minutes to complete this test. Write your answers in the admin booklet provided.

A. Define the following terms (2 points each).
   1. Region
   2. Economic geography
   3. Territoriality
   4. Spatial distribution
   5. Gross national product

B. Write an essay response to one of the following questions. Your essay should contain relevant supporting details. (20 points)
   6. Define and contrast an open city with a closed city.
   7. Discuss industrial location theories in geography, and divide the theories into groups.
   8. Explain the steps needed to complete a geographical survey. List the steps in order of importance.

Schedule Your Time and Determine Point Values

1. What is the total point value of the exam? _____

2. How many questions do you have to answer? _____

3. Which part of the exam would you do first? Explain why. _____
_____

4. Schedule your time. How much time would you spend on each part of the exam?

   Part A: _____   Part B: _____

   Explain your reasoning. _____
_____
_____

Carefully Read the Exam Questions

5. Identify key words in Part B. What important information is in the instructions?
_____

6. What two things must you do in question 6?

   a. _____   b. _____

7. What type of essay is required to answer question 7?

   a. Comparison and contrast

   b. Classification

   c. Process

8. What type of essay is required to answer question 8?

   a. Comparison and contrast

   b. Classification

   c. Process

Spelling, Grammar, and Vocabulary Logs

In the first few pages of your writing portfolio or on the next pages, keep spelling, grammar, and vocabulary logs to help you stop repeating errors in your writing. Each time you write new assignments, consult your logs. You will notice which words you commonly misspell or misuse, and each time you correct them, you will begin developing better spelling, grammar, and vocabulary habits.

Spelling Log

Every time you misspell a word, record both the mistake and the correction in your spelling log. Then, before you hand in a writing assignment, check your spelling log to make sure you are spelling all words correctly.

EXAMPLE:

Incorrect	Correct
realy	really
exagerated	exaggerated

Grammar Log

Each time a writing assignment is returned to you, identify one or two repeated errors and add them to your grammar log. Then, before you hand in writing assignments, consult the grammar log in order to avoid making the same errors. For each type of grammar error, you could do the following:

- Identify the assignment and write down the type of error.
- In your own words, write a rule about the error.
- Include an example from your writing assignment.

EXAMPLE: <u>Illustration Paragraph</u> (Feb. 12) Run-On

Do not connect two complete sentences with a comma.

accidents. Other

Bad drivers cause accidents, other drivers do not expect sudden lane changes.

Vocabulary Log

Every time you read a text, you will learn new vocabulary words. Keep a record of the most interesting and useful vocabulary words and expressions. Write a synonym or definition next to each new word.

EXAMPLE: Exasperating means "annoying."

Spelling Log

Grammar Log

Vocabulary Log

Credits

PHOTOS

Index

Revising Checklist for a Paragraph

Does the topic sentence

- ❏ make a point about the topic?
- ❏ express a complete thought?
- ❏ make a direct statement and not contain expressions such as *I think that* or *I will explain*?

Does the body

- ❏ have **adequate support**? Are there enough details to support the topic sentence?
- ❏ have **coherence**? Are ideas presented in an effective and logical manner?
- ❏ have **unity**? Is the paragraph unified around one central topic?
- ❏ have **style**? Are sentences varied in length? Is the language creative and precise?

Does the concluding sentence

- ❏ bring the paragraph to a satisfactory close?
- ❏ avoid introducing new or contradictory information? (Note: Not all paragraphs have concluding sentences.)

Revising Checklist for an Essay

Does the introduction

- ❏ contain a clearly identifiable thesis statement?
- ❏ build up to the thesis statement?

Does the thesis statement

- ❏ convey the essay's controlling idea?
- ❏ make a valid and supportable point?
- ❏ appear as the last sentence in the introduction?
- ❏ make a direct point and not contain expressions such as *I think that* or *I will explain*?

Do the body paragraphs

- ❏ have **adequate support**? Does each body paragraph have a topic sentence that clearly supports the thesis statement? Are there enough details to support each paragraph's topic sentence?
- ❏ have **coherence**? Are ideas presented in an effective and logical manner? Do transitional words and phrases help the ideas flow smoothly?
- ❏ have **unity**? Is the essay unified around one central topic? Does each body paragraph focus on one topic?
- ❏ have **style**? Are sentences varied in length? Is the language creative and precise?

Does the conclusion

- ❏ bring the essay to a satisfactory end?
- ❏ briefly summarize the ideas that the writer discusses in the essay?
- ❏ avoid introducing new or contradictory ideas?
- ❏ possibly end with a quotation, suggestion, or prediction?